**Donated by
Mrs. John Pisani
in memory of
Rosemary Pisani**
Florissant Valley faculty member
1966 - 1982

CHARACTERS

WERLE, *a merchant, manufacturer, etc.*
GREGERS WERLE, *his son.*
OLD EKDAL.
HIALMAR EKDAL, *his son, a photographer.*
GINA EKDAL, *Hjalmar's wife.*
HEDVIG, *their daughter, a girl of fourteen.*
MRS. SÖRBY, *Werle's housekeeper.*
RELLING, *a doctor.*
MOLVIK, *student of theology.*
GRÅBERG, *Werle's bookkeeper.*
PETTERSEN, *Werle's servant.*
JENSEN, *a hired waiter.*
A FLABBY GENTLEMAN.
A THIN-HAIRED GENTLEMAN.
A SHORT-SIGHTED GENTLEMAN.
SIX OTHER GENTLEMEN, *guests at Werle's dinner-party.*
SEVERAL HIRED WAITERS.

The first act passes in WERLE'S *house, the remaining acts at* HJALMAR EKDAL'S.

Pronunciation of Names: GREGERS WERLE = Grayghers Verlë; HIALMAR EKDAL = Yalmar Aykdal; GINA = Cheena; GRÅBERG = Groberg; JENSEN = Yensen.

THE WILD DUCK
PLAY IN FIVE ACTS

Engstrand. Lord, how you talk, Regina. (*Takes a few limping steps forward.*) What I wanted to tell you was this—

Regina. Don't clump about like that, stupid! The young master is lying asleep upstairs.

Engstrand. Asleep still? In the middle of the day?

Regina. Well, it's no business of yours.

Engstrand. I was out on the spree last night—

Regina. I don't doubt it.

Engstrand. Yes, we are poor weak mortals, my girl—

Regina. We are indeed.

Engstrand. —and the temptations of the world are manifold, you know—but, for all that, here I was at my work at half-past five this morning.

Regina. Yes, yes, but make yourself scarce now. I am not going to stand here as if I had a *rendez-vous* with you.

Engstrand. As if you had a what?

Regina. I am not going to have any one find you here; so now you know, and you can go.

Engstrand (*coming a few steps nearer*). Not a bit of it! Not before we have had a little chat. This afternoon I shall have finished my job down at the school house, and I shall be off home to town by to-night's boat.

Regina (*mutters*). Pleasant journey to you!

Engstrand. Thanks, my girl. To-morrow is the opening of the Orphanage, and I expect there will be a fine kick-up here and plenty of good strong drink, don't you know. And no one shall say of Jacob Engstrand that he can't hold off when temptation comes in his way.

Regina. Oho!

Engstrand. Yes, because there will be a lot of fine folk here to-morrow. Parson Manders is expected from town, too.

Regina. What is more, he's coming to-day.

Engstrand. There you are! And I'm going to be precious careful he doesn't have anything to say against me, do you see?

Regina. Oh, that's your game, is it?

Engstrand. What do you mean?

Regina (*with a significant look at him*). What is it you want to humbug Mr. Manders out of, this time?

GHOSTS

DRAMATIS PERSONÆ

Mrs. Alving (a widow).
Oswald Alving (her son, an artist).
Manders (the Pastor of the parish).
Engstrand (a carpenter).
Regina Engstrand (his daughter, in Mrs. Alving's
service).

(*The action takes place at Mrs. Alving's house on one of the
larger fjords of western Norway.*)

ACT I

(SCENE.—*A large room looking upon a garden. A door
in the left-hand wall, and two in the right. In the middle
of the room, a round table with chairs set about it, and
books, magazines and newspapers upon it. In the foreground on the left, a window, by which is a small sofa with
a work-table in front of it. At the back the room opens
into a conservatory rather smaller than the room. From
the right-hand side of this a door leads to the garden.
Through the large panes of glass that form the outer wall
of the conservatory, a gloomy fjord landscape can be dis-
cerned, half obscured by steady rain.*

ENGSTRAND *is standing close up to the garden door. His
left leg is slightly deformed, and he wears a boot with a
clump of wood under the sole.* REGINA, *with an empty
garden-syringe in her hand, is trying to prevent his coming
in.*)

Regina (*below her breath*). What is it you want? Stay
where you are. The rain is dripping off you.
Engstrand. God's good rain, my girl.
Regina. The Devil's own rain, that's what it is!

Contents

Contents

Printed in the United States of America

THE PLAYS OF
HENRIK
IBSEN

———

AUTHORIZED TRANSLATION

TUDOR PUBLISHING COMPANY

NEW YORK

1934

THE PLAYS OF
HENRIK IBSEN

WITH LOVE

TO

ELSIE

FROM

MARIE

CHRISTMAS
1934

ACT I

At WERLE'S *house. A richly and comfortably furnished study; bookcases and upholstered furniture; a writing-table, with papers and documents, in the centre of the room; lighted lamps with green shades, giving a subdued light. At the back, open folding-doors with curtains drawn back. Within is seen a large and handsome room, brilliantly lighted with lamps and branching candle-sticks. In front, on the right (in the study), a small baize door leads into* WERLE'S *office. On the left, in front, a fireplace with a glowing coal fire, and farther back a double door leading into the dining-room.*

WERLE'S *servant,* PETTERSEN, *in livery, and* JENSEN, *the hired waiter, in black, are putting the study in order. In the large room, two or three other hired waiters are moving about, arranging things and lighting more can-dles. From the dining-room, the hum of conversation and laughter of many voices are heard; a glass is tapped with a knife; silence follows, and a toast is proposed; shouts of "Bravo!" and then again a buzz of conver-sation.*

Pettersen (lights a lamp on the chimney-place and places a shade over it). Hark to them, Jensen! now the old man's on his legs holding a long palaver about Mrs. Sörby.

Jensen (pushing forward an arm-chair). Is it true, what folks say, that they're—very good friends, eh?

Petterson. Lord knows.

Jensen. I've heard tell as he's been a lively customer in his day.

3

Petterson. May be.

Jensen. And he's giving this spread in honour of his son, they say.

Pettersen. Yes. His son came home yesterday.

Jensen. This is the first time I ever heard as Mr. Werle had a son.

Pettersen. Oh yes, he has a son, right enough. But he's a fixture, as you might say, up at the Höidal works. He's never once come to town all the years I've been in service here.

A Waiter (in the doorway of the other room). Pettersen, here's an old fellow wanting——

Pettersen (mutters). The devil—who's this now?

OLD EKDAL *appears from the right, in the inner room. He is dressed in a threadbare overcoat with a high collar; he wears woollen mittens, and carries in his hand a stick and a fur cap. Under his arm, a brown paper parcel. Dirty red-brown wig and small grey moustache.*

Pettersen (goes towards him). Good Lord—what do you want here?

Ekdal (in the doorway). Must get into the office, Pettersen.

Petterson. The office was closed an hour ago, and——

Ekdal. So they told me at the front door. But Gråberg's in there still. Let me slip in this way, Pettersen; there's a good fellow. *(Points towards the baize door.)* It's not the first time I've come this way.

Pettersen. Well, you may pass. *(Opens the door.)* But mind you go out again the proper way, for we've got company.

Ekdal. I know, I know—h'm! Thanks, Pettersen, good old friend! Thanks! *(Mutters softly.)* Ass!

[*He goes into the office;* PETTERSEN *shuts the door after him.*

Jensen. Is he one of the office people?

Pettersen. No he's only an outside hand that does odd

jobs of copying. But he's been a tip-topper in his day, has old Ekdal.

Jensen. You can see he's been through a lot.

Pettersen. Yes; he was an army officer, you know.

Jensen. You don't say so?

Pettersen. No mistake about it. But then he went into the timber trade or something of the sort. They say he once played Mr. Werle a very nasty trick. They were partners in the Höidal works at the time. Oh, I know old Ekdal well, I do. Many a nip of bitters and bottle of ale we two have drunk at Madam Eriksen's.

Jensen. He don't look as if he'd much to stand treat with.

Pettersen. Why, bless you, Jensen, it's me that stands treat. I always think there's no harm in being a bit civil to folks that have seen better days.

Jensen. Did he go bankrupt then?

Pettersen. Worse than that. He went to prison.

Jensen. To prison!

Pettersen. Or perhaps it was the Penitentiary. *(Listens.)* Sh! They're leaving the table.

The dining-room door is thrown open from within, by a couple of waiters. MRS. SÖRBY *comes out conversing with two gentlemen. Gradually the whole company follows, amongst them* WERLE. *Last come* HIALMAR EKDAL *and* GREGERS WERLE.

Mrs. Sörby (in passing, to the servant). Tell them to serve the coffee in the music-room, Pettersen.

Pettersen. Very well, Madam.

[*She goes with the two Gentlemen into the inner room, and thence out to the right.* PETTERSEN *and* JENSEN *go out the same way.*

A Flabby Gentleman (to a THIN-HAIRED GENTLEMAN*).* Whew! What a dinner!—It was no joke to do it justice!

The Thin-haired Gentleman. Oh, with a little good-will one can get through a lot in three hours.

The Flabby Gentleman. Yes, but afterwards, afterwards, my dear Chamberlain!

A Third Gentleman. I hear the coffee and maraschino are to be served in the music-room.

The Flabby Gentleman. Bravo! Then perhaps Mrs. Sörby will play us something.

The Thin-haired Gentleman (in a low voice). I hope Mrs. Sörby mayn't play us a tune we don't like, one of these days!

The Flabby Gentleman. Oh no, not she! Bertha will never turn against her old friends.

[*They laugh and pass into the inner room.*

Werle (in a low voice, dejectedly). I don't think anybody noticed it, Gregers.

Gregers (looks at him). Noticed what?

Werle. Did you not notice it either?

Gregers. What do you mean?

Werle. We were thirteen at table.

Gregers. Indeed? Were there thirteen of us?

Werle (glances towards HIALMAR EKDAL*).* Our usual party is twleve. *(To the others.)* This way, gentlemen!

[WERLE *and the others, all except* HIALMAR *and* GREGERS, *go out by the back, to the right.*

Hialmar (who has overheard the conversation). You ought not to have invited me, Gregers.

Gregers. What! Not ask my best and only friend to a party supposed to be in my honour——?

Hialmar. But I don't think your father likes it. You see I am quite outside his circle.

Gregers. So I hear. But I wanted to see you and have a talk with you, and I certainly shan't be staying long.—Ah, we two old schoolfellows have drifted far apart from each other. It must be sixteen or seventeen years since we met.

Hialmar. Is it so long?

Gregers. It is indeed. Well, how goes it with you? You look well. You have put on flesh, and grown almost stout.

Hialmar. Well, "stout" is scarcely the word; but I daresay I look a little more of a man than I used to.

Gregers. Yes, you do; your outer man is in first-rate condition.

Hialmar (in a tone of gloom). Ah, but the inner man! That is a very different matter, I can tell you! Of course you know of the terrible catastrophe that has befallen me and mine since last we met.

Gregers (more softly). How are things going with your father now?

Hialmar. Don't let us talk of it, old fellow. Of course my poor unhappy father lives with me. He hasn't another soul in the world to care for him. But you can understand that this is a miserable subject for me.—Tell me, rather, how you have been getting on up at the works.

Gregers. I have had a delightfully lonely time of it— plenty of leisure to think and think about things. Come over here; we may as well make ourselves comfortable.

[*He seats himself in an arm-chair by the fire and draws* HIALMAR *down into another alongside of it.*

Hialmar (sentimentally). After all, Gregers, I thank you for inviting me to your father's table; for I take it as a sign that you have got over your feeling against me.

Gregers (surprised). How could you imagine I had any feeling against you?

Hialmar. You had at first, you know.

Gregers. How at first?

Hialmar. After the great misfortune. It was natural enough that you should. Your father was within an ace of being drawn into that—well, that terrible business.

Gregers. Why should that give me any feeling against you? Who can have put that into your head?

Hialmar. I know it did, Gregers; your father told me so himself.

Gregers (starts). My father! Oh indeed. H'm.—Was that why you never let me hear from you?—not a single word.

Hialmar. Yes.

Gregers. Not even when you made up your mind to become a photographer?

Hialmar. Your father said I had better not write to you at all, about anything.

Gregers (looking straight before him). Well well, perhaps he was right.—But tell me now, Hialmar: are you pretty well satisfied with your present position?

Hialmar (with a little sigh). Oh yes, I am; I have really no cause to complain. At first, as you may guess, I felt it a little strange. It was such a totally new state of things for me. But of course my whole circumstances were totally changed. Father's utter, irretrievable ruin,—the shame and disgrace of it, Gregers——

Gregers (affected). Yes, yes; I understand.

Hialmar. I couldn't think of remaining at college; there wasn't a shilling to spare; on the contrary, there were debts —mainly to your father I believe——

Gregers. H'm——

Hialmar. In short, I thought it best to break, once for all, with my old surroundings and associations. It was your father that specially urged me to it; and since he interested himself so much in me——

Gregers. My father did?

Hialmar. Yes, you surely knew that, didn't you? Where do you suppose I found the money to learn photography, and to furnish a studio and make a start? All that costs a pretty penny, I can tell you.

Gregers. And my father provided the money?

Hialmar. Yes, my dear fellow, didn't you know? I understood him to say he had written to you about it.

Gregers. Not a word about his part in the business. He must have forgotten it. Our correspondence has always been purely a business one. So it was my father that——!

Hialmar. Yes, certainly. He didn't wish it to be generally known; but he it was. And of course it was he, too, that put me in a position to marry. Don't you—don't you know about that either?

Gregers. No, I haven't heard a word of it. *(Shakes him by the arm).* But, my dear Hialmar, I can't tell you what pleasure all this gives me—pleasure, and self-reproach. I have perhaps done my father injustice after all—in some things. This proves that he has a heart. It shows a sort of compunction——

Hialmar. Compunction——?

Gregers. Yes, yes—whatever you like to call it. Oh, I can't tell you how glad I am to hear this of father.—So you are a married man, Hialmar! That is further than I shall ever get. Well, I hope you are happy in your married life?

Hialmar. Yes, thoroughly happy. She is as good and capable a wife as any man could wish for. And she is by no means without culture.

Gregers (rather surprised). No, of course not.

Hialmar. You see, life is itself an education. Her daily intercourse with me—— And then we know one or two rather remarkable men, who come a good deal about us. I assure you, you would hardly know Gina again.

Gregers. Gina?

Hialmar. Yes; had you forgotten that her name was Gina?

Gregers. Whose name? I haven't the slightest idea——

Hialmar. Don't you remember that she used to be in service here?

Gregers (looks at him.) Is it Gina Hansen——?

Hialmar. Yes, of course it is Gina Hansen.

Gregers. ——who kept house for us during the last year of my mother's illness?

Hialmar. Yes, exactly. But, my dear friend, I'm quite sure your father told you that I was married.

Gregers (who has risen). Oh yes, he mentioned it; but not that—— *(Walking about the room.)* Stay—perhaps he did—now that I think of it. My father always writes such short letters. *(Half seats himself on the arm of the chair.)* Now, tell me, Hialmar—this is interesting—how did you come to know Gina—your wife?

Hialmar. The simplest thing in the world. You know Gina did not stay here long, everything was so much upset at that time, owing to your mother's illness and so forth, that Gina was not equal to it all; so she gave notice and left. That was the year before your mother died—or it may have been the same year.

Gregers. It was the same year. I was up at the works then. But afterwards——?

Hialmar. Well, Gina lived at home with her mother, Madam Hansen, an excellent hard-working woman, who kept a little eating-house. She had a room to let too; a very nice comfortable room.

Gregers. And I suppose you were lucky enough to secure it?

Hialmar. Yes; in fact, it was your father that recommended it to me. So it was there, you see, that I really came to know Gina.

Gregers. And then you got engaged?

Hialmar. Yes. It doesn't take young people long to fall in love——; h'm——

Gregers (rises and moves about a little). Tell me: was it after your engagement—was it then that my father—I mean was it then that you began to take up photography?

Hialmar. Yes, precisely. I wanted to make a start, and to set up house as soon as possible; and your father and I agreed that this photography business was the readiest way. Gina thought so too. Oh, and there was another thing in its favour, by-the-bye: it happened, luckily, that Gina had learnt to retouch

Gregers. That chimed in marvellously.

Hialmar (pleased, rises). Yes, didn't it? Don't you think it was a marvellous piece of luck?

Gregers. Oh, unquestionably. My father seems to have been almost a kind of providence for you.

Hialmar (with emotion). He did not forsake his old friend's son in the hour of his need. For he has a heart. you see.

Mrs. Sörby (enters, arm-in-arm with WERLE*).* Nonsense, my dear Mr. Werle; you mustn't stop there any longer staring at all the lights. It's very bad for you.

Werle (lets go her arm and passes his hand over his eyes). I daresay you are right.

[PETTERSEN *and* JENSEN *carry round refreshment trays.*

Mrs. Sörby (to the Guests in the other room). This way, if you please, gentlemen. Whoever wants a glass of punch must be so good as to come in here.

The Flabby Gentleman (comes up to MRS. SÖRBY*).* Surely, it isn't possible that you have suspended our cherished right to smoke?

Mrs. Sörby. Yes. No smoking here, in Mr. Werle's sanctum, Chamberlain.

The Thin-haired Gentleman. When did you enact these stringent amendments on the cigar law, Mrs. Sörby?

Mrs. Sörby. After the last dinner, Chamberlain, when certain persons permitted themselves to overstep the mark.

The Thin-haired Gentleman. And may one never overstep the mark a little bit, Madame Bertha? Not the least little bit?

Mrs. Sörby. Not in any respect whatsoever, Mr. Balle.

[*Most of the Guests have assembled in the study; servants hand round glasses of punch.*

Werle (to HIALMAR, *who is standing beside a table).* What are you studying so intently, Ekdal?

Hialmar. Only an album, Mr. Werle.

The Thin-haired Gentleman (who is wandering about). Ah, photographs! They are quite in your line of course.

The Flabby Gentleman (in an arm-chair). Haven't you brought any of your own with you?

Hialmar. No, I haven't.

The Flabby Gentleman. You ought to have; it's very good for the digestion to sit and look at pictures.

The Thin-haired Gentleman. And it contributes to the entertainment, you know.

The Short-sighted Gentleman. And all contributions are thankfully received.

Mrs. Sörby. The Chamberlains think that when one is invited out to dinner, one ought to exert oneself a little in return, Mr. Ekdal.

The Flabby Gentleman. Where one dines so well, that duty becomes a pleasure.

The Thin-haired Gentleman. And when it's a case of the struggle for existence, you know——

Mrs. Sörby. I quite agree with you!

[*They continue the conversation, with laughter and joking.*

Gregers (softly). You must join in, Hialmar.

Hialmar (writhing). What am I to talk about?

The Flabby Gentleman. Don't you think, Mr. Werle, that Tokay may be considered one of the more wholesome sorts of wine?

Werle (by the fire). I can answer for the Tokay you had to-day, at any rate; it's one of the very finest seasons. Of course you would notice that.

The Flabby Gentleman. Yes, it had a remarkably delicate flavour.

Hialmar (shyly). Is there any difference between the seasons?

The Flabby Gentleman (laughs). Come! That's good!

Werle (smiles). It really doesn't pay to set fine wine before you.

The Thin-haired Gentleman. Tokay is like photographs, Mr. Ekdal: they both need sunshine. Am I not right?

Hialmar. Yes, light is important no doubt.

Mrs. Sörby. And it's exactly the same with Chamberlains—they, too, depend very much on sunshine,* as the saying is.

The Thin-haired Gentleman. Oh fie! That's a very threadbare sarcasm!

The Short-sighted Gentleman. Mrs. Sörby is coming out——

The Flabby Gentleman. ——and at our expense, too. *(Holds up his finger reprovingly.)* Oh, Madame Bertha, Madame Bertha!

Mrs. Sörby. Yes, and there's not the least doubt that the seasons differ greatly. The old vintages are the finest.

The Short-sighted Gentleman. Do you reckon me among the old vintages?

Mrs. Sörby. Oh, far from it.

The Thin-haired Gentleman. There now! But me, dear Mrs. Sörby——?

The Flabby Gentleman. Yes, and me? What vintage should you say that we belong to?

Mrs. Sörby. Why, to the sweet vintages, gentlemen.

[*She sips a glass of punch. The gentlemen laugh and flirt with her.*

Werle. Mrs. Sörby can always find a loop-hole—when she wants to. Fill your glasses, gentlemen! Pettersen, will you see to it——! Gregers, suppose we have a glass together. *(Gregers does not move.)* Won't you join us, Ekdal? I found no opportunity of drinking with you at table.

———

* The "sunshine" of Court favour.

[GRÅBERG, *the Bookkeeper, looks in at the baize door.*

Gråberg. Excuse me, sir, but I can't get out.

Werle. Have you been locked in again?

Gråberg. Yes, and Flakstad has carried off the keys.

Werle. Well, you can pass out this way.

Gråberg. But there's some one else——

Werle. All right; come through, both of you. Don't be afraid.

[GRÅBERG *and* OLD EKDAL *come out of the office.*

Werle (involuntarily). Ugh!

[*The laughter and talk among the Guests cease.*
HIALMAR *starts at the sight of his father, puts down his glass, and turns towards the fireplace.*

Ekdal (does not look up, but makes little bows to both sides as he passes, murmuring). Beg pardon, come the wrong way. Door locked—door locked. Beg pardon.

[*He and* GRÅBERG *go out by the back, to the right.*

Werle (between his teeth). That idiot Gråberg.

Gregers (open-mouthed and staring, to HIALMAR). Why surely that wasn't——!

The Flabby Gentleman. What's the matter? Who was it?

Gregers. Oh, nobody, only the bookkeeper and some one with him.

The Short-sighted Gentleman (to HIALMAR). Did you know that man?

Hialmar. I don't know—I didn't notice——

The Flabby Gentleman. What the deuce has come over every one?

[*He joins another group who are talking softly.*

Mrs. Sörby (whispers to the Servant). Give him something to take with him;—something good, mind.

Pettersen (nods). I'll see to it. [*Goes out.*

Gregers (softly and with emotion, to HIALMAR). So that was really he!

Hialmar.   Yes.

Gregers.   And you could stand there and deny that you knew him!

Hialmar (whispers vehemently).   But how could I——!

Gregers.   ——acknowledge your own father?

Hialmar (with pain).   Oh, if you were in my place——

[*The conversation amongst the Guests, which has been carried on in a low tone, now swells into constrained joviality.*

The Thin-haired Gentleman (approaching HIALMAR *and* GREGERS *in a friendly manner).*   Aha! Reviving old college memories, eh? Don't you smoke, Mr. Ekdal? May I give you a light? Oh, by-the-bye, we mustn't——

Hialmar.   No, thank you, I won't——

The Flabby Gentleman.   Haven't you a nice little poem you could recite to us, Mr. Ekdal? You used to recite so charmingly.

Hialmar.   I am sorry I can't remember anything.

The Flabby Gentleman.   Oh, that's a pity. Well, what shall we do, Balle?

[*Both Gentlemen move away and pass into the other room.*

Hialmar (gloomily).   Gregers—I am going! When a man has felt the crushing hand of Fate, you see—— Say good bye to your father for me.

Gregers.   Yes, yes. Are you going straight home?

Hialmar.   Yes. Why?

Gregers.   Oh, because I may perhaps look in on you later.

Hialmar.   No, you mustn't do that. You must not come to my home. Mine is a melancholy abode, Gregers; especially after a splendid banquet like this. We can always arrange to meet somewhere in the town.

Mrs. Sörby (who has quietly approached).   Are you going, Ekdal?

Hialmar.   Yes.

Mrs. Sörby. Remember me to Gina.

Hialmar. Thanks.

Mrs. Sörby. And say I am coming up to see her one of these days.

Hialmar. Yes, thank you. *(To* GREGERS.*)* Stay here; I will slip out unobserved.

[*He saunters away, then into the other room, and so out to the right.*

Mrs. Sörby (softly to the Servant, who has come back). Well, did you give the old man something?

Pettersen. Yes; I sent him off with a bottle of cognac.

Mrs. Sörby. Oh, you might have thought of something better than that.

Pettersen. Oh no, Mrs. Sörby; cognac is what he likes best in the world.

The Flabby Gentleman (in the doorway with a sheet of music in his hand). Shall we play a duet, Mrs. Sörby?

Mrs. Sörby. Yes, suppose we do.

The Guests. Bravo, bravo!

[*She goes with all the Guests through the back room, out to the right.* GREGERS *remains standing by the fire.* WERLE *is looking for something on the writing-table, and appears to wish that* GREGERS *would go; as* GREGERS *does not move,* WERLE *goes towards the door.*

Gregers. Father, won't you stay a moment?

Werle (stops). What is it?

Gregers. I must have a word with you.

Werle. Can it not wait till we are alone?

Gregers. No, it cannot; for perhaps we shall never be alone together.

Werle (drawing nearer). What do you mean by that?

[*During what follows, the pianoforte is faintly heard from the distant music-room.*

Gregers. How has that family been allowed to go so miserably to the wall?

Werle. You mean the Ekdals, I suppose.

Gregers. Yes, I mean the Ekdals. Lieutenant Ekdal was once so closely associated with you.

Werle. Much too closely; I have felt that to my cost for many a year. It is thanks to him that I—yes *I*—have had a kind of slur cast upon my reputation.

Gregers (softly). Are you sure that he alone was to blame?

Werle. Who else do you suppose——?

Gregers. You and he acted together in that affair of the forests——

Werle. But was it not Ekdal that drew the map of the tracts we had bought—that fraudulent map! It was he who felled all that timber illegally on Government ground. In fact, the whole management was in his hands. I was quite in the dark as to what Lieutenant Ekdal was doing.

Gregers. Lieutenant Ekdal himself seems to have been very much in the dark as to what he was doing.

Werle. That may be. But the fact remains that he was found guilty and I acquitted.

Gregers. Yes, I know that nothing was proved against you.

Werle. Acquittal is acquittal. Why do you rake up these old miseries that turned my hair grey before its time? Is that the sort of thing you have been brooding over up there, all these years? I can assure you, Gregers, here in the town the whole story has been forgotten long ago—so far as *I* am concerned.

Gregers. But that unhappy Ekdal family——

Werle. What would you have had me do for the people?

When Ekdal came out of prison he was a broken-down being, past all help. There are people in the world who dive to the bottom the moment they get a couple of slugs in their body, and never come to the surface again. You may take my word for it, Gregers, I have done all I could without positively laying myself open to all sorts of suspicion and gossip——

Gregers. Suspicion——? Oh, I see.

Werle. I have given Ekdal copying to do for the office, and I pay him far, far more for it than his work is worth——

Gregers (without looking at him). H'm; that I don't doubt.

Werle. You laugh? Do you think I am not telling you the truth? Well, I certainly can't refer you to my books, for I never enter payments of that sort.

Gregers (smiles coldly). No, there are certain payments it is best to keep no account of.

Werle (taken aback). What do you mean by that?

Gregers (mustering up courage). Have you entered what it cost you to have Hialmar Ekdal taught photography?

Werle. I? How "entered" it?

Gregers. I have learnt that it was you who paid for his training. And I have learnt, too, that it was you who enabled him to set up house so comfortably.

Werle. Well, and yet you talk as though I had done nothing for the Ekdals! I can assure you these people have cost me enough in all conscience.

Gregers. Have you entered any of these expenses in your books?

Werle. Why do you ask?

Gregers. Oh, I have my reasons. Now tell me: when you interested yourself so warmly in your old friend's son— it was just before his marriage, was it not?

Werle. Why, deuce take it—after all these years, how can I——?

Gregers. You wrote me a letter about that time—a business letter, of course; and in a postscript you mentioned— quite briefly—that Hialmar Ekdal had married a Miss Hansen.

Werle. Yes, that was quite right. That was her name.

Gregers. But you did not mention that this Miss Hansen was Gina Hansen—our former housekeeper.

Werle (with a forced laugh of derision). No; to tell the truth, it didn't occur to me that you were so particularly interested in our former housekeeper.

Gregers. No more I was. But *(lowers his voice)* there were others in this house who were particularly interested in her.

Werle. What do you mean by that? *(Flaring up.)* You are not alluding to me, I hope?

Gregers (softly but firmly). Yes, I am alluding to you.

Werle. And you dare——! You presume to——! How can that ungrateful hound—that photographer fellow—how dare he go making such insinuations!

Gregers. Hialmar has never breathed a word about this. I don't believe he has the faintest suspicion of such a thing.

Werle. Then where have you got it from? Who can have put such notions in your head?

Gregers. My poor unhappy mother told me; and that the very last time I saw her.

Werle. Your mother! I might have known as much! You and she—you always held together. It was she who turned you against me, from the first.

Gregers. No, it was all that she had to suffer and submit to, until she broke down and came to such a pitiful end.

Werle. Oh, she had nothing to suffer or submit to; not more than most people, at all events. But there's no getting on with morbid, overstrained creatures—that I have learnt to my cost.—And you could go on nursing such a suspicion—burrowing into all sorts of old rumours and slanders against your own father! I must say, Gregers, I really think that at your age you might find something more useful to do.

Gregers. Yes, it is high time.

Werle. Then perhaps your mind would be easier than it seems to be now. What can be your object in remaining up at the works, year out and year in, drudging away like a common clerk, and not drawing a farthing more than the ordinary monthly wage? It is downright folly.

Gregers. Ah, if I were only sure of that.

Werle. I understand you well enough. You want to be independent; you won't be beholden to me for anything. Well, now there happens to be an opportunity for you to become independent, your own master in everything.

Gregers. Indeed? In what way——?

Werle. When I wrote you insisting on your coming to town at once—h'm——

Gregers. Yes, what is it you really want of me? I have been waiting all day to know.

Werle. I want to propose that you should enter the firm, as partner.

Gregers. I! Join your firm? As partner?

Werle. Yes. It would not involve our being constantly together. You could take over the business here in town, and I should move up to the works.

Gregers. You would?

Werle. The fact is, I am not so fit for work as I once was. I am obliged to spare my eyes, Gregers; they have begun to trouble me.

Gregers. They have always been weak.

Werle. Not as they are now. And, besides, circumstances might possibly make it desirable for me to live up there—for a time, at any rate.

Gregers. That is certainly quite a new idea to me.

Werle. Listen, Gregers: there are many things that stand between us; but we are father and son after all. We ought surely to be able to come to some sort of understanding with each other.

Gregers. Outwardly, you mean, of course?

Werle. Well, even that would be something. Think it over, Gregers. Don't you think it ought to be possible? Eh?

Gregers (looking at him coldly). There is something behind all this.

Werle. How so?

Gregers. You want to make use of me in some way.

Werle. In such a close relationship as ours, the one can always be useful to the other.

Gregers. Yes, so people say.

Werle. I want very much to have you at home with me for a time. I am a lonely man, Gregers; I have always felt lonely, all my life through; but most of all now that I am getting up in years. I feel the need of some one about me——

Gregers. You have Mrs. Sörby.

Werle. Yes, I have her; and she has become, I may say, almost indispensable to me. She is lively and even-tempered; she brightens up the house; and that is a very great thing for me.

Gregers. Well then, you have everything just as you wish it.

Werle. Yes, but I am afraid it can't last. A woman so situated may easily find herself in a false position, in the eyes of the world. For that matter it does a man no good, either.

Gregers. Oh, when a man gives such dinners as you give, he can risk a great deal.

Werle. Yes, but how about the woman, Gregers? I fear she won't accept the situation much longer; and even if she did—even if, out of attachment to me, she were to take her chance of gossip and scandal and all that——? Do you think, Gregers—you with your strong sense of justice——

Gregers (interrupts him). Tell me in one word: are you thinking of marrying her?

Werle. Suppose I were thinking of it? What then?

Gregers. That's what I say: what then?

Werle. Should you be inflexibly opposed to it!

Gregers.—Not at all. Not by any means.

Werle. I was not sure whether your devotion to your mother's memory——

Gregers. I am not overstrained.

Werle. Well, whatever you may or may not be, at all events you have lifted a great weight from my mind. I am extremely pleased that I can reckon on your concurrence in this matter.

Gregers (looking intently at him). Now I see the use you want to put me to.

Werle. Use to put you to? What an expression!

Gregers. Oh, don't let us be nice in our choice of words —not when we are alone together, at any rate. *(With a short laugh.)* Well well. So this is what made it absolutely essential that I should come to town in person. For the sake of Mrs. Sörby, we are to get up a pretence at family life in the house—a tableau of filial affection! That will be something new indeed.

Werle. How dare you speak in that tone!

Gregers. Was there ever any family life here? Never since I can remember. But now, forsooth, your plans demand something of the sort. No doubt it will have an excellent effect when it is reported that the son has hastened home, on the wings of filial piety, to the grey-haired father's wedding-feast. What will then remain of all the rumours as to the wrongs the poor dead mother had to submit to? Not a vestige. Her son annihilates them at one stroke.

Werle. Gregers—I believe there is no one in the world you detest as you do me.

Gregers (softly). I have seen you at too close quarters.

Werle. You have seen me with your mother's eyes. *(Lowers his voice a little.)* But you should remember that her eyes were—clouded now and then.

Gregers (quivering). I see what you are hinting at. But who was to blame for mother's unfortunate weakness? Why you, and all those——! The last of them was this woman

that you palmed off upon Hialmar Ekdal, when you were——
Ugh!

Werle (shrugs his shoulders). Word for word as if it
were your mother speaking!

Gregers (without heeding). And there he is now, with
his great, confiding, childlike mind, compassed about with
all this treachery—living under the same roof with such a
creature, and never dreaming that what he calls his home is
built upon a lie! *(Comes a step nearer.)* When I look back
upon your past, I seem to see a battle-field with shattered
lives on every hand.

Werle. I begin to think the chasm that divides us is too
wide.

Gregers (bowing, with self-command). So I have observed; and therefore I take my hat and go.

Werle. You are going! Out of the house?

Gregers. Yes. For at last I see my mission in life.

Werle. What mission?

Gregers. You would only laugh if I told you.

Werle. A lonely man doesn't laugh so easily, Gregers.

Gregers (pointing towards the background). Look, father,
—the Chamberlains are playing blind-man's-buff with Mrs.
Sörby.—Good-night and good-bye.

> [*He goes out by the back to the right. Sounds
> of laughter and merriment from the Company,
> who are now visible in the outer room.*

Werle (muttering contemptuously after GREGERS*).* Ha
——! Poor wretch—and he says he is not overstrained!

ACT SECOND

HIALMAR EKDAL'S *studio, a good-sized room, evidently in the top storey of the building. On the right, a sloping roof of large panes of glass, half-covered by a blue curtain. In the right-hand corner, at the back, the entrance door; farther forward, on the same side, a door leading to the sitting-room. Two doors on the opposite side, and between them an iron stove. At the back, a wide double sliding-door. The studio is plainly but comfortably fitted up and furnished. Between the doors on the right, standing out a little from the wall, a sofa with a table and some chairs; on the table a lighted lamp with a shade; beside the stove an old arm-chair. Photographic instruments and apparatus of different kinds lying about the room. Against the back wall, to the left of the double door, stands a bookcase containing a few books, boxes, and bottles of chemicals, instruments, tools, and other objects. Photographs and small articles, such as camel's-hair pencils, paper, and so forth, lie on the table.*

GINA EKDAL *sits on a chair by the table, sewing.* HEDVIG *is sitting on the sofa, with her hands shading her eyes and her thumbs in her ears, reading a book.*

Gina (*glances once or twice at* HEDVIG, *as if with secret anxiety; then says*): Hedvig!

Hedvig (*does not hear*).

Gina (*repeats more loudly*). Hedvig!

Hedvig (*takes away her hands and looks up*). Yes, mother?

Gina. Hedvig dear, you mustn't sit reading any longer now.

Hedvig. Oh mother, mayn't I read a little more? Just a little bit?

Gina. No, no, you must put away your book now. Father doesn't like it; he never reads hisself in the evening.

Hedvig (shuts the book). No, father doesn't care much about reading.

Gina (puts aside her sewing and takes up a lead pencil and a little account-book from the table). Can you remember how much we paid for the butter to-day?

Hedvig. It was one crown sixty-five.

Gina. That's right. *(Puts it down.)* It's terrible what a lot of butter we get through in this house. Then there was the smoked sausage, and the cheese—let me see— *(Writes)*—and the ham—*(Adds up.)* Yes, that makes just——

Hedvig. And then the beer.

Gina. Yes, to be sure. *(Writes.)* How it do mount up! But we can't manage with no less.

Hedvig. And then you and I didn't need anything hot for dinner, as father was out.

Gina. No; that was so much to the good. And then I took eight crowns fifty for the photographs.

Hedvig. Really! So much as that?

Gina. Exactly eight crowns fifty.

[*Silence.* GINA *takes up her sewing again,* HEDVIG *takes paper and pencil and begins to draw, shading her eyes with her left hand.*

Hedvig. Isn't it jolly to think that father is at Mr. Werle's big dinner-party?

Gina. You know he's not really Mr. Werle's guest. It was the son invited him. *(After a pause.)* We have nothing to do with that Mr. Werle.

Hedvig. I'm longing for father to come home. He promised to ask Mrs. Sörby for something nice for me.

Gina. Yes, there's plenty of good things going in that house, I can tell you.

Hedvig (goes on drawing). And I believe I'm a little hungry too.

[OLD EKDAL, *with the paper parcel under his arm and another parcel in his coat pocket, comes in by the entrance door.*

Gina. How late you are to-day, grandfather!

Ekdal. They had locked the office door. Had to wait in Gråberg's room. And then they let me through—h'm.

Hedvig. Did you get some more copying to do, grandfather?

Ekdal. This whole packet. Just look.

Gina. That's capital.

Hedvig. And you have another parcel in your pocket.

Ekdal. Eh? Oh never mind, that's nothing. *(Puts his stick away in a corner.)* This work will keep me going a long time, Gina. *(Opens one of the sliding-doors in the back wall a little.)* Hush! *(Peeps into the room for a moment, then pushes the door carefully to again.)* Hee-hee! They're fast asleep, all the lot of them. And she's gone into the basket herself. Hee-hee!

Hedvig. Are you sure she isn't cold in that basket, grandfather?

Ekdal. Not a bit of it! Cold? With all that straw? *(Goes towards the farther door on the left.)* There are matches in here, I suppose.

Gina. The matches is on the drawers.

[EKDAL *goes into his room.*

Hedvig. It's nice that grandfather has got all that copying.

Gina. Yes, poor old father; it means a bit of pocket-money for him.

Hedvig. And he won't be able to sit the whole forenoon down at that horrid Madam Eriksen's.

Gina. No more he won't. [*Short silence.*

Hedvig. Do you suppose they are still at the dinner-table?

Gina. Goodness knows; as like as not.

Hedvig. Think of all the delicious things father is having to eat! I'm certain he'll be in splendid spirits when he comes. Don't you think so, mother?

Gina. Yes; and if only we could tell him that we'd got the room let——

Hedvig. But we don't need that this evening.

Gina. Oh, we'd be none the worst of it, I can tell you. It's no use to us as it is.

Hedvig. I mean we don't need it this evening, for father will be in a good humour at any rate. It is best to keep the letting of the room for another time.

Gina (looks across at her). You like having some good news to tell father when he comes home in the evening?

Hedvig. Yes; for then things are pleasanter somehow.

Gina (thinking to herself). Yes, yes, there's something in that.

[OLD EKDAL *comes in again and is going out by the foremost door to the left.*

Gina (half turning in her chair). Do you want something out of the kitchen, grandfather?

Ekdal. Yes, yes, I do. Don't you trouble. *(Goes out.*

Gina. He's not poking away at the fire, is he? *(Waits a moment.)* Hedvig, go and see what he's about.

[EKDAL *comes in again with a small jug of steaming hot water.*

Hedvig. Have you been getting some hot water, grandfather?

Ekdal. Yes, hot water. Want it for something. Want to write, and the ink has got as thick as porridge—h'm.

Gina. But you'd best have your supper, first, grandfather. It's laid in there.

Ekdal. Can't be bothered with supper, Gina. Very

busy, I tell you. No one's to come to my room. No one
—h'm.

> [*He goes into his room;* GINA *and* HEDVIG *look
> at each other.*

Gina (softly). Can you imagine where he's got money
from?

Hedvig. From Gråberg, perhaps.

Gina. Not a bit of it. Gråberg always sends the money
to me.

Hedvig. Then he must have got a bottle on credit somewhere.

Gina. Poor grandfather, who'd give him credit?

HIALMAR EKDAL, *in an overcoat and grey felt hat, comes in
from the right.*

Gina (throws down her sewing and rises). Why, Ekdal,
Is that you already?

Hedvig (at the same time jumping up). Fancy your coming so soon, father!

Hialmar (taking off his hat). Yes, most of the people
were coming away.

Hedvig. So early?

Hialmar. Yes, it was a dinner-party, you know.

> [*Is taking off his overcoat.*

Gina. Let me help you.

Hedvig. Me too.

> [*They draw off his coat;* GINA *hangs it up on the
> back wall.*

Hedvig. Were there many people there, father?

Hialmar. Oh no, not many. We were about twelve or
fourteen at table.

Gina. And you had some talk with them all?

Hialmar. Oh yes, a little; but Gregers took me up most
of the time.

Gina. Is Gregers as ugly as ever?

Hialmar. Well, he's not very much to look at. Hasn't
the old man come home?

Hedvig Yes, grandfather is in his room, writing.

Hialmar. Did he say anything?

Gina. No, what should he say?

Hialmar. Didn't he say anything about——? I heard something about his having been with Gråberg. I'll go in and see him for a moment.

Gina. No, no, better not.

Hialmar. Why not? Did he say he didn't want me to go in?

Gina. I don't think he wants to see nobody this evening——

Hedvig (making signs). H'm—h'm!

Gina (not noticing). ——he has been in to fetch hot water——

Hialmar. Aha! Then he's——

Gina. Yes, I suppose so.

Hialmar. Oh God! my poor old white-haired father!—Well, well; there let him sit and get all the enjoyment he can.

> [OLD EKDAL, *in an indoor coat and with a lighted pipe, comes from his room.*

Ekdal. Got home? Thought it was you I heard talking.

Hialmar. Yes, I have just come.

Ekdal. You didn't see me, did you?

Hialmar. No, but they told me you had passed through —so I thought I would follow you.

Ekdal. H'm, good of you, Hialmar.—Who were they, all those fellows?

Hialmar.—Oh, all sorts of people. There was Chamberlain Flor, and Chamberlain Balle, and Chamberlain Kaspersen, and Chamberlain—this, that, and the other—I don't know who all——

Ekdal (nodding). Hear that, Gina! Chamberlains every one of them!

Gina. Yes, I hear as they're terrible genteel in that house nowadays.

Hedvig. Did the Chamberlains sing, father? Or did they read aloud?

Hialmar. No, they only talked nonsense. They wanted me to recite something for them; but I knew better than that.

Ekdal. You weren't to be persuaded, eh?

Gina. Oh, you might have done it.

Hialmar. No; one mustn't be at everybody's beck and call. *(Walks about the room.)* That's not my way, at any rate.

Ekdal. No, no; Hialmar's not to be had for the asking, he isn't.

Hialmar. I don't see why *I* should bother myself to entertain people on the rare occasions when I go into society. Let the others exert themselves. These fellows go from one great dinner-table to the next and gorge and guzzle day out and day in. It's for them to bestir themselves and do something in return for all the good feeding they get.

Gina. But you didn't say that?

Hialmar (humming). Ho-ho-ho——; faith, I gave them a bit of my mind.

Ekdal. Not the Chamberlains?

Hialmar. Oh, why not? *(Lightly.)* After that, we had a little discussion about Tokay.

Ekdal. Tokay! There's a fine wine for you!

Hialmar (comes to a standstill). It may be a fine wine. But of course you know the vintages differ; it all depends on how much sunshine the grapes have had.

Gina. Why, you know everything, Ekdal.

Ekdal. And did they dispute that?

Hialmar. They tried to; but they were requested to observe that it was just the same with Chamberlains—that with them, too, different batches were of different qualities.

Gina. What things you do think of!

Ekdal. Hee-hee! So they got that in their pipes too?

Hialmar. Right in their teeth.

Ekdal. Do you hear that, Gina? He said it right in the very teeth of all the Chamberlains.

Gina. Fancy——! Right in their teeth!

Hialmar. Yes, but I don't want it talked about. One doesn't speak of such things. The whole affair passed off quite amicably of course. They were nice, genial fellows; I didn't want to wound them—not I!

Ekdal. Right in their teeth, though——!

Hedvig (caressingly). How nice it is to see you in a dress-coat! It suits you so well, father.

Hialmar. Yes, don't you think so? And this one really sits to perfection. It fits almost as if it had been made for me;—a little tight in the arm-holes perhaps;—help me, Hedvig *(takes off the coat).* I think I'll put on my jacket. Where is my jacket, Gina?

Gina. Here it is. *(Brings the jacket and helps him.)*

Hialmar. That's it! Don't forget to send the coat back to Molvik first thing to-morrow morning.

Gina (laying it away). I'll be sure and see to it.

Hialmar (stretching himself). After all, there's a more homely feeling about this. A free-and-easy indoor costume suits my whole personality better. Don't you think so, Hedvig?

Hedvig. Yes, father.

Hialmar. When I loosen my necktie into a pair of flowing ends—like this—eh?

Hedvig. Yes, that goes so well with your moustache and the sweep of your curls.

Hialmar. I should not call them curls exactly; I should rather say locks.

Hedvig. Yes, they are too big for curls.

Hialmar. Locks describes them better.

Hedvig (after a pause, twitching his jacket). **Father!**

Hialmar. Well, what is it?

Hedvig. Oh, you know very well.

Hialmar. No, really I don't——

Hedvig (half laughing, half whispering). Oh, yes, father; now don't tease me any longer!

Hialmar. Why, what do you mean?

Hedvig (shaking him). Oh what nonsense; come, where are they, father? All the good things you promised me, you know?

Hialmar. Oh—if I haven't forgotten all about them!

Hedvig. Now you're only teasing me, father! Oh, it's too bad of you! Where have you put them?

Hialmar. No, I positively forgot to get anything. But wait a little! I have something else for you, Hedvig.

[*Goes and searches in the pockets of the coat.*

Hedvig (skipping and clapping her hands). Oh mother, mother!

Gina. There, you see; if you only give him time——

Hialmar (with a paper). Look, here it is.

Hedvig. That? Why, that's only a paper.

Hialmar. That is the bill of fare, my dear; the whole bill of fare. Here you see: "Menu"—that means bill of fare.

Hedvig. Haven't you anything else?

Hialmar. I forgot the other things, I tell you. But you may take my word for it, these dainties are very unsatisfying. Sit down at the table and read the bill of fare, and then I'll describe to you how the dishes taste. Here you are, Hedvig.

Hedvig (gulping down her tears). Thank you. (*She seats herself, but does not read;* GINA *makes signs to her;* HIALMAR *notices it.*)

Hialmar (pacing up and down the room). It's monstrous what absurd things the father of a family is expected to think of; and if he forgets the smallest trifle, he is treated to sour faces at once. Well, well, one gets used to that too. (*Stops near the stove, by the old man's chair.*) Have you peeped in there this evening, father?

Ekdal. Yes, to be sure I have. She's gone into the basket.

Hialmar. Ah, she has gone into the basket. Then she's beginning to get used to it.

Ekdal. Yes; just as I prophesied. But you know there are still a few little things——

Hialmar. A few improvements, yes.

Ekdal. They've got to be made, you know.

Hialmar. Yes, let us have a talk about the improvements, father. Come, let us sit on the sofa.

Ekdal. All right. H'm—think I'll just fill my pipe first. Must clean it out, too. H'm.   [*He goes into his room.*

Gina (smiling to HIALMAR *).* His pipe!

Hialmar. Oh yes yes, Gina; let him alone—the poor shipwrecked old man.—Yes, these improvements—we had better get them out of hand to-morrow.

Gina. You'll hardly have time to-morrow, Ekdal.

Hedvig (interposing). Oh yes he will, mother!

Gina. ——for remember them prints that has to be retouched; they've sent for them time after time.

Hialmar. There now! those prints again! I shall get them finished all right! Have any new orders come in?

Gina. No, worse luck; to-morrow I have nothing but those two sittings, you know.

Hialmar. Nothing else? Oh no, if people won't set about things with a will——

Gina. But what more can I do? Don't I advertise in the papers as much as we can afford?

Hialmar. Yes, the papers, the papers; you see how much good they do. And I suppose no one has been to look at the room either?

Gina. No, not yet.

Hialmar. That was only to be expected. If people won't keep their eyes open——. Nothing can be done without a real effort, Gina!

Hedvig (going towards him). Shall I fetch you the flute, father?

Hialmar. No; no flute for me; *I* want no pleasures in

this world. *(Pacing about.)* Yes, indeed I will work to-morrow; you shall see if I don't. You may be sure I shall work as long as my strength holds out.

Gina. But my dear good Ekdal, I didn't mean it in that way.

Hedvig. Father, mayn't I bring in a bottle of beer?

Hialmar. No, certainly not. I require nothing, noth-ing—— *(Comes to a standstill.)* Beer? Was it beer you were talking about?

Hedvig (cheerfully). Yes, father; beautiful fresh beer.

Hialmar. Well—since you insist upon it, you may bring in a bottle.

Gina. Yes, do; and we'll be nice and cosy.

[HEDVIG *runs towards the kitchen door.*

Hialmar (by the stove, stops her, looks at her, puts his arm round her neck and presses her to him). Hedvig, Hed-vig!

Hedvig (with tears of joy). My dear, kind father!

Hialmar. No, don't call me that. Here have I been feasting at the rich man's table,—battening at the groaning board——! And I couldn't even——!

Gina (sitting at the table). Oh, nonsense, nonsense, Ek-dal.

Hialmar. It's not nonsense! And yet you mustn't be too hard upon me. You know that I love you for all that.

Hedvig (throwing her arms round him). And we love you, oh, so dearly, father!

Hialmar. And if I am unreasonable once in a while,—why then—you must remember that I am a man beset by a host of cares. There, there! *(Dries his eyes.)* No beer at such a moment as this. Give me the flute.

[HEDVIG *runs to the bookcase and fetches it.*

Hialmar. Thanks! That's right. With my flute in my hand and you two at my side—ah——!

[HEDVIG *seats herself at the table near* GINA; HIAL-MAR *paces backwards and forwards, pipes up vig.*

orously, and plays a Bohemian peasant dance, but in a slow plaintive tempo, and with sentimental expression.

Hialmar (breaking off the melody, holds out his left hand to GINA, *and says with emotion):* Our roof may be poor and humble, Gina; but it is home. And with all my heart I say: here dwells my happiness.

[*He begins to play again; almost immediately after, a knocking is heard at the entrance door.*

Gina (rising). Hush, Ekdal,—I think there's some one at the door.

Hialmar (laying the flute on the bookcase). There! Again! [GINA *goes and opens the door.*

Gregers Werle (in the passage). Excuse me——

Gina (starting back slightly). Oh!

Gregers. ——does not Mr. Ekdal, the photographer, live here?

Gina. Yes, he does.

Hialmar (going towards the door). Gregers! You here after all? Well, come in then.

Gregers (coming in). I told you I would come and look you up.

Hialmar. But this evening——? Have you left the party?

Gregers. I have left both the party and my father's house.—Good evening, Mrs. Ekdal. I don't know whether you recognise me?

Gina. Oh yes; it's not difficult to know young Mr. Werle again.

Gregers. No, I am like my mother; and no doubt you remember her.

Hialmar. Left your father's house, did you say?

Gregers. Yes, I have gone to a hotel.

Hialmar. Indeed. Well, since you're here, take off your coat and sit down.

Gregers. Thanks.

[*He takes off his overcoat. He is now dressed in a plain grey suit of a countrified cut.*

Hialmar. Here, on the sofa. Make yourself comfortable.

[GREGERS *seats himself on the sofa;* HIALMAR *takes a chair at the table.*

Gregers (looking around him). So these are your quarters, Hialmar—this is your home.

Hialmar. This is the studio, as you see——

Gina. But it's the largest of our rooms, so we generally sit here.

Hialmar. We used to live in a better place; but this flat has one great advantage: there are such capital outer rooms——

Gina. And we have a room on the other side of the passage that we can let.

Gregers (to HIALMAR*).* Ah—so you have lodgers too?

Hialmar. No, not yet. They're not so easy to find, you see; you have to keep your eyes open. *(To* HEDVIG.*)* What about that beer, eh?

[HEDVIG *nods and goes out into the kitchen.*

Gregers. So that is your daughter?

Hialmar. Yes, that is Hedvig.

Gregers. And she is your only child?

Hialmar. Yes, the only one. She is the joy of our lives, and—*(lowering his voice)*—at the same time our deepest sorrow, Gregers.

Gregers. What do you mean?

Hialmar. She is in serious danger of losing her eyesight.

Gregers. Becoming blind?

Hialmar. Yes. Only the first symptoms have appeared as yet, and she may not feel it much for some time. But the doctor has warned us. It is coming, inexorably.

Gregers. What a terrible misfortune! How do you account for it?

Hialmar (sighs). Hereditary, no doubt.

Gregers (starting). Hereditary?

Gina. Ekdal's mother had weak eyes.

Hialmar. Yes, so my father says; I can't remember her.

Gregers. Poor child! And how does she take it?

Hialmar. Oh, you can imagine we haven't the heart to tell her of it. She dreams of no danger. Gay and careless and chirping like a little bird, she flutters onward into a life of endless night. *(Overcome.)* Oh, it is cruelly hard on me, Gregers.

[HEDVIG *brings a tray with beer and glasses, which she sets upon the table.*

Hialmar (stroking her hair). Thanks, thanks, Hedvig.

[HEDVIG *puts her arm round his neck and whispers in his ear.*

HIALMAR. No, no bread and butter just now. *(Looks up).* But perhaps you would like some, Gregers.

Gregers (with a gesture of refusal). No, no thank you.

Hialmar (still melancholy). Well, you can bring in a little all the same. If you have a crust, that is all I want. And plenty of butter on it, mind.

[HEDVIG *nods gaily and goes out into the kitchen again.*

Gregers (who has been following her with his eyes). She seems quite strong and healthy otherwise.

Gina. Yes. In other ways there's nothing amiss with her, thank goodness.

Gregers. She promises to be very like you, Mrs. Ekdal. How old is she now?

Gina. Hedvig is close on fourteen; her birthday is the day after to-morrow.

Gregers. She is pretty tall for her age, then.

Gina. Yes, she's shot up wonderful this last year.

Gregers. It makes one realise one's own age to see these young people growing up.—How long is it now since you were married?

Gina. We've been married—let me see—just on fifteen years.

Gregers. Is it so long as that?

Gina (becomes attentive; looks at him). Yes, it is indeed.

Hialmer. Yes, so it is. Fifteen years all but a few months. *(Changing his tone.)* They must have been long years for you, up at the works, Gregers.

Gregers. They seemed long while I was living them; now they are over, I hardly know how the time has gone.

[OLD EKDAL *comes from his room without his pipe, but with his old-fashioned uniform cap on his head; his gait is somewhat unsteady.*

Ekdal. Come now, Hialmar, let's sit down and have a good talk about this—h'm—what was it again?

Hialmar (going towards him). Father, we have a visitor here—Gregers Werle.—I don't know if you remember him.

Ekdal (looking at GREGERS, *who has risen).* Werle? Is that the son? What does he want with me?

Hialmar. Nothing; it's me he has come to see.

Ekdal. Oh! Then there's nothing wrong?

Hialmar. No, no, of course not.

Ekdal (with a large gesture). Not that I'm afraid, you know; but——

Gregers (goes over to him). I bring you a greeting from your old hunting-grounds, Lieutenant Ekdal.

Ekdal. Hunting-grounds?

Gregers. Yes, up in Höidal, about the works, you know.

Ekdal. Oh, up there. Yes, I knew all those places well in the old days.

Gregers. You were a great sportsman then.

Ekdal. So I was, I don't deny it. You're looking at my uniform cap. I don't ask anybody's leave to wear it in the house. So long as I don't go out in the streets with it——

[HEDVIG *brings a plate of bread and butter, which she puts upon the table.*

Hialmar. Sit down, father, and have a glass of beer. Help yourself, Gregers.

[EKDAL *mutters and stumbles over to the sofa.*
GREGERS *seats himself on the chair nearest to
him,* HIALMAR *on the other side of* GREGERS.
GINA *sits a little way from the table, sewing;*
HEDVIG *stands beside her father.*

Gregers. Can you remember, Lieutenant Ekdal, how
Hialmar and I used to come up and visit you in the summer
and at Christmas?

Ekdal. Did you? No, no, no; I don't remember it.
But sure enough I've been a tidy bit of a sportsman in my
day. I've shot bears too. I've shot nine of 'em, no less.

Gregers (looking sympathetically at him). And now you
never get any shooting?

Ekdal. Can't just say that, sir. Get a shot now and
then perhaps. Of course not in the old way. For the
woods you see—the woods, the woods——! *(Drinks.)*
Are the woods fine up there now?

Gregers. Not so fine as in your time. They have been
thinned a good deal.

Ekdal. Thinned? *(More softly, and as if afraid.)* It's
dangerous work that. Bad things come of it. The woods
revenge themselves.

Hialmar (filling up his glass). Come—a little more,
father.

Gregers. How can a man like you—such a man for the
open air—live in the midst of a stuffy town, boxed within
four walls?

Ekdal (laughs quietly and glances at HIALMAR*).* Oh, it's
not so bad here. Not at all so bad.

Gregers. But don't you miss all the things that used to
be a part of your very being—the cool sweeping breezes,
the free life in the woods and on the uplands, among beasts
and birds——?

Ekdal (smiling). Hialmar, shall we let him see it?

Hialmar (hastily and a little embarrassed). Oh, no no,
father; not this evening.

Gregers. What does he want to show me?

Hialmar. Oh, it's only something—you can see it another time.

Gregers (continues, to the old man). You see I have been thinking, Lieutenant Ekdal, that you should come up with me to the works; I am sure to be going back soon. No doubt you could get some copying there too. And here, you have nothing on earth to interest you—nothing to liven you up.

Ekdal (stares in astonishment at him). Have *I* nothing on earth to——!

Gregers. Of course you have Hialmar; but then he has his own family. And a man like you, who has always had such a passion for what is free and wild——

Ekdal (thumps the table). Hialmar, he shall see it!

Hialmar. Oh, do you think it's worth while, father? It's all dark.

Ekdal. Nonsense; it's moonlight. *(Rises).* He shall see it, I tell you. Let me pass! Come and help me, Hialmar.

Hedvig. Oh yes, do, father!

Hialmar (rising). Very well then.

Gregers (to GINA*).* What is it?

Gina. Oh, nothing so very wonderful, after all.

[EKDAL *and* HIALMAR *have gone to the back wall and are each pushing back a side of the sliding door;* HEDVIG *helps the old man;* GREGERS *remains standing by the sofa;* GINA *sits still and sews. Through the open doorway a large, deep irregular garret is seen with odd nooks and corners; a couple of stove-pipes running through it, from rooms below. There are skylights through which clear moonbeams shine in on some parts of the great room; others lie in deep shadow.*

Ekdal (to GREGERS*).* You may come close up if you like.

Gregers (going over to them). Why, what is it?

Ekdal. Look for yourself. H'm.

Hialmar (somewhat embarrassed). This belongs to father, you understand.

Gregers (at the door, looks into the garret). Why, you keep poultry, Lieutenant Ekdal.

Ekdal. Should think we did keep poultry. They've gone to roost now. But you should just see our fowls by daylight, sir!

Hedvig. And there's a——

Ekdal. Sh—sh! don't say anything about it yet.

Gregers. And you have pigeons too, I see.

Ekdal. Oh yes, haven't we just got pigeons! They have their nest-boxes up there under the roof-tree; for pigeons like to roost high, you see.

Hialmar. They aren't all common pigeons.

Ekdal. Common! Should think not indeed! We have tumblers, and a pair of pouters, too. But come here! Can you see that hutch down there by the wall?

Gregers. Yes; what do you use it for?

Ekdal. That's where the rabbits sleep, sir.

Gregers. Dear me; so you have rabbits too?

Ekdal. Yes, you may take my word for it, we have rabbits! He wants to know if we have rabbits, Hialmar! H'm! But now comes the thing, let me tell you! Here we have it! Move away, Hedvig. Stand here; that's right, —and now look down there.—Don't you see a basket with straw in it?

Gregers. Yes. And I can see a fowl lying in the basket.

Ekdal. H'm—"a fowl"——

Gregers. Isn't it a duck?

Ekdal (hurt). Why, of course it's a duck.

Hialmar. But what kind of duck, do you think?

Hedvig. It's not just a common duck——

Ekdal. Sh!

Gregers. And it's not a Muscovy duck either.

Ekdal. No, Mr.—Werle; it's not a Muscovy duck; for it's a wild duck!

Gregers. Is it really? A wild duck?

Ekdal. Yes, that's what it is. That "fowl" as you call it—is the wild duck. It's our wild duck, sir.

Hedvig. My wild duck. It belongs to me.

Gregers. And can it live up here in the garret? Does it thrive?

Ekdal. Of course it has a trough of water to splash about in, you know.

Hialmar. Fresh water every other day.

Gina (turning towards HIALMAR*).* But my dear Ekdal, it's getting icy cold here.

Ekdal. H'm, we had better shut up then. It's as well not to disturb their night's rest, too. Close up, Hedvig.

[HIALMAR *and* HEDVIG *push the garret doors together.*

Ekdal. Another time you shall see her properly. *(Seats himself in the arm-chair by the stove.)* Oh, they're curious things, these wild ducks, I can tell you.

Gregers. How did you manage to catch it, Lieutenant Ekdal?

Ekdal. *I* didn't catch it. There's a certain man in this town whom we have to thank for it.

Gregers (starts slightly). That man was not my father, was he?

Ekdal. You've hit it. Your father and no one else. H'm.

Hialmar. Strange that you should guess that, Gregers.

Gregers. You were telling me that you owed so many things to my father; and so I thought perhaps——

Gina. But we didn't get the duck from Mr. Werle himself——

Ekdal. It's Håkon Werle we have to thank for her, all

the same, Gina. *(To* GREGERS.*)* He was shooting from a
boat, you see, and he brought her down. But your father's
sight is not very good now. H'm; she was only wounded.

Gregers. Ah! She got a couple of slugs in her body, I
suppose.

Hialmar. Yes, two or three.

Hedvig. She was hit under the wing, so that she couldn't
fly.

Gregers. And I suppose she dived to the bottom, eh?

Ekdal (sleepily, in a thick voice). Of course. Always
do that, wild ducks do. They shoot to the bottom as deep
as they can get, sir—and bite themselves fast in the tangle
and seaweed—and all the devil's own mess that grows down
there. And they never come up again.

Gregers. But your wild duck came up again, Lieutenant
Ekdal.

Ekdal. He had such an amazingly clever dog, your
father had. And that dog—he dived in after the duck and
fetched her up again.

Gregers (who has turned to HIALMAR*).* And then she
was sent to you here?

Hialmar. Not at once; at first your father took her
home. But she wouldn't thrive there; so Pettersen was told
to put an end to her——

Ekdal (half asleep). H'm—yes—Pettersen—that ass——

Hialmar (speaking more softly). That was how we got
her, you see; for father knows Pettersen a little; and when
he heard about the wild duck he got him to hand her over
to us.

Gregers. And now she thrives as well as possible in the
garret there?

Hialmar. Yes, wonderfully well. She has got fat. You
see, she has lived in there so long now that she has forgotten her natural wild life; and it all depends on that.

Gregers. You are right there, Hialmar. Be sure you

never let her get a glimpse of the sky and the sea——.
But I mustn't stay any longer; I think your father is
asleep.

Hialmar. Oh, as for that——

Gregers. But, by-the-bye—you said you had a room to
let—a spare room?

Hialmar. Yes; what then? Do you know of anybody——?

Gregers. Can *I* have that room?

Hialmar. You?

Gina. Oh no, Mr. Werle, you——

Gregers. May I have the room? If so, I'll take possession first thing to-morrow morning.

Hialmar. Yes, with the greatest pleasure——

Gina. But, Mr. Werle, I'm sure it's not at all the sort
of room for you.

Hialmar. Why, Gina! how can you say that?

Gina. Why, because the room's neither large enough
nor light enough, and——

Gregers. That really doesn't matter, Mrs. Ekdal.

Hialmar. I call it quite a nice room, and not at all badly
furnished either.

Gina. But remember the pair of them underneath.

Gregers. What pair?

Gina. Well, there's one as has been a tutor——

Hialmar. That's Molvik—Mr. Molvik, B.A.

Gina. And then there's a doctor, by the name of Relling.

Gregers. Relling? I know him a little; he practised for
a time up in Höidal.

Gina. They're a regular rackety pair, they are. As often
as not, they're out on the loose in the evenings; and then
they come home at all hours, and they're not always just——

Gregers. One soon gets used to that sort of thing. I daresay I shall be like the wild duck——

Gina. H'm; I think you ought to sleep upon it first, anyway.

Gregers. You seem very unwilling to have me in the house, Mrs. Ekdal.

Gina. Oh, no! What makes you think that?

Hialmar. Well, you really behave strangely about it, Gina. *(To* GREGERS.*)* Then I suppose you intend to remain in the town for the present?

Gregers (putting on his overcoat). Yes, now I intend to remain here.

Hialmar. And yet not at your father's? What do you propose to do, then?

Gregers. Ah, if I only knew that, Hialmar, I shouldn't be so badly off! But when one has the misfortune to be called Gregers—! "Gregers"—and then "Werle" after it; did you ever hear anything so hideous?

Hialmar. Oh, I don't think so at all.

Gregers. Ugh! Bah! I feel I should like to spit upon the fellow that answers to such a name. But when a man is once for all doomed to be Gregers—Werle in this world, as I am——

Hialmar (laughs). Ha, ha! If you weren't Gregers Werle, what would you like to be?

Gregers. If I should choose, I should like best to be a clever dog.

Gina. A dog!

Hedvig (involuntarily). Oh, no!

Gregers. Yes, an amazingly clever dog; one that goes to the bottom after wild ducks when they dive and bite themselves fast in tangle and sea-weed, down among the ooze.

Hialmar. Upon my word now, Gregers—I don't in the least know what you're driving at.

Gregers. Oh, well, you might not be much the wiser if you did. It's understood, then, that I move in early to-morrow morning. *(To* GINA.*)* I won't give you any trouble; I do everything for myself. *(To* HIALMAR.*)* We can talk about the rest to-morrow.—Good-night, Mrs. Ekdal. *(Nods to* HEDVIG.*)* Good-night.

Gina. Good-night, Mr. Werle.

Hedvig. Good-night.

Hialmar (who has lighted a candle). Wait a moment; I must show you a light; the stairs are sure to be dark.

[GREGERS *and* HIALMAR *go out by the passage door.*

Gina (looking straight before her, with her sewing in her lap). Wasn't that queer-like talk about wanting to be a dog?

Hedvig. Do you know, mother—I believe he meant something quite different by that.

Gina. Why, what should he mean?

Hedvig. Oh, I don't know; but it seemed to me he meant something different from what he said—all the time.

Gina. Do you think so? Yes, it was sort of queer.

Hialmar (comes back). The lamp was still burning. *(Puts out the candle and sets it down).* Ah, now one can get a mouthful of food at last. *(Begins to eat the bread and butter.)* Well, you see, Gina—if only you keep your eyes open——

Gina. How, keep your eyes open——?

Hialmar. Why, haven't we at last had the luck to get the room let? And just think—to a person like Gregers—a good old friend.

Gina. Well, I don't know what to say about it.

Hedvig. Oh, mother, you'll see; it'll be such fun!

Hialmar. You're very strange. You were so bent upon getting the room let before; and now you don't like it.

Gina. Yes I do, Ekdal; if it had only been to some one else—— But what do you suppose Mr. Werle will say?

Hialmar. Old Werle? It doesn't concern him.

Gina. But surely you can see that there's something amiss between them again, or the young man wouldn't be leaving home. You know very well those two can't get on with each other.

Hialmar. Very likely not, but——

Gina. And now Mr. Werle may fancy it's you that has egged him on——

Hialmar. Let him fancy so, then! Mr. Werle has done a great deal for me; far be it from me to deny it. But that doesn't make me everlastingly dependent upon him.

Gina. But, my dear Ekdal, maybe grandfather'll suffer for it. He may lose the little bit of work he gets from Gråberg.

Hialmar. I could almost say: so much the better! Is it not humiliating for a man like me to see his grey-haired father treated as a pariah? But now I believe the fulness of time is at hand. (*Takes a fresh piece of bread and butter.*) As sure as I have a mission in life, I mean to fulfil it now!

Hedvig. Oh, yes, father, do!

Gina. Hush! Don't wake him!

Hialmar (more softly). I will fulfil it, I say. The day shall come when—— And that is why I say it's a good thing we have let the room; for that makes me more independent. The man who has a mission in life must be independent. (*By the arm-chair, with emotion.*) Poor old white-haired father! Rely on your Hialmar. He has broad shoulders— strong shoulders, at any rate. You shall yet wake up some fine day and—— (*To* GINA.) Do you not believe it?

Gina (rising). Yes, of course I do; but in the meantime suppose we see about getting him to bed.

Hialmar. Yes, come.

[*They take hold of the old man carefully.*

ACT THIRD

HIALMAR EKDAL'S *studio. It is morning: the daylight shines through the large window in the slanting roof; the curtain is drawn back.*

HIALMAR *is sitting at the table, busy retouching a photograph; several others lie before him. Presently* GINA, *wearing her hat and cloak, enters by the passage door; she has a covered basket on her arm.*

Hialmar. Back already, Gina?

Gina. Oh, yes, one can't let the grass grow under one's feet.

> [*Sets her basket on a chair, and takes off her things.*

Hialmar. Did you look in at Gregers' room?

Gina. Yes, that I did. It's a rare sight, I can tell you; he's made a pretty mess to start off with.

Hialmar. How so?

Gina. He was determined to do everything for himself, he said; so he sets to work to light the stove, and what must he do but screw down the damper till the whole room is full of smoke. Ugh! There was a smell fit to——

Hialmar. Well, really!

Gina. But that's not the worst of it; for then he thinks he'll put out the fire, and goes and empties his water-jug into the stove, and so makes the whole floor one filthy puddle.

Hialmar. How annoying!

Gina. I've got the porter's wife to clear up after him, pig

48

that he is! But the room won't be fit to live in till the afternoon.

Hialmar. What's he doing with himself in the meantime?

Gina. He said he was going out for a little while.

Hialmar. I looked in upon him, too, for a moment—after you had gone.

Gina. So I heard. You've asked him to lunch.

Hialmar. Just to a little bit of early lunch, you know. It's his first day—we can hardly do less. You've got something in the house, I suppose?

Gina. I shall have to find something or other.

Hialmar. And don't cut it too fine, for I fancy Relling and Molvik are coming up, too. I just happened to meet Relling on the stairs, you see; so I had to——

Gina. Oh, are we to have those two as well?

Hialmar. Good Lord—a couple more or less can't make any difference.

Old Ekdal (opens his door and looks in). I say, Hialmar—— *(Sees* GINA.*)* Oh!

Gina. Do you want anything, grandfather?

Ekdal. Oh, no, it doesn't matter. H'm!

[*Retires again.*

Gina (takes up the basket). Be sure you see that he doesn't go out.

Hialmar. All right, all right. And, Gina, a little herring-salad wouldn't be a bad idea; Relling and Molvik were out on the loose again last night.

Gina. If only they don't come before I'm ready for them——

Hialmar. No, of course they won't; take your own time.

Gina. Very well; and meanwhile you can be working a bit.

Hialmar. Well, I am working! I am working as hard as I can!

Gina. Then you'll have that job off your hands, you see.

[*She goes out to the kitchen with her basket.*
HIALMAR *sits for a time pencilling. away at the
photograph, in an indolent and listless manner.*
Ekdal (peeps in, looks round the studio, and says softly):
Are you busy?

Hialmar. Yes, I'm toiling at these wretched pictures——

Ekdal. Well, well, never mind,—since you're so busy—
h'm! [*He goes out again; the door stands open.*

*Hialmar (continues for some time in silence; then he lays
down his brush and goes over to the door).* Are you busy,
father?

Ekdal (in a grumbling tone, within). If you're busy, I'm
busy, too. H'm!

Hialmar. Oh, very well, then.

[*Goes to his work again.*

Ekdal (presently, coming to the door again). H'm; I
say, Hialmar, I'm not so very busy, you know.

Hialmar. I thought you were writing.

Ekdal. Oh, devil take it! can't Gråberg wait a day or
two? After all, it's not a matter of life and death.

Hialmar. No; and you're not his slave either.

Ekdal. And about that other business in there——

Hialmar. Just what I was thinking of. Do you want to
go in? Shall I open the door for you?

Ekdal. Well, it wouldn't be a bad notion.

Hialmar (rises). Then we'd have that off our hands.

Ekdal. Yes, exactly. It's got to be ready first thing to-
morrow. It is to-morrow, isn't it? H'm?

Hialmar. Yes, of course it's to-morrow.

[HIALMAR *and* EKDAL *push aside each his half of
the sliding door. The morning sun is shining in
through the skylights; some doves are flying
about; others sit cooing, upon the perches; the
hens are heard clucking now and then, further
back in the garret.*

Hialmar. There; now you can get to work, father.

Ekdal (goes in). Aren't you coming, too?

Hialmar. Well, really, do you know——; I almost think—— *(Sees* GINA *at the kitchen door.)* I? No; 1 naven't time; I must work.—But now for our new contrivance——

> [*He pulls a cord, a curtain slips down inside, the lower part consisting of a piece of old sailcloth, the upper part of a stretched fishing net. The floor of the garret is thus no longer visible.*

Hialmar (goes to the table). So! Now, perhaps I can sit in peace for a little while.

Gina. Is he rampaging in there again?

Hialmar. Would you rather have had him slip down to Madam Eriksen's? *(Seats himself.)* Do you want anything? You know you said——

Gina. I only wanted to ask if you think we can lay the table for lunch here?

Hialmar. Yes; we have no early appointment, I suppose?

Gina. No, I expect no one to-day except those two sweethearts that are to be taken together.

Hialmar. Why the deuce couldn't they be taken together another day!

Gina. Don't you know, I told them to come in the afternoon, when you are having your nap.

Hialmar. Oh, that's capital. Very well, let us have lunch here then.

Gina. All right; but there's no hurry about laying the cloth; you can have the table for a good while yet.

Hialmar. Do you think I am not sticking at my work? I'm at it as hard as I can!

Gina. Then you'll be free later on, you know.

> [*Goes out into the kitchen again. Short pause.*

Ekdal (in the garret doorway, behind the net). Hialmar!

Hialmar. Well?

Ekdal. Afraid we shall have to move the water-trough, after all.

Hialmar. What else have I been saying all along?

Ekdal. H'm—h'm—h'm.

[*Goes away from the door again.* HIALMAR *goes on working a little; glances towards the garret and half rises.* HEDVIG *comes in from the kitchen.*

Hialmar (sits down again hurriedly). What do you want?

Hedvig. I only wanted to come in beside you, father.

Hialmar (after a pause). What makes you go prying around like that? Perhaps you are told off to watch me?

Hedvig. No, no.

Hialmar. What is your mother doing out there?

Hedvig. Oh, mother's in the middle of making the herring-salad. *(Goes to the table).* Isn't there any little thing I could help you with, father?

Hialmar. Oh, no. It is right that I should bear the whole burden—so long as my strength holds out. Set your mind at rest, Hedvig; if only your father keeps his health——

Hedvig. Oh, no, father! You mustn't talk in that horrid way.

[*She wanders about a little, stops by the doorway and looks into the garret.*

Hialmar. Tell me, what is he doing?

Hedvig. I think he's making a new path to the water-trough.

Hialmar. He can never manage that by himself! And here am I doomed to sit——!

Hedvig (goes to him). Let me take the brush, father; I can do it, quite well.

Hialmar. Oh, nonsense; you will only hurt your eyes.

Hedvig. Not a bit. Give me the brush.

Hialmar (rising). Well, it won't take more than a minute or two.

Hedvig. Pooh, what harm can it do then? *(Takes the brush.)* There! *(Seats herself.)* I can begin upon this one.

Hialmar. But mind you don't hurt your eyes! Do you hear? *I* won't be answerable; you do it on your own responsibility—understand that.

Hedvig (retouching). Yes, yes, I understand.

Hialmar. You are quite clever at it, Hedvig. Only a minute or two, you know.

> [*He slips through by the edge of the curtain into the garret.* HEDVIG *sits at her work.* HIALMAR *and* EKDAL *are heard disputing inside.*

Hialmar (appears behind the net). I say, Hedvig—give me those pincers that are lying on the shelf. And the chisel. *(Turns away inside.)* Now you shall see, father. Just let me show you first what I mean!

> [HEDVIG *has fetched the required tools from the shelf, and hands them to him through the net.*

Hialmar. Ah, thanks. I didn't come a moment too soon.

> [*Goes back from the curtain again; they are heard carpentering and talking inside.* HEDVIG *stands looking in at them. A moment later there is a knock at the passage door; she does not notice it.*

Gregers Werle (bareheaded, in indoor dress, enters and stops near the door). H'm——!

Hedvig (turns and goes towards him). Good morning. Please come in.

Gregers. Thank you. *(Looking towards the garret.)* You seem to have workpeople in the house.

Hedvig. No, it is only father and grandfather. I'll tell them you are here.

Gregers. No, no, don't do that; I would rather wait a little. *[Seats himself on the sofa.*

Hedvig. It looks so untidy here——

> [*Begins to clear away the photographs.*

Gregers. Oh, don't take them away. Are those prints that have to be finished off?

Hedvig. Yes, they are a few I was helping father with.

Gregers. Please don't let me disturb you.

Hedvig. Oh, no.

> [*She gathers the things to her and sits down to work;* GREGERS *looks at her, meanwhile, in silence.*

Gregers. Did the wild duck sleep well last night?

Hedvig. Yes, I think so, thanks.

Gregers (turning towards the garret). It looks quite different by day from what it did last night in the moonlight.

Hedvig. Yes, it changes ever so much. It looks different in the morning and in the afternoon; and it's different on rainy days from what it is in fine weather.

Gregers. Have you noticed that?

Hedvig. Yes, how could I help it?

Gregers. Are you, too, fond of being in there with the wild duck?

Hedvig. Yes, when I can manage it——

Gregers. But I suppose you haven't much spare time; you go to school, no doubt.

Hedvig. No, not now; father is afraid of my hurting my eyes.

Gregers. Oh; then he reads with you himself?

Hedvig. Father has promised to read with me; but he has never had time yet.

Gregers. Then is there nobody else to give you a little help?

Hedvig. Yes, there is Mr. Molvik; but he is not always exactly—quite——

Gregers. Sober?

Hedvig. Yes, I suppose that's it!

Gregers. Why, then you must have any amount of time

on your hands. And in there I suppose it is a sort world
by itself?

Hedvig. Oh, yes, quite. And there are such lots of wonderful things.

Gregers. Indeed?

Hedvig. Yes, there are big cupboards full of books; and
a great many of the books have pictures in them.

Gregers. Aha!

Hedvig. And there's an old bureau with drawers and
flaps, and a big clock with figures that go out and in. But
the clock isn't going now.

Gregers. So time has come to a standstill in there—in
the wild duck's domain.

Hedvig. Yes. And then there's an old paint-box and
things of that sort; and all the books.

Gregers. And you read the books, I suppose?

Hedvig. Oh, yes, when I get the chance. Most of them
are English though, and I don't understand English. But
then I look at the pictures.—There is one great big book
called "Harrison's History of London."* It must be a hundred years old; and there are such heaps of pictures in it.
At the beginning there is Death with an hour-glass and a
woman. I think that is horrid. But then there are all the
other pictures of churches, and castles, and streets, and great
ships sailing on the sea.

Gregers. But tell me, where did all those wonderful things
come from?

Hedvig. Oh, an old sea captain once lived here, and he
brought them home with him. They used to call him "The
Flying Dutchman." That was curious, because he wasn't
a Dutchman at all.

Gregers. Was he not?

---

* *A New and Universal History of the Cities of London and
Westminster,* by Walter Harrison. London, 1775, folio.

Hedvig. No. But at last he was drowned at sea; and so he left all those things behind him.

Gregers. Tell me now—when you are sitting in there looking at the pictures, don't you wish you could travel and see the real world for yourself?

Hedvig. Oh, no! I mean always to stay at home and help father and mother.

Gregers. To retouch photographs?

Hedvig. No, not only that. I should love above everything to learn to engrave pictures like those in the English books.

Gregers. H'm. What does your father say to that?

Hedvig. I don't think father likes it; father is strange about such things. Only think, he talks of my learning basket-making, and straw-plaiting! But I don't think that would be much good.

Gregers. Oh, no, I don't think so either.

Hedvig. But father was right in saying that if I had learnt basket-making I could have made the new basket for the wild duck.

Gregers. So you could; and it was you that ought to have done it, wasn't it?

Hedvig. Yes, for it's my wild duck.

Gregers. Of course it is.

Hedvig. Yes, it belongs to me. But I lend it to father and grandfather as often as they please.

Gregers. Indeed? What do they do with it?

Hedvig. Oh, they look after it, and build places for it, and so on.

Gregers. I see; for no doubt the wild duck is by far the most distinguished inhabitant of the garret?

Hedvig. Yes, indeed she is; for she is a real wild fowl, you know. And then she is so much to be pitied; she has no one to care for, poor thing.

Gregers. She has no family, as the rabbits have——

Hedvig. No. The hens too, many of them, were chickens together; but she has been taken right away from all her friends. And then there is so much that is strange about the wild duck. Nobody knows her, and nobody knows where she came from either.

Gregers. And she has been down in the depths of the sea.

Hedvig (with a quick glance at him, represses a smile and asks): Why do you say "depths of the sea"?

Gregers. What else should I say?

Hedvig. You could say "the bottom of the sea."*

Gregers. Oh, mayn't I just as well say the depths of the sea?

Hedvig. Yes; but it sounds so strange to me when other people speak of the depths of the sea.

Gregers. Why so? Tell me why?

Hedvig. No, I won't; it's so stupid.

Gregers. Oh, no, I am sure it's not. Do tell me why you smiled.

Hedvig. Well, this is the reason: whenever I come to realise suddenly—in a flash—what is in there, it always seems to me that the whole room and everything in it should be called "the depths of the sea."—But that is so stupid.

Gregers. You mustn't say that.

Hedvig. Oh, yes, for you know it is only a garret.

Gregers (looks fixedly at her). Are you so sure of that?

Hedvig (astonished). That it's a garret?

Gregers. Are you quite certain of it?

[HEDVIG *is silent, and looks at him open-mouthed.* GINA *comes in from the kitchen with the table things.*

Gregers (rising). I have come in upon you too early.

----

* Gregers here uses the old-fashioned expression "havsens bund," while Hedvig would have him use the more commonplace "havets bund" or "havbunden."

Gina. Oh, you must be somewhere; and we're nearly ready now, any way. Clear the table, Hedvig.

> [HEDVIG *clears away her things; she and* GINA *lay the cloth during what follows.* GREGERS *seats himself in the arm-chair, and turns over an album.*

Gregers. I hear you can retouch, Mrs. Ekdal.

Gina (with a side glance). Yes, I can.

Gregers. That was exceedingly lucky.

Gina. How—lucky?

Gregers. Since Ekdal took to photography, I mean.

Hedvig. Mother can take photographs, too.

Gina. Oh, yes; I was bound to learn that.

Gregers. So it is really you that carry on the business, I suppose?

Gina. Yes, when Ekdal hasn't time himself——

Gregers. He is a great deal taken up with his old father, I daresay.

Gina. Yes; and then you can't expect a man like Ekdal to do nothing but take car-de-visits of Dick, Tom and Harry.

Gregers. I quite agree with you; but having once gone in for the thing——

Gina. You can surely understand, Mr. Werle, that Ekdal's not like one of your common photographers.

Gregers. Of course not; but still——

> [*A shot is fired within the garret.*

Gregers (starting up). What's that?

Gina. Ugh! now they're firing again!

Gregers. Have they firearms in there?

Hedvig. They are out shooting.

Gregers. What! *(At the door of the garret.)* Are you shooting, Hialmar?

Hialmar (inside the net). Are you there? I didn't know;

I was so taken up—— *(To* HEDVIG.*)* Why did you not let us know? *[Comes into the studio.*

Gregers. Do you go shooting in the garret?

Hialmar (showing a double-barrelled pistol). Oh, only with this thing.

Gina. Yes, you and grandfather will do yourselves a mischief some day with that there pigstol.

Hialmar (with irritation). I believe I have told you that this kind of firearm is called a pistol.

Gina. Oh, that doesn't make it much better, that I can see.

Gregers. So you have become a sportsman, too, Hialmar?

Hialmar. Only a little rabbit-shooting now and then. Mostly to please father, you understand.

Gina. Men are strange beings; they must always have something to pervert theirselves with.

Hialmar (snappishly). Just so; we must always have something to divert ourselves with.

Gina. Yes, that's just what I say.

Hialmar. H'm. *(To* GREGERS*).* You see the garret is fortunately so situated that no one can hear us shooting. *(Lays the pistol on the top shelf of the bookcase.)* Don't touch the pistol, Hedvig! One of the barrels is loaded; remember that.

Gregers (looking through the net). You have a fowling-piece too, I see.

Hialmar. That is father's old gun. It's of no use now; something has gone wrong with the lock. But it's fun to have it all the same; for we can take it to pieces now and then, and clean and grease it, and screw it together again.—Of course, it's mostly father that fiddle-faddles with all that sort of thing.

Hedvig (beside GREGERS*).* Now you can see the wild duck properly.

Gregers. I was just looking at her. One of her wings seems to me to droop a bit.

Hedvig. Well, no wonder; her wing was broken, you know.

Gregers. And she trails one foot a little. Isn't that so?

Hialmar. Perhaps a very little bit.

Hedvig. Yes, it was by that foot the dog took hold of her.

Hialmar. But otherwise she hasn't the least thing the matter with her; and that is simply marvellous for a creature that has a charge of shot in her body, and has been between a dog's teeth——

Gregers (with a glance at HEDVIG*)*——and that has lain in the depths of the sea—so long.

Hedvig (smiling). Yes.

Gina (laying the table). That blessëd wild duck! What a lot of fuss you do make over her.

Hialmar. H'm;—will lunch soon be ready?

Gina. Yes, directly. Hedvig, you must come and help me now.

[GINA *and* HEDVIG *go out into the kitchen.*

Hialmar (in a low voice). I think you had better not stand there looking in at father; he doesn't like it. (GREGERS *moves away from the garret door.*) Besides, I may as well shut up before the others come. (*Claps his hands to drive the fowls back.*) Shh—shh, in with you! (*Draws up the curtain and pulls the doors together.*) All the contrivances are my own invention. It's really quite amusing to have things of this sort to potter with, and to put to rights when they get out of order. And it's absolutely necessary, too; for Gina objects to having rabbits and fowls in the studio.

Gregers. To be sure; and I suppose the studio is your wife's special department?

Hialmar. As a rule, I leave the everyday details of business to her; for then I can take refuge in the parlour and give my mind to more important things.

Gregers. What things may they be, Hialmar?

Hialmar. I wonder you have not asked that question

sooner. But perhaps you haven't heard of the invention?

Gregers. The invention? No.

Hialmar. Really? Have you not? Oh, no, out there in the wilds——

Gregers. So you have invented something, have you?

Hialmar. It is not quite completed yet; but I am working at it. You can easily imagine that when I resolved to devote myself to photography, it wasn't simply with the idea of taking likenesses of all sorts of commonplace people.

Gregers. No; your wife was saying the same thing just now.

Hialmar. I swore that if I consecrated my powers to this handicraft, I would so exalt it that it should become both an art and a science. And to that end I determined to make this great invention.

Gregers. And what is the nature of the invention? What purpose does it serve?

Hialmar. Oh, my dear fellow, you mustn't ask for details yet. It takes time, you see. And you must not think that my motive is vanity. It is not for my own sake that I am working. Oh, no; it is my life's mission that stands before me night and day.

Gregers. What is your life's mission?

Hialmar. Do you forget the old man with the silver hair?

Gregers. Your poor father? Well, but what can you do for him?

Hialmar. I can raise up his self-respect from the dead, by restoring the name of Ekdal to honour and dignity.

Gregers. Then that is your life's mission?

Hialmar. Yes. I will rescue the shipwrecked man. For shipwrecked he was, by the very first blast of the storm. Even while those terrible investigations were going on, he was no longer himself. That pistol there—the one we use to shoot rabbits with—has played its part in the tragedy of the house of Ekdal.

Gregers. The pistol? Indeed?

Hialmar. When the sentence of imprisonment was passed —he had the pistol in his hand——

Gregers. Had he——?

Hialmar. Yes; but he dared not use it. His courage failed him. So broken, so demoralised was he even then! Oh, can you understand it? He, a soldier; he, who had shot nine bears, and who was descended from two lieutenant-colonels—one after the other, of course. Can you understand it, Gregers?

Gregers. Yes, I understand it well enough.

Hialmar. I cannot. And once more the pistol played a part in the history of our house. When he had put on the grey clothes and was under lock and key—oh, that was a terrible time for me, I can tell you. I kept the blinds drawn down over both my windows. When I peeped out, I saw the sun shining as if nothing had happened. I could not understand it. I saw people going along the street, laughing and talking about indifferent things. I could not understand it. It seemed to me that the whole of existence must be at a standstill—as if under an eclipse.

Gregers. I felt that, too, when my mother died.

Hialmar. It was in such an hour that Hialmar Ekdal pointed the pistol at his own breast.

Gregers. You, too, thought of——!

Hialmar. Yes.

Gregers. But you did not fire?

Hialmar. No. At the decisive moment I won the victory over myself. I remained in life. But I can assure you it takes some courage to choose life under circumstances like those.

Gregers. Well, that depends on how you look at it.

Hialmar. Yes, indeed, it takes courage. But I am glad I was firm: for now I shall soon perfect my invention; and Dr. Relling thinks, as I do myself, that father may be allowed to wear his uniform again. I will demand that as my sole reward.

Gregers. So that is what he meant about his uniform——?

Hialmar. Yes, that is what he most yearns for. You can't think how my heart bleeds for him. Every time we celebrate any little family festival—Gina's and my wedding-day, or whatever it may be—in comes the old man in the lieutenant's uniform of happier days. But if he only hears a knock at the door—for he daren't show himself to strangers, you know—he hurries back to his room again as fast as his old legs can carry him. Oh, it's heart-rending for a son to see such things!

Gregers. How long do you think it will take you to finish your invention?

Hialmar. Come now, you mustn't expect me to enter into particulars like that. An invention is not a thing completely under one's own control. It depends largely on inspiration —on intuition—and it is almost impossible to predict when the inspiration may come.

Gregers. But it's advancing?

Hialmar. Yes, certainly, it is advancing. I turn it over in my mind every day; I am full of it. Every afternoon, when I have had my dinner, I shut myself up in the parlour, where I can ponder undisturbed. But I can't be goaded to it; it's not a bit of good; Relling says so, too.

Gregers. And you don't think that all that business in the garret draws you off and distracts you too much?

Hialmar. No, no, no; quite the contrary. You mustn't say that. I cannot be everlastingly absorbed in the same laborious train of thought. I must have something alongside of it to fill up the time of waiting. The inspiration, the intuition, you see—when it comes, it comes, and there's an end of it.

Gregers. My dear Hialmar, I almost think you have something of the wild duck in you.

Hialmar. Something of the wild duck? How do you mean?

Gregers. You have dived down and bitten yourself fast in the undergrowth.

Hialmar. Are you alluding to the well-nigh fatal shot that has broken my father's wing—and mine, too?

Gregers. Not exactly to that. I don't say that your wing has been broken; but you have strayed into a poisonous marsh, Hialmar; an insidious disease has taken hold of you, and you have sunk down to die in the dark.

Hialmar. I? To die in the dark? Look here, Gregers, you must really leave off talking such nonsense.

Gregers. Don't be afraid; I shall find a way to help you up again. I, too, have a mission in life now; I found it yesterday.

Hialmar. That's all very well; but you will please leave me out of it. I can assure you that—apart from my very natural melancholy, of course—I am as contented as any one can wish to be.

Gregers. Your contentment is an effect of the marsh poison.

Hialmar. Now, my dear Gregers, pray do not go on about disease and poison; I am not used to that sort of talk. In my house nobody ever speaks to me about unpleasant things.

Gregers. Ah, that I can easily believe.

Hialmar. It's not good for me, you see. And there are no marsh poisons here, as you express it. The poor photographer's roof is lowly, I know—and my circumstances are narrow. But I am an inventor, and I am the bread-winner of a family. That exalts me above my mean surroundings.—Ah, here comes lunch!

GINA *and* HEDVIG *bring bottles of ale, a decanter of brandy,
    glasses, etc. At the same time,* RELLING *and* MOLVIK
    *enter from the passage; they are both without hat or
    overcoat.* MOLVIK *is dressed in black.*

Gina (placing the things upon the table). Ah, you two have come in the nick of time.

Relling. Molvik got it into his head that he could smell herring-salad, and then there was no holding him.—Good morning again, Ekdal.

Hialmar. Gregers, let me introduce you to Mr. Molvik. Doctor—— Oh, you know Relling, don't you?

Gregers. Yes, slightly.

Relling. Oh, Mr. Werle, junior! Yes, we two have had one or two little skirmishes up at the Höidal works. You've just moved in?

Gregers. I moved in this morning.

Relling. Molvik and I live right under you; so you haven't far to go for the doctor and the clergyman, if you should need anything in that line.

Gregers. Thanks, it's not quite unlikely; for yesterday we were thirteen at table.

Hialmar. Oh, come now, don't let us get upon unpleasant subjects again!

Relling. You may make your mind easy, Ekdal; I'll be hanged if the finger of fate points to you.

Hialmar. I should hope not, for the sake of my family. But let us sit down now, and eat and drink and be merry.

Gregers. Shall we not wait for your father?

Hialmar. No, his lunch will be taken in to him later. Come along!

> [*The men seat themselves at table, and eat and drink.* GINA *and* HEDVIG *go in and out and wait upon them.*

Relling. Molvik was frightfully screwed yesterday, Mrs Ekdal.

Gina. Really? Yesterday again?

Relling. Didn't you hear him when I brought him home last night?

Gina. No, I can't say I did.

Relling. That was a good thing, for Molvik was disgusting last night.

Gina. Is that true, Molvik?

Molvik. Let us draw a veil over last night's proceedings. That sort of thing is totally foreign to my better self.

Relling (to Gregers*).* It comes over him like a sort of possession, and then I have to go out on the loose with him. Mr. Molvik is dæmonic, you see.

Gregers. Dæmonic?

Relling. Molvik is dæmonic, yes.

Gregers. H'm.

Relling. And dæmonic natures are not made to walk straight through the world; they must meander a little now and then.——Well, so you still stick up there at those horrible grimy works?

Gregers. I have stuck there until now.

Relling. And did you ever manage to collect that claim you went about presenting?

Gregers. Claim? *(Understands him.)* Ah, I see.

Hialmar. Have you been presenting claims, Gregers?

Gregers. Oh, nonsense.

Relling. Faith, but he has, though! He went round to all the cottars' cabins presenting something he called "the claim of the ideal."

Gregers. I was young then.

Relling. You're right; you were very young. And as for the claim of the ideal—you never got it honoured while *I* was up there.

Gregers. Nor since either.

Relling. Ah, then you've learnt to knock a little discount off, I expect.

Gregers. Never, when I have a true man to deal with.

Hialmar. No, I should think not, indeed. A little butter, Gina.

Relling. And a slice of bacon for Molvik.

Molvik. Ugh; not bacon!

[*A knock at the garret door.*

Hialmar. Open the door, Hedvig; father wants to come out.

[HEDVIG *goes over and opens the door a little way;* EKDAL *enters with a fresh rabbit-skin; she closes the door after him.*

Ekdal.   Good morning, gentlemen!   Good sport to-day. Shot a big one.

Hialmar.   And you've gone and skinned it without waiting for me——!

Ekdal.   Salted it, too.   It's good tender meat, is rabbit; it's sweet; it tastes like sugar.   Good appetite to you, gentlemen!   [*Goes into his room.*

Molvik (rising).   Excuse me——; I can't——; I must get downstairs immediately——

Relling.   Drink some soda water, man!

Molvik (hurrying away).   Ugh—ugh!

[*Goes out by the passage door.*

Relling (to HIALMAR*).*   Let us drain a glass to the old hunter.

Hialmar (clinks glasses with him).   To the undaunted sportsman who has looked death in the face!

Relling.   To the grey-haired—— *(Drinks.)*   By-the-bye, is his hair grey or white?

Hialmar.   Something between the two, I fancy; for that matter, he has very few hairs left of any colour.

Relling.   Well, well, one can get through the world with a wig.   After all, you are a happy man, Ekdal; you have your noble mission to labour for——

Hialmar.   And I do labour, I can tell you.

Relling.   And then you have your excellent wife, shuffling quietly in and out in her felt slippers, with that see-saw walk of hers, and making everything cosy and comfortable about you.

Hialmar.   Yes, Gina—*(nods to her)*—you were a good helpmate on the path of life.

Gina.   Oh, don't sit there cricketising me.

Relling.   And your Hedvig, too, Ekdal!

Hialmar (affected).   The child, yes!   **The child before** everything! Hedvig, come here to me. *(Strokes her hair.)* What day is it to-morrow, eh?

Hedvig (shaking him). Oh, no, you're not to say anything, father.

Hialmar. It cuts me to the heart when I think what a poor affair it will be; only a little festivity in the garret——

Hedvig. Oh, but that's just what I like!

Relling. Just you wait till the wonderful invention sees the light, Hedvig!

Hialmar. Yes, indeed—then you shall see——! Hedvig, I have resolved to make your future secure. You shall live in comfort all your days. I will demand—something or other—on your behalf. That shall be the poor inventor's sole reward.

Hedvig (whispering, with her arms round his neck). Oh, you dear, kind father!

Relling (to GREGERS *).* Come now, don't you find it pleasant, for once in a way, to sit at a well-spread table in a happy family circle?

Hialmar. Ah, yes, I really prize these social hours.

Gregers. For my part, I don't thrive in marsh vapours.

Relling. Marsh vapours?

Hialmar. Oh, don't begin with that stuff again!

Gina. Goodness knows there's no vapours in this house, Mr. Werle; I give the place a good airing every blessed day.

Gregers (leaves the table). No airing you can give will drive out the taint I mean.

Hialmar. Taint!

Gina. Yes, what do you say to that, Ekdal!

Relling. Excuse me—may it not be you yourself that have brought the taint from those mines up there?

Gregers. It is like you to call what I bring into this house a taint.

Relling (goes up to him). Look here, Mr. Werle, junior: I have a strong suspicion that you are still carrying about that "claim of the ideal" large as life, in your coat-tail pocket.

Gregers. I carry it in my breast.

Relling. Well, wherever you carry it, I advise you not to come dunning us with it here, so long as *I* am on the premises.

Gregers. And if I do so none the less?

Relling. Then you'll go head-foremost down the stairs; now I've warned you.

Hialmar (rising). Oh, but Relling——!

Gregers. Yes, you may turn me out——

Gina (interposing between them). We can't have that, Relling. But I must say, Mr. Werle, it ill becomes you to talk about vapours and taints, after all the mess you made with your stove. [*A knock at the passage door.*

Hedvig. Mother, there's somebody knocking.

Hialmar. There now, we're going to have a whole lot of people!

Gina. I'll go—— *(Goes over and opens the door, starts, and draws back.)* Oh—oh, dear!

[WERLE, *in a fur coat, advances one step into the room.*

Werle. Excuse me; but I think my son is staying here.

Gina (with a gulp). Yes.

Hialmar (approaching him). Won't you do us the honour to——?

Werle. Thank you, I merely wish to speak to my son.

Gregers. What is it? Here I am.

Werle. I want a few words with you, in your room.

Gregers. In my room? Very well—— [*About to go.*

Gina. No, no, your room's not in a fit state——

Werle. Well then, out in the passage here; I want to have a few words with you alone.

Hialmar. You can have them here, sir. Come into the parlour, Relling.

[HIALMAR *and* RELLING *go off to the right.* GINA *takes* HEDVIG *with her into the kitchen.*

Gregers (after a short pause). Well, now we are alone.

Werle. From something you let fall last evening, and from your coming to lodge with the Ekdals, I can't help inferring that you intend to make yourself unpleasant to me, in one way or another.

Gregers. I intend to open Hialmar Ekdal's eyes. He shall see his position as it really is—that is all.

Werle. Is that the mission in life you spoke of yesterday?

Gregers. Yes. You have left me no other.

Werle. Is it I, then, that have crippled your mind, Gregers?

Gregers. You have crippled my whole life. I am not thinking of all that about mother—— But it's thanks to you that I am continually haunted and harassed by a guilty conscience.

Werle. Indeed! It is your conscience that troubles you, is it?

Gregers. I ought to have taken a stand against you when the trap was set for Lieutenant Ekdal. I ought to have cautioned him; for I had a misgiving as to what was in the wind.

Werle. Yes, that was the time to have spoken.

Gregers. I did not dare to, I was so cowed and spiritless. I was mortally afraid of you—not only then, but long afterwards.

Werle. You have got over that fear now, it appears.

Gregers. Yes, fortunately. The wrong done to old Ekdal, both by me and by—others, can never be undone; but Hialmar I can rescue from all the falsehood and deception that are bringing him to ruin.

Werle. Do you think that will be doing him a kindness?

Gregers. I have not the least doubt of it.

Werle. You think our worthy photographer is the sort of man to appreciate such friendly offices?

Gregers. Yes, I do.

Werle. H'm—we shall see.

Gregers. Besides, if I am to go on living, I must try to find some cure for my sick conscience.

Werle. It will never be sound. Your conscience has been sickly from childhood. That is a legacy from your mother, Gregers—the only one she left you.

Gregers (with a scornful half-smile). Have you not yet forgiven her for the mistake you made in supposing she would bring you a fortune?

Werle. Don't let us wander from the point.—Then you hold to your purpose of setting young Ekdal upon what you imagine to be the right scent?

Gregers. Yes, that is my fixed resolve.

Werle. Well, in that case I might have spared myself this visit; for, of course, it is useless to ask whether you will return home with me?

Gregers. Quite useless.

Werle. And I suppose you won't enter the firm either?

Gregers. No.

Werle. Very good. But as I am thinking of marrying again, your share in the property will fall to you at once.*

Gregers (quickly). No, I do not want that.

Werle. You don't want it?

Gregers. No, I dare not take it, for conscience' sake.

Werle (after a pause). Are you going up to the works again?

Gregers. No; I consider myself released from your service.

Werle. But what are you going to do?

Gregers. Only to fulfil my mission; nothing more.

---

* By Norwegian law, before a widower can marry again, a certain proportion of his property must be settled on his children by his former marriage.

Werle. Well but afterwards? What are you going to live upon?

Gregers. I have laid by a little out of my salary.

Werle. How long will that last?

Gregers. I think it will last my time.

Werle. What do you mean?

Gregers. I shall answer no more questions.

Werle. Good-bye then, Gregers.

Gregers. Good-bye.   [WERLE *goes.*

Hialmar (peeping in). He's gone, isn't he?

Gregers. Yes.

HIALMAR *and* RELLING *enter; also* GINA *and* HEDVIG *from the kitchen.*

Relling. That luncheon-party was a failure.

Gregers. Put on your coat, Hialmar; I want you to come for a long walk with me.

Hialmar. With pleasure. What was it your father wanted? Had it anything to do with me?

Gregers. Come along. We must have a talk. I'll go and put on my overcoat.

[*Goes out by the passage door.*

Gina. You shouldn't go out with him, Ekdal.

Relling. No, don't you do it. Stay where you are.

Hialmar (gets his hat and overcoat). Oh, nonsense! When a friend of my youth feels impelled to open his mind to me in private——

Relling. But devil take it—don't you see that the fellow's mad, cracked, demented!

Gina. There, what did I tell you! His mother before him had crazy fits like that sometimes.

Hialmar. The more need for a friend's watchful eye. *(To* GINA.*)* Be sure you have dinner ready in good time. Good-bye for the present.

[*Goes out by the passage door.*

Relling. It's a thousand pities the fellow didn't go to hell through one of the Höidal mines.

Gina. Good Lord! what makes you say that?

Relling (muttering). Oh, I have my own reasons.

Gina. Do you think young Werle is really mad?

Relling. No, worse luck; he's no madder than most other people. But one disease he has certainly got in his system.

Gina. What is it that's the matter with him?

Relling. Well, I'll tell you, Mrs. Ekdal. He is suffering from an acute attack of integrity.

Gina. Integrity?

Hedvig. Is that a kind of disease?

Relling. Yes, it's a national disease; but it only appears sporadically. *(Nods to* GINA.*)* Thanks for your hospitality. [*He goes out by the passage door.*

Gina (moving restlessly to and fro). Ugh, that Gregers Werle—he was always a wretched creature.

Hedvig (standing by the table, and looking searchingly at her). I think all this is very strange.

ACT FOURTH.

HIALMAR EKDAL'S *studio. A photograph has just been taken; a camera with the cloth over it, a pedestal, two chairs, a folding table, etc., are standing out in the room. Afternoon light; the sun is going down; a little later it begins to grow dusk.*

GINA *stands in the passage doorway, with a little box and a wet glass plate in her hand, and is speaking to somebody outside.*

Gina. Yes, certainly. When I make a promise I keep it. The first dozen shall be ready on Monday. Good afternoon.

> [*Someone is heard going downstairs.* GINA *shuts the door, slips the plate into the box, and puts it into the covered camera.*

Hedvig (comes in from the kitchen). Are they gone?

Gina (tidying up). Yes, thank goodness, I've got rid of them at last.

Hedvig. But can you imagine why father hasn't come home yet?

Gina. Are you sure he's not down in Relling's room?

Hedvig. No, he's not; I ran down the kitchen stair just now and asked.

Gina. And his dinner standing and getting cold, too.

Hedvig. Yes, I can't understand it. Father's always so careful to be home to dinner!

Gina. Oh, he'll be here directly, you'll see.

Hedvig. I wish he would come; everything seems so queer to-day.

Gina (calls out). There he is!

HIALMAR EKDAL *comes in at the passage door.*

Hedvig (going to him). Father! Oh, what a time we've been waiting for you!

Gina (glancing sidelong at him). You've been out a long time, Ekdal.

Hialmar (without looking at her). Rather long, yes.

> [*He takes off his overcoat;* GINA *and* HEDVIG *go to help him; he motions them away.*

Gina. Perhaps you've had dinner with Werle?

Hialmar (hanging up his coat). No.

Gina (going towards the kitchen door). Then I'll bring some in for you.

Hialmar. No; let the dinner alone. I want nothing to eat.

Hedvig (going nearer to him). Are you not well, father?

Hialmar. Well? Oh, yes, well enough. We have had a tiring walk, Gregers and I.

Gina. You didn't ought to have gone so far, Ekdal; you're not used to it.

Hialmar. H'm; there's many a thing a man must get used to in this world. *(Wanders about the room.)* Has any one been here whilst I was out?

Gina. Nobody but the two sweethearts.

Hialmar. No new orders?

Gina. No, not to-day.

Hedvig. There will be some to-morrow, father, you'll see.

Hialmar. I hope there will; for to-morrow I am going to set to work in real earnest.

Hedvig. To-morrow! Don't you remember what day it is to-morrow?

Hialmar. Oh, yes, by-the-bye——. Well, the day after,

then. Henceforth I mean to do everything myself; I shall take all the work into my own hands.

Gina. Why, what can be the good of that, Ekdal? It'll only make your life a burden to you. I can manage the photography all right; and you can go on working at your invention.

Hedvig. And think of the wild duck, father,—and all the hens and rabbits and——!

Hialmar. Don't talk to me of all that trash! From to-morrow I will never set foot in the garret again.

Hedvig. Oh, but father, you promised that we should have a little party——

Hialmar. H'm, true. Well, then, from the day after to-morrow. I should almost like to wring that cursed wild duck's neck!

Hedvig (shrieks). The wild duck!

Gina. Well I never!

Hedvig (shaking him). Oh, no, father; you know it's my wild duck!

Hialmar. That is why I don't do it. I haven't the heart to—for your sake, Hedvig. But in my inmost soul I feel that I ought to do it. I ought not to tolerate under my roof a creature that has been through those hands.

Gina. Why, good gracious, even if grandfather did get it from that poor creature, Pettersen——

Hialmar (wandering about). There are certain claims— what shall I call them?—let me say claims of the ideal— certain obligations, which a man cannot disregard without injury to his soul.

Hedvig (going after him). But think of the wild duck, —the poor wild duck!

Hialmar (stops). I tell you I will spare it—for your sake. Not a hair of its head shall be—I mean, it shall be spared. There are greater problems than that to be dealt with. But you should go out a little now, Hedvig, as usual; it is getting dusk enough for you now.

Hedvig. No, I don't care about going out now.

Hialmar. Yes, do; it seems to me your eyes are blinking a great deal; all these vapours in here are bad for you. The air is heavy under this roof.

Hedvig. Very well, then, I'll run down the kitchen stair and go for a little walk. My cloak and hat?—oh, they're in my own room. Father—be sure you don't do the wild duck any harm whilst I'm out.

Hialmar. Not a feather of its head shall be touched. *(Draws her to him.)* You and I, Hedvig—we two——! Well, go along.

> [HEDVIG *nods to her parents and goes out through the kitchen.*

Hialmar (walks about without looking up). Gina.

Gina. Yes?

Hialmar. From to-morrow—or, say, from the day after to-morrow—I should like to keep the household account-book myself.

Gina. Do you want to keep the accounts too, now?

Hialmar. Yes; or to check the receipts at any rate.

Gina. Lord help us! that's soon done.

Hialmar. One would hardly think so; at any rate you seem to make the money go a very long way. *(Stops and looks at her.)* How do you manage it?

Gina. It's because me and Hedvig, we need so little.

Hialmar. Is it the case that father is very liberally paid for the copying he does for Mr. Werle?

Gina. I don't know as he gets anything out of the way. I don't know the rates for that sort of work.

Hialmar. Well, what does he get, about? Let me hear!

Gina. Oh, it varies; I daresay it'll come to about as much as he costs us, with a little pocket-money over.

Hialmar. As much as he costs us! And you have never told me this before!

Gina. No, how could I tell you? It pleased you so much to think he got everything from you.

Hialmar. And he gets it from Mr. Werle.

Gina. Oh, well, he has plenty and to spare, he has.

Hialmar. Light the lamp for me, please!

Gina (lighting the lamp). And, of course, we don't know as it's Mr. Werle himself; it may be Gråberg——

Hialmar. Why attempt such an evasion?

Gina. I don't know; I only thought——

Hialmar. H'm!

Gina. It wasn't me that got grandfather that copying. It was Bertha, when she used to come about us.

Hialmar. It seems to me your voice is trembling.

Gina (putting the lamp-shade on). Is it?

Hialmar. And your hands are shaking, are they not?

Gina (firmly). Come right out with it, Ekdal. What has he been saying about me?

Hialmar. Is it true—can it be true that—that there was an—an understanding between you and Mr. Werle, while you were in service there?

Gina. That's not true. Not at that time. Mr. Werle did come after me, that's a fact. And his wife thought there was something in it, and then she made such a hocus-pocus and hurly-burly, and she hustled me and bustled me about so that I left her service.

Hialmar. But afterwards, then?

Gina. Well, then I went home. And mother—well, she wasn't the woman you took her for, Ekdal; she kept on worrying and worrying at me about one thing and another— for Mr. Werle was a widower by that time.

Hialmar. Well, and then?

Gina. I suppose you've got to know it. He gave me no peace until he'd had his way.

Hialmar (striking his hands together). And this is the mother of my child! How could you hide this from me?

Gina. Yes, it was wrong of me; I ought certainly to have told you long ago.

Hialmar. You should have told me at the very first;—

then I should have known the sort of woman you were.

Gina. But would you have married me all the same?

Hialmar. How can you dream that I would?

Gina. That's just why I didn't dare tell you anything, then. For I'd come to care for you so much, you see; and I couldn't go and make myself utterly miserable——

Hialmar (walks about). And this is my Hedvig's mother And to know that all I see before me——(*kicks at a chair*)— all that I call my home—I owe to a favoured predecessor! Oh, that scoundrel Werle!

Gina. Do you repent of the fourteen—the fifteen years we've lived together?

Hialmar (placing himself in front of her). Have you not every day, every hour, repented of the spider's-web of deceit you have spun around me? Answer me that! How could you help writhing with penitence and remorse?

Gina Oh, my dear Ekdal, I've had all I could do to look after the house and get through the day's work——

Hialmar. Then you never think of reviewing your past?

Gina. No; Heaven knows I'd almost forgotten those old stories.

Hialmar. Oh, this dull, callous contentment! To me there is something revolting about it. Think of it—never so much as a twinge of remorse!

Gina. But tell me, Ekdal—what would have become of you if you hadn't had a wife like me?

Hialmar. Like you——!

Gina. Yes; for you know I've always been a bit more practical and wide-awake than you. Of course I'm a year or two older.

Hialmar. What would have become of me!

Gina. You'd got into all sorts of bad ways when first you met me; that you can't deny.

Hialmar. "Bad ways" do you call them? Little do you know what a man goes through when he is in grief and despair—especially a man of my fiery temperament.

Gina. Well, well, that may be so. And I've no reason to crow over you, neither; for you turned a moral of a husband, that you did, as soon as ever you had a house and home of your own.—-And now we'd got everything so nice and cosy about us; and me and Hedvig was just thinking we'd soon be able to let ourselves go a bit, in the way of both food and clothes.

Hialmar. In the swamp of deceit, yes.

Gina. I wish to goodness that detestable thing had never set his foot inside our doors!

Hialmar. And I, too, thought my home such a pleasant one. That was a delusion. Where shall I now find the elasticity of spirit to bring my invention into the world of reality? Perhaps it will die with me; and then it will be your past, Gina, that will have killed it.

Gina (nearly crying). You mustn't say such things, Ekdal. Me, that has only wanted to do the best I could for you, all my days!

Hialmar. I ask you, what becomes of the breadwinner's dream? When I used to lie in there on the sofa and brood over my invention, I had a clear enough presentiment that it would sap my vitality to the last drop. I felt even then that the day when I held the patent in my hand—that day—would bring my—release. And then it was my dream that you should live on after me, the dead inventor's well-to-do widow.

Gina (drying her tears). No, you mustn't talk like that, Ekdal. May the Lord never let me see the day I am left a widow!

Hialmar. Oh, the whole dream has vanished. It is all over now. All over!

GREGERS WERLE *opens the passage door cautiously and looks in.*

Gregers. May I come in?

Hialmar. Yes, come in.

Gregers (comes forward, his face beaming with satisfac-

tion, and holds out both his hands to them). Well, dear friends——! *(Looks from one to the other, and whispers to* HIALMAR.*)* Have you not done it yet?

Hialmar (aloud). It is done.

Gregers. It is?

Hialmar. I have passed through the bitterest moments of my life.

Gregers. But also, I trust, the most ennobling.

Hialmar. Well, at any rate, we have got through it for the present.

Gina. God forgive you, Mr. Werle.

Gregers (in great surprise). But I don't understand this.

Hialmar. What don't you understand?

Gregers. After so great a crisis—a crisis that is to be the starting-point of an entirely new life—of a communion founded on truth, and free from all taint of deception——

Hialmar. Yes, yes, I know; I know that quite well.

Gregers. I confidently expected, when I entered the room, to find the light of transfiguration shining upon me from both husband and wife. And now I see nothing but dulness, oppression, gloom——

Gina. Oh, is that it? [*Takes off the lamp-shade.*

Gregers. You will not understand me, Mrs. Ekdal. Ah, well, you, I suppose, need time to——. But you, Hialmar? Surely you feel a new consecration after the great crisis.

Hialmar. Yes, of course I do. That is—in a sort of way.

Gregers. For surely nothing in the world can compare with the joy of forgiving one who has erred, and raising her up to oneself in love.

Hialmar. Do you think a man can so easily throw off the bitter cup I have drained?

Gregers. No, not a common man, perhaps. But a man like you——!

Hialmar. Good God! I know that well enough. But you must keep me up to it, Gregers. It takes time, you know.

Gregers. You have much of the wild duck in you, Hialmar.

RELLING *has come in at the passage door.*

Relling. Oho! is the wild duck to the fore again?

Hialmar. Yes; Mr. Werle's wing-broken victim.

Relling. Mr. Werle's——? So it's him you are talking about?

Hialmar. Him and—ourselves.

Relling (in an undertone to GREGERS*).* May the devil fly away with you!

Hialmar. What is that you are saying?

Relling. Only uttering a heartfelt wish that this quacksalver would take himself off. If he stays here, he is quite equal to making an utter mess of life, for both of you.

Gregers. These two will not make a mess of life, Mr. Relling. Of course I won't speak of Hialmar—him we know. But she, too, in her innermost heart, has certainly something loyal and sincere——

Gina (almost crying). You might have let me alone for what I was, then.

Relling (to GREGERS*).* Is it rude to ask what you really want in this house?

Gregers. To lay the foundations of a true marriage.

Relling. So you don't think Ekdal's marriage is good enough as it is?

Gregers. No doubt it is as good a marriage as most others, worse luck. But a true marriage it has yet to become.

Hialmar. You have never had eyes for the claims of the ideal, Relling.

Relling. Rubbish, my boy!—but excuse me, Mr. Werle: how many—in round numbers—how many true marriages have you seen in the course of your life?

Gregers. Scarcely a single one.

Relling. Nor I either.

Gregers. But I have seen innumerable marriages of the opposite kind. And it has been my fate to see at close quarters what ruin such a marriage can work in two human souls.

Hialmar. A man's whole moral basis may give away beneath his feet; that is the terrible part of it.

Relling. Well, I can't say I've ever been exactly married, so I don't pretend to speak with authority. But this I know, that the child enters into the marriage problem. And you must leave the child in peace.

Hialmar. Oh—Hedvig! my poor Hedvig!

Relling. Yes, you must be good enough to keep Hedvig outside of all this. You two are grown-up people; you are free, in God's name, to make what mess and muddle you please of your life. But you must deal cautiously with Hedvig, I tell you; else you may do her a great injury.

Hialmar. An injury!

Relling. Yes, or she may do herself an injury—and perhaps others, too.

Gina. How can you know that, Relling?

Hialmar. Her sight is in no immediate danger, is it?

Relling. I am not talking about her sight. Hedvig is at a critical age. She may be getting all sorts of mischief into her head.

Gina. That's true—I've noticed it already! She's taken to carrying on with the fire, out in the kitchen. She calls it playing at house-on-fire. I'm often scared for fear she really sets fire to the house.

Relling. You see; I thought as much.

Gregers (to RELLING*).* But how do you account for that?

Relling (sullenly). Her constitution's changing, sir.

Hialmar. So long as the child has me——! So long as *I* am above ground——!   [*A knock at the door.*

Gina. Hush, Ekdal; there's some one in the passage. *(Calls out.)* Come in!

[MRS. SÖRBY, *in walking dress, comes in.*

Mrs. Sörby. Good evening.

Gina (going towards her). Is it really you, Bertha?

Mrs. Sörby. Yes, of course it is. But I'm disturbing you, I'm afraid?

Hialmar. No, not at all; an emissary from that house——

Mrs. Sörby (to GINA*).* To tell the truth, I hoped your men-folk would be out at this time. I just ran up to have a little chat with you, and to say good-bye.

Gina. Good-bye? Are you going away, then?

Mrs. Sörby. Yes, to-morrow morning,—up to Höidal. Mr. Werle started this afternoon. *(Lightly to* GREGERS.*)* He asked me to say good-bye for him.

Gina. Only fancy——!

Hialmar. So Mr. Werle has gone? And now you are going after him?

Mrs. Sörby. Yes, what do you say to that, Ekdal?

Hialmar. I say: beware!

Gregers. I must explain the situation. My father and Mrs. Sörby are going to be married.

Hialmar. Going to be married!

Gina. Oh, Bertha! So it's come to that at last!

Relling (his voice quivering a little). This is surely not true?

Mrs. Sörby. Yes, my dear Relling, it's true enough.

Relling. You are going to marry again?

Mrs. Sörby. Yes, it looks like it. Werle has got a special licence, and we are going to be married quite quietly, up at the works.

Gregers. Then I must wish you all happiness, like a dutiful stepson.

Mrs. Sörby. Thank you very much—if you mean what you say. I certainly hope it will lead to happiness, both for Werle and for me.

Relling. You have every reason to hope that. Mr. Werle never gets drunk—so far as I know; and I don't suppose he's in the habit of thrashing his wives, like the late lamented horse-doctor.

Mrs. Sörby. Come now, let Sörby rest in peace. He had his good points, too.

Relling. Mr. Werle has better ones, I have no doubt.

Mrs. Sörby. He hasn't frittered away all that was good in him, at any rate. The man who does that must take the consequences.

Relling. I shall go out with Molvik this evening.

Mrs. Sörby. You mustn't do that, Relling. Don't do it— for my sake.

Relling. There's nothing else for it. *(To* HIALMAR.*)* If you're going with us, come along.

Gina. No, thank you. Ekdal doesn't go in for that sort of dissertation.

Hialmar (half aloud, in vexation). Oh, do hold your tongue!

Relling. Good-bye, Mrs.—Werle.

[*Goes out through the passage door.*

Gregers (to MRS. SÖRBY*).* You seem to know Dr. Relling pretty intimately.

Mrs. Sörby. Yes, we have known each other for many years. At one time it seemed as if things might have gone further between us.

Gregers. It was surely lucky for you that they did not.

Mrs. Sörby. You may well say that. But I have always been wary of acting on impulse. A woman can't afford absolutely to throw herself away.

Gregers. Are you not in the least afraid that I may let my father know about this old friendship?

Mrs. Sörby. Why, of course, I have told him all about it myself.

Gregers. Indeed?

Mrs. Sörby. Your father knows every single thing that can, with any truth, be said about me. I have told him all; it was the first thing I did when I saw what was in his mind.

Gregers. Then you have been franker than most people, I think.

Mrs. Sörby. I have always been frank. We women find that the best policy.

Hialmar. What do you say to that, Gina?

Gina. Oh, we're not all alike, us women aren't. Some are made one way, some another.

Mrs. Sörby. Well, for my part, Gina, I believe it's wisest to do as I've done. And Werle has no secrets either, on his side. That's really the great bond between us, you see. Now he can talk to me as openly as a child. He has never had the chance to do that before. Fancy a man like him, full of health and vigour, passing his whole youth and the best years of his life in listening to nothing but penitential sermons! And very often the sermons had for their text the most imaginary offences—at least so I understand.

Gina. That's true enough.

Gregers. If you ladies are going to follow up this topic, I had better withdraw.

Mrs. Sörby. You can stay as far as that's concerned. I shan't say a word more. But I wanted you to know that I had done nothing secretly or in an underhand way. I may seem to have come in for a great piece of luck; and so I have, in a sense. But after all, I don't think I am getting any more than I am giving. I shall stand by him always, and I can tend and care for him as no one else can, now that he is getting helpless.

Hialmar. Getting helpless?

Gregers (to Mrs. Sörby*).* Hush, don't speak of that here.

Mrs. Sörby. There is no disguising it any longer, however much he would like to. He is going blind.

Hialmar (starts). Going blind? That's strange. He, too, going blind!

Gina. Lots of people do.

Mrs. Sörby. And you can imagine what that means to a business man. Well, I shall try as well as I can to make my eyes take the place of his. But I mustn't stay any longer; I

have heaps of things to do.—Oh, by-the-bye, Ekdal, I was
to tell you that if there is anything Werle can do for you,
you must just apply to Gråberg.

Gregers. That offer I am sure Hialmar Ekdal will decline
with thanks.

Mrs. Sörby. Indeed? I don't think he used to be so——

Gina. No, Bertha, Ekdal doesn't need anything from
Mr. Werle now.

Hialmar (slowly, and with emphasis). Will you present
my compliments to your future husband, and say that I
intend very shortly to call upon Mr. Gråberg——

Gregers. What! You don't really mean that?

Hialmar. To call upon Mr. Gråberg, I say, and obtain an
account of the sum I owe his principal. I will pay that debt
of honour—ha ha ha! a debt of honour, let us call it! In
any case, I will pay the whole with five per cent. interest.

Gina. But, my dear Ekdal, God knows we haven't got
the money to do it.

Hialmar. Be good enough to tell your future husband
that I am working assiduously at my invention. Please tell
him that what sustains me in this laborious task is the wish
to free myself from a torturing burden of debt. That is my
reason for proceeding with the invention. The entire profits
shall be devoted to releasing me from my pecuniary obligations to your future husband.

Mrs. Sörby. Something has happened here.

Hialmar. Yes, you are right.

Mrs. Sörby. Well, good-bye. I had something else to
speak to you about, Gina; but it must keep till another time.
Good-bye.

> [HIALMAR *and* GREGERS *bow silently.* GINA *fol-
> lows* MRS. SÖRBY *to the door.*

Hialmar. Not beyond the threshold, Gina!

> [MRS. SÖRBY *goes;* GINA *shuts the door after her.*

Hialmar. There now, Gregers; I have got that burden of
debt off my mind.

Gregers. You soon will, at all events.

Hialmar. I think my attitude may be called correct.

Gregers. You are the man I have always taken you for.

Hialmar. In certain cases, it is impossible to disregard the claim of the ideal. Yet, as the breadwinner of a family, I cannot but writhe and groan under it. I can tell you it is no joke for a man without capital to attempt the repayment of a long-standing obligation, over which, so to speak, the dust of oblivion had gathered. But it cannot be helped: the Man in me demands his rights.

Gregers (laying his hand on HIALMAR'S *shoulder).* My dear Hialmar—was it not a good thing I came?

Hialmar. Yes.

Gregers. Are you not glad to have had your true position made clear to you?

Hialmar (somewhat impatiently). Yes, of course I am. But there is one thing that is revolting to my sense of justice.

Gregers. And what is that?

Hialmar. It is that—but I don't know whether I ought to express myself so unreservedly about your father.

Gregers. Say what you please, so far as I am concerned.

Hialmar. Well, then, is it not exasperating to think that it is not I, but he, who will realise the true marriage?

Gregers. How can you say such a thing?

Hialmar. Because it is clearly the case. Isn't the marriage between your father and Mrs. Sörby founded upon complete confidence, upon entire and unreserved candour on both sides? They hide nothing from each other, they keep no secrets in the background; their relation is based, if I may put it so, on mutual confession and absolution.

Gregers. Well, what then?

Hialmar. Well, is not that the whole thing? Did you not yourself say that this was precisely the difficulty that had to be overcome in order to found a true marriage?

Gregers. But this is a totally different matter, Hialmar.

You surely don't compare either yourself or your wife with those two——? Oh, you understand me well enough.

Hialmar. Say what you like, there is something in all this that hurts and offends my sense of justice. It really looks as if there were no just providence to rule the world.

Gina. Oh, no, Ekdal; for God's sake don't say such things.

Gregers. H'm; don't let us get upon those questions.

Hialmar. And yet, after all, I cannot but recognise the guiding finger of fate. He is going blind.

Gina. Oh, you can't be sure of that.

Hialmar. There is no doubt about it. At all events there ought not to be; for in that very fact lies the righteous retribution. He has hoodwinked a confiding fellow creature in days gone by——

Gregers. I fear he has hoodwinked many.

Hialmar. And now comes inexorable, mysterious Fate, and demands Werle's own eyes.

Gina. Oh, how dare you say such dreadful things! You make me quite scared.

Hialmar. It is profitable, now and then, to plunge deep into the night side of existence.

HEDVIG, *in her hat and cloak, comes in by the passage door. She is pleasurably excited and out of breath.*

Gina. Are you back already?

Hedvig. Yes, I didn't care to go any farther. It was a good thing, too; for I've just met some one at the door.

Hialmar. It must have been that Mrs. Sörby.

Hedvig. Yes.

Hialmar (walks up and down). I hope you have seen her for the last time.

[*Silence.* HEDVIG, *discouraged, looks first at one and then at the other, trying to divine their frame of mind.*

Hedvig (approaching, coaxingly). Father.

Hialmar. Well—what is it, Hedvig?

Hedvig. Mrs. Sörby had something with her for me.

Hialmar (stops). For you?

Hedvig. Yes. Something for to-morrow.

Gina. Bertha has always given you some little thing on your birthday.

Hialmar. What is it?

Hedvig. Oh, you mustn't see it now. Mother is to give it to me to-morrow morning before I'm up.

Hialmar. What is all this hocus-pocus that I am to be in the dark about!

Hedvig (quickly). Oh, no, you may see it if you like. It's a big letter.

[*Takes the letter out of her cloak pocket.*

Hialmar. A letter, too?

Hedvig. Yes, it is only a letter. The rest will come afterwards, I suppose. But fancy—a letter! I've never had a letter before. And there's "Miss" written upon it. *(Reads.)* "Miss Hedvig Ekdal." Only fancy—that's me!

Hialmar. Let me see that letter.

Hedvig (hands it to him). There it is.

Hialmar. That is Mr. Werle's hand.

Gina. Are you sure of that, Ekdal?

Hialmar. Look for yourself.

Gina. Oh, what do *I* know about such-like things?

Hialmar. Hedvig, may I open the letter—and read it?

Hedvig. Yes, of course you may, if you want to.

Gina. No, not to-night, Ekdal; it's to be kept till to-morrow.

Hedvig (softly). Oh, can't you let him read it! It's sure to be something good; and then father will be glad, and everything will be nice again.

Hialmar. I may open it then?

Hedvig. Yes, do, father. I'm so anxious to know what it is.

Hialmar. Well and good. *(Opens the letter, takes out*

a paper, reads it through, and appears bewildered.) What is
this——!

Gina. What does it say?

Hedvig. Oh, yes, father—tell us!

Hialmar. Be quiet. *(Reads it through again; he has
turned pale, but says with self-control:)* It is a deed of gift,
Hedvig.

Hedvig. Is it? What sort of gift am I to have?

Hialmar. Read for yourself.

[HEDVIG *goes over and reads for a time by the
lamp.*

Hialmar (half-aloud, clenching his hands). The eyes!
The eyes—and then that letter!

Hedvig (leaves off reading). Yes, but it seems to me
that it's grandfather that's to have it.

Hialmar (takes letter from her). Gina—can you understand this?

Gina. I know nothing whatever about it; tell me what's
the matter.

Hialmar. Mr. Werle writes to Hedvig that her old grandfather need not trouble himself any longer with the copying, but that he can henceforth draw on the office for a
hundred crowns a month——

Gregers. Aha!

Hedvig. A hundred crowns, mother! I read that.

Gina. What a good thing for grandfather!

Hialmar. ——a hundred crowns a month so long as he
needs it—that means, of course, so long as he lives.

Gina. Well, so he's provided for, poor dear.

Hialmar. But there is more to come. You didn't read
that, Hedvig. Afterwards this gift is to pass on to you.

Hedvig. To me! The whole of it?

Hialmar. He says that the same amount is assured to
you for the whole of your life. Do you hear that, Gina?

Gina. Yes, I hear.

Hedvig. Fancy—all that money for me! *(Shakes him.)* Father, father, aren't you glad——?

Hialmar (eluding her). Glad! *(Walks about.)* Oh what vistas—what perspectives open up before me! It is Hedvig, Hedvig that he showers these benefactions upon!

Gina. Yes, because it's Hedvig's birthday——

Hedvig. And you'll get it all the same, father! You know quite well I shall give all the money to you and mother.

Hialmar. To mother, yes! There we have it.

Gregers. Hialmar, this is a trap he is setting for you.

Hialmar. Do you think it's another trap?

Gregers. When he was here this morning he said: Hialmar Ekdal is not the man you imagine him to be.

Hialmar. Not the man——!

Gregers. That you shall see, he said.

Hialmar. He meant you should see that I would let myself be bought off——!

Hedvig. Oh mother, what does all this mean?

Gina. Go and take off your things.

[HEDVIG *goes out by the kitchen door, half-crying.*

Gregers. Yes, Hialmar—now is the time to show who was right, he or I.

Hialmar (slowly tears the paper across, lays both pieces on the table, and says): Here is my answer.

Gregers. Just what I expected.

Hialmar (goes over to GINA, *who stands by the stove, and says in a low voice):* Now please make a clean breast of it. If the connection between you and him was quite over when you—came to care for me, as you call it—why did he place us in a position to marry?

Gina. I suppose he thought as he could come and go in our house.

Hialmar. Only that? Was not he afraid of a possible contingency?

Gina. I don't know what you mean.

Hialmar. I want to know whether—your child has the right to live under my roof.

Gina (draws herself up; her eyes flash). You ask that!

Hialmar. You shall answer me this one question: Does Hedvig belong to me—or——? Well!

Gina (looking at him with cold defiance). I don't know.

Hialmar (quivering a little). You don't know!

Gina. How should *I* know. A creature like me——

Hialmar (quietly turning away from her). Then I have nothing more to do in this house.

Gregers. Take care, Hialmar! Think what you are doing!

Hialmar (puts on his overcoat). In this case, there is nothing for a man like me to think twice about.

Gregers. Yes indeed, there are endless things to be considered. You three must be together if you are to attain the true frame of mind for self-sacrifice and forgiveness.

Hialmar. I don't want to attain it. Never, never! My hat! *(Takes his hat.)* My home has fallen in ruins about me. *(Bursts into tears.)* Gregers, I have no child!

Hedvig (who has opened the kitchen door). What is that you're saying? *(Coming to him.)* Father, father!

Gina. There, you see!

Hialmar. Don't come near me, Hedvig! Keep far away. I cannot bear to see you. Oh! those eyes——! Good-bye.
[*Makes for the door.*

Hedvig (clinging close to him and screaming loudly). No! no! Don't leave me!

Gina (cries out). Look at the child, Ekdal! Look at the child!

Hialmar. I will not! I cannot! I must get out—away from all this!

[*He tears himself away from* HEDVIG, *and goes out by the passage door.*

Hedvig (with despairing eyes). He is going away from

us, mother! He is going away from us! He will never come back again!

Gina. Don't cry, Hedvig. Father's sure to come back again.

Hedvig (throws herself sobbing on the sofa). No, no, he'll never come home to us any more.

Gregers. Do you believe I meant all for the best, Mrs. Ekdal?

Gina. Yes, I daresay you did; but God forgive you, all the same.

Hedvig (lying on the sofa). Oh, this will kill me! What have I done to him? Mother, you must fetch him home again!

Gina. Yes yes yes; only be quiet, and I'll go out and look for him. *(Puts on her outdoor things.)* Perhaps he's gone in to Relling's. But you mustn't lie there and cry. Promise me!

Hedvig (weeping convulsively). Yes, I'll stop, I'll stop; if only father comes back!

Gregers (to Gina, *who is going).* After all, had you not better leave him to fight out his bitter fight to the end?

Gina. Oh, he can do that afterwards. First of all, we must get the child quieted. *(Goes out by the passage door.*

Hedvig (sits up and dries her tears). Now you must tell me what all this means. Why doesn't father want me any more?

Gregers. You mustn't ask that till you are a big girl— quite grown-up.

Hedvig (sobs). But I can't go on being as miserable as this till I'm grown-up.—I think I know what it is.—Perhaps I'm not really father's child.

Gregers (uneasily). How could that be?

Hedvig. Mother might have found me. And perhaps father has just got to know it; I've read of such things.

Gregers. Well, but if it were so——

Hedvig. I think he might be just as fond of me for all

that. Yes, fonder almost. We got the wild duck in a present, you know, and I love it so dearly all the same.

Gregers (turning the conversation). Ah, the wild duck, by-the-bye! Let us talk about the wild duck a little, Hedvig.

Hedvig. The poor wild duck! He doesn't want to see it any more either. Only think, he wanted to wring its neck!

Gregers. Oh, he won't do that.

Hedvig. No; but he said he would like to. And I think it was horrid of father to say it; for I pray for the wild duck every night, and ask that it may be preserved from death and all that is evil.

Gregers (looking at her). Do you say your prayers every night?

Hedvig. Yes.

Gregers. Who taught you to do that?

Hedvig. I myself; one time when father was very ill, and had leeches on his neck, and said that death was staring him in the face.

Gregers. Well?

Hedvig. Then I prayed for him as I lay in bed; and since then I have always kept it up.

Gregers. And now you pray for the wild duck too?

Hedvig. I thought it was best to bring in the wild duck; for she was so weakly at first.

Gregers. Do you pray in the morning, too?

Hedvig. No, of course not.

Gregers. Why not in the morning as well?

Hedvig. In the morning it's light, you know, and there's nothing in particular to be afraid of.

Gregers. And your father was going to wring the neck of the wild duck that you love so dearly?

Hedvig. No; he said he ought to wring its neck, but he would spare it for my sake; and that was kind of father.

Gregers (coming a little nearer). But suppose you were to sacrifice the wild duck of your own free will for his sake.

Hedvig (rising). The wild duck!

Gregers. Suppose you were to make a free-will offering, for his sake, of the dearest treasure you have in the world!

Hedvig. Do you think that would do any good?

Gregers. Try it, Hedvig.

Hedvig (softly, with flashing eyes). Yes, I will try it.

Gregers. Have you really the courage for it, do you think?

Hedvig. I'll ask grandfather to shoot the wild duck for me.

Gregers. Yes, do. But not a word to your mother about it.

Hedvig. Why not?

Gregers. She doesn't understand us.

Hedvig. The wild duck! I'll try it to-morrow morning.

[GINA *comes in by the passage door.*

Hedvig (going towards her). Did you find him, mother?

Gina. No, but I heard as he had called and taken Relling with him.

Gregers. Are you sure of that?

Gina. Yes, the porter's wife said so. Molvik went with them too, she said.

Gregers. This evening, when his mind so sorely needs to wrestle in solitude——!

Gina (takes off her things). Yes, men are strange creatures, so they are. The Lord only knows where Relling has dragged him to! I ran over to Madam Eriksen's, but they weren't there.

Hedvig (struggling to keep back her tears). Oh, if he should never come home any more!

Gregers. He will come home again. I shall have news to give him to-morrow; and then you shall see how he comes home. You may rely upon that, Hedvig, and sleep in peace. Good-night. [*He goes out by the passage door.*

Hedvig (throws herself sobbing on GINA'S *neck).* Mother, mother!

Gina (pats her shoulder and sighs). Ah yes; Relling was right, he was. That's what comes of it when crazy creatures go about presenting the claims of the—what-you-may-call-it.

ACT FIFTH

HIALMAR EKDAL'S *studio. Cold, grey morning light. Wet snow lies upon the large panes of the sloping roof-window.*

GINA *comes from the kitchen with an apron and bib on, and carrying a dusting-brush and a duster; she goes towards the sitting-room door. At the same moment* HEDVIG *comes hurriedly in from the passage.*

Gina (stops). Well?

Hedvig. Oh, mother, I almost think he's down at Relling's——

Gina. There, you see!

Hedvig. ——because the porter's wife says she could hear that Relling had two people with him when he came home last night.

Gina. That's just what I thought.

Hedvig. But it's no use his being there, if he won't come up to us.

Gina. I'll go down and speak to him at all events.

OLD EKDAL, *in dressing-gown and slippers, and with a lighted pipe, appears at the door of his room.*

Ekdal. Hialmar—— Isn't Hialmar at home?

Gina. No, he's gone out.

Ekdal. So early? And in such a tearing snowstorm? Well well; just as he pleases; I can take my morning walk alone.

> [*He slides the garret door aside;* HEDVIG *helps him; he goes in; she closes it after him.*

Hedvig (in an undertone). Only think, mother, when poor grandfather hears that father is going to leave us.

Gina. Oh, nonsense; grandfather mustn't hear anything about it. It was a heaven's mercy he wasn't at home yesterday in all that hurly-burly.

Hedvig. Yes, but——

[GREGERS *comes in by the passage door.*

Gregers. Well, have you any news of him?

Gina. They say he's down at Relling's.

Gregers. At Relling's! Has he really been out with those creatures?

Gina. Yes, like enough.

Gregers. When he ought to have been yearning for solitude, to collect and clear his thoughts——

Gina. Yes, you may well say so.

RELLING *enters from the passage.*

Hedvig (going to him). Is father in your room?

Gina (at the same time). Is he there?

Relling. Yes, to be sure he is.

Hedvig. And you never let us know!

Relling. Yes; I'm a brute. But in the first place I had to look after the other brute; I mean our dæmonic friend, of course; and then I fell so dead asleep that——

Gina. What does Ekdal say to-day?

Relling. He says nothing whatever.

Hedvig. Doesn't he speak?

Relling. Not a blessed word.

Gregers. No no; I can understand that very well.

Gina. But what's he doing then?

Relling. He's lying on the sofa, snoring.

Gina. Oh is he? Yes, Ekdal's a rare one to snore.

Hedvig. Asleep? Can he sleep?

Relling. Well, it certainly looks like it.

Gregers. No wonder, after the spiritual conflict that has rent him——

Gina. And then he's never been used to gadding about out of doors at night.

Hedvig. Perhaps it's a good thing that he's getting sleep, mother.

Gina. Of course it is; and we must take care we don't wake him up too early. Thank you, Relling. I must get the house cleaned up a bit now, and then—— Come and help me, Hedvig.

[Gina *and* Hedvig *go into the sitting-room.*

Gregers (turning to Relling*).* What is your explanation of the spiritual tumult that is now going on in Hialmar Ekdal?

Relling. Devil a bit of a spiritual tumult have *I* noticed in him.

Gregers. What! Not at such a crisis, when his whole life has been placed on a new foundation——? How can you think that such an individuality as Hialmar's——?

Relling. Oh, individuality—he! If he ever had any tendency to the abnormal developments you call individuality, I can assure you it was rooted out of him while he was still in his teens.

Gregers. That would be strange indeed,—considering the loving care with which he was brought up.

Relling. By those two high-flown, hysterical maiden aunts, you mean?

Gregers. Let me tell you that they were women who never forgot the claim of the ideal—but of course you will only jeer at me again.

Relling. No, I'm in no humour for that. I know all about those ladies; for he has ladled out no end of rhetoric on the subject of his "two soul-mothers." But I don't think he has much to thank them for. Ekdal's misfortune is that in his own circle he has always been looked upon as a shining light——

Gregers. Not without reason, surely. Look at the depth of his mind!

Relling. *I* have never discovered it. That his father believed in it I don't so much wonder; the old lieutenant has been an ass all his days.

Gregers. He has had a child-like mind all his days; that is what you cannot understand.

Relling. Well, so be it. But then, when our dear, sweet Hialmar went to college, he at once passed for the great light of the future amongst his comrades too. He was handsome, the rascal—red and white—a shop-girl's dream of manly beauty; and with his superficially emotional temperament, and his sympathetic voice, and his talent for declaiming other people's verses and other people's thoughts——

Gregers (indignantly). Is it Hialmar Ekdal you are talking about in this strain?

Relling. Yes, with your permission; I am simply giving you an inside view of the idol you are grovelling before.

Gregers. I should hardly have thought I was quite stone blind.

Relling. Yes you are—or not far from it. You are a sick man, too, you see.

Gregers. You are right there.

Relling. Yes. Yours is a complicated case. First of all there is that plaguy integrity-fever; and then—what's worse —you are always in a delirium of hero-worship; you must always have something to adore, outside yourself.

Gregers. Yes, I must certainly seek it outside myself.

Relling. But you make such shocking mistakes about every new phœnix you think you have discovered. Here again you have come to a cotter's cabin with your claim of the ideal; and the people of the house are insolvent.

Gregers. If you don't think better than that of Hialmar Ekdal, what pleasure can you find in being everlastingly with him?

Relling. Well, you see, I'm supposed to be a sort of a doctor—save the mark! I can't but give a hand to the poor sick folk who live under the same roof with me.

Gregers. Oh, indeed! Hialmar Ekdal is sick too, is he!

Relling. Most people are, worse luck.

Gregers. And what remedy are you applying in Hialmar's case?

Relling. My usual one. I am cultivating the life-illusion * in him.

Gregers. Life—illusion? I didn't catch what you said.

Relling. Yes, I said illusion. For illusion, you know, is the stimulating principle.

Gregers. May I ask with what illusion Hialmar is inoculated?

Relling. No, thank you; I don't betray professional secrets to quacksalvers. You would probably go and muddle his case still more than you have already. But my method is infallible. I have applied it to Molvik as well. I have made him "dæmonic." That's the blister I have to put on his neck.

Gregers. Is he not really dæmonic then?

Relling. What the devil do you mean by dæmonic! It's only a piece of gibberish I've invented to keep up a spark of life in him. But for that, the poor harmless creature would have succumbed to self-contempt and despair many a long year ago. And then the old lieutenant! But he has hit upon his own cure, you see.

Gregers. Lieutenant Ekdal? What of him?

Relling. Just think of the old bear-hunter shutting himself up in that dark garret to shoot rabbits! I tell you there is not a happier sportsman in the world than that old man pottering about in there among all that rubbish. The four or five withered Christmas-trees he has saved up are the same to him as the whole great fresh Höidal forest; the cock and the hens are big game-birds in the fir-tops; and the rabbits that flop about the garret floor are the bears

---

* "Livslögnen," literally "the life-lie."

he has to battle with—the mighty hunter of the mountains!

Gregers. Poor unfortunate old man! Yes; he has indeed had to narrow the ideals of his youth.

Relling. While I think of it, Mr. Werle, junior—don't use that foreign word: ideals. We have the excellent native word: lies.

Gregers. Do you think the two things are related?

Relling. Yes, just about as closely as typhus and putrid fever.

Gregers. Dr. Relling, I shall not give up the struggle until I have rescued Hialmar from your clutches!

Relling. So much the worse for him. Rob the average man of his life-illusion, and you rob him of his happiness at the same stroke. *(To* HEDVIG, *who comes in from the sitting-room.)* Well, little wild-duck-mother, I'm just going down to see whether papa is still lying meditating upon that wonderful invention of his. [*Goes out by passage door.*

Gregers (approaches HEDVIG*).* I can see by your face that you have not yet done it.

Hedvig. What? Oh, that about the wild duck! No.

Gregers. I suppose your courage failed when the time came.

Hedvig. No, that wasn't it. But when I awoke this morning and remembered what we had been talking about, it seemed so strange.

Gregers. Strange?

Hedvig. Yes, I don't know—— Yesterday evening, at the moment, I thought there was something so delightful about it; but since I have slept and thought of it again, it somehow doesn't seem worth while.

Gregers. Ah, I thought you could not have grown up quite unharmed in this house.

Hedvig. I don't care about that, if only father would come up——

Gregers. Oh, if only your eyes had been opened to that

which gives life its value—if you possessed the true, joy-ous, fearless spirit of sacrifice, you would soon see how he would come up to you.—But I believe in you still, Hedvig.

> [*He goes out by the passage door.* HEDVIG *wan-ders about the room for a time; she is on the point of going into the kitchen when a knock is heard at the garret door.* HEDVIG *goes over and opens it a little; old* EKDAL *comes out; she pushes the door to again.*

Ekdal. H'm, it's not much fun to take one's morning walk alone.

Hedvig. Wouldn't you like to go shooting, grandfather?

Ekdal. It's not the weather for it to-day. It's so dark there, you can scarcely see where you're going.

Hedvig. Do you never want to shoot anything besides the rabbits?

Ekdal. Do you think the rabbits aren't good enough?

Hedvig. Yes, but what about the wild duck?

Ekdal. Ho-ho! are you afraid I shall shoot your wild duck? Never in the world. Never.

Hedvig. No, I suppose you couldn't; they say it's very difficult to shoot wild ducks.

Ekdal. Couldn't! Should rather think I could.

Hedvig. How would you set about it, grandfather?—I don't mean with my wild duck, but with others?

Ekdal. I should take care to shoot them in the breast, you know; that's the surest place. And then you must shoot against the feathers, you see—not the way of the feathers.

Hedvig. Do they die then, grandfather?

Ekdal. Yes, they die right enough—when you shoot properly. Well, I must go and brush up a bit. H'm— understand—h'm. [*Goes into his room.*

> [HEDVIG *waits a little, glances towards the sitting-room door, goes over to the book-case, stands on tip-toe, takes the double-barrelled pistol down*

from the shelf, and looks at it. GINA, *with
brush and duster, comes from the sitting-room.*
HEDVIG *hastily lays down the pistol, unobserved.*

Gina. Don't stand raking amongst father's things,
Hedvig.

Hedvig (goes away from the bookcase). I was only going
to tidy up a little.

Gina. You'd better go into the kitchen, and see if the
coffee's keeping hot; I'll take his breakfast on a tray, when
I go down to him.

> [HEDVIG *goes out.* GINA *begins to sweep and
> clean up the studio. Presently the passage door
> is opened with hesitation, and* HIALMAR EKDAL
> *looks in. He has on his overcoat, but not his
> hat; he is unwashed, and his hair is dishevelled
> and unkempt. His eyes are dull and heavy.*

*Gina (standing with the brush in her hand, and looking
at him).* Oh, there now, Ekdal—so you've come after all?

Hialmar (comes in and answers in a toneless voice). I
come—only to depart again immediately.

Gina. Yes, yes, I suppose so. But, Lord help us! what
a sight you are!

Hialmar. A sight?

Gina. And your nice winter coat too! Well, that's done
for.

Hedvig (at the kitchen door). Mother, hadn't I better——? *(Sees* HIALMAR, *gives a loud scream of joy, and
runs to him.)* Oh, father, father!

Hialmar (turns away and makes a gesture of repulsion).
Away, away, away! *(To* GINA.*)* Keep her away from me,
I say!

Gina (in a low tone). Go into the sitting-room, Hedvig.
> [HEDVIG *does so without a word.*

Hialmar (fussily pulls out the table-drawer). I must have
my books with me. Where are my books?

Gina. Which books?

Hialmar. My scientific books, of course; the technical magazines I require for my invention.

Gina (searches in the bookcase). Is it these here paper-covered ones?

Hialmar. Yes, of course.

Gina (lays a heap of magazines on the table). Shan't I get Hedvig to cut them for you?

Hialmar. I don't require to have them cut for me.

[*Short silence.*

Gina. Then you're still set on leaving us, Ekdal?

Hialmar (rummaging amongst the books). Yes, that is a matter of course, I should think.

Gina. Well, well.

Hialmar (vehemently). How can I live here, to be stabbed to the heart every hour of the day?

Gina. God forgive you for thinking such vile things of me.

Hialmar. Prove——!

Gina. I think it's you as has got to prove.

Hialmar. After a past like yours? There are certain claims—I may almost call them claims of the ideal——

Gina. But what about grandfather? What's to become of him, poor dear?

Hialmar. I know my duty; my helpless father will come with me. I am going out into the town to make arrangements—— H'm—(*hesitatingly*)—has any one found my hat on the stairs?

Gina. No. Have you lost your hat?

Hialmar. Of course I had it on when I came in last night; there's no doubt about that; but I couldn't find it this morning.

Gina. Lord help us! where have you been to with those two ne'er-do-weels?

Hialmar. Oh, don't bother me about trifles. Do you suppose I am in the mood to remember details?

Gina. If only you haven't caught cold, Ekdal——

> [*Goes out into the kitchen.*

Hialmar (talks to himself in a low tone of irritation, whilst he empties the table-drawer). You're a scoundrel, Relling!—You're a low fellow!—Ah, you shameless tempter! —I wish I could get some one to stick a knife into you!

> [*He lays some old letters on one side, finds the torn document of yesterday, takes it up and looks at the pieces; puts it down hurriedly as* GINA *enters.*

Gina (sets a tray with coffee, etc., on the table). Here's a drop of something hot, if you'd fancy it. And there's some bread and butter and a snack of salt meat.

Hialmar (glancing at the tray). Salt meat? Never under this roof! It's true I have not had a mouthful of solid food for nearly twenty-four hours; but no matter.—My memoranda! The commencement of my autobiography! What has become of my diary, and all my important papers? *(Opens the sitting-room door but draws back.)* She is there too!

Gina. Good Lord! the child must be somewhere!

Hialmar. Come out.

> [*He makes room,* HEDVIG *comes, scared, into the studio.*

Hialmar (with his hand upon the door-handle, says to GINA*):* In these, the last moments I spend in my former home, I wish to be spared from interlopers——

> [*Goes into the room.*

Hedvig (with a bound towards her mother, asks softly, trembling). Does that mean me?

Gina. Stay out in the kitchen, Hedvig; or, no—you'd best go into your own room. *(Speaks to* HIALMAR *as she goes in to him.)* Wait a bit, Ekdal; don't rummage so in the drawers; *I* know where everything is.

Hedvig (stands a moment immovable, in terror and perplexity, biting her lips to keep back the tears; then she

lenches her hands convulsively, and says softly): The
wild duck.

> [*She steals over and takes the pistol from the
> shelf, opens the garret door a little way, creeps
> in, and draws the door to after her.*
>
> [HIALMAR *and* GINA *can be heard disputing in
> the sitting-room.*

*Hialmar (comes in with some manuscript books and old
loose papers, which he lays upon the table).* That portmanteau is of no use! There are a thousand and one things
I must drag with me.

Gina (following with the portmanteau). Why not leave
all the rest for the present, and only take a shirt and a pair
of woollen drawers with you?

Hialmar. Whew!—all these exhausting preparations——!

> [*Pulls off his overcoat and throws it upon the sofa.*

Gina. And there's the coffee getting cold.

Hialmar. H'm.

> [*Drinks a mouthful without thinking of it, and
> then another.*

Gina (dusting the backs of the chairs). A nice job you'll
have to find such another big garret for the rabbits.

Hialmar. What! Am I to drag all those rabbits with me
too?

Gina. You don't suppose grandfather can get on without his rabbits.

Hialmar. He must just get used to doing without them.
Have not *I* to sacrifice very much greater things than
rabbits!

Gina (dusting the bookcase). Shall I put the flute in
the portmanteau for you?

Hialmar. No. No flute for me. But give me the pistol!

Gina. Do you want to take the pigstol with you?

Hialmar. Yes. My loaded pistol.

Gina (searching for it). It's gone. He must have taken
it in with him.

Hialmar. Is he in the garret?

Gina. Yes, of course he's in the garret.

Hialmar. H'm—poor lonely old man.

> [*He takes a piece of bread and butter, eats it,
> and finishes his cup of coffee.*

Gina. If we hadn't have let that room, you could have moved in there.

Hialmar. And continued to live under the same roof with——! Never,—never!

Gina. But couldn't you put up with the sitting-room for a day or two? You could have it all to yourself.

Hialmar. Never within these walls!

Gina. Well then, down with Relling and Molvik.

Hialmar. Don't mention those wretches' names to me! The very thought of them almost takes away my appetite.— Oh no, I must go out into the storm and the snow-drift,— go from house to house and seek shelter for my father and myself.

Gina. But you've got no hat, Ekdal! You've been and lost your hat, you know.

Hialmar. Oh those two brutes, those slaves of all the vices! A hat must be procured. (*Takes another piece of bread and butter.*) Some arrangements must be made. For I have no mind to throw away my life, either.

> [*Looks for something on the tray.*

Gina. What are you looking for?

Hialmar. Butter.

Gina. I'll get some at once. [*Goes out into the kitchen.*

Hialmar (calls after her). Oh it doesn't matter; dry bread is good enough for me.

Gina (brings a dish of butter). Look here; this is fresh churned.

> [*She pours out another cup of coffee for him; he
> seats himself on the sofa, spreads more butter
> on the already buttered bread, and eats and
> drinks awhile in silence.*

Hialmar. Could I, without being subject to intrusion—intrusion of any sort—could I live in the sitting-room there for a day or two?

Gina. Yes, to be sure you could, if you only would.

Hialmar. For I see no possibility of getting all father's things out in such a hurry.

Gina. And, besides, you've surely got to tell him first as you don't mean to live with us others no more.

Hialmar (pushes away his coffee cup). Yes, there is that too; I shall have to lay bare the whole tangled story to him—— I must turn matters over; I must have breathing-time; I cannot take all these burdens on my shoulders in a single day.

Gina. No, especially in such horrible weather as it is outside.

Hialmar (touching WERLE's *letter).* I see that paper is still lying about here.

Gina. Yes, *I* haven't touched it.

Hialmar. So far as I am concerned it is mere waste paper——

Gina. Well, *I* have certainly no notion of making any use of it.

Hialmar. ——but we had better not let it get lost all the same;—in all the upset when I move, it might easily——

Gina. I'll take good care of it, Ekdal.

Hialmar. The donation is in the first instance made to father, and it rests with him to accept or decline it.

Gina (sighs). Yes, poor old father——

Hialmar. To make quite safe—— Where shall I find some gum?

Gina (goes to the bookcase). Here's the gum-pot.

Hialmar. And a brush?

Gina. The brush is here too. [*Brings him the things.*

Hialmar (takes a pair of scissors). Just a strip of paper at the back——(*Clips and gums.*) Far be it from me to lay hands upon what it not my own—and least of all upon what belongs to a destitute old man—and to—the other as well.—There now. Let it lie there for a time; and when it is dry, take it away. I wish never to see that document again. Never!

GREGERS WERLE *enters from the passage.*

Gregers (somewhat surprised). What,—are you sitting here, Hialmar?

Hialmar (rises hurriedly). I had sunk down from fatigue

Gregers. You have been having breakfast, I see.

Hialmar. The body sometimes makes its claims felt too.

Gregers. What have you decided to do?

Hialmar. For a man like me, there is only one course possible. I am just putting my most important things together. But it takes time, you know.

Gina (with a touch of impatience). Am I to get the room ready for you, or am I to pack your portmanteau?

Hialmar (after a glance of annoyance at GREGERS*).* Pack —and get the room ready!

Gina (takes the portmanteau). Very well; then I'll put in the shirt and the other things.

[*Goes into the sitting-room and draws the door to after her.*

Gregers (after a short silence). I never dreamed that this would be the end of it. Do you really feel it a necessity to leave house and home?

Hialmar (wanders about restlessly). What would you have me do?—I am not fitted to bear unhappiness, Gregers. I must feel secure and at peace in my surroundings.

Gregers. But can you not feel that here? Just try it. I should have thought you had firm ground to build upon now—if only you start afresh. And, remember, you have your invention to live for.

Hialmar. Oh don't talk about my invention. It's perhaps still in the dim distance.

Gregers. Indeed!

Hialmar. Why, great heavens, what would you have me

invent? Other people have invented almost everything already. It becomes more and more difficult every day——

Gregers. And you have devoted so much labour to it.

Hialmar. It was that blackguard Relling that urged me to it.

Gregers. Relling?

Hialmar. Yes, it was he that first made me realise my aptitude for making some notable discovery in photography.

Gregers. Aha—it was Relling!

Hialmar. Oh, I have been so truly happy over it! Not so much for the sake of the invention itself, as because Hedvig believed in it—believed in it with a child's whole eagerness of faith.—At least, I have been fool enough to go and imagine that she believed in it.

Gregers. Can you really think Hedvig has been false towards you?

Hialmar. I can think anything now. It is Hedvig that stands in my way. She will blot out the sunlight from my whole life.

Gregers. Hedvig! Is it Hedvig you are talking of? How should she blot out your sunlight?

Hialmar (without answering). How unutterably I have loved that child! How unutterably happy I have felt every time I came home to my humble room, and she flew to meet me, with her sweet little blinking eyes. Oh, confiding fool that I have been! I loved her unutterably;—and I yielded myself up to the dream, the delusion, that she loved me unutterably in return.

Gregers. Do you call that a delusion?

Hialmar. How should I know? I can get nothing out of Gina; and besides, she is totally blind to the ideal side of these complications. But to you I feel impelled to open my mind, Gregers. I cannot shake off this frightful doubt—perhaps Hedvig has never really and honestly loved me.

Gregers. What would you say if she were to give you a

proof of her love? *(Listens.)* What's that? I thought I heard the wild duck——?

Hialmar. It's the wild duck quacking. Father's in the garret.

Gregers. Is he? *(His face lights up with joy.)* I say you may yet have proof that your poor misunderstood Hedvig loves you!

Hialmar. Oh, what proof can she give me? I dare not believe in any assurance from that quarter.

Gregers. Hedvig does not know what deceit means.

Hialmar. Oh Gregers, that is just what I cannot be sure of. Who knows what Gina and that Mrs. Sörby may many a time have sat here whispering and tattling about? And Hedvig usually has her ears open, I can tell you. Perhaps the deed of gift was not such a surprise to her, after all. In fact, I'm not sure but that I noticed something of the sort.

Gregers. What spirit is this that has taken possession of you?

Hialmar. I have had my eyes opened. Just you notice; —you'll see, the deed of gift is only a beginning. Mrs. Sörby has always been a good deal taken up with Hedvig; and now she has the power to do whatever she likes for the child. They can take her from me whenever they please.

Gregers. Hedvig will never, never leave you.

Hialmar. Don't be so sure of that. If only they beckon to her and throw out a golden bait——! And oh! I have loved her so unspeakably! I would have counted it my highest happiness to take her tenderly by the hand and lead her, as one leads a timid child through a great dark empty room!—I am cruelly certain now that the poor photographer in his humble attic has never really and truly been anything to her. She has only cunningly contrived to keep on a good footing with him until the time came.

Gregers. You don't believe that yourself, Hialmar.

Hialmar. That is just the terrible part of it—I don't

know what to believe,—I never can know it. But can you really doubt that it must be as I say? Ho-ho, you have far too much faith in the claim of the ideal, my good Gregers! If those others came, with the glamour of wealth about them, and called to the child:—"Leave him: come to us: here life awaits you——!"

Gregers (quickly). Well, what then?

Hialmar. If I then asked her: Hedvig, are you willing to renounce that life for me? *(Laughs scornfully.)* No thank you! You would soon hear what answer I should get. [*A pistol shot is heard from within the garret.*

Gregers (loudly and joyfully). Hialmar!

Hialmar. There now; he must needs go shooting too.

Gina (comes in). Oh Ekdal, I can hear grandfather blazing away in the garret by hisself.

Hialmar. I'll look in——

Gregers (eagerly, with emotion). Wait a moment! Do you know what that was?

Hialmar. Yes, of course I know.

Gregers. No you don't know. But *I* do. That was the proof!

Hialmar. What proof?

Gregers. It was a child's free-will offering. She has got your father to shoot the wild duck.

Hialmar. To shoot the wild duck!

Gina. Oh, think of that——!

Hialmar. What was that for?

Gregers. She wanted to sacrifice to you her most cherished possession; for then she thought you would surely come to love her again.

Hialmar (tenderly, with emotion). Oh, poor child!

Gina. What things she does think of!

Gregers. She only wanted your love again, Hialmar. She could not live without it.

Gina (struggling with her tears). There, you can see for yourself, Ekdal.

Hialmar. Gina, where is she?

Gina (sniffs). Poor dear, she's sitting out in the kitchen, I dare say.

Hialmar (goes over, tears open the kitchen door, and says): Hedvig, come, come in to me! *(Looks around.)* No, she's not here.

Gina. Then she must be in her own little room.

Hialmar (without). No, she's not here either. *(Comes in.)* She must have gone out.

Gina. Yes, you wouldn't have her anywheres in the house.

Hialmar. Oh, if she would only come home quickly, so that I can tell her—— Everything will come right now, Gregers; now I believe we can begin life afresh.

Gregers (quietly). I knew it; I knew the child would make amends.

OLD EKDAL *appears at the door of his room; he is in full uniform, and is busy buckling on his sword.*

Hialmar (astonished). Father! Are you there?

Gina. Have you been firing in your room?

Ekdal (resentfully, approaching). So you go shooting alone, do you, Hialmar?

Hialmar (excited and confused). Then it wasn't you that fired that shot in the garret?

Ekdal. Me that fired? H'm.

Gregers (calls out to HIALMAR*).* She has shot the wild duck herself!

Hialmar. What can it mean? *(Hastens to the garret door, tears it aside, looks in and calls loudly):* Hedvig!

Gina (runs to the door). Good God, what's that!

Hialmar (goes in). She's lying on the floor!

Gregers. Hedvig! lying on the floor!

[*Goes in to* HIALMAR

Gina (at the same time). Hedvig! *(Inside the garret.)* No, no, no!

Ekdal. Ho-ho! does she go shooting, too, now?

[HIALMAR, GINA *and* GREGERS *carry* HEDVIG *into the studio; in her dangling right hand she holds the pistol fast clasped in her fingers.*

Hialmar (distracted). The pistol has gone off. She has wounded herself. Call for help! Help!

Gina (runs into the passage and calls down). Relling! Relling! Doctor Relling; come up as quick as you can!

[HIALMAR *and* GREGERS *lay* HEDVIG *down on the sofa.*

Ekdal (quietly). The woods avenge themselves.

Hialmar (on his knees beside HEDVIG*).* She'll soon come to now. She's coming to——; yes, yes, yes.

Gina (who has come in again). Where has she hurt herself? I can't see anything——

[RELLING *comes hurriedly, and immediately after him* MOLVIK; *the latter without his waistcoat and necktie, and with his coat open.*

Relling. What's the matter here?

Gina. They say Hedvig has shot herself.

Hialmar. Come and help us!

Relling. Shot herself!

[*He pushes the table aside and begins to examine her.*

Hialmar (kneeling and looking anxiously up at him). It can't be dangerous? Speak, Relling! She is scarcely bleeding at all. It can't be dangerous?

Relling. How did it happen?

Hialmar. Oh, we don't know——

Gina. She wanted to shoot the wild duck.

Relling. The wild duck?

Hialmar. The pistol must have gone off.

Relling. H'm. Indeed.

Ekdal. The woods avenge themselves. But I'm not afraid, all the same.

[*Goes into the garret and closes the door after him.*

Hialmar. Well, Relling,—why don't you say something?

Relling. The ball has entered the breast.

Hialmar. Yes, but she's coming to!

Relling. Surely you can see that Hedvig is dead.

Gina (bursts into tears). Oh my child, my child——

Gregers (huskily). In the depths of the sea——

Hialmar (jumps up). No, no, she must live! Oh, for God's sake, Relling—only a moment—only just till I can tell her how unspeakably I loved her all the time!

Relling. The bullet has gone through her heart. Internal hemorrhage. Death must have been instantaneous.

Hialmar. And I! I hunted her from me like an animal! And she crept terrified into the garret and died for love of me! *(Sobbing.)* I can never atone to her! I can never tell her——! *(Clenches his hands and cries, upwards.)* O thou above——! If thou be indeed! Why hast thou done this thing to me?

Gina. Hush, hush, you mustn't go on that awful way. We had no right to keep her, I suppose.

Molvik. The child is not dead, but sleepeth.

Relling. Bosh.

Hialmar (becomes calm, goes over to the sofa, folds his arms, and looks at HEDVIG *).* There she lies so stiff and still.

Relling (tries to loosen the pistol). She's holding it so tight, so tight.

Gina. No, no, Relling, don't break her fingers; let the pigstol be.

Hialmar. She shall take it with her.

Gina. Yes, let her. But the child mustn't lie here for a show. She shall go to her own room, so she shall. Help me, Ekdal. [HIALMAR *and* GINA *take* HEDVIG *between them.*

Hialmar (as they are carrying her). Oh, Gina, Gina, can you survive this!

Gina. We must help each other to bear it. For now at least she belongs to both of us.

Molvik (stretches out his arms and mumbles). Blessed be the Lord; to earth thou shalt return; to earth thou shalt return——

Relling (whispers). Hold your tongue, you fool; you're drunk.

[HIALMAR *and* GINA *carry the body out through the kitchen door.* RELLING *shuts it after them.* MOLVIK *slinks out into the passage.*

Relling (goes over to GREGERS *and says):* No one shall ever convince me that the pistol went off by accident.

Gregers (who has stood terrified, with convulsive twitchings). Who can say how the dreadful thing happened?

Relling. The powder has burnt the body of her dress. She must have pressed the pistol right against her breast and fired.

Gregers. Hedvig has not died in vain. Did you not see how sorrow set free what is noble in him?

Relling. Most people are ennobled by the actual presence of death. But how long do you suppose this nobility will last in him?

Gregers. Why should it not endure and increase throughout his life?

Relling. Before a year is over, little Hedvig will be nothing to him but a pretty theme for declamation.

Gregers. How dare you say that of Hialmar Ekdal?

Relling. We will talk of this again, when the grass has first withered on her grave. Then you'll hear him spouting about "the child too early torn from her father's heart;" then you'll see him steep himself in a syrup of sentiment and self-admiration and self-pity. Just you wait!

Gregers. If you are right and I am wrong, then life is not worth living.

Relling. Oh, life would be quite tolerable, after all, if only we could be rid of the confounded duns that keep on pestering us, in our poverty, with the claim of the ideal.

Gregers (looking straight before him). In that case, I am glad that my destiny is what is.

Relling. May I inquire,—what is your destiny?

Gregers (going). To be the thirteenth at table.

Relling. The devil it is.

THE END

THE LEAGUE OF YOUTH
(1869)

CHARACTERS

CHAMBERLAIN BRATSBERG,* *owner of iron-works.*
ERIK BRATSBERG, *his son, a merchant.*
THORA, *his daughter.*
SELMA, *Erik's wife.*
DOCTOR FIELDBO, *physician at the Chamberlain's works.*
STENSGÅRD,† *a lawyer.*
MONS MONSEN, *of Stonelee.‡*
BASTIAN MONSEN, *his son.*
RAGNA, *his daughter.*
HELLE,§ *student of theology, tutor at Stonelee.*
RINGDAL, *manager of the iron-works.*
ANDERS LUNDESTAD, *landowner.*
DANIEL HEIRE.¶
MADAM ‖ RUNDHOLMEN, *widow of a storekeeper and publican.*
ASLAKSEN, *a printer.*
A MAID-SERVANT AT THE CHAMBERLAIN'S.
A WAITER.
A WAITRESS AT MADAM RUNDHOLMEN'S.
Townspeople, Guests at the Chamberlain's, etc., etc.

The action takes place in the neighbourhood of the iron-works, not far from a market town in Southern Norway.

---

* "Chamberlain" (Kammerherre) is a title conferred by the King of Norway upon men of wealth and position. Hereditary nobility was abolished in 1821. † Pronounce *Staynsgore.* ‡ In the original "Storli." § Pronounce *Hellë.* ¶ Heire (pronounce *Heirë*) = Heron. ‖ Married women and widows of the lower middle-class are addressed as Madam in Norway.

THE LEAGUE OF YOUTH

ACT FIRST

The Seventeenth of May.* *A popular fête in the Chamber-*
lain's grounds. Music and dancing in the background,
Coloured lights among the trees. In the middle, some-
what towards the back, a rostrum. To the right, the
entrance to a large refreshment-tent; before it, a table
with benches. In the foreground on the left, another
table, decorated with flowers and surrounded with
lounging-chairs.

A Crowd of People. LUNDESTAD, *with a committee-badge*
at his button-hole, stands on the rostrum. RINGDAL,
also with a committee-badge, at the table on the left.

Lundestad. . . . Therefore, friends and fellow citizens, I
drink to our freedom! As we have inherited it from our
fathers, so will we preserve it for ourselves and for our children! Three cheers for the day! Three cheers for the
Seventeenth of May!

The Crowd. Hurrah! hurrah! hurrah!

Ringdal (as LUNDESTAD *descends from the rostrum).*
And one cheer more for old Lundestad!

Some of the Crowd (hissing). Ss! Ss!

Many Voices (drowning the others). Hurrah for Lundestad! Long live old Lundestad! Hurrah!

> [*The* CROWD *gradually disperses.* MONSEN, *his*
> *son* BASTIAN, STENSGÅRD, *and* ASLAKSEN *make*
> *their way forward through the throng.*

---

* The Norwegian "Independence Day."

123

Monsen. 'Pon my soul, it's time he was laid on the shelf!

Aslaksen. It was the local situation * he was talking about! Ho-ho!

Monsen. He has made the same speech year after year as long as I can remember. Come over here.

Stensgård. No, no, not that way, Mr. Monsen. We are quite deserting your daughter.

Monsen. Oh, Ragna will find us again.

Bastian. She's all right; young Helle is with her.

Stensgård. Helle?

Monsen. Yes, Helle. But *(nudging* STENSGÅRD *familiarly)* you have me here, you see, and the rest of us. Come on! Here we shall be out of the crowd, and can discuss more fully what——

> [*Has meanwhile taken a seat beside the table on the left.*

Ringdal (approaching). Excuse me, Mr. Monsen—that table is reserved——

Stensgård. Reserved? For whom?

Ringdal. For the Chamberlain's party.

Stensgård. Oh, confound the Chamberlain's party! There's none of them here.

Ringdal. No, but we expect them every minute.

Stensgård. Then let them sit somewhere else.

> [*Takes a chair.*

Lundestad (laying his hand on the chair). No, the table is reserved, and there's an end of it.

Monsen (rising). Come, Mr. Stensgård; there are just as good seats over there. *(Crosses to the right.)* Waiter! Ha, no waiters either. The Committee should have seen to that in time. Oh, Aslaksen, just go in and get us four

---

* "Local situation" is a very ineffectual rendering of Aslaksen's phrase, "lokale forholde"—German, *Verhältnisse*—but there seems to be no other which will fit into all the different contexts in which it occurs. It reappears in *An Enemy of the People,* Act v.

bottles of champagne. Order the dearest; tell them to put
it down to Monsen!

> [ASLAKSEN *goes into the tent; the three others
> seat themselves.*

Lundestad (goes quietly over to them and addresses STENS-
GÅRD*).* I hope you won't take it ill——

Monsen. Take it ill! Good gracious, no! Not in the
least.

Lunestad (still to STENSGÅRD*).* It's not my doing; it's
the Committee that decided——

Monsen. Of course. The Committee orders, and we
must obey.

Lundestad (as before). You see, we are on the Chamberlain's own ground here. He has been so kind as to throw
open his park and garden for this evening; so we thought——

Stensgård. We're extremely comfortable here, Mr. Lundestad—if only people would leave us in peace—the crowd,
I mean.

Lundestad (unruffled). Very well; then it's all right.

> [*Goes towards the back.*

Aslaksen (entering from the tent). The waiter is just
coming with the wine.   [*Sits.*

Monsen. A table apart, under special care of the Committee! And on our Independence Day of all others!
There you have a specimen of the way things go.

Stensgård. But why on earth do you put up with all this,
you good people?

Monsen. The habit of generations, you see.

Aslaksen. You're new to the district, Mr. Stensgård. If
only you knew a little of the local situation——

A Waiter (brings champagne). Was it you that ordered——?

Aslaksen. Yes, certainly; open the bottle.

The Waiter (pouring out the wine). It goes to your account, Mr. Monsen?

Monsen. The whole thing; don't be afraid.

[*The* WAITER *goes.*

Monsen (clinks glasses with STENSGÅRD*).* Here's welcome among us, Mr. Stensgård! It gives me great pleasure to have made your acquaintance; I cannot but call it an honour to the district that such a man should settle here. The newspapers have made us familiar with your name, on all sorts of public occasions. You have great gifts of oratory, Mr. Stensgård, and a warm heart for the public weal. I trust you will enter with life and vigour into the— h'm, into the——

Aslaksen. The local situation.

Monsen. Oh yes, the local situation. I drink to that.

[*They drink.*

Stensgård. Whatever I do, I shall certainly put life and vigour into it.

Monsen. Bravo! Hear, hear! Another glass in honour of that promise.

Stensgård. No, stop; I've already——

Monsen. Oh, nonsense! Another glass, I say—to seal the bond!

[*They clink glasses and drink. During what follows* BASTIAN *keeps on filling the glasses as soon as they are empty.*

Monsen. However—since we have got upon the subject —I must tell you that it's not the Chamberlain himself that keeps everything under his thumb. No, sir—old Lundestad is the man that stands behind and drives the sledge.

Stensgård. So I am told in many quarters. I can't understand how a Liberal like him——

Monsen. Lundestad? Do you call Anders Lundestad a Liberal? To be sure, he professed Liberalism in his young days, when he was still at the foot of the ladder. And then he inherited his seat in Parliament from his father. Good Lord! everything runs in families here.

Stensgård. But there must be some means of putting a stop to all these abuses.

Aslaksen. Yes, damn it all, Mr. Stensgård—see if you can't put a stop to them!

Stensgård. I don't say that I——

Aslaksen. Yes, you! You are just the man. You have the gift of gab, as the saying goes; and what's more: you have the pen of a ready writer. My paper's at your disposal, you know.

Monsen. If anything is to be done, it must be done quickly. The preliminary election * comes on in three days now.

Stensgård. And if you were elected, your private affairs would not prevent your accepting the charge?

Monsen. My private affairs would suffer, of course; but if it appeared that the good of the community demanded the sacrifice, I should have to put aside all personal considerations.

Stensgård. Good; that's good. And you have a party already: that I can see clearly.

Monsen. I flatter myself the majority of the younger, go-ahead generation——

Aslaksen. H'm, h'm! 'ware spies!

DANIEL HEIRE *enters from the tent; he peers about short-sightedly, and approaches.*

Heire. May I beg for the loan of a spare seat; I want to sit over there.

Monsen. The benches are fastened here, you see; but won't you take a place at this table?

Heire. Here? At this table? Oh, yes, with pleasure. *(Sits.)* Dear, dear! Champagne, I believe.

---

* The system of indirect election obtains in Norway. The constituencies choose a College of Electors, who, in turn, choose the Members of the Storthing or Parliament. It is the preliminary "Election of Electors" to which Monsen refers.

Monsen. Yes; won't you join us in a glass?

Heire. No, thank you! Madam Rundholmen's champagne—— Well, well, just half a glass to keep you company. If only one had a glass, now.

Monsen. Bastian, go and get one.

Bastian. Oh, Aslaksen, just go and fetch a glass.

[ASLAKSEN *goes into the tent. A pause.*

Heire. Don't let me interrupt you, gentlemen. I wouldn't for the world——! Thanks, Aslaksen. *(Bows to* STENSGÅRD.) A strange face—a recent arrival! Have I the pleasure of addressing our new legal luminary, Mr. Stensgård?

Monsen. Quite right. *(Introducing them.)* Mr. Stensgård, Mr. Daniel Heire——

Bastian. Capitalist.

Heire. Ex-capitalist, you should rather say. It's all gone now; slipped through my fingers, so to speak. Not that I'm bankrupt—for goodness' sake don't think that.

Monsen. Drink, drink, while the froth is on it.

Heire. But rascality, you understand—sharp practice and so forth—— I say no more. Well, well, I am confident it is only temporary. When I get my outstanding law-suits and some other little matters off my hands, I shall soon be on the track of our aristocratic old Reynard the Fox. Let us drink to that—— You won't, eh?

Stensgård. I should like to know first who your aristocratic old Reynard the Fox may be.

Heire. Hee-hee; you needn't look so uncomfortable, man. You don't suppose I'm alluding to Mr. Monsen. No one can accuse Mr. Monsen of being aristocratic. No; it's Chamberlain Bratsberg, my dear young friend.

Stensgård. What! In money matters the Chamberlain is surely above reproach.

Heire. You think so, young man? H'm; I say no more. *(Draws nearer.)* Twenty years ago I was worth no end of money. My father left me a great fortune. You've heard of my father, I daresay? No? Old Hans Heire? They called him Gold Hans. He was a shipowner: made heaps of money in the blockade time; had his window-frames and door-posts gilded; he could afford it—— I say no more; so they called him Gold Hans.

Aslaksen. Didn't he gild his chimney-pots too?

Heire. No; that was only a penny-a-liner's lie; invented long before your time, however. But he made the money fly; and so did I in my time. My visit to London, for instance—haven't you heard of my visit to London? I took a prince's retinue with me. Have you really not heard of it, eh? And the sums I have lavished on art and science! And on bringing rising talent to the front!

Aslaksen (rises). Well, good-bye, gentlemen.

Monsen. What? Are you leaving us?

Aslaksen. Yes; I want to stretch my legs a bit. [*Goes.*

Heire (speaking low). He was one of them—just as grateful as the rest, hee-hee! Do you know, I kept him a whole year at college?

Stensgård. Indeed? Has Aslaksen been to college?

Heire. Like young Monsen. He made nothing of it; also like—— I say no more. Had to give him up, you see; he had already developed his unhappy taste for spirits——

Monsen. But you've forgotten what you were going to tell Mr. Stensgård about the Chamberlain.

Heire. Oh, it's a complicated business. When my father was in his glory, things were going downhill with the old Chamberlain—this one's father, you understand; he was a Chamberlain too.

Bastian. Of course; everything runs in families here.

Heire. Including the social graces—— I say no more. The conversion of the currency, rash speculations, extravagances he launched out into, in the year 1816 or thereabouts, forced him to sell some of his land.

Stensgård. And your father bought it?

Heire. Bought and paid for it. Well, what then? I come into my property; I make improvements by the thousand——

Bastian. Of course.

Heire. Your health, my young friend!—Improvements by the thousand, I say—thinning the woods, and so forth. Years pass; and then comes Master Reynard—the present one, I mean—and repudiates the bargain!

Stensgård. But, my dear Mr. Heire, you could surely have snapped your fingers at him.

Heire. Not so easily! Some small formalities had been overlooked, he declared. Besides, I happened then to be in temporary difficulties, which afterwards became permanent. And what can a man do nowadays without capital?

Monsen. You're right there, by God! And in many ways you can't do very much with capital either. That I know to my cost. Why, even my innocent children——

Bastian (thumps the table). Ugh, father! if I only had certain people here!

Stensgård. Your children, you say?

Monsen. Yes; take Bastian, for example. Perhaps I haven't given him a good education?

Heire. A threefold education! First for the University; then for painting; and then for—what is it?—it's a civil engineer he is now, isn't it?

Bastian. Yes, that I am, by the Lord!

Monsen. Yes, that he is; I can produce his bills and his certificates to prove it! But who gets the town business? Who has got the local road-making—especially these last two years? Foreigners, or at any rate strangers—in short, people no one knows anything about!

Heire. Yes; it's shameful the way things go on. Only last New Year, when the managership of the Savings Bank fell vacant, what must they do but give Monsen the go-by, and choose an individual that knew—*(Coughs)*—that knew how to keep his purse-strings drawn—which our princely host obviously does not. Whenever there's a post of confidence going, it's always the same! Never Monsen—always some one that enjoys the confidence—of the people in power. Well, well; *commune suffragium*, as the Roman Law puts it; that means shipwreck in the Common Council, sir.* It's a shame! Your health!

Monsen. Thanks! But, to change the subject—how are all your law-suits getting on?

Heire. They are still pending; I can say no more for the present. What endless annoyance they do give me! Next week I shall have to summon the whole Town Council before the Arbitration Commission.†

Bastian. Is it true that you once summoned yourself before the Arbitration Commission?

Heire. Myself? Yes; but I didn't put in an appearance.

Monsen. Ha, ha! You didn't, eh?

Heire. I had a sufficient excuse: had to cross the river, and it was unfortunately the very year of Bastian's bridge—plump! down it went, you know——

Bastian. Why, confound it all——!

Heire. Take it coolly, young man! You are not the first that has bent the bow till it breaks. Everything runs in families, you know—— I say no more.

Monsen. Ho ho ho! You say no more, eh? Well, drink, then, and say no more! (*To* STENSGÅRD.) You see, Mr. Heire's tongue is licensed to wag as it pleases.

---

* In this untranslatable passage Daniel Heire seems to be making a sort of pun on *suffragium* and *naufragium*.

† In Norway, before an action comes into Court, the parties are bound to appear in person before a commission of Arbitration or Conciliation. If the Commission can suggest an arrangement acceptable to both sides, this arrangement has the validity of a judgment, and the case goes no further. Counsel are not allowed to appear before the Commission.

Heire. Yes, freedom of speech is the only civic right I really value.

Stensgård. What a pity the law should restrict it.

Heire. Hee-hee! Our legal friend's mouth is watering for a nice action for slander, eh? Make your mind easy, my dear sir! I'm an old hand, let me tell you!

Stensgård. Especially at slander?

Heire. Your pardon, young man! That outburst of indignation does honour to your heart. I beg you to forget an old man's untimely frankness about your absent friends.

Stensgård. Absent friends?

Heire. I have nothing to say against the son, of course —nor against the daughter. And if I happened to cast a passing slur upon the Chamberlain's character——

Stensgård. The Chamberlain's? Is it the Chamberlain's family you call my friends?

Heire. Well, you don't pay visits to your enemies, I presume?

Bastian. Visits?

Monsen. What?

Heire. Ow, ow, ow! Here am I letting cats out of bags——!

Monsen. Have you been paying visits at the Chamberlain's?

Stensgård. Nonsense! A misunderstanding——

Heire. A most unhappy slip on my part. But how was I to know it was a secret? *(To* MONSEN.*)* Besides, you mustn't take my expressions too literally. When I say a visit, I mean only a sort of formal call; a frock-coat and yellow gloves affair——

Stensgård. I tell you I haven't exchanged a single word with any of that family!

Heire. Is it possible? Were you not received the second time either? I know they were "not at home" the first time.

Stensgård (to MONSEN*).* I had a letter to deliver from a friend in Christiania—that was all.

Heire (rising). I'll be hanged if it isn't positively revolting! Here is a young man at the outset of his career; full of simple-minded confidence, he seeks out the experienced man-of-the-world and knocks at his door; turns to him, who has brought his ship to port, to beg for—— I say no more! The man-of-the-world shuts the door in his face; is not at home; never is at home when it's his duty to be—— I say no more! *(With indignation.)* Was there ever such shameful insolence!

Stensgård. Oh, never mind that stupid business.

Heire. Not at home! He, who goes about professing that he is always at home to reputable people!

Stensgård. Does he say that?

Heire. A mere empty phrase. He's not at home to Mr. Monsen either. But I can't think what has made him hate you so much. Yes, hate you, I say; for what do you think I heard yesterday?

Stensgård. I don't want to know what you heard yesterday.

Heire. Then I say no more. Besides, the expressions didn't surprise me—coming from the Chamberlain, I mean. Only I can't understand why he should have added "demagogue."

Stensgård. Demagogue!

Heire. Well, since you insist upon it, I must confess that the Chamberlain called you an adventurer and demagogue.

Stensgård (jumps up). What!

Heire. Adventurer and demagogue—or demagogue and adventurer; I won't answer for the order.

Stensgård. And you heard that?

Heire. I? If I had been present, Mr. Stensgård, you may be sure I should have stood up for you as you deserve.

Monsen. There, you see what comes of——

Stensgård. How dare the old scoundrel——?

Heire. Come, come, come! Keep your temper. Very likely it was a mere figure of speech—a harmless little joke, I have no doubt. You can demand an explanation to-morrow; for I suppose you are going to the great dinner-party, eh?

Stensgård. I am not going to any dinner-party.

Heire. Two calls and no invitation——!

Stensgård. Demagogue and adventurer! What can he be thinking of?

Monsen. Look there! Talk of the devil——! Come, Bastian.   [*Goes off with* BASTIAN.

Stensgård. What did he mean by it, Mr. Heire?

Heire. Haven't the ghost of an idea.—It pains you? Your hand, young man! Pardon me if my frankness has wounded you. Believe me, you have yet many bitter lessons to learn in this life. You are young; you are confiding; you are trustful. It is beautiful; it is even touching; but— but—trustfulness is silver, experience is gold: that's a proverb of my own invention, sir! God bless you!   [*Goes.*

CHAMBERLAIN BRATSBERG, *his daughter* THORA, *and* DOCTOR FIELDBO *enter from the left.*

Lundestad (strikes the bell on the rostrum). Silence for Mr. Ringdal's speech!

Stensgård (shouts). Mr. Lundestad, I demand to be heard.

Lundestad. Afterwards.

Stensgård. No, now! at once!

Lundestad. You can't speak just now. Silence for Mr. Ringdal!

Ringdal (on the rostrum). Ladies and gentlemen! We have at this moment the honour of seeing in our midst the man with the warm heart and the open hand—the man we have all looked up to for many a year, as to a father—the man who is always ready to help us, both in word and deed —the man whose door is never closed to any reputable citizen—the man who—who—ladies and gentlemen, **our honoured** guest is no lover of long speeches; so, without more words, I call for three cheers for Chamberlain Bratsberg and his family! Long life to them! Hurrah!

The Crowd. Hurrah! hurrah! hurrah!

> [*Great enthusiasm; people press around the* CHAMBERLAIN, *who thanks them and shakes hands with those nearest him.*

Stensgård. Now may I speak?

Lundestad. By all means. The platform is at your service.

Stensgård (*jumps upon the table*). I shall choose my own platform!

The Young Men (*crowding around him*). Hurrah!

The Chamberlain (*to the* DOCTOR). Who is this obstreperous personage?

Fieldbo. Mr. Stensgård.

The Chamberlain. Oh, it's he, is it?

Stensgård. Listen to me, my glad-hearted brothers and sisters! Hear me, all you who have in your souls—though it may not reach your lips—the exultant song of the day, the day of our freedom! I am a stranger among you——

Aslaksen. No!

Stensgård. Thanks for that "No!" I take it as the utterance of a longing, an aspiration. A stranger I am, however; but this I swear, that I come among you with a great and open-hearted sympathy for your sorrows and your joys, your victories and defeats. If it lay in my power——

Aslaksen. It does, it does!

Lundestad. No interruptions! You have no right to speak.

Stensgård. You still less! I abolish the Committee! Freedom on the day of freedom, boys!

The Young Men. Hurrah for freedom!

Stensgård. They deny you the right of speech! You hear it—they want to gag you! Away with this tyranny! I won't stand here declaiming to a flock of dumb animals. I will talk; but you shall talk, too. We will talk to each other, from the heart!

The Crowd (with growing enthusiasm). Hurrah!

Stensgård. We will have no more of these barren, white-chokered festivities! A golden harvest of deeds shall here-after shoot up from each Seventeenth of May. May! Is it not the season of bud and blossom, the blushing maiden-month of the year? On the first of June I shall have been just two months among you; and in that time what great-ness and littleness, what beauty and deformity, have I not seen?

The Chamberlain. What on earth is he talking about, Doctor?

Fieldbo. Aslaksen says it's the local situation.

Stensgård. I have seen great and brilliant possibilities among the masses; but I have seen, too, a spirit of corrup-tion brooding over the germs of promise and bringing them to nought. I have seen ardent and trustful youth rush yearn-ing forth—and I have seen the door shut in its face.

Thora. Oh, Heaven!

The Chamberlain. What does he mean by that?

Stensgård. Yes, my brothers and sisters in rejoicing! There hovers in the air an Influence, a Spectre from the dead and rotten past, which spreads darkness and oppression where there should be nothing but buoyancy and light. We must lay that Spectre; down with it!

The Crowd. Hurrah! Hurrah for the Seventeenth of May!

Thora. Come away, father——!

The Chamberlain. What the deuce does he mean by a spectre? Who is he talking about, Doctor?

Fieldbo (quickly). Oh, it's about——

[*Whispers a word or two.*

The Chamberlain. Aha! So that's it!

Thora (softly to FIELDBO*).* Thanks!

Stensgård. If no one else will crush the dragon, I will! But we must hold together, boys!

Many Voices. Yes! yes!

Stensgård. We are young! The time belongs to us; but we also belong to the time. Our right is our duty! Elbow-room for faculty, for will, for power! Listen to me! We must form a League. The money-bag has ceased to rule among us!

The Chamberlain. Bravo! *(To the* DOCTOR*).* He said the money-bag; so no doubt you're right——

Stensgård. Yes, boys; we, we are the wealth of the country, if only there's metal in us. Our will is the ringing gold that shall pass from man to man. War to the knife against whoever shall deny its currency!

The Crowd. Hurrah!

Stensgård. A scornful "bravo" has been flung in my teeth——

The Chamberlain. No, no!

Stensgård. What care I! Thanks and threats alike are powerless over the perfect will. And now, God be with us! For we are going about His work, with youth and faith to help us. Come, then, into the refreshment-tent—our League shall be baptised this very hour.

The Crowd. Hurrah! Carry him! Shoulder high with him! [*He is lifted shoulder high.*

Voices. Speak on! More! More!

Stensgård. Let us hold together, I say! Providence is on the side of the League of Youth. It lies with us to rule the world—here in the district!

[*He is carried into the tent amid wild enthusiasm.*

Madam Rundholmen (wiping her eyes). Oh, Lord, how beautifully he does speak! Don't you feel as if you could kiss him, Mr. Heire?

Heire. Thank you, I'd rather not.

Madam Rundholmen. Oh, you! I daresay not.

Heire. Perhaps you would like to kiss him, Madam Rundholmen.

Madam Rundholmen. Ugh, how horrid you are!

[*She goes into the tent;* HEIRE *follows her.*

The Chamberlain. Spectre—and dragon—and money-
bag! It was horribly rude—but well deserved!

Lundestad (approaching). I'm heartily sorry, Chamberlain——

The Chamberlain. Yes, where was your knowledge of
character, Lundestad? Well, well; we are none of us infallible. Good-night, and thanks for a pleasant evening.
[*Turns to* THORA *and the* DOCTOR.*)* But bless me, I've been
positively rude to that fine young fellow!

Fieldbo. How so?

Thora. His call, you mean——?

The Chamberlain. He called twice. It's really Lundestad's fault. He told me he was an adventurer and—and I
forget what else. Fortunately I can make up for it.

Thora. How?

The Chamberlain. Come, Thora; let us see to it at
once——

Fieldbo. Oh, do you think it's worth while, Chamberlain——?

Thora (softly). Hush!

The Chamberlain. When one has done an injustice one
should lose no time in undoing it; that's a plain matter of
duty. Good-night, Doctor. After all, I've spent an amusing
hour; and that's more than I have to thank you for to-day.

Fieldbo. Me, Chamberlain?

The Chamberlain. Yes, yes, yes—you and others.

Fieldbo. May I ask what I——?

The Chamberlain. Don't be curious, Doctor. I am never
curious. Come, come—no offence—good-night!

[THE CHAMBERLAIN *and* THORA *go out to the left;*
FIELDBO *gazes thoughtfully after them.*

Aslaksen (from the tent). Hei, waiter! Pen and ink! Things are getting lively, Doctor!

Fieldbo. What things?

Aslaksen. He's founding the League. It's nearly founded.

Lundestad (who has quietly drawn near). Are many putting down their names?

Aslaksen. We've enrolled about seven-and-thirty, not counting widows and so forth. Pen and ink, I say! No waiters to be found!—that's the fault of the local situation.

[*Goes off behind the tent.*

Lundestad. Puh! It has been hot to-day.

Fieldbo. I'm afraid we have hotter days to come.

Lundestad. Do you think the Chamberlain was very angry?

Fieldbo. Oh, not in the least; you could see that, couldn't you? But what do you say to the new League?

Lundestad. H'm; I say nothing. What is there to be said?

Fieldbo. It's the beginning of a struggle for power here in the district.

Lundestad. Well, well; no harm in a fight. He has great gifts, that Stensgård.

Fieldbo. He is determined to make his way.

Lundestad. Youth is always determined to make its way. I was, when I was young; no one can object to that. But mightn't we look in and see——

Heire (from the tent). Well, Mr. Lundestad, are you going to move the previous question, eh? To head the opposition? Hee-hee! You must make haste!

Lundestad. Oh, I daresay I shall be in time.

Heire. Too late, sir! Unless you want to stand godfather. *(Cheering from the tent.)* There, they're chanting Amen; the baptism is over.

Lundestad. I suppose one may be permitted to listen; I shall keep quiet. [*Enters the tent.*

Heire. There goes one of the falling trees! There will

be a rare uprooting, I can tell you! The place will soon look like a wood after a tornado. Won't I chuckle over it!

Fieldbo. Tell me, Mr. Heire, what interest have you in the matter?

Heire. Interest? I am entirely disinterested, Doctor! If I chuckle, it is on behalf of my fellow citizens. There will be life, spirit, go, in things. For my own part—good Lord, it's all the same to me; I say, as the Grand Turk said of the Emperor of Austria and the King of France—I don't care whether the pig eats the dog or the dog the pig.

[*Goes toward the back on the right.*

The Crowd (in the tent). Long live Stensgård! Hurrah! Hurrah for the League of Youth! Wine! Punch! Hei, hei! Beer! Hurrah!

Bastian (comes from the tent). God bless you and every one. *(With tears in his voice.)* Oh, Doctor, I feel so strong this evening; I must do something.

Fieldbo. Don't mind me. What would you like to do?

Bastian. I think I'll go down to the dancing-room and fight one or two fellows. [*Goes out behind the tent.*

Stensgård (comes from the tent without his hat, and greatly excited). My dear Fieldbo, is that you?

Fieldbo. At your service, Tribune of the People! For I suppose you've been elected——?

Stensgård. Of course; but——

Fieldbo. And what is to come of it all? What nice little post are you to have? The management of the Bank? Or perhaps——

Stensgård. Oh, don't talk to me like that! I know you don't mean it. You are not so empty and wooden as you like to appear.

Fieldbo. Empty and wooden, eh?

Stensgård. Fieldbo! Be my friend as you used to be! We have not understood each other of late. You have wounded and repelled me with your ridicule and irony. Be-

lieve me, it was wrong of you. *(Embraces him.)* **Oh, my**
great God! how happy I am!

Fieldbo. You too? So am I, so am I!

Stensgård. Yes, I should be the meanest hound on earth
if all heaven's bounty didn't make me good and true. How
have I deserved it, Fieldbo? What have I, sinner that I
am, done to be so richly blessed?

Fieldbo. There is my hand! This evening I am your
friend indeed!

Stensgård. Thanks! Be faithful and true, as I shall be!
—Oh, isn't it an unspeakable joy to carry all that multitude
away and along with you? How can you help becoming good
from mere thankfulness? And how it makes you love all
your fellow creatures! I feel as if I could clasp them all in
one embrace, and weep, and beg their forgiveness because
God has been so partial as to give me more than them.

Fieldbo (quietly). Yes, treasures without price may fall
to one man's lot. This evening I would not crush an insect,
not a green leaf upon my path.

Stensgård. You?

Fieldbo. Never mind. That's apart from the question. I
only mean that I understand you.

Stensgård. What a lovely night! Listen to the music
and merriment floating out over the meadows. And how
still it is in the valley! I tell you the man whose life is not
reconsecrated in such an hour, does not deserve to live on
God's earth!

Fieldbo. Yes; but tell me now: what do you mean to
build up out of it—to-morrow, and through the working-days
to come?

Stensgård. To build up? We have to tear down first.—
Fieldbo, I had once a dream—or did I see it? No; it was a
dream, but such a vivid one! I thought the Day of Judgment was come upon the world. I could see the whole curve
of the hemisphere. There was no sun, only a livid storm-
light. A tempest arose; it came rushing from the west and

swept everything before it: first withered leaves, then men; but they kept on their feet all the time, and their garments clung fast to them, so that they seemed to be hurried along sitting. At first they looked like townspeople running after their hats in a wind; but when they came nearer they were emperors and kings; and it was their crowns and orbs they were chasing and catching at, and seemed always on the point of grasping, but never grasped. Oh, there were hundreds and hundreds of them, and none of them understood in the least what was happening; but many bewailed themselves, and asked: "Whence can it come, this terrible storm?" Then there came the answer: "One Voice spoke, and the storm is the echo of that one Voice."

Fieldbo. When did you dream that?

Stensgård. Oh, I don't remember when; several years ago.

Fieldbo. There were probably disturbances somewhere in Europe, and you had been reading the newspapers after a heavy supper.

Stensgård. The same shiver, the same thrill, that then ran down my back, I felt again to-night. Yes, I will give my whole soul utterance. I will be the Voice——

Fieldbo. Come, my dear Stensgård, pause and reflect. You will be the Voice, you say. Good! But where will you be the Voice? Here in the parish? Or at most here in the county! And who will echo you and raise the storm? Why, people like Monsen and Aslaksen, and that fat-headed genius, Mr. Bastian. And instead of the flying emperors and kings, we shall see old Lundestad rushing about after his lost seat in Parliament. Then what will it all amount to? Just what you at first saw in your dream—townsfolk in a wind.

Stensgård. In the beginning, yes. But who knows how far the storm may sweep?

Fieldbo. Fiddlesticks with you and your storm! And the first thing you go and do, hoodwinked and blinded and gulled as you are, is to turn your weapons precisely against all that is worthy and capable among us——

Stensgård. That is not true.

Fieldbo. It is true! Monsen and the Stonelee gang got hold of you the moment you came here; and if you don't shake him off it will be your ruin. Chamberlain Bratsberg is a man of honour; that you may rely on. Do you know why the great Monsen hates him? Why, because——

Stensgård. Not a word more! I won't hear a word against my friends!

Fieldbo. Look into yourself, Stensgård! Is Mr. Monsen really your friend?

Stensgård. Mr. Monsen has most kindly opened his doors to me——

Fieldbo. To people of the better sort he opens his doors in vain.

Stensgård. Oh, whom do you call the better sort? A few stuck-up officials! I know all about it. As for me, I have been received at Stonelee with so much cordiality and appreciation——

Fieldbo. Appreciation? Yes, unfortunately—there we are at the root of the matter.

Stensgård. Not at all! I can see with unprejudiced eyes. Mr. Monsen has abilities, he has reading, he has a keen sense for public affairs.

Fieldbo. Abilities? Oh, yes, in a way. Reading, too: he takes in the papers, and has read your speeches and articles. And his sense for public affairs he has, of course, proved by applauding the said articles and speeches.

Stensgård. Now, Fieldbo, up come the dregs of your nature again. Can you never shake off that polluting habit of thought? Why must you always assume mean or ridiculous motives for everything? Oh, you are not serious! Now you look good and true again. I'll tell you the real root of the matter. Do you know Ragna?

Fieldbo. Ragna Monsen? Oh, after a fashion—at second hand.

Stensgård. Yes, I know she is sometimes at the Chamberlain's.

Fieldbo. In a quiet way, yes. She and Miss Bratsberg are old schoolfellows.

Stensgård. And what do you think of her?

Fieldbo. Why, from all I have heard she seems to be a very good girl.

Stensgård. Oh, you should see her in her home! She thinks of nothing but her two little sisters. And how devotedly she must have nursed her mother! You know the mother was out of her mind for some years before she died.

Fieldbo. Yes; I was their doctor at one time. But surely, my dear fellow, you don't mean that——

Stensgård. Yes, Fieldbo, I love her truly; to you I can confess it. Oh, I know what you are surprised at. You think it strange that so soon after—of course you know that I was engaged to Christiania?

Fieldbo. Yes, so I was told.

Stensgård. The whole thing was a disappointment. I had to break it off; it was best for all parties. Oh, how I suffered in that affair! The torture, the sense of oppression I endured——! Now, thank heaven, I am out of it all. That was my reason for leaving town.

Fieldbo. And with regard to Ragna Monsen, are you quite sure of yourself?

Stensgård. Yes, I am, indeed. There's no mistake possible in this case.

Fieldbo. Well, then, in heaven's name, go in and win! It means your life's happiness! Oh, there's so much I could say to you——

Stensgård. Really? Has she said anything? Has she confided in Miss Bratsberg?

Fieldbo. No; that's not what I mean. But how can you, in the midst of your happiness, go and fuddle yourself in these political orgies? How can town tattle take any hold upon a mind that is——

Stensgård. Why not? Man is a complex machine—I am, at any rate. Besides, my way to her lies through these very party turmoils.

Fieldbo. A terribly prosaic way.

Stensgård. Fieldbo, I am ambitious; you know I am. I must make my way in the world. When I remember that I'm thirty, and am still on the first round of the ladder, I feel my conscience gnawing at me.

Fieldbo. Not with its wisdom teeth.

Stensgård. It's of no use talking to you. You have never felt the spur of ambition. You have dawdled and drifted all your days—first at college, then abroad, now here.

Fieldbo. Perhaps; but at least it has been delightful. And no reaction follows, like what you feel when you get down from the table after——

Stensgård. Stop that! I can bear anything but that. You are doing a bad action—you are damping my ardour.

Fieldbo. Oh, come! If your ardour is so easily damped——

Stensgård. Stop, I say! What right have you to break in upon my happiness? Do you think I am not sincere?

Fieldbo. Yes, I am sure you are.

Stensgård. Well, then, why go and make me feel empty, and disgusted, and suspicious of myself? *(Shouts and cheers from the tent.)* There—listen! They are drinking my health. An idea that can take such hold upon people—by God, it must have truth in it!

THORA BRATSBERG, RAGNA MONSEN, *and* MR. HELLE *enter from the left and cross, half-way back.*

Helle. Look, Miss Bratsberg; there is Mr. Stensgård.

Thora. Then I won't go any further. Good-night, Ragna dear.

Helle and Miss Monsen. Good-night, good-night.

[*They go out to the right*

Thora (advancing). I am Miss Bratsberg. I have a let‐ ter for you, from my father.

Stensgård. For me?

Thora. Yes; here it is.   [*Going.*

Fieldbo. May I not see you home?

Thora. No, thank you. I can go alone. Good-night.
                                   [*Goes out to the left.*

Stensgård (reading the letter by a Chinese lantern). What is this!

Fieldbo. Well—what has the Chamberlain to say to you?

Stensgård (bursts into loud laughter). I must say I didn't expect this!

Fieldbo. Tell me——?

Stensgård. Chamberlain Bratsberg is a pitiful creature.

Fieldbo. You dare to——

Stensgård. Pitiful! Pitiful! Tell any one you please that I said so. Or rather, say nothing about it—— *(Puts the letter in his pocket.)* Don't mention this to any one!
                      [*The* COMPANY *come out from the tent.*

Monsen. Mr. President! Where is Mr. Stensgård?

The Crowd. There he is! Hurrah!

Lundestad. Mr. President has forgotten his hat.
                                   [*Hands it to him.*

Aslaksen. Here; have some punch! Here's a whole bowlful!

Stensgård. Thanks, no more.

Monsen. And the members of the League will recollect that we meet to-morrow at Stonelee——

Stensgård. To-morrow? It wasn't to-morrow, was it——?

Monsen. Yes, certainly; to draw up the manifesto——

Stensgård. No, I really can't to-morrow—I shall see about it the day after to-morrow, or the day after that. Well, good-night, gentlemen; hearty thanks all round, and hurrah for the future!

The Crowd.   Hurrah!   Let's take him home in triumph!

Stensgård.   Thanks, thanks!   But you really mustn't——

Aslaksen.   We'll all go with you.

Stensgård.   Very well, come along.   Good-night, Fieldbo; you're not coming with us?

Fieldbo.   No; but let me tell you, what you said about Chamberlain Bratsberg——

Stensgård.   Hush, hush!   It was an exaggeration—I withdraw it!   Well, my friends, if you're coming, come; I'll take the lead.

Monsen.   Your arm, Stensgård!

Bastian.   A song!   Strike up!   Something thoroughly patriotic!

The Crowd.   A song!   A song!   Music!

[*A popular air is played and sung.   The procession marches out by the back to the right.*

Fieldbo (to LUNDESTAD, *who remains behind).*   A gallant procession.

Lundestad.   Yes—and with a gallant leader.

Fieldbo.   And where are you going, Mr. Lundestad?

Lundestad.   I?   I'm going home to bed.

[*He nods and goes off.*   DOCTOR FIELDBO *remains behind alone.*

ACT SECOND.

A garden-room at the Chamberlain's, elegantly furnished with a piano, flowers, and rare plants. Entrance door at the back. On the left, a door leading to the dining-room; on the right, several glass doors lead out to the garden.

ASLAKSEN *stands at the entrance door.* A MAID-SERVANT *is carrying some dishes of fruit into the dining-room.*

The Maid. Yes, but I tell you they're still at table; you must call again.

Aslaksen. I'd rather wait, if I may.

The Maid. Oh, yes, if you like. You can sit there for the present.

> [*She goes into the dining-room.* ASLAKEN *takes a seat near the door. Pause.* DR. FIELDBO *enters from the back.*

Fieldbo. Ah, good evening, Aslaksen: are you here?

The Maid (returning). You're late this evening, sir.

Fieldbo. I was called to see a patient.

The Maid. The Chamberlain and Miss Bratsberg have both been inquiring about you.

Fieldbo. Indeed?

The Maid. Yes. Won't you go in at once, sir; or shall I say that——?

Fieldbo. No, no; never mind. I can have a snack afterwards; I shall wait here in the meantime.

The Maid. Dinner will soon be over.

> [*She goes out by the back.*

148

Aslaksen (after a pause). How can you resist such a dinner, Doctor—with dessert, and fine wines, and all sorts of good things?

Fieldbo. Why, man, it seems to me we get too many good things hereabouts, rather than too few.

Aslaksen. There I can't agree with you.

Fieldbo. H'm. I suppose you are waiting for some one.

Aslaksen. Yes, I am.

Fieldbo. And are things going tolerably at home? Your wife——?

Aslaksen. In bed, as usual; coughing and wasting away.

Fieldbo. And your second child?

Aslaksen. Oh, he's a cripple for the rest of his days; you know that. That's our luck, you see; what the devil's the use of talking about it?

Fieldbo. Let me look at you, Aslaksen!

Aslaksen. Well; what do you want to see?

Fieldbo. You've been drinking to-day.

Aslaksen. Yes, and yesterday, too.

Fieldbo. Well, yesterday there was some excuse for it; but to-day——

Aslaksen. What about your friends in there, then? Aren't they drinking, too?

Fieldbo. Yes, my dear Aslaksen; that's a fair retort; but circumstances differ so in this world.

Aslaksen. I didn't choose my circumstances.

Fieldbo. No; God chose them for you.

Aslaksen. No, he didn't—men chose them. Daniel Heire chose, when he took me from the printing-house and sent me to college. And Chamberlain Bratsberg chose, when he ruined Daniel Heire and sent me back to the printing-house.

Fieldbo. Now you know that's not true. The Chamberlain did not ruin Daniel Heire; Daniel Heire ruined himself.

Aslaksen. Perhaps! But how dared Daniel Heire ruin,

himself, in the face of his responsibilities towards me? God's partly to blame, too, of course. Why should he give me talent and ability? Well, of course, I could have turned them to account as a respectable handicraftsman; but then comes that tattling old fool——

Fieldbo. It's base of you to say that. Daniel Heire acted with the best intentions.

Aslaksen. What good do his "best intentions" do me? You hear them in there, clinking glasses and drinking healths? Well, I, too, have sat at that table in my day, dressed in purple and fine linen, like the best of them——! That was just the thing for me, that was—for me, that has read so much and had thirsted so long to have my share in all the good things of life. Well, well; how long was Jeppe in Paradise?* Smash, crash! down you go—and my fine fortunes fell to pi, as we printers say.

Fieldbo. But, after all, you were not so badly off; you had your trade to fall back upon.

Aslaksen. That's easily said. After getting out of your class you can't get into it again. They took the ground from under my feet, and shoved me out on the slippery ice— and then they abuse me because I stumble.

Fieldbo. Well, far be it from me to judge you harshly——

Aslaksen. No; you have no right to.—What a queer jumble it is! Daniel Heire, and Providence, and the Chamberlain, and Destiny, and Circumstance—and I myself in the middle of it! I've often thought of unravelling it all and writing a book about it; but it's so cursedly entangled that—— *(Glances towards the door on the left.)* Ah! They're rising from table.

---

* An allusion to Holberg's comedy, *Jeppe pa Bierget,* which deals with the theme of Abou Hassan, treated by Shakespeare in the Induction to *The Taming of the Shrew,* and by Hauptmann in *Schluck und Jau.*

[*The party, ladies and gentlemen, pass from the dining-room into the garden, in lively conversation. Among the guests is* STENSGÅRD, *with* THORA *on his left arm and* SELMA *on his right.* FIELDBO *and* ASLAKSEN *stand beside the door at the back.*

Stensgård. I don't know my way here yet; you must tell me where I am to take you, ladies.

Selma. Out into the air; you must see the garden.

Stensgård. Oh, that will be delightful.

[*They go out by the foremost glass door on the right.*

Fieldbo. Why, by all that's wonderful, there's Stensgård!

Aslaksen. It's him I want to speak to. I've had a fine chase after him; fortunately I met Daniel Heire——

DANIEL HEIRE *and* ERIK BRATSBERG *enter from the dining-room.*

Heire. Hee-hee! Excellent sherry, upon my word. I've tasted nothing like it since I was in London.

Erik. Yes, it's good, isn't it? It puts life into you.

Heire. Well, well—it's a real pleasure to see one's money so well spent.

Erik. How so? (*Laughing.*) Oh, yes; I see, I see.

[*They go into the garden.*

Fieldbo. You want to speak to Stensgård. you say?

Aslaksen. Yes.

Fieldbo. On business?

Aslaksen. Of course; the report of the fête——

Fieldbo. Well, then, you must wait out there in the meantime.

Aslaksen. In the passage?

Fieldbo. In the anteroom. This is scarcely the time or

place—but the moment I see Stensgård alone, I'll tell
him——

Aslaksen. Very well; I'll bide my time.

[*Goes out by the back.*

CHAMBERLAIN BRATSBERG, LUNDESTAD, RINGDAL, *and one
or two other gentlemen come out of the dining-room.*

The Chamberlain (conversing with LUNDESTAD). Violent,
you say? Well, perhaps the form wasn't all that could be
desired; but there were real gems in the speech, I can assure
you.

Lundestad. Well, if you are satisfied, Chamberlain, I
have no right to complain.

The Chamberlain. Why should you? Ah, here's the
Doctor! Starving, I'll be bound.

Fieldbo. It doesn't matter, Chamberlain. The servants
will attend to me. I feel myself almost at home here, you
know.

The Chamberlain. Oh, you do, do you? I wouldn't be
in too great a hurry.

Fieldbo. What? Am I taking too great a liberty? You
yourself permitted me to——

The Chamberlain. What I permitted, I permitted. Well,
well, make yourself at home, and forage for something to
eat. (*Slaps him lightly on the shoulder and turns to* LUNDE-
STAD.) Now, here's one you may call an adventurer and
—and the other thing I can't remember.

Fieldbo. Why, Chamberlain——!

Lundestad. No, I assure you——

The Chamberlain. No arguments after dinner; it's bad
for the digestion. They'll serve the coffee outside presently.

[*Goes with the guests into the garden.*

Lundestad (to FIELDBO). Did you ever see the Chamberlain so strange as he is to-day?

Fieldbo. I noticed it yesterday evening.

Lundestad. He will have it that I called Mr. Stensgård an adventurer and something else of that sort.

Fieldbo. Oh, well, Mr. Lundestad, what if you did? Excuse me; I must go and talk to the ladies.

[*Goes out to the right.*

Lundestad (*to* RINGDAL, *who is arranging a card table*). How do you account for Mr. Stensgård's appearance here to-day?

Ringdal. Yes, how? He wasn't on the original list.

Lundestad. An afterthought, then? After his attack on the Chamberlain yesterday——?

Ringdal. Yes, can you understand it?

Lundestad. Understand it? Oh, yes, I suppose I can.

Ringdal (*more softly*). You think the Chamberlain is afraid of him?

Lundestad. I think he is prudent—that's what I think.

[*They go up to the back conversing, and so out into the garden. At the same time* SELMA *and* STENSGÅRD *enter by the foremost door on the right.*

Selma. Yes, just look—over the tops of the trees you can see the church tower and all the upper part of the town.

Stensgård. So you can; I shouldnt' have thought so.

Selma. Don't you think it's a beautiful view?

Stensgård. Everything is beautiful here: the garden, and the view, and the sunshine, and the people! Great heaven, how beautiful it all is! And you live here all the summer?

Selma. No, not my husband and I; we come and go. We have a big, showy house in town, much finer than this; you'll see it soon.

Stensgård. Perhaps your family live in town?

Selma. My family? Who are my family?

Stensgård. Oh, I didn't know——

Selma. We fairy princesses have no family.

Stensgård. Fairy princesses?

Selma. At most we have a wicked stepmother——

Stensgård. A witch, yes! So you are a princess!

Selma. Princess of all the sunken palaces, whence you hear the soft music on midsummer nights. Doctor Fieldbo thinks it must be pleasant to be a princess; but I must tell you——

Erik Bratsberg (coming from the garden). Ah, at last I find the little lady!

Selma. The little lady is telling Mr. Stensgård the story of her life.

Erik. Oh, indeed. And what part does the husband play in the little lady's story?

Selma. The Prince, of course. *(To* Stensgård.*)* You know the prince always comes and breaks the spell, and then all ends happily, and every one calls and congratulates, and the fairy-tale is over.

Stensgård. Oh, it's too short.

Selma. Perhaps—in a way.

Erik (putting his arm round her waist). But a new fairy-tale grows out of the old one, and in it the Princess becomes a Queen!

Selma. On the same conditions as real Princesses?

Erik. What condition?

Selma. They must go into exile—to a foreign kingdom.

Erik. A cigar, Mr. Stensgård?

Stensgård. Thank you, not just now.

Doctor Fieldbo *and* Thora *enter from the garden.*

Selma (Going toward them). Is that you, Thora dear? I hope you're not ill?

Thora. I? No.

Selma. Oh, but I'm sure you must be; you seem to be always consulting the doctor of late.

Thora. No, I assure you——

Selma. Nonsense; let me feel your pulse! You are

burning. My dear Doctor, don't you think the fever will pass over?

Fieldbo. Everthing has its time.

Thora. Would you rather have me freezing——?

Selma. No, a medium temperature is the best—ask my husband.

The Chamberlain (enters from the garden). The whole family gathered in secret conclave? That's not very polite to the guests.

Thora. I am just going, father dear——

The Chamberlain. Aha, it is you the ladies are paying court to, Mr. Stensgård! I must look to this.

Thora (softly to FIELDBO*).* Remain here!

[*She goes into the garden.*

Erik (offers SELMA *his arm).* Has Madame any objection——?

Selma. Come!   [*They go out to the right.*

The Chamberlain (looking after them). It's impossible to get these two separated.

Fieldbo. It would be sinful to try.

The Chamberlain. Fools that we are! How Providence blesses us in spite of ourselves. *(Calls out.)* Thora, Thora, do look after Selma! Get a shawl for her, and don't let her run about so: she'll catch cold! How short-sighted we mortals are, Doctor! Do you know any cure for that disease?

Fieldbo. The spectacles of experience; through them you will see more clearly a second time.

The Chamberlain. You don't say so! Thanks for the advice. But since you feel yourself at home here, you must really pay a little attention to your guests.

Fieldbo. Certainly; come, Stensgård, shall we——?

The Chamberlain. Oh, no, no—there's my old friend Heire out there——

Fieldbo. He thinks himself at home here, too.

The Chamberlain. Ha, ha, ha! So he does.

Fieldbo. Well, we two will join forces, and do our best.
[*Goes into the garden.*

Stensgård. You were speaking of Daniel Heire, Chamberlain. I must say I was rather surprised to see him here.

The Chamberlain. Were you? Mr. Heire and I are old school and college friends. Besides, we have had a good deal to do with each other in many ways since——

Stensgård. Yes, Mr. Heire was good enough to give his own account of some of these transactions, yesterday evening.

The Chamberlain. H'm!

Stensgård. Had it not been for him, I certainly should not have let myself boil over as I did. But he has a way of speaking of people and things, that—in short, he has a vile tongue in his head.

The Chamberlain. My dear young friend—Mr. Heire is my guest; you must not forget that. My house is liberty hall, with only one reservation: my guests must not be discussed to their disadvantage.

Stensgård. I beg your pardon, I'm sure——!

The Chamberlain. Oh, never mind; you belong to the younger generation, that's not so punctilious. As for Mr. Heire, I don't think you really know him. I, at any rate, owe Mr. Heire a great deal.

Stensgård. Yes, he gave one to understand; but I didn't think——

The Chamberlain. I owe him the best part of our domestic happiness, Mr. Stensgård! I owe him my daughter-in-law. Yes, that is really so. Daniel Heire was kind to her in her childhood. She was a youthful prodigy; she gave concerts when she was only ten years old. I daresay you have heard her spoken of—Selma Sjöblom.*

Stensgård. Sjöblom? Yes, of course; her father was Swedish?

---

* Pronounce "Shöblom"—the modified "ö" much as in German.

The Chamberlain. Yes, a music-teacher. He came here many years ago. Musicians, you know, are seldom millionaires; and their habits are not always calculated to——; in short, Mr. Heire has always had an eye for talent; he was struck with the child, and had her sent to Berlin; and then, when her father was dead and Heire's fortunes were on the wane, she returned to Christiania, where she was, of course, taken up by the best people. That was how my son happened to fall in with her.

Stensgård. Then in that way old Daniel Heire has indeed been an instrument for good——

The Chamberlain. That is how one thing leads to another in this life, you see. We are all instruments, Mr. Stensgård; you, like the rest of us; an instrument of wrath, I suppose——

Stensgård. Oh, don't speak of it, Chamberlain. I am utterly ashamed——

The Chamberlain. Ashamed?

Stensgård. It was most unbecoming——

The Chamberlain. The form was perhaps open to criticism, but the intention was excellent. And now I want to ask you, in future, when you are contemplating any move of the sort, just to come to me and tell me of it openly, and without reserve. You know we all want to act for the best; and it is my duty——

Stensgård. You will permit me to speak frankly to you?

The Chamberlain. Of course I will. Do you think I haven't long realised that matters here have in some ways taken a most undesirable turn? But what was I to do? In the late King's time I lived for the most part in Stockholm. I am old now; and besides, it is not in my nature to take the lead in reforms, or to throw myself personally into the turmoil of public affairs. You, on the other hand, Mr. Stensgård, have every qualification for them; so let us hold together.

Stensgård. Thanks, Chamberlain; many, many thanks!

RINGDAL *and* DANIEL HEIRE *enter from the garden.*

Ringdal. And I tell you it must be a misunderstanding.

Heire. Indeed? I like that! How should I misunderstand my own ears?

The Chamberlain. Anything new, Heire?

Heire. Only that Anders Lundestad is going over to the Stonelee party.

The Chamberlain. Oh, you're joking!

Heire. I beg your pardon, my dear sir; I have it from his own lips. Mr. Lundestad intends, on account of failing health, to retire from political life; you can draw your own conclusions from that.

Stensgård. He told you so himself?

Heire. Of course he did. He made the momentous announcement to an awe-struck circle down in the garden; hee-hee!

The Chamberlain. Why, my dear Ringdal, what can be the meaning of this?

Heire. Oh, it's not difficult to guess.

The Chamberlain. Indeed it is, though. This is a most important affair for the district. Come along, Ringdal; we must find the man himself.

[*He and* RINGDAL *go down the garden.*

Fieldbo (entering by the furthest back garden-door). Has the Chamberlain gone out?

Heire. Sh! The sages are deliberating! Great news Doctor! Lundestad is going to resign.

Fieldbo. Oh, impossible!

Stensgård. Can you understand it?

Heire. Ah, now we may look out for real sport. It's the League of Youth that's beginning to work, Mr. Stensgård. Do you know what you should call your League? I'll tell you some other time.

Stensgård. Do you think it's really our League——?

Heire. Not the least doubt about it. So we're to have the pleasure of sending our respected friend Mr. Mons Monsen to Parliament! I wish he were off already;—I'd give him a lift with pleasure—— I say no more; hee-hee!

> [*Goes into the garden.*

Stensgård. Tell me, Fieldbo—how do you explain all this?

Fieldbo. There are other things still more difficult to explain. How come you to be here?

Stensgård. I? Like the rest, of course—by invitation.

Fieldbo. I hear you were invited yesterday evening— after your speech——

Stensgård. What then?

Fieldbo. How could you accept the invitation?

Stensgård. What the deuce was I to do? I couldn't insult these good people.

Fieldbo. Indeed! You couldn't? What about your speech then?

Stensgård. Nonsense! It was principles I attacked in my speech, not persons.

Fieldbo. And how do you account for the Chamberlain's invitation?

Stensgård. Why, my dear friend, there can only be one way of accounting for it.

Fieldbo. Namely, that the Chamberlain is afraid of you?

Stensgård. By heaven, he shall have no reason to be! He is a gentleman.

Fieldbo. That he is.

Stensgård. Isn't it touching the way the old man has taken this affair? And how lovely Miss Bratsberg looked when she brought me the letter!

Fieldbo. But look here—they haven't mentioned the scene of yesterday, have they?

Stensgård. Not a word; they have far too much tact for

that. But I am filled with remorse; I must find an opportunity of apologising——

Fieldbo. I strongly advise you not to! You don't know the Chamberlain——

Stensgård. Very well; then my acts shall speak for me.

Fieldbo. You won't break with the Stonelee party?

Stensgård. I shall bring about a reconciliation. I have my League; it's a power already, you see.

Fieldbo. By-the-bye, while I remember—we were speaking of Miss Monsen—I advised you to go in and win——

Stensgård. Oh, there's no hurry——

Fieldbo. But listen; I have been thinking it over: you had better put all that out of your head.

Stensgård. I believe you are right. If you marry into an underbred family, you marry the whole tribe of them.

Fieldbo. Yes, and there are other reasons——

Stensgård. Monsen is an underbred fellow; I see that now.

Fieldbo. Well, polish is not his strong point.

Stensgård. No, indeed it's not! He goes and speaks ill of his guests; that's ungentlemanly. His rooms all reek of stale tobacco——

Fieldbo. My dear fellow, how is it you haven't noticed the stale tobacco before?

Stensgård. It's the contrast that does it. I made a false start when I settled here. I fell into the clutches of a clique, and they bewildered me with their clamour. But there shall be an end to that! I won't go and wear my life out as a tool in the hands of self-interest or coarse stupidity.

Fieldbo. But what will you do with your League?

Stensgård. The League shall remain as it is; it's founded on a pretty broad basis. Its purpose is to counteract noxious influences; and I am just beginning to realise what side the noxious influences come from.

Fieldbo. But do you think the "Youth" will see it in the same light?

Stensgård. They shall! I have surely a right to expect fellows like that to bow before my superior insight.

Fieldbo. But if they won't?

Stensgård. Then they can go their own way. I have done with them. You don't suppose I am going to let my life slip into a wrong groove, and never reach the goal, for the sake of mere blind, pig-headed consistency!

Fieldbo. What do you call the goal?

Stensgård. A career that gives scope for my talents, and fulfils my aspirations.

Fieldbo. No vague phrases! What do you mean by your goal?

Stensgård. Well, to you I can make a clean breast of it. My goal is this: in the course of time to get into Parliament, perhaps into the Ministry, and to marry happily into a family of means and position.

Fieldbo. Oh, indeed! And by help of the Chamberlain's social connections you intend to——?

Stensgård. I intend to reach the goal by my own exertions! I must and will reach it; and without help from any one. It will take time, I daresay; but never mind! Meanwhile I shall enjoy life here, drinking in beauty and sunshine——

Fieldbo. Here?

Stensgård. Yes, here! Here there are fine manners; life moves gracefully here; the very floors seem laid to be trodden only by lacquered shoes. Here the arm-chairs are deep and the ladies sink exquisitely into them. Here conversation moves lightly and elegantly, like a game at battledore; here no blunders come plumping in to make an awkward silence. Oh, Fieldbo—here I feel for the first time what distinction means! Yes, we have indeed an aristocracy of our own; a little circle; an aristocracy of culture; and to it I will belong. Don't you yourself feel the refining influence of this place? Don't you feel that wealth here loses its grossness? When I think of Monsen's money, I seem to see piles of fetid bank-notes and greasy mortgages—but here! here it is shimmering silver! And the people are the same. Look at the Chamberlain—what a fine high-bred old fellow!

Fieldbo. He is, indeed.

Stensgård. And the son—alert, straightforward, capable!

Fieldbo. Certainly.

Stensgård. And then the daughter-in-law! Isn't she a pearl? Good God, what a rich, what a fascinating nature!

Fieldbo. Thora—Miss Bratsberg has that, too.

Stensgård. Oh, yes; but she is less remarkable.

Fieldbo. Oh, you don't know her. You don't know how deep, and steadfast, and true her nature is.

Stensgård. But, oh, the daughter-in-law! So frank, almost reckless; and yet so appreciative, so irresistible——

Fieldbo. Why, I really believe you're in love with her.

Stensgård. With a married woman? Are you crazy? What good would that do me? No, but I am falling in love —I can feel that plainly. Yes, she is indeed deep, and steadfast, and true.

Fieldbo. Who?

Stensgård. Miss Bratsberg, of course.

Fieldbo. What? You're never thinking of——?

Stensgård. Yes, by heaven I am!

Fieldbo. I assure you it's quite out of the question.

Stensgård. Ho-ho! Will rules the world, my dear fellow! We shall see if it doesn't.

Fieldbo. Why, this is the merest extravagance! Yesterday it was Miss Monsen——

Stensgård. Oh, I was too hasty about that; besides, you yourself advised me not to——

Fieldbo. I advise you most emphatically to dismiss all thought of either of them.

Stensgård. Indeed! Perhaps you yourself think of throwing the handkerchief to one of them?

Fieldbo. I? No, I assure you——

Stensgård. Well, it wouldn't have mattered if you had. If people stand in my way and want to balk me of my future, why, I stick at nothing.

Fieldbo. Take care I don't say the same!

Stensgård. You! What right have you to pose as guardian and protector to Chamberlain Bratsberg's family?

Fieldbo. I have at least the right of a friend.

Stensgård. Pooh! that sort of talk won't do with me. Your motive is mere self-interest! It gratifies your petty vanity to imagine yourself cock-of-the-walk in this house; and so I am to be kept outside the pale.

Fieldbo. That is the best thing that could happen to you. Here you are standing on hollow ground.

Stensgård. Am I indeed? Many thanks. I shall manage to prop it up.

Fieldbo. Try; but I warn you, it will fall through with you first.

Stensgård. Ho-ho! So you are intriguing against me, are you? I'm glad I have found it out. I know you now; you are my enemy, the only one I have here.

Fieldbo. Indeed I am not.

Stensgård. Indeed you are! You have always been so, ever since our school-days. Just look around here and see how every one appreciates me, stranger as I am. You, on the other hand, you who know me, have never appreciated me. That is the radical weakness of your character—you can never appreciate any one. What did you do in Christiania but go about from tea-party to tea-party, spreading yourself out in little witticisms? That sort of thing brings its own punishment! You dull your sense for all that makes life worth living, for all that is ennobling and inspiring; and presently you get left behind, fit for nothing.

Fieldbo. Am I fit for nothing?

Stensgård. Have you ever been fit to appreciate me?

Fieldbo. What was I to appreciate in you?

Stensgård. My will, if nothing else. Every one else appreciates it—the crowd at the fête yesterday—Chamberlain Bratsberg and his family——

Fieldbo. Mr. Mons Monsen and his ditto——! And by-the-bye, that reminds me—there's some one out here waiting for you——

Stensgård. Who?

Fieldbo (going towards the back). One who appreciates you. *(Opens the door and calls.)* Aslaksen, come in!

Stensgård. Aslaksen?

Aslaksen (entering). Ah, at last!

Fieldbo. Good-bye for the present; I won't intrude upon friends in council.   [*Goes into the garden.*

Stensgård. What in the devil's name do you want here?

Aslaksen. I must speak to you. You promised me yesterday an account of the founding of the League, and——

Stensgård. I can't give it you; it must wait till another time.

Aslaksen. Impossible, Mr. Stensgård; the paper appears to-morrow morning.

Stensgård. Nonsense! It has all to be altered. The matter has entered on a new phase; new forces have come into play. What I said about Chamberlain Bratsberg must be entirely recast before it can appear.

Aslaksen. Oh, that about the Chamberlain, that's in type already.

Stensgård. Then it must come out of type again.

Aslaksen. Not go in?

Stensgård. I won't have it published in that form. Why do you stare at me? Do you think I don't know how to manage the affairs of the League?

Aslaksen. Oh, certainly; but you must let me tell you——

Stensgård. Not arguing, Aslaksen; that I can't stand and won't stand!

Aslaksen. Do you know, Mr. Stensgård, that you are

doing your best to take the bread out of my mouth? Do you know that?

Stensgård. No; I know nothing of the sort.

Aslaksen. But you are. Last winter, before you came here, my paper was looking up. I edited it myself, I must tell you, and I edited it on a principle.

Stensgård. You?

Aslaksen. Yes, I!—I said to myself: it's the great public that supports a paper; now the great public is the bad public—that comes of the local situation; and the bad public will have a bad paper. So you see I edited it——

Stensgård. Badly! Yes, that's undeniable.

Aslaksen. Well, and I prospered by it. But then you came and brought ideas into the district. The paper took on a colour, and then Lundestad's supporters all fell away. The subscribers that are left won't pay their subscriptions——

Stensgård. Ah, but the paper has become a good one.

Aslaksen. I can't live on a good paper. You were to make things lively; you were to grapple with abuses, as you promised yesterday. The bigwigs were to be pilloried; the paper was to be filled with things people were bound to read—and now, you leave me in the lurch——

Stensgård. Ho-ho! You think I am going to keep you supplied with libels! No, thank you, my good sir!

Aslaksen. Mr. Stensgård, you mustn't drive me to desperation, or you'll repent it.

Stensgård. What do you mean?

Aslaksen. I mean that I must make the paper pay in another way. Heaven knows I should be sorry to do it. Before you came I made an honest living out of accidents and suicides and other harmless things, that often hadn't even happened. But now you have turned everything topsy-turvy; people now want very different fare——

Stensgård. Just let me tell you this: if you break loose

in any way, if you go a single step beyond my orders, and try to exploit the movement in your own dirty interests, I'll go to the opposition printer and start a new paper. We have money, you must know! We can bring your rag to ruin in a fortnight.

Aslaksen (pale). You wouldn't do that!

Stensgård. Yes, I would; and you'll see I can edit a paper so as to appeal to the great public.

Aslaksen. Then I'll go this instant to Chamberlain Bratsberg——

Stensgård. You? What have you to do with him?

Aslaksen. What have you to do with him? Do you think I don't know why you are invited here? It's because he is afraid of you, and of what you may do; and you are making capital of that. But if he's afraid of what you may do, he'll be no less afraid of what I may print; and *I* will make capital of that!

Stensgård. Would you dare to? A wretched creature like you——!

Aslaksen. I'll soon show you. If your speech is to be kept out of the paper, the Chamberlain shall pay me for keeping it out.

Stensgård. Try it; just try it! You're drunk, fellow——!

Aslaksen. Only in moderation. But I'll fight like a lion if you try to take my poor crust out of my mouth. Little you know what sort of a home mine is: a bedridden wife, a crippled child——

Stensgård. Off with you! Do you think I want to be soiled with your squalor? What are your bedridden wives and deformed brats to me? If you stand in my way, if you dare so much as to obstruct a single one of my prospects, you shall be on the parish before the year's out!

Aslaksen. I'll wait one day——

Stensgård. Ah, you're coming to your senses.

Aslaksen. I shall announce to the subscribers in a hand-bill that in consequence of an indisposition contracted at the fête, the editor——

Stensgård. Yes, do so; I daresay, later on, we shall come to an understanding.

Aslaksen. I trust we may.—Rememer this, Mr. Stensgård: that paper is my one ewe lamb.

[*Goes out by the back.*

Lundestad (at the foremost garden door). Ah, Mr. Stensgård!

Stensgård. Ah, Mr. Lundestad!

Lundestad. You here alone? If you have no objection, I should like to have a little talk with you.

Stensgård. With pleasure.

Lundestad. In the first place, let me say that if any one has told you that I have said anything to your disadvantage, you mustn't believe it.

Stensgård. To my disadvantage? What do you mean?

Lundestad. Oh, nothing; nothing, I assure you. You see, there are so many busybodies here, that go about doing nothing but setting people by the ears.

Stensgård. Well, on the whole—I'm afraid our relations are a little strained.

Lundestad. They are quite natural relations, Mr. Stensgård: the relation of the old to the new; it is always so.

Stensgård. Oh, come, Mr. Lundestad, you are not so old as all that.

Lundestad. Yes, indeed, I'm getting old. I have held my seat ever since 1839. It's time I should be relieved.

Stensgård. Relieved?

Lundestad. Times change, you see. New problems arise, and for their solution we want new forces.

Stensgård. Now, frankly, Mr. Lundestad—are you really going to give up your seat to Monsen?

Lundestad. To Monsen? No, certainly not to Monsen.

Stensgård. Then I don't understand——

Lundestad. Suppose, now, I did retire in Monsen's favour: do you think he would be elected?

Stensgård. It's hard to say. As the preliminary election comes on the day after to-morrow, there may scarcely be time to prepare the public mind; but——

Lundestad. I don't believe he would manage it. The Chamberlain's party, my party, would not vote for him. Of course "my party" is a figure of speech; I mean the men of property, the old families, who are settled on their own land and belong to it. They won't have anything to do with Monsen. Monsen is a newcomer; no one really knows anything about Monsen and his affairs. And then he has had to cut down so much to clear a place for himself—to fell both trees and men, you may say.

Stensgård. Well, then, if you think he has no chance——

Lundestad. H'm! You are a man of rare gifts, Mr. Stensgård. Providence has dealt lavishly with you. But it has made one little oversight: it ought to have given you one thing more.

Stensgård. And what might that be?

Lundestad. Tell me—why do you never think of yourself? Why have you no ambition?

Stensgård. Ambition? I?

Lunestad. Why do you waste all your strength on other people? In one word—why not go into Parliament yourself?

Stensgård. I? You are not serious?

Lundestad. Why not? You have qualified, I hear. And if you don't seize this opportunity, then some one else will come in; and when once he is firm in the saddle, it may not be so easy to unseat him.

Stensgård. Great heavens, Mr. Lundestad! do you really mean what you say?

Lundestad. Oh, I don't want to commit you; if you don't care about it——

Stensgård. Not care about it! Well, I must confess I'm not so utterly devoid of ambition as you suppose. But do you really think it possible?

Lunestad. Oh, there's nothing impossible about it. I should do my best, and so, no doubt, would the Chamberlain; he knows your oratorical gifts. You have the young men on your side——

Stensgård. Mr. Lundestad, by heaven, you are my true friend!

Lundestad. Oh, you don't mean much by that. If you really looked upon me as a friend, you would relieve me of this burden. You have young shoulders; you could bear it so easily.

Stensgård. I place myself entirely at your disposal; I will not fail you.

Lundestad. Then you are really not disinclined to——

Stensgård. Here's my hand on it!

Lundestad. Thanks! Believe me, Mr. Stensgård, you will not regret it. But now we must go warily to work. We must both of us take care to be on the electoral college—— I to propose you as my successor, and put you through your facings before the rest; and you to give an account of your views——

Stensgård. If we once get so far, we are safe. In the electoral college you are omnipotent.

Lundestad. There is a limit to omnipotence. You must of course bring your oratory into play; you must take care to explain away anything that might seem really awkward or objectionable——

Stensgård. You don't mean that I am to break with my party?

Lundestad. Now just look at the thing reasonably. What do we mean when we talk of two parties? We have, on the one hand, certain men or families who are in possession of the common civic advantages—I mean property, independence, and power. That is the party I belong to. On the other hand, we have the mass of our younger fellow citizens who want to share in these advantages. That is your party. But that party you will quite naturally and properly pass out of when you get into power—to say nothing of taking up a solid position as a man of property—for, of course, that is essential, Mr. Stensgård.

Stensgård. Yes, I believe it is. But the time is short; and such a position is not to be attained in a day.

Lundestad. That's true; but perhaps the prospect of such a position would be enough——

Stensgård. The prospect——?

Lundestad. Have you any rooted objection to a good marriage, Mr. Stensgård? There are heiresses in the country-side. A man like you, with a future before him—a man who can reckon on attaining the highest offices—believe me, you needn't fear a repulse if you play your cards neatly.

Stensgård. Then, for heaven's sake, help me in the game! You open wide vistas to me—great visions! All that I have hoped and longed for, and that seemed so dreamlike and far away, stands suddenly before me in living reality—to lead the people forward towards emancipation, to——

Lundestad. Yes, we must keep our eyes open, Mr. Stensgård. I see your ambition is already on the alert. That's well. The rest will come of itself.—In the meantime, thanks! I shall never forget your readiness to take the burden of office from my shoulders.

[*The whole party gradually enters from the garden. Two maid-servants bring in candles and hand round refreshments during the following scene.*

Selma (goes towards the piano at the back, left). Mr. Stensgård, you must join us; we are going to have a game of forfeits.

Stensgård. With pleasure; I am just in the mood.

[*Follows her towards the back, makes arrangements with her, places chairs, etc., etc.*

Erik Bratsberg (in an undertone). What the deuce is this
my father is saying, Mr. Heire? What speech has Mr. Stensgård been making yesterday?

Heire. Hee-hee! Don't you know about it?

Erik. No; we townspeople had our dinner and ball at
the Club. My father declares Mr. Stensgård has entirely
broken with the Stonelee gang—that he was frightfully rude
to Monsen——

Heire. To Monsen! No, you must have misunderstood
him, my dear sir.

Erik. Well, there were a whole lot of people about, so
that I couldn't quite follow what he said; but I certainly
heard——

Heire. Wait till to-morrow—— I say no more. You'll
have the whole story with your coffee, in Aslaksen's paper.

[*They separate.*

The Chamberlain. Well, my dear Lundestad, are you
sticking to those crotchets of yours?

Lundestad. They are no crotchets, Chamberlain; rather
than be ousted, one should give way gracefully.

The Chamberlain. Nonsense; who is dreaming of ousting
you?

Lundestad. H'm; I'm an old weather-prophet. There
has been a change in the wind. Besides, I have my successor ready. Mr. Stensgård is willing——

The Chamberlain. Mr. Stensgård?

Lundestad. Wasn't that what you meant? I took it for
a hint when you said he was a man we must make friends
with and support.

The Chamberlain. I meant in his onslaught upon all the
corruption and swindling that goes on at Stonelee.

Lundestad. But how could you count so confidently upon
his breaking with that crew?

The Chamberlain. He did it openly enough last evening, my dear fellow.

Lundestad. Last evening?

The Chamberlain. Yes, when he spoke of Monsen's deplorable influence in the district.

Lundestad (open-mouthed). Of Monsen's——?

The Chamberlain. Of course; that time on the table——

Lundestad. On the table? Yes?

The Chamberlain. He was frightfully rude; called him a money-bag, and a griffin or a basilisk, or something. Ha-ha!—it was great sport to hear him.

Lundestad. Great sport, was it?

The Chamberlain. Yes, I own I'm not sorry to see these people a little roughly handled. But now we must back him up; for after such a savage attack——

Lundestad. As that of yesterday, you mean?

The Chamberlain. Of course.

Lundestad. Upon the table?

The Chamberlain. Yes, upon the table.

Lundestad. Against Monsen?

The Chamberlain. Yes, against Monsen and his set. Of course they'll try to have their revenge; you can't blame them——

Lundestad (decidedly). Mr. Stensgård must be supported—that is clear.

Thora. Father dear, you must join in the game.

The Chamberlain. Oh, nonsense, child——

Thora. Yes, indeed you must; Selma insists upon it.

The Chamberlain. Very well, I suppose I must give in. *(In an undertone as they go towards the back.)* I'm quite distressed about Lundestad; he is really failing; fancy, he didn't in the least understand what Stensgård——

Thora. Oh, come, come; they've begun the game.

[*She drags him into the circle of young people where the game is in full swing.*

Erik (calls from his place). Mr. Heire, you are appointed forfeit-judge.

Heire. Hee-hee! It's the first appointment I ever had.

Stensgård (also in the circle). On account of your legal experience, Mr. Heire.

Heire. Oh, my amiable young friends, I should be delighted to sentence you all—— I say no more!

Stensgård (slips up to LUNDESTAD, *who stands in front on the left).* You were speaking to the Chamberlain. What about? Was it about me?

Lundestad. Unfortunately it was—about that affair of yesterday evening——

Stensgård (writhing). Oh, confound it all!

Lundestad. He said you had been frightfully rude.

Stensgård. Do you think it isn't a torture to me?

Lundestad. Now is your chance to atone for it.

Erik (calls). Mr. Stensgård, it's your turn.

Stensgård. Coming. *(Quickly to* LUNDESTAD.*)* What do you mean?

Lundestad. Find an opportunity and apologise to the Chamberlain.

Stensgård. By heaven, I will!

Selma. Make haste, make haste!

Stensgård. I'm coming! Here I am!

> [*The game goes on with noise and laughter. Some elderly gentlemen play cards on the right.* LUNDESTAD *takes a seat on the left;* DANIEL HEIRE *near him.*

Heire. That whelp twits me with my legal experience, does he?

Lundestad. He's rather free with his tongue, that's certain.

Heire. And so the whole family goes and fawns upon him. Hee-hee! They're pitifully afraid of him.

Lundestad. No, there you are wrong, Mr. Heire; the Chamberlain is not afraid of him.

Heire. Not afraid? Do you think I'm blind, my good sir?

Lundestad. No, but—I can trust you to keep the secret? Well, I'll tell you all about it. The Chamberlain thinks it was Monsen he was attacking.

Heire. Monsen? Oh, absurd!

Lundestad. Fact, Mr. Heire! Ringdal or Miss Thora must have got him persuaded that——

Heire. And so he goes and asks him to a state dinner-party! Deuce take me, if that isn't the best thing I've heard for long! No, really now, I can't keep that bottled up.

Lundestad. Sh, sh! Remember your promise. The Chamberlain's your old school-fellow; and even if he has been a little hard upon you——

Heire. Hee-hee! I'll pay him back with interest!

Lundestad. Take care! The Chamberlain is powerful. Don't play tricks in the lion's den!

Heire. Bratsberg a lion? Pooh, he's a blockhead, sir, and I am not. Oh, won't I get a rare crop of taunts, and jibes, and innuendoes out of this, when once our great suit comes on!

Selma (calls from the circle). Learned judge, what shall the owner of this forfeit do?

Erik (unnoticed, to HEIRE*).* It's Stensgård's! Think of something amusing.

Heire. That forfeit? Hee-hee, let me see; he might, for example—yes—he shall make a speech!

Selma. It's Mr. Stensgård's forfeit.

Erik. Mr. Stensgård is to make a speech.

Stensgård. Oh no, spare me that; I came off badly enough last night.

The Chamberlain. Excellently, Mr. Stensgård; I know something of public speaking.

Lundestad (to HEIRE*).* If only he doesn't put his foot in it now.

Heire. Put his foot in it? Hee-hee! You're a sharp one! That's an inspiration! *(In an undertone to* STENS-GÅRD.*)* If you came off badly last night, why not put yourself right again to-night?

Stensgård (seized with a sudden idea). Lundestad, here is the opportunity!

Lundestad (evasively). Play your cards neatly.

[*Looks for his hat and slips quietly towards the door.*

Stensgård. Yes, I will make a speech!

The Young Ladies. Bravo! Bravo!

Stensgård. Fill your glasses, ladies and gentlemen! I am going to make a speech which shall begin with a fable; for here I seem to breathe the finer air of fable-land.

Erik (to the LADIES*).* Hush! Listen!

[*The* CHAMBERLAIN *takes his glass from the card-table on the right, beside which he remains standing.* RINGDAL, FIELDBO, *and one or two other gentlemen come in from the garden.*

Stensgård. It was in the spring time. There came a young cuckoo flying over the uplands. Now the cuckoo is an adventurer. There was a great Bird-Parliament on the meadow beneath him, and both wild and tame fowl flocked to it. They came tripping out of the hen-yards; they waddled up from the goose-ponds; down from Stonelee hulked a fat capercailzie, flying low and noisily; he settled down, and ruffled his feathers and flapped his wings, and made himself even broader than he was; and every now and then he crowed, "Krak, krak, krak!" as much as to say: I'm the game-cock from Stonelee, I am!

The Chamberlain. Capital! Hear, hear!

Stensgård. And then there was an old woodpecker. He bustled up and down the tree-trunks, pecking with his pointed beak, and gorging himself with grubs and everything that turns to gall. To right and left you heard him going: prik, prik, prik! And that was the woodpecker.

Erik. Excuse me, wasn't it a stork, or a——? *

Heire. Say no more!

Stensgård. That was the old woodpecker. But now there came life into the crew; for they found something to cackle evil about. And they flustered together, and cackled in chorus, until at last the young cuckoo began to join in the cackling——

Fieldbo (unnoticed). For God's sake, man, be quiet!

Stensgård. Now it was an eagle they cackled about—an eagle who dwelt in lonely dignity upon a beetling cliff.† They were all agreed about him. "He's a bugbear to the neighbourhood," croaked a hoarse raven. But the eagle swooped down into their midst, seized the cuckoo, and bore him aloft to his eyrie.—Heart conquered heart! From that clear summit the adventurer-cuckoo looked far and wide over the lowlands; there he found sunshine and peace; and there he learned to judge aright the swarm from the hen-yards and the clearings——

Fieldbo (loudly). Bravo, bravo! And now some music.

The Chamberlain. Hush! Don't interrupt him.

Stensgård. Chamberlain Bratsberg—here my fable ends; and here I stand before you, in the presence of every one, to beg your forgiveness for last night.

The Chamberlain (falls a step backwards). Mine——?

Stensgård. I thank you for the magnanimous vengeance you have taken for my senseless words. In me you have henceforth a faithful champion. And now, ladies and gentlemen, I drink the health of the eagle on the mountain-top —the health of Chamberlain Bratsberg.

The Chamberlain (clutching at the table). Thank you, Mr.—Mr. Stensgård.

* As before stated, "Heire" means a heron.

† "Et brat fjeld"—an allusion to the name Bratsberg.

The Guests (for the most part in painful embarrassment). The Chamberlain!   Chamberlain Bratsberg!

The Chamberlain.   Ladies! Gentlemen!   *(Softly.)* Thora!

Thora.   Father!

The Chamberlain.   Oh, Doctor, Doctor, what have you done——?

Stensgård (with his glass in his hand, radiant with self-satisfaction).   Now to our places again!   Hullo, Fieldbo! Come, join in—join in the League of Youth!   The game's going merrily!

Heire (in front, on the left).   Yes, on my soul, the game's going merrily!

[LUNDESTAD *slips out by the door in the back.*

ACT THIRD

*An elegant morning-room, with entrance-door in the back.
On the left, the door of the* CHAMBERLAIN'S *study;
further back, a door leading to the drawing-room. On
the right, a door leading to* RINGDAL'S *offices; further
forward, a window.*

THORA *is seated on the sofa, left, weeping. The* CHAMBER-
LAIN *paces angrily up and down.*

The Chamberlain. Yes, now we have the epilogue—tears
and lamentations——

Thora. Oh, that we had never seen that man!

The Chamberlain. What man?

Thora. That wretched Mr. Stensgård, of course.

The Chamberlain. You should rather say: Oh, that we
had never seen that wretched Doctor.

Thora. Doctor Fieldbo?

The Chamberlain. Yes, Fieldbo, Fieldbo! Wasn't it he
that palmed off a parcel of lies upon me——?

Thora. No, my dear father, it was I.

The Chamberlain. You? Well, then, both of you! You
were his accomplice—behind my back. A nice state of
affairs!

Thora. Oh, father, if you only knew——

The Chamberlain. Oh, I know enough; more than
enough; much more!

DR. FIELDBO *enters from the back.*

Fieldbo. Good morning, Chamberlain! Good morning,
Miss Bratsberg!

178

The Chamberlain (still pacing the room). So you are there, are you—bird of evil omen!

Fieldbo. Yes, it was a very unpleasant affair.

The Chamberlain (looking out at the window). Oh, you think so?

Fieldbo. You must have noticed how I kept my eye upon Stensgård all the evening. Unfortunately, when I heard there was to be a game of forfeits, I thought there was no danger——

The Chamberlain (stamping on the floor). To be made a laughing-stock by such a windbag! What must my guests have thought of me? That I was mean enough to want to buy this creature, this—this —— as Lundestad calls him!

Fieldbo. Yes, but——

Thora (unnoticed by her father). Don't speak.

The Chamberlain (after a short pause, turns to FIELDBO*).* Tell me frankly, Doctor:—Am I really denser than the gen eral run of people?

Fieldbo. How can you ask such a question, Chamberlain?

The Chamberlain. Then how did it happen that I was probably the only person there who didn't understand that that confounded speech was meant for me?

Fieldbo. Shall I tell you why?

The Chamberlain. Certainly.

Fieldbo. It is because you yourself regard your position in the district differently from other people.

The Chamberlain. I regard my position as my father before me regarded his. No one would ever have ventured to treat him so.

Fieldbo. Your father died about the year 1830.

The Chamberlain. Oh, yes; many a barrier has broken down since that time. But, after all, it's my own fault. I have mixed myself up too much with these good people. So now I must be content to have my name coupled with Anders Lundestad's!

Fieldbo. Well, frankly, I see no disgrace in that.

The Chamberlain. Oh, you know quite well what I mean. Of course I don't plume myself on rank, or titles, or anything of that sort. But what I hold in honour, and expect others to hold in honour, is the integrity handed down in our family from generation to generation. What I mean is that when a man like Lundestad goes into public life, he cannot keep his character and his conduct entirely free from stain. In the general mud-throwing, he is sure to find himself bespattered. But they might leave me in peace; I stand outside their parties.

Fieldbo. Not so entirely, Chamberlain; at least you were delighted so long as you thought it was Monsen that was attacked.

The Chamberlain. Don't mention that fellow!—It is he that has relaxed the moral sense of the district. And now he has gone and turned my son's head, confound him!

Thora. Erik's?

Fieldbo. Your son's?

The Chamberlain. Yes; what tempted him to go and set up in business? It leads to nothing.

Fieldbo. Why, my dear Chamberlain, he must live and——

The Chamberlain. Oh, with economy he could quite well live on the money that came to him from his mother.

Fieldbo. He might perhaps live on it; but what could he live for?

The Chamberlain. For? Well, if he absolutely must have something to live for, hasn't he qualified as a lawyer? He might live for his profession.

Fieldbo. No, that he couldn't do; it is against his nature. Then there was no official appointment he could well hope for; you have kept the management of your property in your own hands; and your son has no children to educate. Under these circumstances, when he sees tempting examples around him—people who have started from nothing and are worth their half million——

The Chamberlain. Their half million! Oh, come now, let us keep to the hundred thousands. But neither the half million nor the hundred thousands can be scraped together with perfectly clean hands:—I don't mean in the eyes of the world; Heaven knows it is easy enough to keep within the law; but in respect to one's own conscience. Of course my son cannot descend to anything questionable; so you may be quite sure Mr. Erik Bratsberg's financial operations won't bring in any half millions.

SELMA, *in walking dress, enters from the back.*

Selma. Good-morning! Is Erik not here?

The Chamberlain. Good-morning, child! Are you looking for your husband?

Selma. Yes, he said he was coming here. Mr. Monsen called upon him early this morning, and then——

The Chamberlain. Monsen? Does Monsen come to your house?

Selma. Now and then; generally on business. Why, my dear Thora, what's the matter? Have you been crying?

Thora. Oh, it's nothing.

Selma. No, it's not nothing! At home Erik was out of humour, and here—— I can see it in your looks: there is something wrong. What is it?

The Chamberlain. Nothing you need trouble about, at any rate. You are too dainty to carry burdens, my little Selma. Go into the drawing-room for the present. If Erik said he was coming, he will be here soon, no doubt.

Selma. Come, Thora—and be sure you don't let me sit in a draught! *(Embracing her.)* Oh, I could hug the life out of you, my sweet Thora!

[*The two ladies go off to the left.*

The Chamberlain. So they are hand in glove, are they, the two speculators! They should go into partnership. Monsen and Bratsberg—how nice it would sound! *(A knock at the door in the back.)* Come in!

STENSGÅRD *enters.*

The Chamberlain (recoiling a step). What is this?

Stensgård. Yes, here I am again, Chamberlain!

The Chamberlain. So I see.

Fieldbo. Are you mad, Stensgård?

Stensgård. You retired early yesterday evening. When Fieldbo had explained to me how matters stood, you had already——

The Chamberlain. Excuse me—all explanations are superfluous——

Stensgård. I understand that; therefore I have not come to make any.

The Chamberlain. Oh, indeed?

Stensgård. I know I have insulted you.

The Chamberlain. I know that too; and before I have you turned out, perhaps you will be good enough to tell me why you are here.

Stensgård. Because I love your daughter, Chamberlain.

Fieldbo. What——!

The Chamberlain. What does he say, Doctor?

Stensgård. Ah, you can't grasp the idea, Chamberlain. You are an old man; you have nothing to fight for——

The Chamberlain. And you presume to——?

Stensgård. I am here to ask for your daughter's hand, Chamberlain.

The Chamberalin. You—— you——? Won't you sit down?

Stensgård. Thanks, I prefer to stand.

The Chamberlain. What do you say to this, Doctor?

Stensgård. Oh, Fieldbo is on my side; he is my friend; the only true friend I have.

Fieldbo. No, no, man! Never in this world, if you——

The Chamberlain. Perhaps it was with this view that Doctor Fieldbo secured his friend's introduction into my house?

Stensgård. You know me only by my exploits of yester-

day and the day before. That is not enough. Besides, I
am not the same man to-day that I was then. My intercourse with you and yours has fallen like spring showers
upon my spirit, making it put forth new blossoms in a single
night! You must not hurl me back into my sordid past.
Till now, I have never been at home with the beautiful in
life; it has always been beyond my reach——

The Chamberlain. But my daughter——?

Stensgård. Oh, I shall win her.

The Chamberlain. Indeed? H'm!

Stensgård. Yes, for I have will on my side. Remember
what you told me yesterday. You were opposed to your
son's marriage—and see how it has turned out! You must
put on the glasses of experience, as Fieldbo said——

The Chamberlain. Ah, that was what you meant?

Fieldbo. Not in the least! My dear Chamberlain, let
me speak to him alone——

Stensgård. Nonsense; I have nothing to speak to you
about. Now, pray be reasonable, Chamberlain! A family
like yours needs new alliances, or its brains stagnate——

The Chamberlain. Oh, this is too much!

Stensgård. Now, now, don't be angry! These high-and-
mighty airs are unworthy of you—of course you know they
are all nonsense at bottom. You shall see how much you'll
value me when you come to know me. Yes, yes; you shall
value me—both you and your daughter! I will make
her——

The Chamberlain. What do you think of this, Doctor?

Fieldbo. I think it's madness.

Stensgård. Yes, it would be in you; but I, you see—I
have a mission to fulfil on God's beautiful earth;—I am
not to be deterred by nonsensical prejudices——

The Chamberlain. Mr. Stensgård, there is the door.

Stensgård. You show me——?

The Chamberlain. The door!

Stensgård. Don't do that!

The Chamberlain. Out with you! You are an adventurer, an a—a—confound my memory! You're a——

Stensgård. What am I?

The Chamberlain. You are—that other thing—it's on the tip of my tongue——

Stensgård. Beware how you block my career!

The Chamberlain. Beware? Of what?

Stensgård. I will attack you in the papers, persecute you, libel you, do all I can to undermine your reputation. You shall shriek under the lash. You shall seem to see spirits in the air raining blows upon you. You shall huddle together in dread, and crouch with your arms bent over your head to ward off the strokes—you shall try to creep into shelter——

The Chamberlain. Creep into shelter yourself—in a mad-house; that is the proper place for you!

Stensgård. Ha-ha; that is a cheap retort; but you know no better, Mr. Bratsberg! I tell you the wrath of the Lord is in me. It is His will you are opposing. He has destined me for the light—beware how you cast a shadow!—Well, I see I shall make no way with you to-day; but that matters nothing. I only ask you to speak to your daughter—to prepare her—to give her the opportunity of choosing! Reflect, and look around you. Where can you expect to find a son-in-law among these plodding dunces? Fieldbo says she is deep and steadfast and true. So now you know just how matters stand. Good-bye, Chamberlain—I leave you to choose between my friendship and my enmity. Good-bye!

[*Goes out by the back.*

The Chamberlain. So it has come to this! This is how they dare to treat me in my own house!

Fieldbo. Stensgård dares; no one else would.

The Chamberlain. He to-day; others to-morrow.

Fieldbo. Let them come; I shall keep them off; I would go through fire and water for you——

The Chamberlain. Yes, you who have caused all the mischief!—H'm; that Stensgård is the most impudent scoun-

drel I have ever known! And yet, after all—deuce take me
if there isn't something I like about him.

Fieldbo. He has possibilities——

The Chamberlain. He has openness, Dr. Fieldbo! He
doesn't go playing his own game behind one's back, like so
many other people; he-he——!

Fieldbo. It's not worth disputing about. Only be firm,
Chamberlain; no, and no again, to Stensgård——!

The Chamberlain. Oh, keep your advice to yourself!
You may rely upon it that neither he nor anyone
else——

Ringdal (enters by the door on the right). Excuse me,
Chamberlain; one word——   [*Whispers.*

The Chamberlain. What? In your room?

Ringdal. He came in by the back way, and begs you to
see him.

The Chamberlain. H'm.—Oh, Doctor, just go into the
drawing-room for a moment; there's some one here who——
But don't say a word to Selma of Mr. Stensgård and his
visit. She must be kept outside all this business. As for my
daughter, I should prefer that you should say nothing to her
either; but—— Oh, what's the use——? Please go now.

  [FIELDBO *goes into the drawing-room.* RINGDAL
          has, in the meantime, gone back to his office,
          whence MONSEN *presently enters.*

Monsen (at the door). I beg ten thousand pardons,
sir——

The Chamberlain. Oh, come in, come in!

Monsen. I trust your family is in good health?

The Chamberlain. Thank you. Is there anything you
want?

Monsen. I can't quite put it that way. Thank heaven,
I'm one of those that have got pretty nearly all they can
want.

The Chamberlain. Oh, indeed? That is a good deal to
say.

Monsen. But I've had to work for it, Chamberlain. Oh, I know you regard my work with no very friendly eye.

The Chamberlain. I cannot suppose that your work is in any way affected by my way of regarding it.

Monsen. Who knows? At any rate, I'm thinking of gradually withdrawing from business.

The Chamberlain. Really?

Monsen. The luck has been on my side, I may tell you. I've gone ahead as far as I care to; so now I think it's about time to slack off a little——

The Chamberlain. Well, I congratulate both you—and other people.

Monsen. And if I could at the same time do you a service, Chamberlain——

The Chamberlain. Me?

Monsen. When the Langerud woods were put up to auction five years ago, you made a bid for them——

The Chamberlain. Yes, but you outbade me, and they were knocked down to you.

Monsen. You can have them now, with the saw-mills and all appurtenances——

The Chamberlain. After all your sinful cutting and hacking——!

Monsen. Oh, they're worth a good deal still; and with your method of working, in a few years——

The Chamberlain. Thank you; unfortunately I must decline the proposal.

Monsen. There's a great deal of money in it, Chamberlain. As for me,—I may tell you I have a great speculation on hand; the stakes are large; I mean there's a big haul to be made—a hundred thousand or so——

The Chamberlain. A hundred thousand? That is certainly no trifle.

Monsen. Ha ha ha! A nice round sum to add to the pile. But when you're going into a great battle you need

reserve forces, as the saying goes. There's not much ready
money about; the names that are worth anything are rather
used up——

The Chamberlain. Yes, certain people have taken care
of that.

Monsen. It's a case of you scratch me, I scratch you.
Well, Chamberlain, is it to be a bargain? You shall have
the woods at your own figure——

The Chamberlain. I will not have them at any figure,
Mr. Monsen.

Monsen. Well, one good offer deserves another. Will
you help me, sir?

The Chamberlain. What do you mean?

Monsen. Of course I'll give good security. I have
plenty of property. Look here—these papers—just let me
explain my position to you.

The Chamberlain (waving the papers aside). Is it pecuniary aid you want?

Monsen. Not ready money; oh, no! But your support,
Chamberlain. Of course I'll pay for it—and give security,
and——

The Chamberlain. And you come to me with such a proposal as this?

Monsen. Yes, precisely to you. I know you've often let
bygones be bygones when a man was in real straits.

The Chamberlain. Well, in a way, I must thank you for
your good opinion—especially at a time like this; but nevertheless——

Monsen. Won't you tell me, Chamberlain, what sets you
against me?

The Chamberlain. Oh, what would be the use?

Monsen. It might lead to a better understanding between us. I've never stood in your way that I know of.

The Chamberlain. You think not? Then let me tell you
of one case in which you have stood in my way. I founded
the Iron-works Savings Bank for the benefit of my employees

and others. But then you must needs set up as a banker; people take their savings to you——

Monsen. Naturally, sir, for I give higher interest.

The Chamberlain. Yes, but you charge higher interest on loans.

Monsen. But I don't make so many difficulties about security and so forth.

The Chamberlain. That is just the mischief of it; for now we have people making bargains to the tune of ten or twenty thousand dollars,* though neither of the parties has so much as a brass farthing. That is what sets me against you, Mr. Monsen. And there is another thing too that touches me still more nearly. Do you think it was with my good will that my son flung himself into all these wild speculations?

Monsen. But how can I help that?

The Chamberlain. It was your example that infected him, as it did the others. Why could you not stick to your last?

Monsen. Remain a lumberman, like my father?

The Chamberlain. Was it a disgrace to be in my employment? Your father made his bread honourably, and was respected in his own class.

Monsen. Yes, until he'd almost worked his life out, and at last went over the waterfall with his raft. Do you know anything of life in that class, Chamberlain? Have you ever realised what the men have to endure who toil for you deep in the forests, and along the river-reaches, while you sit comfortably at home and fatten on the profits? Can you blame such a man for struggling to rise in the world? I had had a little more schooling than my father; perhaps I had rather more brains too——

———

* The dollar—four crowns—four-and-sixpence, was the unit of coinage at the time this play was written. It has since been replaced by the crown.

The Chamberlain. Very likely. But by what means
have you risen in the world? You began by selling brandy.
Then you bought up doubtful debts, and enforced them
mercilessly;—and so you got on and on. How many people
have you not ruined to push yourself forward!

Monsen. That's the course of business; one up, another
down.

The Chamberlain. But there are different methods of
business. I know of respectable families whom you have
brought to the workhouse.

Monsen. Daniel Heire is not very far from the workhouse.

The Chamberlain. I understand you; but I can justify
my conduct before God and man! When the country was
in distress, after the separation from Denmark, my father
made sacrifices beyond his means. Thus part of our property came into the hands of the Heire family. What was
the result? The people who lived upon the property suffered under Daniel Heire's incompetent management. He
cut down timber to the injury, I may even say to the ruin,
of the district. Was it not my obvious duty to put a stop
to it if I was able? And it happened that I was able;
I had the law on my side; I was well within my rights
when I re-entered upon my family property.

Monsen. I, too, have always had the law on my side.

The Chamberlain. But what about your sense of right,
your conscience, if you have such a thing? And how you
have broken down all social order! How you have im-
paired the respect that should attach to wealth! People
never think of asking nowadays how such and such a fortune was made, or how long it has been in such and such a
family; they only ask: how much is so-and-so worth?—and
they esteem him accordingly. Now I suffer by all this; I
find myself regarded as a sort of associate of yours; people
speak of us in one breath, because we are the two largest
proprietors in the neighbourhood. This state of things I

cannot endure! I tell you once for all: that is why I am set against you.

Monsen. This state of things shall come to an end, sir; I will give up business, and make way for you at every point; but I beg you, I implore you, to help me!

The Chamberlain. I will not.

Monsen. I'm willing to pay you what you like——

The Chamberlain. To pay! And you dare to——!

Monsen. If not for my sake, then for your son's!

The Chamberlain. My son's!

Monsen. Yes, he's in it. I reckon he stands to win some twenty thousand dollars.

The Chamberlain. Stands to win?

Monsen. Yes.

The Chamberlain. Then, good God, who stands to lose all this money?

Monsen. How do you mean?

The Chamberlain. If my son wins, some one or other must lose!

Monsen. It's a good stroke of business; I'm not in a position to say more. But I need a solid name; only just your endorsement——

The Chamberlain. Endorsement! On a bill——?

Monsen. Only for ten or fifteen thousand dollars.

The Chamberlain. Do you suppose for a moment that——? My name! In such an affair! My name? As surety, no doubt?

Monsen. A mere matter of form——

The Chamberlain. A matter of swindling! My name! Not upon any consideration. I have never put my name on other men's paper.

Monsen. Never? That's an exaggeration, Chamberlain.

The Chamberlain. It is the literal truth.

Monsen. No, not literal; I've seen it with my own eyes.

The Chamberlain. What have you seen?

Monsen. Your name—on one bill at least.

The Chamberlain. It is false, I tell you! You have never seen it!

Monsen. I have! On a bill for two thousand dollars. Think again!

The Chamberlain. Neither for two thousand nor for ten thousand! On my sacred word of honour, never!

Monsen. Then it's a forgery.

The Chamberlain. Forgery?

Monsen. Yes, a forgery—for I have seen it.

The Chamberlain. Forgery? Forgery! Where did you see it? In whose hands?

Monsen. That I won't tell you.

The Chamberlain. Ha-ha! We shall soon find that out——

Monsen. Listen to me——!

The Chamberlain. Silence! It has come to this then! Forgery. They must mix me up in their abominations! No wonder, then, that people bracket me with the rest of you. But it is my turn now!

Monsen. Chamberlain—for your own sake and for the sake of others——

The Chamberlain. Off with you! Out of my sight! It is you that are at the root of it all!—Yes you are! Woe unto him from whom offences come. Your home-life is scandalous. What sort of society do you get about you? Persons from Christiania and elsewhere, who think only of eating and drinking, and do not care in what company they gorge themselves. Silence! I have seen with my own eyes your distinguished guests tearing along the roads at Christmas-time like a pack of howling wolves. And there is worse behind. You have had scandals with your own maid-servants. You drove your wife out of her mind by your ill-treatment and debauchery.

Monsen. Come, this is going too far! You shall pay for these words!

The Chamberlain. Oh, to the deuce with your threats!

What harm can you do to me? Me? You asked what I had to say against you. Well, I have said it. Now you know why I have kept you out of decent society.

Monsen. Yes, and now I'll drag your decent society down——

The Chamberlain. That way!

Monsen. I know my way, Chamberlain!

[*Goes out by the back.*

The Chamberlain (opens the door on the right and calls). Ringdal, Ringdal——come here!

Ringdal. What is it, sir?

The Chamberlain (calls into the drawing-room). Doctor, please come this way!——Now, Ringdal, now you shall see my prophecies fulfilled.

Fieldbo (entering). What can I do for you, Chamberlain?

Ringdal. What prophecies, sir?

The Chamberlain. What do you say to this, Doctor? You have always accused me of exaggerating when I said that Monsen was corrupting the neighbourhood.

Fieldbo. Well, what then?

The Chamberlain. We are getting on, I can tell you! What do you think? There are forgeries going about.

Ringdal. Forgeries?

The Chamberlain. Yes, forgeries! And whose name do you think they have forged? Why, mine!

Fieldbo. Who in the world can have done it?

The Chamberlain. How can I tell? I don't know all the scoundrels in the district. But we shall soon find out.—— Doctor, do me a service. The papers must have come into the hands either of the Savings Bank or the Iron-works Bank. Drive up to Lundestad; he is the director who knows most about things. Find out whether there is any such paper——

Fieldbo. Certainly; at once.

Ringdal. Lundestad is here at the works to-day; there's a meeting of the school committee.

The Chamberlain. So much the better. Find him; bring him here.

Fieldbo. I'll go at once.   [*Goes out at the back.*

The Chamberlain. And you, Ringdal, make inquiries at the Iron-works. As soon as we have got to the bottom of the matter, we'll lay an information. No mercy to the scoundrels!

Ringdal. Very good, sir. Bless me, who'd have thought of such a thing?   [*Goes out to the right.*

[*The* CHAMBERLAIN *paces the room once or twice, and is then about to go into his study. At that instant* ERIK BRATSBERG *enters from the back.*

Erik. My dear father——!

The Chamberlain. Oh, are you there?

Erik. I want so much to speak to you.

The Chamberlain. H'm; I'm not much in the humour for speaking to any one. What do you want?

Erik. You know I have never mixed you up in my affairs, father.

The Chamberlain. No; that is an honour I should certainly have declined.

Erik. But now I am forced to——

The Chamberlain. What are you forced to do?

Erik. Father, you must help me!

The Chamberlain. With money! You may be very sure that——

Erik. Only this once! I swear I'll never again—— The fact is, I am under certain engagements to Monsen of Stonelee——

The Chamberlain. I know that. You have a brilliant speculation on hand.

Erik. A speculation? We? No! Who told you so?

The Chamberlain. Monsen himself.

Erik. Has Monsen been here?

The Chamberlain. He has just gone. I showed him the door.

Erik. If you don't help me, father, I am ruined.

The Chamberlain. You?

Erik. Yes. Monsen has advanced me money. I had to pay terribly dear for it; and now the bills have fallen due——

The Chamberlain. There we have it! What did I tell you——?

Erik. Yes, yes; it's too late now——

The Chamberlain. Ruined! In two years! But how could you expect anything else? What had you to do among these charlatans that go about dazzling people's eyes with wealth that never existed! They were no company for you. Among people of that sort you must meet cunning with cunning, or you'll go to the wall; you have learnt that now.

Erik. Father, will you save me or will you not?

The Chamberlain. No; for the last time, no. I will not.

Erik. My honour is at stake——

The Chamberlain. Oh, let us have no big phrases! There's no honour involved in commercial success nowadays; quite the opposite, I had almost said. Go home and make up your accounts; pay every man his due, and have done with it, the sooner the better.

Erik. Oh, you don't know——

Selma *and* Thora *enter from the drawing-room.*

Selma. Is that Erik's voice?—Good heavens, what is the matter?

The Chamberlain. Nothing. Go into the drawing-room again.

Selma. No, I won't go. I will know. Erik, what is it? Tell me!

Erik. It's only that I am ruined!

Thora. Ruined!

The Chamberlain. There, you see!

Selma. What is ruined?

Erik. Everything.

Selma. Do you mean you have lost your money?

Erik. Money, house, inheritance—everything!

Selma. Is that what you call everything?

Erik. Come, let us go, Selma. You are all I have left me. We must bear the blow together.

Selma. The blow? Bear it together? *(With a cry.)* Do you think I am fit for that, now?

The Chamberlain. For heaven's sake——!

Erik. What do you mean?

Thora. Oh, Selma, take care!

Selma. No, I won't take care! I cannot go on lying and shamming any longer! I must speak the truth. I will not "bear" anything!

Erik. Selma!

The Chamberlain. Child, what are you saying?

Selma. Oh, how cruel you have been to me! Shamefully—all of you! It was my part always to accept—never to give. I have been like a pauper among you. You never came and demanded a sacrifice of me; I was not fit to bear anything. I hate you! I loathe you!

Erik. What can this mean?

The Chamberlain. She is ill; she is out of her mind!

Selma. How I have thirsted for a single drop of your troubles, your anxieties! But when I begged for it you only laughed me off. You have dressed me up like a doll; you have played with me as you would play with a child. Oh, what a joy it would have been to me to take my share in your burdens! How I longed, how I yearned, for a large, and high, and strenuous part in life! Now you come to me, Erik, now that you have nothing else left. But I will not be treated simply as a last resource. I will have nothing to do with your troubles now. I won't stay with you! I will rather play and sing in the streets——! Let me be! Let me be! *[She rushes out by the back.*

The Chamberlain. Thora, was there any meaning in all that, or——

Thora. Oh, yes, there was meaning in it; if only I had seen it sooner.   [*Goes out by the back.*

Erik. No! All else I can lose, but not her! Selma, Selma!   [*Follows* THORA *and* SELMA.

Ringdal (enters from the right). Chamberlain!

The Chamberlain. Well, what is it?

Ringdal. I have been to the Bank——

The Chamberlain. The Bank? Oh, yes, about the bill——

Ringdal. It's all right; they have never had any bill endorsed by you——

FIELDBO *and* LUNDESTAD *enter by the back.*

Fieldbo. False alarm, Chamberlain!

The Chamberlain. Indeed? Not at the Savings Bank either?

Lundestad. Certainly not. During all the years I've been a director I have never once seen your name; except, of course, on your son's bill.

The Chamberlain. My son's bill?

Lundestad. Yes, the bill you accepted for him early this spring.

The Chamberlain. My son? My son? Do you dare to tell me——?

Lundestad. Why, bless me, just think a moment; the bill for two thousand dollars drawn by your son——

The Chamberlain (groping for a chair). Oh, my God——!

Fieldbo. For heaven's sake——!

Ringdal. It's not possible that——!

The Chamberlain (who has sunk down on a chair). Quietly, quietly! Drawn by my son, you say? Accepted by me? For two thousand dollars?

Fieldbo (to LUNDESTAD*).* And this bill is in the Savings Bank?

Lundestad. Not now; it was redeemed last week by Monsen——

The Chamberlain. By Monsen——?

Ringdal. Monsen may still be at the works; I'll go——.

The Chamberlain. Stop here!

DANIEL HEIRE *enters by the back.*

Heire. Good-morning, gentlemen! Good-morning, Chamberlain! Thank you so much for the delightful evening we spent yesterday. What do you think I've just heard——?

Ringdal. Excuse me; we are busy——

Heire. So are other people, I can tell you; our friend from Stonelee, for example——

The Chamberlain. Monsen?

Heire. Hee-hee; it's a pretty story! The electioneering intrigues are in full swing. And what do you think is the last idea? They are going to bribe you, Chamberlain!

Lundestad. To bribe——?

The Chamberlain. They judge the tree by its fruit.

Heire. Deuce take me if it isn't the most impudent thing I ever heard of! I just looked in at Madam Rundholmen's to have a glass of bitters. There sat Messrs. Monsen and Stensgård drinking port—filthy stuff! I wouldn't touch it; but they might have had the decency to offer me a glass, all the same. However, Monsen turned to me and said, "What do you bet that Chamberlain Bratsberg won't go with our party at the preliminary election to-morrow?" "Indeed," said I, "how's that to be managed?" "Oh," he said, "this bill will persuade him——"

Fieldbo. Bill——?

Lundestad. At the election——?

The Chamberlain. Well? What then?

Heire. Oh, I know no more. They said something about two thousand dollars. That's the figure they rate a gentleman's conscience at! Oh, it's abominable, I say!

The Chamberlain. A bill for two thousand dollars?

Ringdal. And Monsen has it?

Heire. No, he handed it over to Stensgård.

Lundestad. Indeed!

Fieldbo. To Stensgård?

The Chamberlain. Are you sure of that?

Heire. Quite certain. "You can make what use you please of it," he said. But I don't understand——

Lundestad. I want to speak to you, Mr. Heire—and you too, Ringdal.

[*The three converse in a whisper at the back.*

Fieldbo. Chamberlain!

The Chamberlain. Well?

Fieldbo. Your son's bill is genuine, of course——?

The Chamberlain. One would suppose so.

Fieldbo. Of course. But now if the forged bill were to turn up——?

The Chamberlain. I will lay no information.

Fieldbo. Naturally not;—but you must do more.

The Chamberlain (rising). I can do no more.

Fieldbo. Yes, for heaven's sake, you can and must. You must save the poor fellow——

The Chamberlain. In what way?

Fieldbo. Quite simply: by acknowledging the signature.

The Chamberlain. Then you think, Doctor, that we stick at nothing in our family?

Fieldbo. I am trying to think for the best, Chamberlain.

The Chamberlain. And do you believe for a moment that I can tell a lie?—that I can play into the hands of forgers?

Fieldbo. And do you realise what will be the consequences if you do not?

The Chamberlain. The offender must settle that with the law.   [*He goes out to the left.*

ACT FOURTH

A public room in MADAM RUNDHOLMEN'S *hotel.* **Entrance**
*door in the back; a smaller door on either side. A
window on the right; before it, a table with writing
materials; further back, in the middle of the room,
another table.*

*Madam Rundholmen (within, on the left, heard talking
loudly).* Oh, let them go about their business! Tell them
they've come here to vote and not to drink. If they won't
wait, they can do the other thing.

Stensgård (enters by the back). Good-morning! H'm,
h'm, Madam Rundholmen! *(Goes to the door on the left
and knocks.)* Good-morning, Madam Rundholmen!

Madam Rundholmen (within). Oh! Who's there?

Stensgård. It is I—Stensgård. May I come in?

Madam Rundholmen. No, indeed, you mustn't! No!
I'm not dress'd.

Stensgård. What? Are you so late to-day?

Madam Rundholmen. Oh, I can tell you I've been up
since all hours; but one must look a little decent, you know.
(Peeps out, with a kerchief over her head.) Well, what is
it? No, you really mustn't look at me, Mr. Stensgård.—
Oh, there's some one else!

> [*Disappears, slamming the door to.*

Aslaksen (enters from the back with a bundle of papers).
Good-morning, Mr. Stensgård.

Stensgård. Well, is it in?

Aslaksen. Yes, here it is. Look—"The Independence Day Celebrations—From our Special Correspondent." Here's the founding of the League on the other side, and your speech up here. I've leaded all the abuse.

Stensgård. It seems to me it's all leaded.

Aslaksen. Pretty nearly.

Stensgård. And the extra number was of course distributed yesterday?

Aslaksen. Of course; all over the district, both to subscribers and others. Would you like to see it?

[*Hands him a copy.*

Stensgård (running his eye over the paper). "Our respected member, Mr. Lundestad, proposes to resign . . . long and faithful service . . . in the words of the poet: 'Rest, patriot, it, is thy due!' " H'm! "The association founded on Independence Day!: the League of Youth . . . Mr. Stensgård, the guiding intelligence of the League . . . timely reforms, credit on easier terms." Ah, that's very good. Has the polling begun?

Aslaksen. It's in full swing. The whole League is on the spot—both voters and others.

Stensgård. Oh, deuce take the others—between ourselves, of course. Well, you go down and talk to the waverers.

Aslaksen. All right.

Stensgård. You can tell them that I am pretty much at one with Lundestad——

Aslaksen. Trust to me; I know the local situation.

Stensgård. One thing more; just to oblige me, Aslaksen, don't drink to-day.

Aslaksen. Oh, what do you mean——!

Stensgård. We'll have a jolly evening when it's all over; but remember what you, as well as I, have at stake; your paper—— Come, now, my good fellow, let me see that you can——

Aslaksen. There, that's enough now; I'm old enough to look after myself. [*Goes out to the right.*

Madam Rundholmen (enters from the left, elaborately dressed). Now, Mr. Stensgård, I'm at your service. Is it anything of importance——?

Stensgård. No, only that I want you to be good enough to let me know when Mr. Monsen comes.

Madam Rundholmen. He won't be here to-day.

Stensgård. Not to-day?

Madam Rundholmen. No; he drove past here at four this morning; he's always driving about nowadays. What's more, he came in and roused me out of bed—he wanted to borrow money, you must know.

Stensgård. Monsen did?

Madam Rundholmen. Yes. He's a tremendous man to get through money is Monsen. I hope things may turn out all right for him. And I say the same to you; for I hear you're going into Parliament.

Stensgård. I? Nonsense. Who told you so?

Madam Rundholmen. Oh, some of Mr. Lundestad's people.

Daniel Heire (enters from the back). Hee-hee! Good-morning! I'm not in the way, am I?

Madam Rundholmen. Gracious, no!

Heire. Good God, how resplendent! Can it be for me that you've got yourself up like this?

Madam Rundholmen. Of course. It's for you bachelors we get ourselves up, isn't it?

Heire. For marrying men, Madam Rundholmen; for marrying men! Unfortunately, my law-suits take up all my time——

Madam Rundholmen. Oh, nonsense; you've always plenty of time to get married.

Heire. No; deuce take me if I have! Marriage is a thing you've got to give your whole mind to. Well, well— if you can't have me, you must put up with somebody else. For you ought to marry again.

Madam Rundholmen. Now, do you know, I'm sometimes of the same opinion.

Heire. Naturally; when once one has tasted the joys of matrimony—— Of course, poor Rundholmen was one in a thousand——

Madam Rundholmen. Well, I won't go so far as that; he was a bit rough, and rather too fond of his glass; but a husband's always a husband.

Heire. Very true, Madam Rundholmen; a husband's a husband, and a widow's a widow——

Madam Rundholmen. And business is business. Oh, when I think of all I've got to attend to, I don't know whether I'm on my heels or my head. Every one wants to buy; but when it comes to paying, I've got to go in for summonses and executions, and Lord knows what. Upon my word, I'll soon have to engage a lawyer all to myself.

Heire. I'll tell you what, Madam Rundholmen, you should retain Mr. Stensgård; he's a bachelor.

Madam Rundholmen. Oh, how you do talk! I won't listen to a word more.   [*Goes out to the right.*

Heire. A substantial woman, sir! Comfortable and well-preserved; no children up to date; money well invested. Education too; she's widely read, sir.

Stensgård. Widely read, eh?

Heire. Hee-hee; she ought to be; she had charge of Alm's circulating library for a couple of years. But your head's full of other things to-day, I daresay.

Stensgård. Not at all; I don't even know that I shall vote. Who are you going to vote for, Mr. Heire?

Heire. Haven't got a vote, sir. There was only one kennel that would qualify in the market, and that you bought.

Stensgård. If you're at a loss for a lodging, I'll give it up to you.

Heire. Hee-hee, you're joking. Ah, youth, youth! What a pleasant humour it has! But now I must be off and have a look at the menagerie. I'm told your whole League is afoot. *(Sees* FIELDBO, *who enters from the back.)* Here's the Doctor, too! I suppose you have come on a scientific mission?

Fieldbo. A scientific mission?

Heire. Yes, to study the epidemic; you've heard of the virulent *rabies agitatoria* that has broken out? God be with you, my dear young friends?   [*Goes out to the right.*

Stensgård. Tell me quickly—have you seen the Chamberlain to-day?

Fieldbo. Yes.

Stensgård. And what did he say?

Fieldbo. What did he say?

Stensgård. Yes; you know I have written to him.

Fielabo. Have you? What did you write?

Stensgård. That I am still of the same mind about his daughter; that I want to talk the matter over with him; and that I propose to call on him to-morrow.

Fieldbo. If I were you, I should at least defer my visit. It is the Chamberlain's birthday to-morrow; a crowd of people will be there——

Stensgård. That's all right; the more the better. I hold big cards in my hand, let me tell you.

Fieldbo. And perhaps you have bluffed a little with your big cards?

Stensgård. How do you mean?

Fieldbo. I mean you have perhaps embellished your declaration of love with a few little threats or so?

Stensgård. Fieldbo, you have seen the letter!

Fieldbo. No, I assure you——

Stensgård. Well, then, frankly—I have threatened him.

Fieldbo. Ah! Then I have, in a way, an answer to your letter.

Stensgård. An answer? Out with it, man!

Fieldbo (shows him a sealed paper). Look here—the Chamberlain's proxy.

Stensgård. And who does he vote for?

Fieldbo. Not for you, at any rate.

Stensgård. For whom then? For whom?

Fieldbo. For the Sheriff and the Provost.*

Stensgård. What! Not even for Lundestad?

Fieldbo. No. And do you know why? Because Lundestad is going to propose you as his successor.

Stensgård. He dares to do this!

Fieldbo. Yes, he does. And he added: "If you see Stensgård, you can tell him how I am voting; it will show him on what footing we stand."

Stensgård. Good; since he will have it so!

Fieldbo. Take care; it's dangerous to tug at an old tower—it may come down on your head.

Stensgård. Oh, I have learnt wisdom in these two days.

Fieldbo. Indeed? You're not so wise but that you let old Lundestad lead you by the nose.

Stensgård. Do you think I haven't seen through Lundestad? Do you think I don't understand that he took me up because he thought I had won over the Chamberlain, and because he wanted to break up our League and keep Monsen out?

Fieldbo. But now that he knows you haven't won over the Chamberlain——

Stensgård. He has gone too far to draw back; and I've made good use of the time, and scattered announcements broadcast. Most of his supporters will abstain from voting; mine are all here——

Fieldbo. It's a big stride from the preliminary election to the final election.

Stensgård. Lundestad knows very well that if he fails me

---

* "Amtmanden og provsten." The "Amtmand" is the chief magistrate of an "Amt" or county; the "Provst" is an ecclesiastical functionary, perhaps equivalent to a rural dean.

in the College of Electors, I'll soon agitate him out of the town Council.

Fieldbo. Not a bad calculation. And to succeed in all this, you feel that you must strike root here more firmly than you have as yet done?

Stensgård. Yes, these people always demand material guarantees, community of interests——

Fieldbo. Just so; and therefore Miss Bratsberg is to be sacrificed?

Stensgård. Sacrificed? If that were so, I should be no better than a scoundrel. But it will be for her happiness, that I'm convinced. What now? Fieldbo, why do you look like that? You have some underhand scheme of your own——

Fieldbo. I?

Stensgård. Yes, you have! You are intriguing against me, behind my back. Why do you do that? Be open with me—will you?

Fieldbo. Frankly, I won't. You are so dangerous, so unscrupulous—well, so reckless at any rate, that one dare not be open with you. Whatever you know, you make use of without hesitation. But this I say to you as a friend: put Miss Bratsberg out of your head.

Stensgård. I cannot. I must extricate myself from these sordid surroundings. I can't go on living in this hugger-mugger way. Here have I got to be hail-fellow-well-met with Dick, Tom, and Harry; to whisper in corners with them, to hob-nob with them, to laugh at their beery witticisms; to be hand in glove with hobbledehoys and unlicked cubs. How can I keep my love of the People untarnished in the midst of all this? I feel as if all the electricity went out of my words. I have no elbow-room, no fresh air to breathe. Oh, a longing comes over me at times for exquisite women! I want something that brings beauty with it! I lie here in a sort of turbid eddy, while out there the clear

blue current sweeps past me—— But what can you understand of all this!

Lundestad (enters from the back) Ah, here we are.
Good-morning, gentlemen.

Stensgård. I have news for you, Mr. Lundestad! **Do**
you know who the Chamberlain is voting for?

Fieldbo. Silence! It's dishonourable of you.

Stensgård. What do I care? He is voting for the Sheriff
and the Provost.

Lundestad. Oh, that was to be expected. You went and
ruined your chances with him—though I implored you to
play your cards neatly.

Stensgård. I shall play them neatly enough—in future.

Fieldbo. Take care—two can play at that game.
[*Goes out to the right.*

Stensgård. That fellow has something up his sleeve.
Have you any idea what it can be?

Lundestad. No, I haven't. But, by-the-bye, I see you
are flourishing in the paper to-day.

Stensgård. I?

Lundestad. Yes, with a nice little epitaph on me.

Stensgård. Oh, that's that beast Aslaksen, of course——

Lundestad. Your attack on the Chamberlain is in too.

Stensgård. I don't know anything about that. If it's to
be war between the Chamberlain and me, I have sharper
weapons.

Lundestad. Indeed!

Stensgård. Have you ever seen this bill? Look at it. Is
it good?

Lundestad. Good, you say? This bill here?

Stensgård. Yes; look closely at it.

Heire (enters from the right). Why, what the deuce can
be the meaning of—— Ah, how interesting! Do remain
as you are, gentlemen, I beg! Do you know what you irre-
sistibly remind me of? Of a summer night in the Far North.

Lundestad. That's a curious simile.

Heire. A very obvious one—the setting and the rising sun together. Delightful, delightful! But, talking of that, what the deuce is the matter outside there? Your fellow citizens are scuttling about like frightened fowls, cackling and crowing and not knowing what perch to settle on.

Stensgård. Well, it's an occasion of great importance.

Heire. Oh, you and your importance! No, it's something quite different, my dear friends. There are whispers of a great failure; a bankruptcy—oh, not political, Mr. Lundestad; I don't mean that!

Stensgård. A bankruptcy?

Heire. Hee-hee! That puts life into our legal friend. Yes, a bankruptcy; some one is on his last legs; the axe is laid to the root of the tree—— I say no more! Two strange gentlemen have been seen driving past; but where to? To whose address? Do you know anything, Mr. Lundestad?

Lundestad. I know how to hold my tongue, Mr. Heire.

Heire. Of course; you are a statesman, a diplomatist. But I must be off and find out all I can about it. It's such sport with these heroes of finance: they are like beads on a string—when one slips off, all the rest follow.

[*Goes out by the back.*

Stensgård. Is there any truth in all this gossip?

Lundestad. You showed me a bill; I thought I saw young Mr. Bratsberg's name upon it?

Stensgård. The Chamberlain's too.

Lundestad. And you asked me if it was good?

Stensgård. Yes; just look at it.

Lundestad. It's perhaps not so good as it might be.

Stensgård. You see it then?

Lundestad. What?

Stensgård. That is is a forgery.

Lundestad. A forgery? Forged bills are often the safest; people redeem them first.

Stensgård. But what do you think? Isn't it a forgery?

Lundestad. I don't much like the look of it.

Stensgård. How so?

Lundestad. I'm afraid there are too many of these about, Mr. Stensgard.

Stensgård. What! It's not possible that——?

Lundestad. If young Mr. Bratsberg slips off the string, those nearest him are only too likely to follow.

Stensgård (seizes his arm). What do you mean by those nearest him?

Lundestad. Who can be nearer than father and son?

Stensgård. Why, good God——!

Lundestad. Remember, I say nothing! It was Daniel Heire that was talking of failure and bankruptcy and——

Stensgård. This is a thunderbolt to me.

Lundestad. Oh, many a man that seemed solid enough has gone to the wall before now. Perhaps he's too good-natured; goes and backs bills; ready money isn't always to be had; property has to be sold for an old song——

Stensgård. And of course this falls on—falls on the children as well.

Lundestad. Yes, I'm heartily grieved for Miss Bratsberg. She didn't get much from her mother; and heaven knows if even the little she has is secured.

Stensgård. Oh, now I undertsand Fieldbo's advice! He's a true friend, after all.

Lundestad. What did Doctor Fieldbo say?

Stensgård. He was too loyal to say anything, but I understand him all the same. And now I understand you too, Mr. Lundestad.

Lundestad. Have you not understood me before?

Stensgård. Not thoroughly. I forget the proverb about the rats and the sinking ship.

Lundestad. That's not a very nice way to put it. But what's the matter with you? You look quite ill. Good God, I haven't gone and blasted your hopes, have I?

Stensgård.—How do you mean?

Lundestad. Yes, yes—I see it all. Old fool that I am! My dear Mr. Stensgård, if you really love the girl, what does it matter whether she is rich or poor?

Stensgård. Matter? No, of course——

Lundestad. Good Lord, we all know happiness isn't a matter of money.

Stensgård. Of course not.

Lundestad. And with industry and determination you'll soon be on your feet again. Don't let poverty frighten you. I know what love is; I went into all that in my young days A happy home; a faithful woman——! My dear young friend, beware how you take any step that may involve you in life-long self-reproach.

Stensgård. But what will become of your plans?

Lundestad. Oh, they must go as best they can. I couldn't think of demanding the sacrifice of your heart!

Stensgård. But I will make the sacrifice. Yes, I will show you that I have the strength for it. Think of the longing multitude out there: they claim me with a sort of voiceless pathos. I cannot, I dare not, fail them!

Lundestad. Yes, but the stake in the district——?

Stensgård. I shall take measures to fulfil the demands of my fellow citizens in that respect, Mr. Lundestad. I see a way, a new way; and I will follow it up. I renounce the happiness of toiling in obscurity for the woman I love. I say to my fellow countrymen: "Here I am—take me!"

Lundestad (looks at him in quiet admiration and presses his hand). You are indeed a man of rare gifts, Mr. Stensgård.   [*Goes out to the right.*

[STENSGÅRD *paces the room several times, now stopping for a moment at the window, now running his fingers through his hair. Presently* BASTIAN MONSEN *enters from the back.*

Bastian. Here I am, my dear friend.*

---

* Bastian now says "thou" (du) to Stensgard—*il le tutoie.*

Stensgård. Where have you come from?

Bastian. From the Nation.

Stensgård. The Nation? What does that mean?

Bastian. Don't you know what the Nation means? It means the People; the common people; those who have nothing, and are nothing; those who lie chained——

Stensgård. What monkey-tricks are these, I should like to know?

Bastian. Monkey-tricks?

Stensgård. I have noticed lately that you go about mimicking me; you imitate even my clothes and my handwriting. Be kind enough to stop that.

Bastian. What do you mean? Don't we belong to the same party?

Stensgård. Yes, but I won't put up with this—you make yourself ridiculous——

Bastian. By being like you?

Stensgård. By aping me. Be sensible now, Monsen, and give it up. It's quite disgusting. But look here—can you tell me when your father is coming back?

Bastian. I have no idea. I believe he's gone to Christiania; he may not be back for a week or so.

Stensgård. Indeed? I'm sorry for that. He has a big stroke of business on hand, I hear.

Bastian. I have a big stroke of business on hand too. Look here, Stensgård, you must do me a service.

Stensgård. Willingly. What is it?

Bastian. I feel so full of energy. I have to thank you for that; you have stimulated me. I feel I must do something, Stensgård:—I want to get married.

Stensgård. To get married? To whom?

Bastian. Sh! Some one in this house.

Stensgård. Madam Rundholmen?

Bastian. Sh! Yes, it's her. Put in a good word for me, do! This sort of thing is just the thing for me. She's in the swim, you know; she's on the best of terms with the

Chamberlain's people, ever since her sister was housekeeper there. If I get her, perhaps I shall get the town-contracts too. So that on the whole—damn it, I love her!

Stensgård. Oh, love, love! Have done with that sickening hypocrisy.

Bastian. Hypocrisy!

Stensgård. Yes; you are lying to yourself, at any rate. You talk in one breath of town-contracts and of love. Why not call a spade a spade? There's something sordid about all this; I will have nothing to do with it.

Bastian. But listen——!

Stensgård. Do your dirty work yourself, I say! *(To* FIELDBO, *who enters from the right.)* Well, how goes the election?

Fieldbo. Excellently for you, it appears. I saw Lundestad just now; he said you were getting all the votes.

Stensgård. Am I indeed?

Fieldbo. But what good will they do you? Since you're not a man of property——

Stensgård (between his teeth). Isn't it confounded!

Fieldbo. Well, you can't do two things at once. If you win on the one side, you must be content to lose on the other. Good-bye! *[Goes out by the back.*

Bastian. What did he mean by winning and losing?

Stensgård. I'll tell you afterwards. But now, my dear Monsen—to return to what we were talking about—I promised to put in a good word for you——

Bastian. You promised? On the contrary, I thought you said——?

Stensgård. Oh, nonsense; you didn't let me explain myself fully. What I meant was that there is something sordid in mixing up your love with town-contracts and so forth; it is an offence against all that is noblest in your nature. So, my dear friend, if you really love the girl——

Bastian. The widow——

Stensgård. Yes, yes; it's all the same. I mean when one

really loves a woman, that in itself should be a conclusive reason——

Bastian. Yes, that's just what I think. So you'll speak for me, will you?

Stensgård. Yes, with great pleasure—but on one condition.

Bastian. What's that?

Stensgård. Tit for tat, my dear Bastian—you must put in a word for me too.

Bastian. I? With whom?

Stensgård. Have you really not noticed anything? Yet it's before your very nose.

Bastian. You surely don't mean——?

Stensgård. Your sister Ragna? Yes, it is she. Oh, you don't know how I have been moved by the sight of her quiet, self-sacrificing devotion to her home——

Bastian. Do you really mean to say so?

Stensgård. And you, with your penetrating eye, have suspected nothing?

Bastian. Yes, at one time I did think——; but now people are talking of your hanging about the Chamberlain's——

Stensgård. Oh, the Chamberlain's! Well, Monsen, I'll tell you frankly that for a moment I did hesitate; but, thank goodness, that is over; now I see my way quite clear before me.

Bastian. There's my hand. I'll back you up, you may be sure. And as for Ragna—why, she daren't do anything but what I and father wish.

Stensgård. Yes, but your father—that's just what I wanted to say——

Bastian. Sh! There—I hear Madam Rundholmen. Now's your chance to speak for me, if she's not too busy; for then she's apt to be snappish. You do your best, my dear fellow, and leave the rest to me. Do you happen to have seen Aslaksen?

Stensgård. He's probably at the polling-booth.

[BASTIAN *goes out by the back, as* MADAM RUND-
HOLMEN *enters from the right.*

Madam Rundholmen.   Things are going as smooth as possible, Mr. Stensgård; every one is voting for you.

Stensgård. That's very odd.

Madam Rundholmen. Goodness knows what Monsen of
Stonelee will say.

Stensgård. I want a word with you, Madam Rundholmen.

Madam Rundholmen. Well, what is it?

Stensgård. Will you lisen to me?

Madam Rundholmen. Lord yes, that I will.

Stensgård. Well then: you were talking just now about
being alone in the world——

Madam Rundholmen. Oh, it was that horrid old
Heire——

Stensgård. You were saying how hard it is for an un-
protected widow——

Madam Rundholmen. Yes, indeed; you should just try
it, Mr. Stensgård!

Stensgård. But now if there came a fine young man——

Madam Rundholmen. A fine young man?

Stensgård. One who had long loved you in secret——

Madam Rundholmen. Oh, come now, Mr. Stensgård, I
won't hear any more of your nonsense.

Stensgård. You must! A young man who, like yourself, finds it hard to be alone in the world——

Madam Rundholmen. Well, what then? I don't understand you at all.

Stensgård. If you could make two people happy, Madam
Rundholmen—yourself and——

Madam Rundholmen. And a fine young man?

Stensgård. Just so; now, answer me——

Madam Rundholmen. Mr. Stensgård, you can'l be in
earnest?

Stensgård. You don't suppose I would jest on such a subject? Should you be disposed——?

Madam Rundholmen. Yes, that I am, the Lord knows! Oh, you dear, sweet——

Stensgård (recoiling a step). What is this?

Madam Rundholmen. Bother, here comes some one!

RAGNA MONSEN *enters hastily, and in evident disquietude, from the back.*

Ragna. I beg your pardon—isn't my father here?

Madam Rundholmen. Your father? Yes; no;—I—I don't know—excuse me——

Ragna. Where is he?

Madam Rundholmen. Your father? Oh, he drove past here——

Stensgård. Towards Christiania.

Ragna. No; it's impossible——

Madam Rundholmen. Yes, I know for certain he drove down the road. Oh, my dear Miss Monsen, you can't think how happy I am! Wait a moment—I'll just run to the cellar, and fetch up a bottle of the real thing.

[*Goes out to the left.*

Stensgård. Tell me, Miss Monsen—is it really your father you are looking for?

Ragna. Yes, of course it is.

Stensgård. And you didnt know that he had gone away?

Ragna. Oh, how should I know? They tell me nothing. But to Christiania——? That's impossible; they would have met him. Good-bye!

Stensgård (intercepts her). Ragna! Tell me! Why are you so changed towards me?

Ragna. I? Let me pass! Let me go!

Stensgård. No, you shall not go! I believe Providence guided you here at this moment. Oh, why do you shrink from me? You used not to.

Ragna. Ah, that is all over, thank God!

Stensgård. But why?

Ragna. I have learnt to know you better; it is well that I learned in time.

Stensgård. Oh, that is it? People have been lying about me? Perhaps I am to blame too; I have been lost in a maze of perplexities. But that is past now. Oh, the very sight of you makes a better man of me. It is you I care for, deeply and truly; it is you I love, Ragna—you and no other!

Ragna. Let me pass! I am afraid of you——

Stensgård. Oh, but to-morrow, Ragna—may I come and speak to you to-morrow?

Ragna. Yes, yes, if you must; only for heaven's sake not to-day.

Stensgård. Only not to-day! Hurrah! I have won; now I am happy!

Madam Rundholmen (enters from the left with cake and wine). Come now, we must drink a glass for luck.

Stensgård. For luck in love! Here's to love and happiness! Hurrah for to-morrow!   [*He drinks.*

Helle (entering, from the right, to RAGNA). Have you found him?

Ragna. No, he is not here. Come, come!

Madam Rundholmen. Heaven help us, what's the matter?

Helle. Nothing; only some visitors have arrived at Stonelee——

Ragna. Thanks for all your kindness, Madam Rundholmen——

Madam Rundholmen. Oh, have you got visitors on your hands again?

Ragna. Yes, yes; excuse me; I must go home. Goodbye!

Stensgård. Good-bye—till to-morrow!

[RAGNA *and* HELLE *go out by the back.*
DANIEL HEIRE *enters from the right.*

Heire. Ha-ha! It's going like a house on fire! They're all cackling Stensgård, Stensgård, Stensgård! They're all plumping for you. Now you should plump for him too, Madam Rundholmen!

Madam Rundholmen. Hey, that's an idea! Are they all voting for him?

Heire. Unanimously—Mr. Stensgård enjoys the confidence of the constituency, as the saying is. Old Lundestad is going about with a face like a pickled cucumber. Oh, it's a pleasure to see it all.

Madam Rundholmen. They shan't regret having voted for him. If I can't vote, I can stand treat.

[*Goes out to the left.*

Heire. Ah, you are the man for the widows, Mr. Stensgård! I'll tell you what—if you can only get hold of her, you're a made man, sir!

Stensgård. Get hold of Madam Rundholmen?

Heire. Yes, why not? She's a substantial woman in every sense of the word. She'll be mistress of the situation as soon as the Stonelee card-castle has come to grief.

Stensgård. There's nothing wrong at Stonelee, is there?

Heire. Isn't there? You have a short memory, my dear sir. Didn't I tell you there were rumours of failure, and bankruptcy, and——?

Stensgård. Well, what then?

Heire. What then? That's just what we want to know. There's a hue and cry after Monsen; two men have come to Stonelee——

Stensgård. Yes, I know—a couple of visitors——

Heire. Uninvited visitors, my dear young friend; there are whispers of the police and infuriated creditors—there's something queer about the accounts, you must know! Talking of that—what paper was that Monsen gave you yesterday?

Stensgård. Oh, just a paper—— Something queer about the accounts, you say? Look here! you know Chamberlain Bratsberg's signature?

Heire. Hee-hee! I should rather think I did.

Stensgård (produces the bill). Well, look at this.

Heire. Give it here—I'm rather short-sighted, you know. *(After examining it.)* That, my dear sir? That's not the Chamberlain's hand.

Stensgård. Not? Then it is——?

Heire. And it's drawn by Monsen?

Stensgård. No, by young Mr. Bratsberg.

Heire. Nonsense! Let me see. *(Looks at the paper and hands it back again.)* You can light your cigar with this.

Stensgård. What! The drawer's name too——?

Heire. A forgery, young man; a forgery, as sure as my name's Daniel. You have only to look at it with the keen eye of suspicion——

Stensgård. But how can that be? Monsen can't have known——

Heire. Monsen? No, he knows nothing about either his own paper or other people's. But I'm glad it has come to an end, Mr. Stensgård!—It's a satisfaction to one's moral sense. Ah, I have often glowed with a noble indignation, if I may say so, at having to stand by and see—— I say no more! But the best of it all is that now Monsen is down he'll drag young Bratsberg after him; and the son will bring the father down——

Stensgård Yes, so Lundestad said.

Heire. But of course there's method even in bankruptcy. You'll see; I am an old hand at prophecy. Monsen will go to prison; young Bratsberg will compound with his creditors; and the Chamberlain will be placed under trustees; that's to say, his creditors will present him with an annuity of a couple of thousand dollars. That's how things go, Mr. Stensgård, I know it, I know it! What says the classic? *Fiat justitia, pereat mundus;* which means: Fie on what's called justice in this wicked world, sir!

Stensgård (pacing the room). One after the other! Both ways barred!

Heire. What the deuce——?

Stensgård. And now too! Just at this moment!

Aslaksen (enters from the right). I congratulate you, chosen of the people!

Stensgård. Elected!

Aslaksen. Elected by 117 votes, and Lundestad by 53. The rest all nowhere.

Heire. Your first step on the path of glory, Mr. Stensgård.

Aslaksen. And it shall cost you a bowl of punch——

Heire. Well, it's the first step that costs, they say.

Aslaksen (goes off to the left, shouting). Punch, Madam Rundholmen! A bowl of punch! The chosen of the people stands treat!

LUNDESTAD, *and after him several* ELECTORS,
enter from the right.

Heire (in a tone of condolence to LUNDESTAD*).* Fifty-three! That's the grey-haired patriot's reward!

Lundestad (whispers to STENSGÅRD*).* Are you firm in your resolve?

Stensgård. What's the use of being firm when everything is tumbling about your ears?

Lundestad. Do you think the game is lost?

Aslaksen (returning by the left). Madam Rundholmen stands treat herself. She says she has the best right to.

Stensgård (struck by an idea). Madam Rundholmen!— has the best right to——!

Lundestad. What?

Stensgård. The game is not lost, Mr. Lundestad!

[*Sits at the right-hand table and writes.*

Lundestad (in a low voice). Oh, Aslaksen—can you get something into your next paper for me?

Aslaksen. Of course I can. Is it libellous?

Lundestad. No, certainly not!

Aslaksen. Well, never mind; I'll take it all the same.

Lundestad. It is my political last will and testament; I shall write it to-night.

A Maid-servant (enters from the left). The punch, with Madam Rundholmen's compliments.

Aslaksen. Hurrah! Now there's some life in the local situation.

> [*He places the punch-bowl on the middle table, serves the others, and drinks freely himself during the following scene.* BASTIAN MONSEN *has meanwhile entered from the right.*

Bastian (softly). You won't forget my letter?

Aslaksen. Don't be afraid. *(Taps his breast pocket.)* I have it here.

Bastian. You'll deliver it as soon as you can—when you see she's disengaged, you understand.

Aslaksen. I understand. *(Calls.)* Come, now, the glasses are filled.

Bastian. You shan't do it for nothing, I promise you.

Aslaksen. All right, all right. *(To the servant.)* A lemon, Karen—quick as the wind!   [BASTIAN *retires.*

Stensgård. A word, Aslaksen; shall you be passing here to-morrow evening?

Aslaksen. To-morrow evening? I can, if you like.

Stensgård. Then you might look in and give Madam Rundholmen this letter.

Aslaksen. From you?

Stensgård. Yes. Put it in your pocket. There now. To-morrow evening, then?

Aslaksen. All right; trust to me.

> [*The servant brings the lemon;* STENSGÅRD *goes towards the window.*

Bastian. Well—have you spoken to Madam Rundholmen?

Stensgård. Spoken? Oh yes, I said a word or two——

Bastian. And what do you think?

Stensgård. Oh—well—we were interrupted. I can't say anything definite.

Bastian. I'll take my chance all the same; she's always

complaining of her loneliness. My fate shall be sealed within an hour.

Stensgård. Within an hour?

Bastian (sees MADAM RUNDHOLMEN, *who enters from the left).* Sh! Not a word to any one!

[*Goes towards the back.*

Stensgård (whispers to ASLAKSEN*).* Give me back the letter.

Aslaksen. Do you want it back?

Stensgård. Yes, at once; I shall deliver it myself.

Aslaksen. Very well; here it is.

[STENSGÅRD *thrusts the letter into his pocket, and mixes with the rest.*

Madam Rundholmen (to BASTIAN*).* What do you say to the election, Mr. Bastian?

Bastian. I'm delighted. Stensgård and I are bosom friends, you know. I shouldn't be surprised if he got into Parliament.

Madam Rundholmen. But your father wouldn't much like that.

Bastian. Oh, father has so many irons in the fire. Besides, if Stensgård's elected, it will still be all in the family, I daresay.

Madam Rundholmen. How so?

Bastian. He wants to marry——

Madam Rundholmen. Lord! Has he said anything?

Bastian. Yes; and I've promised to put in a word for him. It'll be all right. I'm sure Ragna likes him.

Madam Rundholmen. Ragna!

Lundestad (approaching). What is interesting you so deeply, Madam Rundholmen?

Madam Rundholmen. What do you think he says? Why, that Mr. Stensgård's making up to——

Lundestad. Yes, but he won't find the Chamberlain so easy to deal with.

Bastian. The Chamberlain?

Lundestad. He probably thinks her too good a match for a mere lawyer——

Madam Rundholmen. Who? Who?

Lundestad. Why, his daughter, Miss Bratsberg, of course.

Bastian. He's surely not making love to Miss Bratsberg?

Lundestad. Yes, indeed he is.

Madam Rundholmen. You are quite sure of that?

Bastian. And he told me——! Oh, I want to say a word to you!

[LUNDESTAD *and* BASTIAN *go towards the back.*

Madam Rundholmen (approaching STENSGÅRD*).* You must be on your guard, Mr. Stensgård.

Stensgård. Against whom?

Madam Rundholmen. Against malicious people who are slandering you.

Stensgård. Why, let them—so long as one person doesn't believe their slanders.

Madam Rundholmen. And who may that one person be?

Stensgård (slips the letter into her hand). Take this· read it when you are alone.

Madam Rundholmen. Ah, I knew it!

[*Goes off to the left.*

Ringdal (enters from the right). Well, I hear you have won a brilliant victory, Mr. Stensgård.

Stensgård. Yes, I have, Mr. Ringdal, in spite of your noble chief's endeavours.

Ringdal. His endeavours? What to do?

Stensgård. To keep me out.

Ringdal. Like other people, he has a right to vote as he pleases.

Stensgård. It's a pity he is not likely to retain that right for long.

Ringdal. What do you mean?

Stensgård. I mean, since his affairs are not so straight as they might be——

Ringdal. His affairs! What affairs! What have you got into your head?

Stensgård. Oh, you needn't pretend ignorance. Isn't there a storm brewing?—a great crash impending?

Ringdal. Yes, so I hear on all sides.

Stensgård. And aren't both the Bratsbergs involved in it?

Ringdal. My dear sir, are you crazy?

Stensgård. Oh, you naturally want to keep it dark.

Ringdal. What good would that be? That sort of thing can't be kept dark.

Stensgård. Is it not true then?

Ringdal. Not a word of it, so far as the Chamberlain is concerned. How could you believe such nonsense? Who has been humbugging you?

Stensgård. I won't tell you just yet.

Ringdal. Well, you needn't; but whoever it was must have had a motive.

Stensgård. A motive——!

Ringdal. Yes, just think: is there no one who has an interest in keeping you and the Chamberlain apart?

Stensgård. Yes, on my soul, but there is though!

Ringdal. The Chamberlain in reality thinks very highly of you——

Stensgård. Does he?

Ringdal. Yes, and that's why people want to make mischief between you. They reckon on your ignorance of the situation, on your impulsiveness and your confiding disposition——

Stensgård. Oh, the vipers! And Madam Rundholmen has my letter!

Ringdal. What letter?

Stensgård. Oh, nothing. But it's not too late! My dear Mr. Ringdal, shall you see the Chamberlain this evening?

Ringdal. In all probability.

Stensgård. Then tell him to think no more of those threats

—he will understand; tell him I shall call to-morrow and explain everything.

Ringdal. You'll call?

Stensgård. Yes, to prove to him—— Ah, a proof! Look here, Mr. Ringdal; will you give the Chamberlain this bill from me?

Ringdal. This bill——?

Stensgård. Yes; it's a matter I can't explain to you; but just you give it to him——

Ringdal. Upon my word, Mr. Stensgård——

Stensgård. And just add these words from me: This is how I treat those who vote against me!

Ringdal. I shan't forget.   [*Goes out at the back.*

Stensgård. I say, Mr. Heire—how could you go and palm off that story about the Chamberlain upon me?

Heire. How could I palm it off on you——?

Stensgård. Yes—it's a lie from beginning to end.

Heire. No! Is it indeed? I'm delighted to hear it. Do you hear, Mr. Lundestad? It's all a lie about the Chamberlain.

Lundestad. Sh! We were on a false scent; it's nearer at hand.

Stensgård. How nearer at hand?

Lundestad. I know nothing for certain; but they talk of Madam Rundholmen——

Stensgård. What!

Heire. Haven't I prophesied it! She has been too much mixed up with our friend at Stonelee——

Lundestad. He drove off this morning before daylight——

Heire. And his family is out hunting for him——

Lundestad. And the son has been doing all he knows to get his sister provided for——

Stensgård. Provided for! "To-morrow" she said; and then her anxiety about her father——!

Heire. Hee-hee! You'll see he's gone and hanged himself, sir!

Aslaksen. Has any one hanged himself?

Lundestad. Mr. Heire says Monsen of Stonelee——

Monsen (enters from the back). A dozen of champagne!

Aslaksen and Others. Monsen!

Monsen. Yes, Monsen! Champagne-Monsen! Money-Monsen! Let's have the wine, confound it all!

Heire. But, my dear sir——

Stensgård. Why, where have you dropped from?

Monsen. I've been doing a stroke of business, sir! Cleared a hundred thousand! Hei! To-morrow I'll give a thundering dinner at Stonelee. I invite you all. Champagne, I say! I congratulate you, Stensgård! I hear you're elected.

Stensgård. Yes; I must explain to you——

Monsen. Pooh; what does it matter to me? Wine, I say! Where is Madam Rundholmen?

[*Makes a motion to go out to the left.*

The Maid-servant (who has just entered, intercepts him). No one can see the mistress just now; she's got a letter——

Bastian. Oh, damn it all! [*Goes out by the back.*

Stensgård. Is she reading it?

Servant. Yes; and it seems quite to have upset her.

Stensgård. Good-bye, Mr. Monsen; dinner at Stonelee to-morrow——?

Monsen. Yes, to-morrow. Good-bye!

Stensgård (whispers). Mr. Heire, will you do me a service?

Heire. Certainly, certainly.

Stensgård. Then just run me down a little to Madam Rundholmen; indulge in an innuendo or two at my expense. You are so good at that sort of thing.

Heire. What the deuce is the meaning of this?

Stensgård. I have my reasons. It's a joke, you know——

a wager with—with some one you have a grudge against.

Heire. Aha, I understand. I say no more!

Stensgård. Don't go too far, you know. Just place me in a more or less equivocal light—make her a little suspicious of me, for the moment.

Heire. Rely upon me; it will be a real pleasure to me.

Stensgård. Thanks, thanks in advance. *(Goes towards the table.)* Mr. Lundestad, we shall meet to-morrow forenoon at the Chamberlain's.

Lundestad. Have you hopes?

Stensgård. A three-fold hope.

Lundestad. Threefold? I don't understand——

Stensgård. You needn't. Henceforth, I will be my own counsellor. [*Goes out by the back.*

Monsen (at the punch-bowl). Another glass, Aslaksen! Where's Bastian?

Aslaksen. He's just gone out. But I have a letter to deliver for him.

Monsen. Have you?

Aslaksen. To Madam Rundholmen.

Monsen. Ah, at last!

Aslaksen. But not till to-morrow evening, he said; to-morrow evening, neither sooner nor later. Here's to you!

Heire (to LUNDESTAD*).* What the deuce is all this business between Stensgård and Madam Rundholmen?

Lundestad (whispers). He's courting her.

Heire. I suspected as much! But he asked me to run him down a bit—to cast a slur on his character——

Lundestad. And you said you would?

Heire. Yes, of course.

Lundestad. I believe he says of you that your word is as good as your bond—and no better.

Heire. Hee-hee—the dear fellow! He shall find out his mistake this time.

Madam Rundholmen (with an open letter in her hand, at the door on the left). Where is Mr. Stensgård?

Heire. He kissed your chambermaid and went, Madam Rundholmen!

ACT FIFTH

Large reception-room at the CHAMBERLAIN'S. *Entrance door*
at the back. Doors right and left.
RINGDAL *stands at a table looking through some papers.* A
knock.

Ringdal. Come in.

Fieldbo (from the back). Good-morning.

Ringdal. Good-morning, Doctor.

Fieldbo. All well, eh?

Ringdal. Oh, yes, well enough; but——

Fieldbo. What?

Ringdal. Of course you've heard the great news?

Fieldbo. No. What is it?

Ringdal. Do you mean to say you haven't heard what
has happened at Stonelee?

Fieldbo. No.

Ringdal. Monsen has absconded.

Fieldbo. Absconded! Monsen?

Ringdal. Absconded.

Fieldbo. Great heavens——!

Ringdal. There were ugly rumours yesterday; but then
Monsen turned up again; he managed to throw dust in people's eyes——

Fieldbo. But the reason? The reason?

Ringdal. Enormous losses in timber, they say. Several
houses in Christiania have stopped payment, and so——

Fieldbo. And so he has gone off!

227

Ringdal. To Sweden, probably. The authorities took possession at Stonelee this morning. Things are being inventoried and sealed up——

Fieldbo. And the unfortunate children——?

Ringdal. The son seems to have kept clear of the business; at least I hear he puts a bold face on it.

Fieldbo. But the daughter?

Ringdal. Sh! The daughter is here.

Fieldbo. Here?

Ringdal. The tutor brought her and the two little ones here this morning. Miss Bratsberg is looking after them, quietly you know.

Fieldbo. And how does she bear it?

Ringdal. Oh, pretty well, I fancy. You may guess, after the treatment she has met with at home— — And, besides, I may tell you she is—— Ah, here's the Chamberlain.

The Chamberlain (from the left). So you are there, my dear Doctor?

Fieldbo. Yes, I am pretty early astir. Let me wish you many happy returns of the day, Chamberlain.

The Chamberlain. Oh, as for happiness——! But thank you, all the same; I know you mean it kindly.

Fieldbo. And may I ask, Chamberlain——?

The Chamberlain. One word: be good enough to drop that title.

Fieldbo. What do you mean?

The Chamberlain. I am an ironmaster, and nothing more.

Fieldbo. Why, what strange notion is this?

The Chamberlain. I have renounced my post and my title. I am sending in my resignation to-day.

Fieldbo. You should sleep upon that.

The Chamberlain. When his Majesty was graciously pleased to assign me a place in his immediate circle, he did so because of the unblemished honour of my family through long generations.

Fieldbo. Well, what then?

The Chamberlain. My family is disgraced, just as much as Mr. Monsen's. Of course, you have heard about Monsen?

Fieldbo. Yes, I have.

The Chamberlain (to RINGDAL*).* Any further news about him?

Ringdal. Only that he brings down with him a good many of the younger men.

The Chamberlain. And my son?

Ringdal. Your son has sent me his balance-sheet. He will be able to pay in full; but there will be nothing over.

The Chamberlain. H'm. Then will you get my resignation copied?

Ringdal. I'll see to it.

[*Goes out by the foremost door on the right.*

Fieldbo. Have you reflected what you are doing? Things can be arranged without any one being a bit the wiser.

The Chamberlain. Indeed! Can I make myself ignorant of what has happened?

Fieldbo. Oh, after all, what has happened? Has not he written to you, acknowledged his fault, and begged for your forgiveness? This is the only time he has done anything of the sort; why not simply blot it out?

The Chamberlain. Would you do what my son has done?

Fieldbo. He won't repeat it; that is the main point.

The Chamberlain. How do you know he will not repeat it?

Fieldbo. If for no other reason, because of what you yourself told me—the scene with your daughter-in-law. Whatever else comes of it, that will steady him.

The Chamberlain (pacing the room). My poor Selma! Our peace and happiness gone!

Fieldbo. There are higher things than peace and happiness. Your happiness has been an illusion. Yes, I must speak frankly to you: in that, as in many other things, you have built on a hollow foundation. You have been short-sighted and over-weening, Chamberlain!

The Chamberlain (stops short). I?

Fieldbo. Yes, you! You have plumed yourself on your family honour; but when has that honour been tried? Are you sure it would have stood the test?

The Chamberlain. You can spare your sermons, Doctor. Do you think I have not learnt a lesson from the events of these days?

Fieldbo. I daresay you have; but prove it, by showing greater tolerance and clearer insight. You reproach your son; but what have you done for him? You have taken care to develop his faculties, but not to form his character. You have lectured him on what he owed to the honour of his family; but you have not guided and moulded him so that honour became to him an irresistible instinct.

The Chamberlain. Do you think so?

Fieldbo. I not only think, I know it. But that is generally the way here: people are bent on learning, not on living. And you see what comes of it; you see hundreds of men with great gifts, who never seem to be more than half ripe; who are one thing in their ideas and feelings, and something quite different in their habits and acts. Just look at Stensgård——

The Chamberlain. Ah, Stensgård now! What do you make of Stensgård?

Fieldbo. A patchwork. I have known him from childhood. His father was a mere rag of a man, a withered weed, a nobody. He kept a little huckster's shop, and eked things out with pawnbroking; or rather his wife did for him. She was a coarse-grained woman, the most unwomanly I ever knew. She had her husband declared incapable;* she had not an ounce of heart in her. And in that home Stensgård passed his childhood. Then he went to the grammar-school. "He shall go to college," said his mother; "I'll make a smart solicitor of him." Squalor at home, high-pressure at school;

---

* "Gjort umyndig"=placed under a legal interdict.

soul, temperament, will, talents, all pulling in different ways
—what could it lead to but disintegration of character?

The Chamberlain. What could it lead to, eh? I should
like to know what is good enough for you. We are to expect
nothing of Stensgård; nothing of my son; but we may look
to you, I suppose—to you——?

Fieldbo. Yes, to me—precisely. Oh, you needn't laugh;
I take no credit to myself; but my lot has been one that be-
gets equilibrium and firmness of character. I was brought
up amid the peace and harmony of a modest middle-class
home. My mother is a woman of the finest type; in our
home we had no desires that outstripped our opportunities,
no cravings that were wrecked on the rocks of circumstance;
and death did not break in upon our circle, leaving emptiness
and longing behind it. We were brought up in the love of
beauty, but it informed our whole view of life, instead of
being a side-interest, a thing apart. We were taught to shun
excesses, whether of the intellect or of the feelings——

The Chamberlain. Bless me! So that accounts for your
being the pink of perfection?

Fieldbo. I am far from thinking so. I only say that fate
had been infinitely kind to me, and that I regard its favours
in the light of obligations.

The Chamberlain. Very well; but if Stensgård is under no
such obligations, it is all the more to his credit that he——

Fieldbo. What? What is to his credit?

The Chamberlain. You have misjudged him, my good
Doctor. Look here. What do you say to this?

Fieldbo. Your son's bill!

The Chamberlain. Yes; he has sent it to me.

Fieldbo. Of his own accord?

The Chamberlain. Of his own accord, and uncondition-
ally. It is fine; it is noble. From this day forth, my house
is open to him.

Fieldbo. Think again! For your own sake, for your
daughter's——

The Chamberlain. Oh, let me alone! He is better than you in many ways. At any rate he is straightforward, while you are underhand in your dealings.

Fieldbo. I?

The Chamberlain. Yes, you! You have made yourself the master of this house; you come and go as you please; I consult you about everything—and yet——

Fieldbo. Well?—And yet?

The Chamberlain. And yet there's always something confoundedly close about you; yes, and something—something uppish that I cannot endure!

Fieldbo. Please explain yourself!

The Chamberlain. I? No, it is you that ought to explain yourself! But now you must take the consequences.

Fieldbo. We don't understand each other, Chamberlain. I have no bill to give up to you; yet, who knows but I may be making a greater sacrifice for your sake?

The Chamberlain. Indeed! How so?

Fieldbo. By holding my tongue.

The Chamberlain. Holding your tongue, indeed! Shall I tell you what I am tempted to do? To forget my manners, use bad language, and join the League of Youth. You are a stiff-necked Pharisee, my good Doctor; and that sort of thing is out of place in our free society. Look at Stensgård; he is not like that; so he shall come here whenever he likes; he shall—he shall——! Oh, what's the use of talking——! You must take the consequences; as you make your bed, so you must lie.

Lundestad (enters from the back). My congratulations, Chamberlain! May you long enjoy the respect and——

The Chamberlain. Oh, go to the devil—I'm almost inclined to say! That's all humbug, my dear Lundestad. There's nothing but humbug in this world.

Lundestad. That is what Mr. Monsen's creditors are saying.

The Chamberlain. Ah, about Monsen—didn't it come upon you like a thunderbolt?

Lundestad. Oh, you have often prophesied it, Chamberlain.

The Chamberlain. H'm, h'm;—yes, to be sure I have. I prophesied it only the day before yesterday; he came here trying to get money out of me——

Fieldbo. It might have saved him.

Lundestad. Impossible; he was too deep in the mire; and whatever is, is for the best.

The Chamberlain. That is your opinion? Was it for the best, then, that you were beaten at the poll yesterday?

Lundestad. I wasn't beaten; everything went just as I wanted. Stensgård is not a man to make an enemy of; he has got what we others have to whistle for.

The Chamberlain. I don't quite understand what you mean——?

Lundestad. He has the power of carrying people away with him. And then he has the luck to be unhampered by either character, or conviction, or social position; so that Liberalism is the easiest thing in the world to him.

The Chamberlain. Well, really, I should have thought we were all Liberals.

Lundestad. Yes, of course we are Liberals, Chamberlain; not a doubt of it. But the thing is that we are Liberal only on our own behalf, whereas Stensgård's Liberalism extends to other people. That's the novelty of the thing.

The Chamberlain. And you are going over to these subversive ideas?

Lundestad. I've read in old story-books about people who could summon up spirits, but could not lay them again.

The Chamberlain. Why, my dear Lundestad, how can a man of your enlightenment——?

Lundestad. I know it's mere popish superstition, Chamberlain. But new ideas are like those spirits: it's not so easy to lay them; the best plan is to compromise with them as best you can.

The Chamberlain. But now that Monsen has fallen, and no doubt his crew of agitators with him——

Lundestad. If Monsen's fall had come two or three days ago, things would have been very different.

The Chamberlain. Yes, unfortunately. You have been too hasty.

Lundestad. Partly out of consideration for you, Chamberlain.

The Chamberlain. For me?

Lundestad. Our party must keep up its reputation in the eyes of the people. We represent the old, deep-rooted Norse sense of honour. If I had deserted Stensgård, you know he holds a paper——

The Chamberlain. Not now.

Lundestad. What?

The Chamberlain. Here it is.

Lundestad. He has given it up to you?

The Chamberlain. Yes. Personally, he is a gentleman; so much I must say for him.

Lundestad (thoughtfully). Mr. Stensgård has rare abil-'ties.

Stensgård (at the back, standing in the doorway). May I come in?

The Chamberlain (going to meet him). I am delighted to see you.

Stensgård. And you will accept my congratulations?

The Chamberlain. With all my heart.

Stensgård. Then with all my heart I wish you happiness! And you must forget all the stupid things I have written.

The Chamberlain. I go by deeds, not words, Mr. Stensgård.

Stensgård. How good of you to say so!

The Chamberlain. And henceforth—since you wish it— you must consider yourself at home here.

Stensgård. May I? May I really?

[*A knock at the door.*

The Chamberlain. Come in.

Several LEADING MEN *of the neighbourhood,* TOWN COUN-
CILLORS, *etc., enter.* THE CHAMBERLAIN *goes to receive them, accepts their congratulations, and converses
with them.*

*Thora (who has meantime entered by the second door on
the left).* Mr. Stensgård, let me thank you.

Stensgård. You, Miss Bratsberg!

Thora. My father has told me how nobly you have acted.

Stensgård. But——?

Thora. Oh, how we have misjudged you!

Stensgård. Have you——?

Thora. It was your own fault—— No, no; it was ours.
Oh, what would I not do to atone for our error.

Stensgård. Would you? You yourself? Would you
really——?

Thora. All of us would; if we only knew——

The Chamberlain. Refreshments for these gentlemen, my
child.

Thora. They are just coming.

[*She retires towards the door again, where a* SER-
*vant at the same moment appears with cake and
wine, which are handed round.*

Stensgård. Oh, my dear Lundestad! I feel like a conquering god.

Lundestad. So you must have felt yesterday, I suppose.

Stensgård. Pooh! This is something quite different;
the final triumph; the crown of all! There is a glory, a halo,
over my life.

Lundestad. Oho; dreams of love!

Stensgård. Not dreams! Realities, glorious realities!

Lundestad. So brother Bastian has brought you the answer?

Stensgård. Bastian——?

Lundestad. Yes, he gave me a hint yesterday; he had promised to plead your cause with a certain young lady.

Stensgård. Oh, what nonsense——

Lundestad. Why make a mystery of it? If you haven't heard already, I can give you the news. You have won the day, Mr. Stensgard; I have it from Ringdal.

Stensgård. What have you from Ringdal?

Lundestad. Miss Monsen has accepted you.

Stensgård. What!

Lundestad. Accepted you, I say

Stensgård. Accepted me! And the father has bolted!

Lundestad. But the daughter hasn't.

Stensgård. Accepted me! In the midst of all this family trouble! How unwomanly! How repellant to any man with the least delicacy of feeling! But the whole thing is a misunderstanding. I never commissioned Bastian—— How could that idiot——? However, it doesn't matter to me; he must answer for his follies himself.

Daniel Heire (enters from the back). Hee-hee! Quite a gathering! Of course, of course! We are paying our respects, propitiating the powers that be, as the saying goes. May I, too——

The Chamberlain. Thanks, thanks, old friend!

Heire. Oh, I protest, my dear sir? That is too much condescension. *(New* GUESTS *arrive.)* Ah, here we have the myrmidons of justice—the executive—— I say no more. *(Goes over to* STENSGÅRD.*)* Ah, my dear fortunate youth, are you there? Your hand! Accept the assurance of an old man's unfeigned rejoicing.

Stensgård. At what?

Heire. You asked me yesterday to run you down a little to her—you know——

Stensgård. Yes, yes; what then?

Heire. It was a heartfelt pleasure to me to oblige you——

Stensgård. Well—and what happened then? How did she take it?

Heire. Like a loving woman, of course—burst into tears; locked herself into her room; would neither answer nor show herself——

Stensgård. Ah, thank goodness!

Heire. It's barbarous to subject a widow's heart to such cruel tests, to go and gloat over her jealous agonies! But love has cat's eyes—— I say no more! For to-day, as I drove past, there stood Madam Rundholmen, brisk and buxom, at her open window, combing her hair. She looked like a mermaid, if you'll allow me to say so. Oh, she's a fine woman!

Stensgård. Well, and then?

Heire. Why, she laughed like one possessed, sir, and waved a letter in the air, and called out "A proposal, Mr. Heire! I'm engaged to be married."

Stensgård. What! Engaged?

Heire. My hearty congratulations, young man; I'm inexpressibly pleased to be the first to announce to you——

Stensgård. It's all rubbish! It's nonsense!

Heire. What is nonsense?

Stensgård. You have misunderstood her; or else she has misunderstood—— Engaged! Preposterous! Now that Monsen's down, she'll probably——

Heire. Not at all, sir, not at all! Madam Rundholmen has solid legs to stand on.

Stensgård. No matter! I have quite other intentions. All that about the letter was only a joke—a wager, as I told you. My dear Mr. Heire, do oblige me by not saying a word to any one of this silly affair.

Heire. I see, I see! It's to be kept secret; it's to be a romance. Ah, youth, youth! it's nothing if not poetical.

Stensgård. Yes, yes; mum's the word. You shan't regret it—I'll take up your cases—— Sh! I rely upon you.

[*He retires.*

The Chamberlain (who has meanwhile been talking to LUNDESTAD*).* No, Lundestad—that I really cannot believe!

Lundestad. I assure you, Chamberlain—Daniel Heire told me so himself.

Heire. What did I tell you, may I inquire?

The Chamberlain. Did Mr. Stensgård show you a bill yesterday?

Heire. Yes, by-the-bye——! What on earth was the meaning of all that?

The Chamberlain. I'll tell you afterwards. And you told him——

Lundestad. You persuaded him it was a forgery?

Heire. Pooh, a mere innocent jest, to bewilder him a little in the hour of triumph.

Lundestad. And you told him both signatures were forged?

Heire. Oh, yes; why not both while I was about it?

The Chamberlain. So that was it!

Lundestad (to the CHAMBERLAIN*).* And when he heard that——

The Chamberlain. He gave the bill to Ringdal!

Lundestad. The bill that was useless as a weapon of offence.

The Chamberlain. He shams magnanimity! Makes a fool of me a second time! Gains admission to my house, and makes me welcome him and thank him—this—this——! And this is the fellow——

Heire. Why, what are you going on about, my dear sir?

The Chamberlain. I'll tell you all about it afterwards. *(Takes* LUNDESTAD *apart.)* And this is the fellow you protect, push forward, help to rise!

Lundestad. Well, he took you in, too!

The Chamberlain. Oh, I should like to——!

Lundestad (pointing to STENSGÅRD, *who is speaking to* THORA*).* Look there! What will people be fancying!

The Chamberlain. I shall soon put a stop to these fancies.

Lundestad. Too late, Chamberlain; he'll worm himself forward by dint of promises and general plausibility——

The Chamberlain. I, too, can manœuvre, Mr. Lundestad.

Lundestad. What will you do?

The Chamberlain. Just watch. (*Goes over to* FIELDBO.) Doctor Fieldbo, will you do me a service?

Fieldbo. With pleasure.

The Chamberlain. Then turn that fellow out of my house.

Fieldbo. Stensgård?

The Chamberlain. Yes, the adventurer; I hate his very name; turn him out!

Fieldbo. But how can I——?

The Chamberlain. This is your affair; I give you a free hand.

Fieldbo. A free hand! Do you mean it? Entirely free?

The Chamberlain. Yes, yes, by all means.

Fieldbo. Your hand on it, Chamberlain!

The Chamberlain. Here it is.

Fieldbo. So be it, then; now or never! (*Loudly.*) May I request the attention of the company for a moment?

The Chamberlain. Silence for Doctor Fieldbo!

Fieldbo. With Chamberlain Bratsberg's consent, I have the pleasure of announcing my engagement to his daughter.

> [*An outburst of astonishment.* THORA *utters a slight scream.* THE CHAMBERLAIN *is on the point of speaking, but refrains. Loud talk and congratulations.*

Stensgård. Engagement! Your engagement——

Heire. With the Chamberlain's——? With your—— What does it mean?

Lundestad. Is the Doctor out of his mind?

Stensgård. But, Chamberlain——?

The Chamberlain. What can I do? I am a Liberal. I join the League of Youth!

Fieldbo. Thanks, thanks—and forgive me!

The Chamberlain. Associations are the order of the day, Mr. Stensgård. There is nothing like free competition!

Thora. Oh, my dear father!

Lundestad. Yes, and engagements are the order of the day. I have another to announce.

Stensgård. A mere invention!

Lundestad. No, not a bit of it; Miss Monsen is engaged to——

Stensgård. False, false, I say!

Thora. No, father, it's true; they are both here.

The Chamberlain. Who? Where?

Thora. Ragna and Mr. Helle. They are in here——
    [*Goes towards the second door on the right.*

Lundestad. Mr. Helle! Then it's he——!

The Chamberlain. Here? In my house? (*Goes towards the door.*) Come in, my dear child.

Ragna (*shrinking back shyly*). Oh, no, no; there are so many people.

The Chamberlain. Don't be bashful; you couldn't help what has happened.

Helle. She is homeless now, Chamberlain.

Ragna. Oh, you must help us!

The Chamberlain. I will, indeed; and thank you for giving me the opportunity.

Heire. You may well say engagements are the order of the day. I have one to add to the list.

The Chamberlain. What? You? At your age?—How rash of you!

Heire. Oh——! I say no more.

Lundestad. The game is up, Mr. Stensgård.

Stensgård. Indeed? (*Loudly.*) *I* have one to add to the list, Mr. Heire! An announcement, gentlemen: I, too, have cast anchor for life.

The Chamberlain. What?

Stensgård. One is now and then forced to play a double

game, to conceal one's true intentions. I regard this as permissible when the general weal is at stake. My life-work lies clear before me, and is all in all to me. I consecrate my whole energies to this district; I find here a ferment of ideas which I must strive to clarify. But this task cannot be accomplished by a mere adventurer. The men of the district must gather round one of themselves. Therefore I have determined to unite my interests indissolubly with yours —to unite them by a bond of affection. If I have awakened any false hopes, I must plead for forgiveness. I too am en-gaged.

The Chamberlain. You?

Fieldbo. Engaged?

Heire. I can bear witness.

The Chamberlain. But how——?

Fieldbo. Engaged? To whom?

Lundestad. It surely can't be——?

Stensgård. It is a union both of the heart and of the understanding. Yes, my fellow citizens, I am engaged to Madam Rundholmen.

Fieldbo. To Madam Rundholmen!

The Chamberlain. The storekeeper's widow!

Lundestad. H'm. Indeed!

The Chamberlain. Why, my head's going round! How could you——?

Stensgård. A manœuvre, Mr. Bratsberg!

Lundestad. He has rare abilities!

Aslaksen (looks in at the door, back). I humbly beg par-don——

The Chamberlain. Oh, come in, Aslaksen! A visit of congratulation, eh?

Aslaksen. Oh, not at all; I wouldn't presume—— But I have something very important to say to Mr. Stensgård.

Stensgård. Another time; you can wait outside.

Aslaksen. No, confound it; I must tell you——

Stensgård. Hold your tongue! What intrusiveness is

this?—Yes, gentlemen, strange are the ways of destiny. The district and I required a bond that should bind us firmly together; and I found on my path a woman of ripened character who could make a home for me. I have put off the adventurer, gentlemen, and here I stand in your midst, as one of yourselves. Take me; I am ready to stand or fall in any post your confidence may assign me.

Lundestad. You have won.

The Chamberlain. Well, really, I must say—— (*To the* MAID, *who has entered from the back.*) Well, what is it? What are you giggling about?

The Servant. Madam Rundholmen——?

The Company. Madam Rundholmen?

The Chamberlain. What about her?

The Servant. Madam Rundholmen is waiting outside with her young man——

The Company (to each other). Her young man? Madam Rundholmen! How's this?

Stensgård. What nonsense!

Aslaksen. Yes, I was just telling you——

The Chamberlain (at the door). Come along, come along!

BASTIAN MONSEN, *with* MADAM RUNDHOLMEN *on his arm, enters from the back. A general movement.*

Madam Rundholmen. I hope I'm not intruding, sir——

The Chamberlain. Not at all, not at all!.

Madam Rundholmen. But I couldn't resist bringing up my young man to show him to you and Miss Bratsberg.

The Chamberlain. Yes, I hear you are engaged; but——

Thora. We didn't know——

Stensgård (to ASLAKSEN). How is all this——?

Aslaksen. I had so much in my head yesterday; so much to think about, I mean——

Stensgard. But I gave her my letter, and——

Aslaksen. No, you gave her Bastian Monsen's; here is yours.

Stensgård. Bastian's? And here——? *(Glances at the address, crumples the letter together, and crams it into his pocket.)* Oh, curse you for a blunderer!

Madam Rundholmen. Of course I was willing enough. There's no trusting the men-folk, I know; but when you have it in black and white that their intentions are honourable—— Why, there's Mr. Stensgård, I declare. Well, Mr. Stensgård, won't you congratulate me?

Heire (to LUNDESTAD*).* How hungrily she glares at him.

The Chamberlain. Of course he will, Madam Rundholmen; but won't you congratulate your sister-in-law to be?

Madam Rundholmen. Who?

Thora. Ragna; she is engaged, too.

Bastian. Are you, Ragna?

Madam Rundholmen. Indeed? Yes, Bastian told me there was something in the wind. I wish you both joy; and welcome into the family, Mr. Stensgård!

Fieldbo. No, no; not Stensgård!

The Chamberlain. No, it's Mr. Helle; an excellent choice. And, by-the-bye, you may congratulate my daughter, too.

Madam Rundholmen. Miss Bratsberg! Ah, so Lundestad was right, after all. I congratulate you, Miss Thora; and you, too, Mr. Stensgård.

Fieldbo. You mean Doctor Fieldbo.

Madam Rundholmen. What?

Fieldbo. I am the happy man.

Madam Rundholmen. Well, now, I don't in the least know where I am.

The Chamberlain. And we have just found out where we are.

Stensgård. Excuse me; I have an appointment——

The Chamberlain (aside). Lundestad, what was the other word?

Lundestad. What other?

The Chamberlain. Not adventurer, but the other——?

Lundestad. Demagogue.

Stensgård.—I take my leave.

The Chamberlain. One word—only one word, Mr. Stensgård—a word which has long been on the tip of my tongue.

Stensgård (at the door). Excuse me; I'm in a hurry.

The Chamberlain (following him). Demagogue!

Stensgård. Good-bye; good-bye!

[*Goes out by the back.*

The Chamberlain (coming forward again). Now the air is pure again, my friends.

Bastian. I hope you don't blame me, sir, for what has happened at home?

The Chamberlain. Every one must bear his own burden.

Bastian. I had really no part in it.

Selma (who, during the preceding scene, has been listening at the second door on the right). Father! Now you are happy;—may he come now?

The Chamberlain. Selma! You! You plead for him? After what happened two days ago——

Selma. Oh, two days are a long time. All is well now. I know now that he can go astray——

The Chamberlain. And that pleases you?

Selma. Yes, that he can; but in future I won't let him.

The Chamberlain. Bring him in then.

[SELMA *goes out again to the right.*

Ringdal (enters by the foremost door on the right). Here is your resignation.

The Chamberlain. Thanks; but you can tear it up.

Ringdal. Tear it up?

The Chamberlain. Yes, Ringdal; I have found another way. I can make atonement without that; I shall set to work in earnest——

Erik (enters with SELMA from the right). Can you forgive me?

The Chamberlain (hands him the bill). I cannot be less merciful than fate.

Erik. Father! I shall retire this very day from the business you dislike so much.

The Chamberlain. No, indeed; you must stick to it. No cowardice! No running away from temptation! But I will stand at your side. *(Loudly.)* News for you, gentlemen! I have entered into partnership with my son.

Several Gentlemen. What? You, Chamberlain?

Heire. You, my dear sir?

The Chamberlain. Yes; it is a useful and honourable calling; or at any rate it can be made so. And now I have no reason to hold aloof any longer.

Lundestad. Well, I'll tell you what, Chamberlain—since you are going to set to work for the good of the district, it would be a shame and disgrace if an old soldier like me were to sulk in his tent.

Erik. Ah, what is this?

Lundestad. I cannot, in fact. After the disappointments in love that have befallen Mr. Stensgård to-day, Heaven forbid we should force the poor fellow into the political mill. He must rest and recover; a change of air is what he wants, and I shall see that he gets it. So if my constituents want me, why, they can have me.

The Gentlemen (shaking hands with him enthusiastically). Thanks, Lundestad! That's a good fellow! You won't fail us!

The Chamberlain. Now, this is as it should be; things are settling down again. But whom have we to thank for all this?

Fieldbo. Come, Aslaksen, you can explain——?

Aslaksen (alarmed). I, Doctor? I'm as innocent as the babe unborn!

Fieldbo. What about that letter, then——?

Aslaksen. It wasn't my fault, I tell you! It was the election and Bastian Monsen, and chance, and destiny, and

Madam Rundholmen's punch—there was no lemon in it—
and there was I, with the whole responsibility of the press
upon me——

The Chamberlain (approaching). What? What's that?

Aslaksen. The press, sir?

The Chamberlain. The press! That's just it! Haven't
I always said that the press has marvellous influence these
days?

Aslaksen. Oh, Chamberlain——

The Chamberlain. No false modesty, Mr. Aslaksen! I
haven't hitherto been in the habit of reading your paper,
but henceforth I will. I shall subscribe for ten copies.

Aslaksen. Oh, you can have twenty, Chamberlain!

The Chamberlain. Very well, then; let me have twenty.
And if you need money, come to me; I mean to support the press; but I tell you once for all—I won't write
for it.

Ringdal. What's this I hear? Your daughter engaged?

The Chamberlain. Yes; what do you say to that?

Ringdal. I am delighted! But when was it arranged?

Fieldbo (quickly). I'll tell you afterwards——

The Chamberlain. Why, it was arranged on the Seventeenth of May.

Fieldbo. What?

The Chamberlain. The day little Miss Ragna was here.

Thora. Father, father; did you know——?

The Chamberlain. Yes, my dear; I have known all along.

Fieldbo. Oh, Chamberlain——!

Thora. Who can have——?

The Chamberlain. Another time, I should advise you
young ladies not to talk so loud when I am taking my siesta
in the bay window.

Thora. Oh! so you were behind the curtains?

Fieldbo. Now I understand!

The Chamberlain. Yes, you are the one to keep your own
counsel——

Fieldbo. Would it have been of any use for me to speak earlier?

The Chamberlain. You are right, Fieldbo. These days have taught me a lesson.

Thora (aside to FIELDBO*).* Yes, you can keep your own counsel. All this about Mr. Stensgård—why did you tell me nothing?

Fieldbo. When a hawk is hovering over the dove-cote, one watches and shields his little dove—one does not alarm her.

[*They are interrupted by* MADAM RUNDHOLMEN.

Heire (to the CHAMBERLAIN*).* I'm sorry to tell you, Chamberlain, that the settlement of our little legal differences will have to be adjourned indefinitely.

The Chamberlain. Indeed; Why so?

Heire. You must know I've accepted a post as society reporter on Aslaksen's paper.

The Chamberlain. I am glad to hear it.

Heire. And of course you'll understand—with so much business on hand——

Madam Rundholmen (to THORA*).* Yes, I can tell you he's cost me many a tear, that bad man. But now I thank the Lord for Bastian. The other was false as the sea-foam; and then he's a terrible smoker, Miss Bratsberg, and frightfully particular about his meals. I found him a regular gourmand.

A Servant (enters from the left). Dinner is on the table.

The Chamberlain. Come along, then, all of you. Mr. Lundestad, you shall sit beside me; and you too, Mr. Aslaksen.

Ringdal. We shall have a lot of toasts to drink after dinner!

Heire. Yes; and perhaps an old man may be allowed to put in a claim for the toast of "Absent Friends."

Lundestad. One absent friend will return, Mr. Heire.

Heire. Stensgård?

Lundestad. Yes; you'll see, gentlemen! In ten or fifteen years, Stensgård will either be in Parliament or in the Ministry—perhaps in both at once.*

Fieldbo. In ten or fifteen years? Perhaps; but then he can scarcely stand at the head of the League of Youth.

Heire. Why not?

Fieldbo. Why, because by that time his youth will be—questionable.

Heire. Then he can stand at the head of the Questionable League, sir. That's what Lundestad means. He says like Napoleon—"It's the questionable people that make politicians"; hee-hee!

Fieldbo. Well, after all is said and done, our League shall last through young days and questionable days as well; and it shall continue to be the League of Youth. When Stensgård founded his League, and was carried shoulder-high amid all the enthusiasm of Independence Day, he said—"Providence is on the side of the League of Youth." I think even Mr. Helle, theologian as he is, will let us apply that saying to ourselves.

The Chamberlain. I think so too, my friends; for truly we have been groping and stumbling in darkness; but good angels guided us.

Lundestad. Oh, for that matter, I think the angels were only middling.

Aslaksen. Yes; that comes of the local situation, Mr. Lundestad.

---

* When this play was written, Ministers did not sit in the Storthing, and were not responsible to it. This state of things was altered—as Ibsen here predicts—in the great constitutional struggle of 1872-84, which ended in the victory of the Liberal party, their leader, Johan Sverdrup, becoming Prime Minister.

THE END

ROSMERSHOLM
(1886)

CHARACTERS

JOHANNES ROSMER, *of Rosmersholm, formerly clergyman of the parish.*

REBECCA WEST, *in charge of Rosmer's household.*

RECTOR * KROLL, *Rosmer's brother-in-law.*

ULRIC BRENDEL.

PETER MORTENSGÅRD.†

MADAM HELSETH, *housekeeper at Rosmersholm.*

The action takes place at Rosmersholm, an old family seat near a small coast town in the west of Norway.

---

* "Rector" in the Scotch and Continental sense of headmaster of a school, not in the English sense of a beneficed clergyman.

† Pronounce *Mortensgore.*

ROSMERSHOLM

PLAY IN FOUR ACTS

ACT FIRST

Sitting-room at Rosmersholm; spacious, old-fashioned, and comfortable. In front, on the right, a stove decked with fresh birch-branches and wild flowers. Farther back, on the same side, a door. In the back wall, folding-doors opening into the hall. To the left, a window, and before it a stand with flowers and plants. Beside the stove a table with a sofa and easy chairs. On the walls, old and more recent portraits of clergymen, officers, and government officials in uniform. The window is open; so are the door into the hall and the house door beyond. Outside can be seen an avenue of fine old trees, leading up to the house. It is a summer evening, after sunset.

REBECCA WEST *is sitting in an easy-chair by the window, and crocheting a large white woollen shawl, which is nearly finished. She now and then looks out expectantly through the leaves of the plants.* MADAM HELSETH *presently enters from the right.*

Madam Helseth. I suppose I had better begin to lay the table, Miss?

Rebecca West. Yes, please do. The Pastor must soon be in now.

Madam Helseth. Don't you feel the draught, Miss, where you're sitting?

Rebecca. Yes, there is a little draught. Perhaps you had better shut the window.

[MADAM HELSETH *shuts the door into the hall, and then comes to the window.*

Madam Helseth (about to shut the window, looks out). Why, isn't that the Pastor over there?

Rebecca (hastily). Where? *(Rises.)* Yes, it is he. *(Behind the curtain.)* Stand aside—don't let him see us.

Madam Helseth (keeping back from the window). Only think, Miss—he's beginning to take the path by the mill again.

Rebecca. He went that way the day before yesterday too. *(Peeps out between the curtains and the window-frame).* But let us see whether——

Madam Helseth. Will he venture across the foot-bridge?

Rebecca. That is what I want to see. *(After a pause.)* No, he is turning. He is going by the upper road again. *(Leaves the window.)* A long way round.

Madam Helseth. Dear Lord, yes. No wonder the Pastor thinks twice about setting foot on that bridge. A place where a thing like that has happened——

Rebecca (folding up her work). They cling to their dead here at Rosmersholm.

Madam Helseth. Now I would say, Miss, that it's the dead that clings to Rosmersholm.

Rebecca (looks at her). The dead?

Madam Helseth. Yes, it's almost as if they couldn't tear themselves away from the folk that are left.

Rebecca. What makes you fancy that?

Madam Helseth. Well, if it wasn't for that, there would be no White Horse, I suppose.

Rebecca. Now what is all this about the White Horse, Madam Helseth?

Madam Helseth. Oh, I don't like to talk about it. And, besides, you don't believe in such things.

Rebecca. Do you believe in it, then?

Madam Helseth (goes and shuts the window). Oh, you'd only be for laughing at me, Miss. *(Looks out.)* Why, isn't that Mr. Rosmer on the mill-path again——?

Rebecca (looks out). That man there? *(Goes to the window.)* No, that's the Rector!

Madam Helseth. Yes, so it is.

Rebecca. This is delightful. You may be sure he's coming here.

Madam Helseth. He goes straight over the foot-bridge, he does. And yet she was his sister, his own flesh and blood. Well, I'll go and lay the table then, Miss West.

> [*She goes out to the right.* REBECCA *stands at the window for a short time; then smiles and nods to some one outside. It begins to grow dark.*

Rebecca (goes to the door on the right). Oh, Madam Helseth, you might let us have some little extra dish for supper. You know what the Rector likes best.

Madam Helseth (outside). Oh yes, Miss, I'll see to it.

Rebecca (opens the door to the hall). At last——! How glad I am to see you, my dear Rector.

Rector Kroll (in the hall, laying down his stick). Thanks. Then I am not disturbing you?

Rebecca. You? How can you ask?

Kroll (comes in). Amiable as ever. *(Looks round.)* Is Rosmer upstairs in his room?

Rebecca. No, he is out walking. He has stayed out rather longer than usual; but he is sure to be in directly. *(Motioning him to sit on the sofa.)* Won't you sit down till he comes?

Kroll (laying down his hat). Many thanks. *(Sits down and looks about him.)* Why, how you have brightened up the old room! Flowers everywhere!

Rebecca. Mr. Rosmer is so fond of having fresh, growing flowers about him.

Kroll. And you are too, are you not?

Rebecca. Yes; they have a delightfully soothing effect

on me. We had to do without them, though, till lately.

Kroll (nods sadly.) Yes, their scent was too much for poor Beata.

Rebecca. Their colours, too. They quite bewildered her——

Kroll. I remember, I remember. *(In a lighter tone.)* Well, how are things going out here?

Rebecca. Oh, everything is going its quiet, jog-trot way. One day is just like another.—And with you? Your wife——?

Kroll. Ah, my dear Miss West, don't let us talk about my affairs. There is always something or other amiss in a family; especially in times like these.

Rebecca (after a pause, sitting down in an easy-chair beside the sofa). How is it you haven't once been near us during the whole of the holidays?

Kroll. Oh, it doesn't do to make oneself a nuisance——

Rebecca. If you knew how we have missed you——

Kroll. And then I have been away——

Rebecca. Yes, for the last week or two. We have heard of you at political meetings.

Kroll (nods). Yes what do you say to that? Did you think I would turn political agitator in my old age, eh?

Rebecca (smiling). Well, you have always been a bit of an agitator, Rector Kroll.

Kroll. Why, yes, just for my private amusement. But henceforth it is to be no laughing matter, I can tell you.— Do you ever see those radical newspapers?

Rebecca. Well yes, my dear Rector, I can't deny that——

Kroll. My dear Miss West, I have nothing to say against it—nothing in your case.

Rebecca. No, surely not. One likes to know what's going on—to keep up with the time——

Kroll. And of course I should not think of expecting you, as a woman, to side actively with either party in the civil contest—I might almost say the civil war—that is raging among us.—But you have seen then, I suppose, how these gentlemen of "the people" have been pleased to treat me? What infamous abuse they have had the audacity to heap on me?

Rebecca. Yes; but it seems to me you gave as good as you got.

Kroll. So I did, though I say it that shouldn't. For now I have tasted blood; and they shall soon find to their cost that I am not the man to turn the other cheek——— *(Breaks off.)* But come come—don't let us get upon that subject this evening—it's too painful and irritating.

Rebecca. Oh no, don't let us talk of it.

Kroll. Tell me now—how do you get on at Rosmersholm, now that you are alone? Since our poor Beata———

Rebecca. Thank you, I get on very well. Of course one feels a great blank in many ways—a great sorrow and longing. But otherwise———

Kroll. And do you think of remaining here?—permanently, I mean.

Rebecca. My dear Rector, I really haven't thought about it, one way or the other. I have got so used to the place now, that I feel almost as if I belonged to it.

Kroll. Why, of course you belong to it.

Rebecca. And so long as Mr. Rosmer finds that I am of any use or comfort to him—why, so long, I suppose, I shall stay here.

Kroll (looks at her with emotion). Do you know,—it is really fine for a woman to sacrifice her whole youth to others as you have done.

Rebecca. Oh, what else should I have had to live for?

Kroll. First, there was your untiring devotion to your paralytic and exacting foster-father———

Rebecca. You mustn't suppose that Dr. West was such a charge when we were up in Finmark. It was those terrible boat-voyages up there that broke him down. But after we came here—well yes, the two years before he found rest were certainly hard enough.

Kroll. And the years that followed—were they not even harder for you?

Rebecca. Oh how can you say such a thing? When I was so fond of Beata—and when she, poor dear, stood so sadly in need of care and forbearance.

Kroll. How good it is of you to think of her with so much kindness!

Rebecca (moves a little nearer). My dear Rector, you say that with such a ring of sincerity that I cannot think there is any ill-feeling lurking in the background.

Kroll. Ill-feeling? Why, what do you mean?

Rebecca. Well, it would be only natural if you felt it painful to see a stranger managing the household here at Rosmersholm.

Kroll. Why, how on earth——!

Rebecca. But you have no such feeling? *(Takes his hand.)* Thanks, my dear Rector; thank you again and again.

Kroll. How on earth did you get such an idea into your head?

Rebecca. I began to be a little afraid when your visits became so rare.

Kroll. Then you have been on a totally wrong scent, Miss West. Besides—after all, there has been no essential change. Even while poor Beata was alive—in her last unhappy days—it was you, and you alone, that managed everything.

Rebecca. That was only a sort of regency in Beata's name.

Kroll. Be that as it may——. Do you know, Miss West —for my part, I should have no objection whatever if you——. But I suppose I mustn't say such a thing.

Rebecca. What must you not say?

Kroll. If matters were to shape so that you took the empty place——

Rebecca. I have the only place I want, Rector.

Kroll. In fact, yes; but not in——

Rebecca (interrupting gravely). For shame, Rector Kroll. How can you joke about such things?

Kroll. Oh well, our good Johannes Rosmer very likely thinks he has had more than enough of married life already. But nevertheless——

Rebecca. You are really too absurd, Rector.

Kroll. Nevertheless——. Tell me, Miss West—if you will forgive the question—what is your age?

Rebecca. I'm sorry to say I am over nine-and-twenty, Rector; I am in my thirtieth year.

Kroll. Indeed. And Rosmer—how old is he? Let me see: he is five years younger than I am, so that makes him well over forty-three. I think it would be most suitable.

Rebecca (rises). Of course, of course; most suitable.— Will you stay to supper this evening?

Kroll. Yes, many thanks; I thought of staying. There is a matter I want to discuss with our good friend.—And I suppose, Miss West, in case you should take fancies into your head again, I had better come out pretty often for the future—as I used to in the old days.

Rebecca. Oh yes, do—do. *(Shakes both his hands.)* Many thanks—how kind and good you are!

Kroll (gruffly). Am I? Well, that's not what they tell me at home.

JOHANNES ROSMER *enters by the door on the right.*

Rebecca. Mr. Rosmer, do you see who is here?

Johannes Rosmer. Madam Helseth told me.

[RECTOR KROLL *has risen.*

Rosmer (gently and softly, pressing his hands). Welcome back to this house, my dear Kroll. *(Lays his hands on* KROLL'S *shoulders and looks into his eyes.)* My dear old friend! I knew that sooner or later things would come all right between us.

Kroll. Why, my dear fellow—do you mean to say you too have been so foolish as to fancy there was anything wrong?

Rebecca (to ROSMER*).* Yes, only think,—it was nothing but fancy after all!

Rosmer. Is that really the case, Kroll? Then why did you desert us so entirely?

Kroll (gravely, in a low voice). Because my presence would always have been reminding you of the years of your happiness, and of—the life that ended in the mill-race.

Rosmer. Well, it was a kind thought—you were always considerate. But it was quite unnecessary to remain away on that account.—Come, sit here on the sofa. *(They sit down.)* No, I assure you, the thought of Beata has no pain for me. We speak of her every day. We feel almost as if she were still one of the household.

Kroll. Do you really?

Rebecca (lighting the lamp). Yes, indeed we do.

Rosmer. It is quite natural. We were both so deeply attached to her. And both Rebec—both Miss West and I know that we did all that was possible for her in her affliction. We have nothing to reproach ourselves with.—So I feel nothing but a tranquil tenderness now at the thought of Beata.

Kroll. You dear, good people! Henceforward, I declare I shall come out and see you every day.

Rebecca (seats herself in an arm chair). Mind, we shall expect you to keep your word.

Rosmer (with some hesitation). My dear Kroll—I wish very much that our intercourse had never been interrupted. Ever since we have known each other, you have seemed predestined to be my adviser—ever since I went to the University.

Kroll. Yes, and I have always been proud of the office. But is there anything particular just now——?

Rosmer. There are many things that I would give a great deal to talk over with you, quite frankly—straight from the heart.

Rebecca. Ah yes, Mr. Rosmer—that must be such a comfort—between old friends——

Kroll. Oh I can tell you I have still more to talk to you about. I suppose you know I have turned a militant politician?

Rosmer. Yes, so you have. How did that come about?

Kroll. I was forced into it in spite of myself. It is impossible to stand idly looking on any longer. Now that the Radicals have unhappily come into power, it is high time something should be done,—so I have got our little group of friends in the town to close up their ranks. I tell you it is high time!

Rebecca (with a faint smile). Don't you think it may even be a little late?

Kroll. Unquestionably it would have been better if we had checked the stream at an earlier point in its course. But who could foresee what was going to happen? Certainly not I. *(Rises and walks up and down.)* But now I have had my eyes opened once for all; for now the spirit of revolt has crept into the school itself.

Rosmer. Into the school? Surely not into your school?

Kroll. I tell you it has—into my own school. What do you think? It has come to my knowledge that the sixth-form boys—a number of them at any rate—have been keeping up a secret society for over six months; and they take in Mortensgård's paper!

Rebecca. The "Beacon"?

Kroll. Yes; nice mental sustenance for future government officials, is it not? But the worst of it is that it's all the cleverest boys in the form that have banded together in this conspiracy against me. Only the dunces at the bottom of the class have kept out of it.

Rebecca. Do you take this so very much to heart, Rector?

Kroll. Do I take it to heart! To be so thwarted and opposed in the work of my whole life! *(Lower.)* But I could almost say I don't care about the school—for there is worse behind. *(Looks round.)* I suppose no one can hear us?

Rebecca. Oh no, of course not.

Kroll. Well, then, I must tell you that dissension and revolt have crept into my own house—into my own quiet home. They have destroyed the peace of my family life.

Rosmer (rises). What! Into your own house——?

Rebecca (goes over to the RECTOR*).* My dear Rector, what has happened?

Kroll. Would you believe that my own children—— In short, it is Laurits that is the ringleader of the school conspiracy; and Hilda has embroidered a red portfolio to keep the "Beacon" in.

Rosmer. I should certainly never have dreamt that, in your own house——

Kroll. No, who would have dreamt of such a thing? In my house, the very home of obedience and order—where one will, and one only, has always prevailed——

Rebecca. How does your wife take all this?

Kroll. Why, that is the most incredible part of it. My wife, who all her life long has shared my opinions and concurred in my views, both in great things and small—she is actually inclined to side with the children on many points. And she blames me for what has happened. She says I tyrannise over the children. As if it weren't necessary to——. Well, you see how my house is divided against itself. But of course I say as little about it as possible. Such things are best kept quiet. *(Wanders up the room.)* Ah, well, well, well.

[*Stands at the window with his hands behind his back, and looks out.*

Rebecca (comes up close to ROSMER, *and says rapidly and in a low voice, so that the* RECTOR *does not hear her).* Do it now!

Rosmer (also in a low voice). Not this evening.

Rebecca (as before). Yes, just this evening.

[*Goes to the table and busies herself with the lamp.*

Kroll (comes forward). Well, my dear Rosmer, now you know how the spirit of the age has overshadowed both my domestic and my official life. And am I to refrain from combating this pernicious, subversive, anarchic spirit, with any weapons I can lay my hands on? Fight it I will, trust me for that; both with tongue and pen.

Rosmer. Have you any hope of stemming the tide in that way?

Kroll. At any rate I shall have done my duty as a citizen in defence of the State. And I hold it the duty of every right-minded man with an atom of patriotism to do likewise. In fact—that was my principal reason for coming out here this evening.

Rosmer. Why, my dear Kroll, what do you mean——? What can I——?

Kroll. You can stand by your old friends. Do as we do. Lend a hand, with all your might.

Rebecca. But, Rector Kroll, you know Mr. Rosmer's distaste for public life.

Kroll. He must get over his distaste.—You don't keep abreast of things, Rosmer. You bury yourself alive here, with your historical collections. Far be it from me to speak disrespectfully of family trees and so forth; but, unfortunately, this is no time for hobbies of that sort. You cannot imagine the state things are in, all over the country. There is hardly a single accepted idea that hasn't been turned topsy-turvy. It will be a gigantic task to get all the errors rooted out again.

Rosmer. I have no doubt of it. But I am the last man to undertake such a task.

Rebecca. And besides, I think Mr. Rosmer has come to take a wider view of life than he used to.

Kroll (with surprise). Wider?

Rebecca. Yes; or freer, if you like—less one-sided.

Kroll. What is the meaning of this? Rosmer—surely you are not so weak as to be influenced by the accident that the leaders of the mob have won a temporary advantage?

Rosmer. My dear Kroll, you know how little I understand of politics. But I confess it seems to me that within the last few years people are beginning to show greater independence of thought.

Kroll. Indeed! And you take it for granted that that must be an improvement! But in any case you are quite mistaken, my friend. Just inquire a little into the opinions that are current among the Radicals, both out here and in the town. They are neither more nor less than the wisdom that's retailed in the "Beacon."

Rebecca. Yes; Mortensgård has great influence over many people hereabouts.

Kroll. Yes, just think of it! A man of his foul antecedents—a creature that was turned out of his place as a schoolmaster on account of his immoral life! A fellow like that sets himself up as a leader of the people! And succeeds too! Actually succeeds! I hear he is going to enlarge his paper. I know on good authority that he is on the lookout for a capable assistant.

Rebecca. I wonder that you and your friends don't set up an opposition to him.

Kroll. That is the very thing we are going to do. We have to-day bought the "County News"; there was no difficulty about the money question. But—— *(Turns to* ROSMER.*)* Now I come to my real errand. The difficulty lies in the conduct of the paper—the editing—— Tell me, Rosmer,—don't you feel it your duty to undertake it, for the sake of the good cause?

Rosmer (almost in consternation). I?

Rebecca. Oh, how can you think of such a thing?

Kroll. I can quite understand your horror of public meetings, and your reluctance to expose yourself to their tender mercies. But an editor's work is less conspicuous, or rather——

Rosmer. No, no, my dear friend, you must not ask me to do this.

Kroll. I should be quite willing to try my own hand at that style of work too; but I couldn't possibly manage it. I have such a multitude of irons in the fire already. But for you, with no profession to tie you down—— Of course the rest of us would give you as much help as we could.

Rosmer. I cannot, Kroll. I am not fitted for it.

Kroll. Not fitted? You said the same thing when your father preferred you to the living here——

Rosmer. And I was right. That was why I resigned it.

Kroll. Oh, if only you are as good an editor as you were a clergyman, we shall not complain.

Rosmer. My dear Kroll—I tell you once for all—I cannot do it.

Kroll. Well, at any rate, you will lend us your name.

Rosmer. My name?

Kroll. Yes, the mere name, Johannes Rosmer, will be a great thing for the paper. We others are looked upon as confirmed partisans—indeed I hear I am denounced as a desperate fanatic—so that if we work the paper in our own names, we can't reckon upon its making much way among the misguided masses. You, on the contrary, have always kept out of the fight. Everybody knows and values your humanity and uprightness—your delicacy of mind—your unimpeachable honour. And then the prestige of your former position as a clergyman still clings to you; and, to crown all, you have your grand old family name!

Rosmer. Oh, my name——

Kroll (points to the portraits). Rosmers of Rosmersholm

—clergymen and soldiers; government officials of high place and trust; gentlemen to the finger-tips, every man of them— a family that for nearly two centuries has held its place as the first in the district. *(Lays his hand on* ROSMER'S *shoulder.)* Rosmer—you owe it to yourself and to the traditions of your race to take your share in guarding all that has hitherto been held sacred in our society. *(Turns round.)* What do you say, Miss West?

Rebecca (laughing softly, as if to herself). My dear Rector—I can't tell you how ludicrous all this seems to me.

Kroll. What do you say? Ludicrous?

Rebecca. Yes, ludicrous. For you must let me tell you frankly——

Rosmer (quickly). No, no—be quiet! Not just now!

Kroll (looks from one to the other). My dear friends, what on earth——? *(Interrupting himself.)* H'm.

MADAME HELSETH *appears in the doorway on the right.*

Madam Helseth. There's a man out in the kitchen passage that says he wants to see the Pastor.

Rosmer (relieved). Ah, very well. Ask him to come in.

Madam Helseth. Into the sitting-room?

Rosmer. Yes, of course.

Madam Helseth. But he looks scarcely the sort of man to bring into the sitting-room.

Rebecca. Why, what does he look like, Madam Helseth?

Madam Helseth. Well, he's not much to look at, Miss, and that's a fact.

Rosmer. Did he not give his name?

Madam Helseth. Yes—I think he said his name was Hekman or something of the sort.

Rosmer. I know nobody of that name.

Madam Helseth. And then he said he was called Uldric too.

Rosmer (in surprise). Ulric Hetman! Was that it?

Madam Helseth. Yes, so it was—Hetman.

Kroll. I've surely heard that name before——

Rebecca. Wasn't that the name he used to write under
—that strange being——

Rosmer (to KROLL*).* It is Ulric Brendel's pseudonym.

Kroll. That black sheep Ulric Brendel's—of course it is.

Rebecca. Then he is still alive.

Rosmer. I heard he had joined a company of strolling
players.

Kroll. When last *I* heard of him, he was in the House
of Correction.

Rosmer. Ask him to come in, Madam Helseth.

Madam Helseth. Oh, very well.   [*She goes out.*

Kroll. Are you really going to let a man like that into
your house?

Rosmer. You know he was once my tutor.

Kroll. Yes, I know he went and crammed your head full
of revolutionary ideas, until your father showed him the
door—with his horsewhip.

Rosmer (with a touch of bitterness). Father was a mar-
tinet at home as well as in his regiment.

Kroll. Thank him in his grave for that, my dear Rosmer.
—Well!

MADAM HELSETH *opens the door on the right for* ULRIC
   BRENDEL, *and then withdraws, shutting the door behind
   him. He is a handsome man, with grey hair and beard;
   somewhat gaunt, but active and well set up. He is
   dressed like a common tramp; threadbare frock-coat;
   worn-out shoes; no shirt visible. He wears an old pair
   of black gloves, and carries a soft, greasy felt hat under
   his arm, and a walking-stick in his hand.*

*Ulric Brendel (hesitates at first, then goes quickly up to
the* RECTOR, *and holds out his hand).* Good evening, Johannes!

Kroll. Excuse me——

Brendel. Did you expect to see me again? And within these hated walls, too?

Kroll. Excuse me—— *(Pointing.)* There——

Brendel (turns). Right. There he is. Johannes—my boy—my best-beloved——!

Rosmer (takes his hand). My old teacher.

Brendel. Notwithstanding certain painful memories, I could not pass by Rosmersholm without paying you a flying visit.

Rosmer. You are heartily welcome here now. Be sure of that.

Brendel. Ah, this charming lady——? *(Bows.)* Mrs. Rosmer, of course.

Rosmer. Miss West.

Brendel. A near relation, no doubt. And yonder unknown——? A brother of the cloth, I see.

Rosmer. Rector Kroll.

Brendel. Kroll? Kroll? Wait a bit?—Weren't you a student of philology in your young days?

Kroll. Of course I was.

Brendel. Why *Donnerwetter,* then I knew you!

Kroll. Pardon me——

Brendel. Weren't you——

Kroll. Pardon me——

Brendel. ——one of those myrmidons of morality that got me turned out of the Debating Club?

Kroll. Very likely. But I disclaim any closer acquaintanceship.

Brendel. Well, well! *Nach Belieben, Herr Doctor.* It's all one to me. Ulric Brendel remains the man he is for all that.

Rebecca. You are on your way into town, Mr. Brendel?

Brendel. You have hit it, gracious lady. At certain intervals, I am constrained to strike a blow for existence. It goes against the grain; but—*enfin*—imperious necessity——

Rosmer. Oh, but, my dear Mr. Brendel, you must allow me to help you. In one way or another, I am sure——

Brendel. Ha, such a proposal to me! Would you desecrate the bond that unites us? Never, Johannes, never!

Rosmer. But what do you think of doing in town? Believe me, you won't find it easy to——

Brendel. Leave that to me, my boy. The die is cast Simple as I stand here before you, I am engaged in a com prehensive campaign—more comprehensive than all my previous excursions put together. (*To* RECTOR KROLL.) Dare I ask the Herr Professor—*unter uns*—have you a tolerably decent, reputable, and commodious Public Hall in your estimable city?

Kroll. The hall of the Workmen's Society is the largest.

Brendel. And has the Herr Professor any official influence in this doubtless most beneficent Society?

Kroll. I have nothing to do with it.

Rebecca (*to* BRENDEL). You should apply to Peter Mortensgård.

Brendel. Pardon, madame—what sort of an idiot is he?

Rosmer. What makes you take him for an idiot?

Brendel. Can't I tell at once by the name that it belongs to a plebeian?

Kroll. I did not expect that answer.

Brendel. But I will conquer my reluctance. There is no alternative. When a man stands—as I do—at a turning-point in his career——. It is settled. I will approach this individual—will open personal negotiations——

Rosmer. Are you really and seriously standing at a turning-point?

Brendel. Surely my own boy knows that, stand he where he may, Ulric Brendel always stands really and seriously.— Yes, Johannes, I am going to put on a new man—to throw off the modest reserve I have hitherto maintained——

Rosmer. How——?

Brendel. I am about to take hold of life with a strong hand; to step forth; to assert myself. We live in a tempestuous, an equinoctial age.—I am about to lay my mite on the altar of Emancipation.

Kroll. You, too?

Brendel (to them all). Is the local public at all familiar with my occasional writings?

Kroll. No, I must candidly confess that——

Rebecca. I have read several of them. My adopted father had them in his library.

Brendel. Fair lady, then you have wasted your time. For, let me tell you, they are so much rubbish.

Rebecca. Indeed!

Brendel. What you have read, yes. My really important works no man or woman knows. No one—except myself.

Rebecca. How does that happen?

Brendel. Because they are not written.

Rosmer. But, my dear Mr. Brendel——

Brendel. You know, my Johannes, that I am a bit of a Sybarite—a *Feinschmecker.* I have been so all my days. I like to take my pleasures in solitude; for then I enjoy them doubly—tenfold. So, you see, when golden dreams descended and enwrapped me—when new, dizzy, far-reaching thoughts were born in me, and wafted me aloft on their sustaining pinions—I bodied them forth in poems, visions, pictures—in the rough, as it were, you understand.

Rosmer. Yes, yes.

Brendel. Oh, what pleasures, what intoxications I have enjoyed in my time! The mysterious bliss of creation—in the rough, as I said—applause, gratitude, renown, the wreath of bays—all these I have garnered with full hands quivering with joy. I have sated myself, in my secret thoughts, with a rapture—oh! so intense, so inebriating——!

Kroll. H'm.

Rosmer. But you have written nothing down?

Brendel. Not a word. The soulless toil of the scrivener has always aroused a sickening aversion in me. And besides, why should I profane my own ideals, when I could enjoy them in their purity by myself? But now they shall be offered up. I assure you I feel like a mother who delivers her tender daughters into their bridegrooms' arms. But I will offer them up, none the less. I will sacrifice them on the altar of Emancipation. A series of carefully elaborated lectures—over the whole country——!

Rebecca (with animation). This is noble of you, Mr. Brendel! You are yielding up the dearest thing you possess.

Rosmer. The only thing.

Rebecca (looking significantly at ROSMER*).* How many are there who do as much—who dare do as much?

Rosmer (returning the look). Who knows?

Brendel. My audience is touched. That does my heart good—and steels my will. So now I will proceed to action. Stay—one thing more. *(To the* RECTOR.*)* Can you tell me, Herr Preceptor,—is there such a thing as a Temperance Society in the town? A Total Abstinence Society? I need scarcely ask.

Kroll. Yes, there is. I am the president, at your service.

Brendel. I saw it in your face! Well, it is by no means impossible that I may come to you and enrol myself as a member for a week.

Kroll. Excuse me—we don't receive members by the week.

Brendel. A la bonne heure, Herr Pedagogue. Ulric Brendel has never forced himself into that sort of Society *(Turns.)* But I must not prolong my stay in this house, so rich in memories. I must get on to the town and select a suitable lodging. I presume there is a decent hotel in the place.

Rebecca. Mayn't I offer you anything before you go?

Brendel. Of what sort, gracious lady?

Rebecca. A cup of tea, or——

Brendel. I thank my bountiful hostess—but I am always loath to trespass on private hospitality. *(Waves his hand.)* Farewell, gentlefolks all! *(Goes towards the door, but turns again.)* Oh, by the way—Johannes—Pastor Rosmer—for the sake of our ancient friendship, will you do your former teacher a service?

Rosmer. Yes, with all my heart.

Brendel. Good. Then lend me—for a day or two—a starched shirt—with cuffs.

Rosmer. Nothing else?

Brendel. For you see I am travelling on foot—at present. My trunk is being sent after me.

Rosmer. Quite so. But is there nothing else?

Brendel. Well, do you know—perhaps you could spare me an oldish, well-worn summer overcoat.

Rosmer. Yes, yes; certainly I can.

Brendel. And if a respectable pair of boots happened to go along with the coat——

Rosmer. That we can manage, too. As soon as you let us know your address, we will send the things in.

Brendel. Not on any account. Pray do not let me give you any trouble! I will take the bagatelles with me.

Rosmer. As you please. Come upstairs with me then.

Rebecca. Let me go. Madam Helseth and I will see to it.

Brendel. I cannot think of suffering this distinguished lady to——

Rebecca. Oh, nonsense! Come along, Mr. Brendel.

[*She goes out to the right.*

Rosmer (detaining him). Tell me—is there nothing else I can do for you?

Brendel. Upon my word, I know of nothing more. Well, yes, damn it all—now that I think of it——! Johannes, do you happen to have eight crowns in your pocket?

Rosmer. Let me see. *(Opens his purse.)* Here are two ten-crown notes.

Brendel. Well, well, never mind! I can take them. I can always get them changed in the town. Thanks in the meantime. Remember it was two tenners you lent me. Good-night my own dear boy. Good-night, respected Sir.

[*Goes out to the right.* ROSMER *takes leave of him, and shuts the door behind him.*

Kroll. Merciful Heaven—so that is the Ulric Brendel people once expected such great things of.

Rosmer (quietly). At least he has had the courage to live his life his own way. I don't think that is such a small matter either.

Kroll. What? A life like his! I almost believe he has it in him to turn your head afresh.

Rosmer. Oh, no. My mind is quite clear now, upon all points.

Kroll. I wish I could believe it, my dear Rosmer. You are so terribly impressionable.

Rosmer. Let us sit down. I want to talk to you.

Kroll. Yes, let us.

[*They seat themselves on the sofa.*

Rosmer (after a slight pause). Don't you think we lead a pleasant and comfortable life here?

Kroll. Yes, your life is pleasant and comfortable now—and peaceful. You have found yourself a home, Rosmer. And I have lost mine.

Rosmer. My dear friend, don't say that. The wound will heal again in time.

Kroll. Never; never. The barb will always rankle. Things can never be as they were.

Rosmer. Listen to me, Kroll. We have been fast friends for many and many a year. Does it seem to you conceivable that our friendship should ever go to wreck?

Kroll. I know of nothing in the world that could estrange us. What puts that into your head?

Rosmer. You attach such paramount importance to uniformity of opinions and views.

Kroll. No doubt; but we two are in practical agreement --at any rate on the great essential questions.

Rosmer (in a low voice). No; not now.

Kroll (tries to spring up). What is this?

Rosmer (holding him). No, you must sit still—I entreat you, Kroll.

Kroll. What can this mean? I don't understand you. Speak plainly.

Rosmer. A new summer has blossomed in my soul. I see with eyes grown young again. And so now I stand——

Kroll. Where—where, Rosmer?

Rosmer. Where your children stand.

Kroll. You? You! Impossible! Where do you say you stand?

Rosmer. On the same side as Laurits and Hilda.

Kroll (bows his head). An apostate! Johannes Rosmer an apostate!

Rosmer. I should have felt so happy—so intensely happy, in what you call my apostasy. But, nevertheless, I suffered deeply; for I knew it would be a bitter sorrow to you.

Kroll. Rosmer—Rosmer! I shall never get over this! *(Looks gloomily at him.)* To think that you, too, can find it in your heart to help on the work of corruption and ruin in this unhappy land.

Rosmer. It is the work of emancipation I wish to help on.

Kroll. Oh, yes, I know. That is what both the tempters and their victims call it. But do you think there is any emancipation to be expected from the spirit that is now poisoning our social life?

Rosmer. I am not in love with the spirit that is in the ascendant, nor with either of the contending parties. I will try to bring together men from both sides—as many as I can—and to unite them as closely as possible. I will devote my life and all my energies to this one thing—the creation of a true democracy in this country.

Kroll. So you don't think we have democracy enough

already! For my part it seems to me we are all in a fair way to be dragged down into the mire, where hitherto only the mob have been able to thrive.

Rosmer. That is just why I want to awaken the democracy to its true task.

Kroll. What task?

Rosmer. That of making all the people of this country noble——

Kroll. All the people——?

Rosmer. As many as possible, at any rate.

Kroll. By what means?

Rosmer. By freeing their minds and purifying their wills.

Kroll. You are a dreamer, Rosmer. Will you free them? Will you purify them?

Rosmer. No, my dear friend—I will only try to arouse them to their task. They themselves must accomplish it.

Kroll. And you think they can?

Rosmer. Yes.

Kroll. By their own strength?

Rosmer. Yes, precisely by their own strength. There is no other.

Kroll (rises). Is this becoming language for a priest?

Rosmer. I am no longer a priest.

Kroll. Well but—the faith of your fathers——?

Rosmer. It is mine no more.

Kroll. No more——!

Rosmer (rises). I have given it up. I had to give it up, Kroll.

Kroll (controlling his agitation). Oh, indeed—— Yes, yes, yes. I suppose one thing goes with another. Was this, then, your reason for leaving the Church?

Rosmer. Yes. As soon as my mind was clear—as soon as I was quite certain that this was no passing attack of scepticism, but a conviction I neither could nor would shake off— then I at once left the Church.

Kroll. So this has been your state of mind all this time! And we—your friends—have heard nothing of it. Rosmer— Rosmer—how could you hide the miserable truth from us!

Rosmer. Because it seemed to me a matter that concerned myself alone. And besides, I did not wish to give you and my other friends any needless pain. I thought I might live on here, as before, quietly, serenely, happily. I wanted to read, to bury myself in all the studies that until then had been sealed books to me. I wanted to make myself thoroughly at home in the great world of truth and freedom that has been revealed to me.

Kroll. Apostate! Every word proves it. But why, then, do you confess your secret apostasy after all? And why just at this time?

Rosmer. You yourself have driven me to it, Kroll.

Kroll. I? Have I driven you——?

Rosmer. When I heard of your violence on the platform —when I read all the rancorous speeches you made—your bitter onslaughts on your opponents—the contemptuous invectives you heaped on them—oh, Kroll, to think that you— you—could come to this!—then my duty stood imperatively before me. Men are growing evil in this struggle. Peace and joy and mutual forbearance must once more enter into our souls. That is why I now intend to step forward and openly avow myself for what I am. I, too, will try my strength. Could not you—from your side—help me in this, Kroll?

Kroll. Never so long as I live will I make peace with the subversive forces in society.

Rosmer. Then at least let us fight with honourable weapons—since fight we must.

Kroll. Whoever is not with me in the essential things of life, him I no longer know. I owe him no consideration.

Rosmer. Does that apply to me, too?

Kroll. It is you that have broken with me, Rosmer.

Rosmer. Is this a breach then?

Kroll. This! It is a breach with all who have hitherto been your friends. You must take the consequences.

REBECCA WEST *enters from the right, and opens the door wide.*

Rebecca. There now; he is on his way to his great sacrifice. And now we can go to supper. Will you come in, Rector?

Kroll (takes up his hat). Good-night, Miss West. I have nothing more to do here.

Rebecca (eagerly). What is this? *(Shuts the door and comes forward.)* Have you spoken?

Rosmer. He knows everything.

Kroll. We will not let you go, Rosmer. We will force you to come back to us.

Rosmer. I can never stand where I did.

Kroll. We shall see. You are not the man to endure standing alone.

Rosmer. I shall not be so completely alone after all.— There are two of us to bear the loneliness together.

Kroll. Ah———. *(A suspicion appears in his face.)* That too! Beata's words———!

Rosmer. Beata's———?

Kroll (shaking off the thought). No, no—that was vile. Forgive me.

Rosmer. What? What do you mean?

Kroll. Don't ask. Bah! Forgive me! Good-bye!

[*Goes towards the entrance door.*

Rosmer (follows him). Kroll! Our friendship must not end like this. I will come and see you to-morrow.

Kroll (in the hall, turns). You shall never cross my threshold again.

[*He takes up his stick and goes out.*
[ROSMER *stands for a moment in the doorway; then shuts the door and walks up to the table.*

Rosmer. It does not matter, Rebecca. We will see it out, we two faithful friends—you * and I.

Rebecca. What do you think he meant when he said "That was vile"?

Rosmer. Don't trouble about that, dear. He himself didn't believe what was in his mind. To-morrow I will go and see him. Good-night!

Rebecca. Are you going upstairs so early to-night? After this?

Rosmer. To-night as usual. I feel so relieved, now it is over. You see—I am quite calm, Rebecca. Do you, too, take it calmly. Good-night!

Rebecca. Good-night, dear friend! Sleep well!

> [ROSMER *goes out by the hall door; his steps are heard ascending the staircase.*

> [REBECCA *goes and pulls a bell-rope near the stove. Shortly after,* MADAM HELSETH *enters from the right.*

Rebecca. You can take away the supper things, Madam Helseth. Mr. Rosmer doesn't want anything, and the Rector has gone home.

Madam Helseth. Has the Rector gone? What was the matter with him?

Rebecca (takes up her crochet work). He said he thought there was a heavy storm brewing——

Madam Helseth. What a strange notion! There's not a cloud in the sky this evening.

Rebecca. Let us hope he mayn't meet the White Horse! I'm afraid we shall soon be hearing something from the bogies now.

Madam Helseth. Lord forgive you, Miss! Don't say such awful things.

---

* From this point, and throughout when alone, Rosmer and Rebecca use the *du* of intimate friendship in speaking to each other.

Rebecca. Well, well, well——

Madam Helseth (softly). Do you really think some one is to go soon, Miss?

Rebecca. No; why should I think so? But there are so many sorts of white horses in this world, Madam Helseth.— Well, good-night. I shall go to my room now.

Madam Helseth. Good-night, Miss.

> [REBECCA *goes out to the right, with her crochet-work.*

Madam Helseth (turns the lamp down, shaking her head and muttering to herself). Lord—Lord! That Miss West! The things she does say!

ACT SECOND.

JOHANNES ROSMER'S *study. Entrance door on the left. At the back, a doorway with a curtain drawn aside, leading into* ROSMER'S *bedroom. On the right a window, and in front of it a writing-table covered with books and papers. Book-shelves and cases round the room. The furniture is simple. On the left, an old-fashioned sofa, with a table in front of it.*

JOHANNES ROSMER, *in an indoor jacket, is sitting in a high-backed chair at the writing-table. He is cutting and turning over the leaves of a pamphlet, and reading a little here and there.*

There is a knock at the door on the left.

Rosmer (without moving). Come in.

Rebecca West (enters, dressed in a morning gown). Good morning.

Rosmer (turning the leaves of the pamphlet). Good morning, dear. Do you want anything?

Rebecca. I only wanted to hear if you had slept well.

Rosmer. Oh, I have had a beautiful, peaceful night. *(Turns.)* And you?

Rebecca. Oh, yes, thanks—towards morning——

Rosmer. I don't know when I have felt so light-hearted as I do now. I am so glad I managed to speak out at last.

Rebecca. Yes, it is a pity you remained silent so long, Rosmer.

Rosmer. I don't understand myself how I could be such a coward.

Rebecca. It wasn't precisely cowardice——

Rosmer. Oh, yes, dear—when I think the thing out, I can see there was a touch of cowardice at the bottom of it.

Rebecca. All the braver, then, to make the plunge at last. *(Sits on a chair at the writing-table, close to him.)* But now I want to tell you of something I have done—and you mustn't be vexed with me about it.

Rosmer. Vexed? How can you think——?

Rebecca. Well, it was perhaps rather indiscreet of me but——

Rosmer. Let me hear what it was.

Rebecca. Yesterday evening, when Ulric Brendel was leaving—I gave him a note to Peter Mortensgård.

Rosmer (a little doubtful). Why, my dear Rebecca—— Well, what did you say?

Rebecca. I said that he would be doing you a service if he would look after that unfortunate creature a little, and help him in any way he could.

Rosmer. Dear, you shouldn't have done that. You have only done Brendel harm. And Mortensgård is not a man I care to have anything to do with. You know of that old episode between us.

Rebecca. But don't you think it would be as well to make it up with him again?

Rosmer. I? With Mortensgård? In what way do you mean?

Rebecca. Well, you know you can't feel absolutely secure now—after this breach with your old friends.

Rosmer (looks at her and shakes his head). Can you really believe that Kroll or any of the others would try to take revenge on me? That they would be capable of——?

Rebecca. In the first heat of anger, dear——. No one can be sure. I think—after the way the Rector took it——

Rosmer. Oh, you ought surely to know him better than that. Kroll is a gentleman, to the backbone. I am going into town this afternoon to talk to him. I will talk to them all. Oh, you shall see how easily it will all go——

MADAM HELSETH *appears at the door on the left.*

Rebecca (rises). What is it, Madam Helseth?
Madam Helseth. Rector Kroll is downstairs in the hall.
Rosmer (rises hastily). Kroll!
Rebecca. The Rector! Is it possible——
Madam Helseth. He wants to know if he may come upstairs, Mr. Rosmer.
Rosmer (to REBECCA). What did I tell you?—Of course he may. *(Goes to the door and calls down the stairs.)* Come up, dear friend! I am delighted to see you.

[ROSMER *stands holding the door open.* MADAM
HELSETH *goes out.* REBECCA *draws the curtain
before the doorway at the back, and then begins
arranging things in the room.*

RECTOR KROLL *enters, with his hat in his hand.*

Rosmer (with quiet emotion). I knew it couldn't be the last time——
Kroll. I see things to-day in quite a different light from yesterday.
Rosmer. Ah yes, Kroll; I was sure you would, now that you have had time to reflect.
Kroll. You misunderstand me completely. *(Lays his hat on the table beside the sofa.)* It is of the utmost importance that I should speak to you, alone.
Rosmer. Why may not Miss West——?
Rebecca. No no, Mr. Rosmer. I will go.
Kroll (looks at her from head to foot). And I must ask Miss West to excuse my coming at such an untimely hour— taking her unawares before she has had time to——
Rebecca (surprised). What do you mean? Do you see

any harm in my wearing a morning gown about the house?

Kroll. Heaven forbid! I know nothing of what may now be customary at Rosmersholm.

Rosmer. Why, Kroll—you are not yourself to-day!

Rebecca. Allow me to wish you good morning, Rector Kroll.   [*She goes out to the left.*

Kroll. By your leave——   [*Sits on the sofa.*

Rosmer. Yes, Kroll, sit down, and let us talk things out amicably.

[*He seats himself in a chair directly opposite to the* RECTOR.

Kroll. I haven't closed an eye since yesterday. I have been lying thinking and thinking all night.

Rosmer. And what do you say to things to-day?

Kroll. It will be a long story, Rosmer. Let me begin with a sort of introduction. I can give you news of Ulric Brendel.

Rosmer. Has he called on you?

Kroll. No. He took up his quarters in a low public-house—in the lowest company of course—and drank and stood treat as long as he had any money. Then he began abusing the whole company as a set of disreputable black-guards—and so far he was quite right—whereupon they thrashed him and pitched him out into the gutter.

Rosmer. So he is incorrigible after all.

Kroll. He had pawned the coat, too; but I am told that has been redeemed for him. Can you guess by whom?

Rosmer. Perhaps by you?

Kroll. No; by the distinguished Mr. Mortensgård.

Rosmer. Ah, indeed.

Kroll. I understand that Mr. Brendel's first visit was to the "idiot" and "plebeian."

Rosmer. Well, it was lucky for him——

Kroll. To be sure it was. (*Leans over the table towards* ROSMER.) And that brings me to a matter it is my duty to warn you about, for our old—for our former friendship's sake.

Rosmer. My dear Kroll, what can that be?

Kroll. It is this: there are things going on behind your back in this house.

Rosmer. How can you think so? Is it Reb—is it Miss West you are aiming at?

Kroll. Precisely. I can quite understand it on her part. She has so long been accustomed to have everything her own way here. But nevertheless——

Rosmer. My dear Kroll, you are utterly mistaken. She and I—we have no concealments from each other on any subject whatever.

Kroll. Has she told you, then, that she has entered into correspondence with the editor of the "Beacon"?

Rosmer. Oh, you are thinking of the few lines she sent by Ulric Brendel?

Kroll. Then you have found it out. And do you approve of her entering into relations with a scurrilous scribbler, who never lets a week pass without holding me up to ridicule, both as a schoolmaster and as a public man?

Rosmer. My dear Kroll, I don't suppose that side of the matter ever entered her head. And besides, of course she has full liberty of action, just as I have.

Kroll. Indeed? Ah, no doubt that follows from your new line of thought. For Miss West presumably shares your present standpoint?

Rosmer. Yes, she does. We two have worked our way forward in faithful comradeship.

Kroll (looks at him and slowly shakes his head). Oh, you blind, deluded being!

Rosmer. I? Why do you say that?

Kroll. Because I dare not—I will not think the worst. No no, let me say my say out.—You really do value my friendship, Rosmer? And my respect too? Do you not?

Rosmer. I surely need not answer that question.

Kroll. Well, but there are other questions that do require an answer—a full explanation on your part.—Will you submit to a sort of investigation——?

Rosmer. Investigation?

Kroll. Yes; will you let me question you about certain things it may pain you to be reminded of? You see—this apostasy of yours—well, this emancipation, as you call it— is bound up with many other things that for your own sake you must explain to me.

Rosmer. My dear Kroll, ask what questions you please. I have nothing to conceal.

Kroll. Then tell me—what do you think was the real, the ultimate reason why Beata put an end to her life?

Rosmer. Can you have any doubt on the subject? Or, rather, can you ask for reasons for what an unhappy, irresponsible invalid may do?

Kroll. Are you certain that Beata was completely irresponsible for her actions? The doctors, at any rate, were by no means convinced of it.

Rosmer. If the doctors had ever seen her as I have so often seen her, for days and nights together, they would have had no doubts.

Kroll. I had no doubts either—then.

Rosmer. Oh, no, unhappily, there wasn't the smallest room for doubt. I have told you of her wild frenzies of passion—which she expected me to return. Oh, how they appalled me! And then her causeless, consuming self-reproaches during the last few years.

Kroll. Yes, when she had learnt that she must remain childless all her life.

Rosmer. Yes, just think of that! Such terrible, haunting agony of mind about a thing utterly beyond her control——! How could you call her responsible for her actions?

Kroll. H'm——. Can you remember whether you had any books in the house at that time treating of the rationale of marriage—according to the "advanced" ideas of the day?

Rosmer. I remember Miss West lending me a work of the kind. The Doctor left her his library, you know. But, my dear Kroll, you surely cannot suppose we were so reckless as to let my poor sick wife get hold of any such ideas? I can solemnly assure you that the fault was not ours. It was her own distempered brain that drove her into these wild aberrations.

Kroll. One thing at any rate I can tell you; and that is, that poor, overstrung, tortured Beata put an end to her life in order that you might live happily—live freely, and—after your own heart.

Rosmer (starts half up from his chair). What do you mean by that?

Kroll. Listen to me quietly, Rosmer; for now I can speak of it. In the last year of her life she came to me twice to pour forth all her anguish and despair.

Rosmer. On this same subject?

Kroll. No. The first time she came, it was to declare that you were on the road to perversion—that you were going to break with the faith of your fathers.

Rosmer (eagerly). What you say is impossible, Kroll Absolutely impossible! You must be mistaken.

Kroll. And why?

Rosmer. Because while Beata was alive I was still wrestling with myself in doubt. And that fight I fought out alone and in utter silence. I don't think even Rebecca——

Kroll. Rebecca?

Rosmer. Oh, well—Miss West. I call her Rebecca for convenience' sake.

Kroll. So I have remarked.

Rosmer. So it is inconceivable to me how Beata could have got hold of the idea. And why did she not speak to me about it? She never did—she never said a single word.

Kroll. Poor creature—she begged and implored me to **talk to you.**

Rosmer. And why did you not?

Kroll. At that time I never for a moment doubted that she was out of her mind. Such an accusation against a man like you!—And then she came again—about a month later. This time she seemed outwardly calmer; but as she was going she said: "They may soon expect the White Horse at Rosmersholm now."

Rosmer. Yes, yes. The White Horse—she often spoke of it.

Kroll. And when I tried to divert her mind from such melancholy fancies, she only answered: "I have not long to live; for Johannes must marry Rebecca at once."

Rosmer (almost speechless). What do you say? I marry——?

Kroll. That was on a Thursday afternoon——. On the Saturday evening she threw herself from the bridge into the mill-race.

Rosmer. And you never warned us——!

Kroll. You know very well how often she used to say that she felt her end was near.

Rosmer. Yes, I know. But nevertheless—you should have warned us!

Kroll. I did think of it; but not till too late.

Rosmer. But afterwards, why did you not——? Why have you said nothing about all this?

Kroll. What good would it have done for me to come torturing and harassing you still further? I took all she said for mere wild, empty ravings—until yesterday evening.

Rosmer. Then you have now changed your opinion?

Kroll. Did not Beata see quite clearly when she declared you were about to desert the faith of your fathers?

Rosmer (looks fixedly, straight before him). I cannot understand it. It is the most incomprehensible thing in the world.

Kroll. Incomprehensible or not—there it is. And now

I ask you, Rosmer,—how much truth is there in her other accusation? The last one, I mean.

Rosmer. Accusation? Was that an accusation?

Kroll. Perhaps you did not notice the way she worded it. She had to go, she said—why?

Rosmer. In order that I might marry Rebecca——

Kroll. These were not precisely her words. Beata used a different expression. She said: "I have not long to live; for Johannes must marry Rebecca at once."

Rosmer (looks at him for a moment; then rises). Now I understand you, Kroll.

Kroll. And what then? What is your answer?

Rosmer (still quiet and self-restrained). To such an unheard-of——? The only fitting answer would be to point to the door.

Kroll (rises). Well and good.

Rosmer (stands in front of him). Listen to me. For more than a year—ever since Beata left us—Rebecca West and I have lived alone here at Rosmersholm. During all that time you have known of Beata's accusation against us. But I have never for a moment noticed that you disapproved of Rebecca's living in my house.

Kroll. I did not know till yesterday evening that it was an unbelieving man who was living with an—emancipated woman.

Rosmer. Ah——! Then you do not believe that purity of mind is to be found among the unbelieving and the emancipated? You do not believe that morality may be an instinctive law of their nature!

Kroll. I have no great faith in the morality that is not founded on the teachings of the Church.

Rosmer. And you mean this to apply to Rebecca and me? To the relation between us two——?

Kroll. Not even out of consideration for you two can I depart from my opinion that there is no unfathomable gulf between free thought and—h'm——

Rosmer. And what?

Kroll. ——and free love,—since you will have it.

Rosmer (in a low voice). And you are not ashamed to say this to me! You, who have known me from my earliest youth!

Kroll. For that very reason. I know how easily you are influenced by the people you associate with. And this Rebecca of yours—well, Miss West then—we really know little or nothing about her. In short, Rosmer—I will not give you up. And you—you must try to save yourself in time.

Rosmer. Save myself? How——?

MADAM HELSETH *peeps in at the door on the left.*

Rosmer. What do you want?

Madam Helseth. I wanted to ask Miss West to step downstairs.

Rosmer. Miss West is not up here.

Madam Helseth. Isn't she? *(Looks round the room.)* Well, that's strange.   [*She goes.*

Rosmer. You were saying——?

Kroll. Listen to me. I am not going to inquire too closely into the secret history of what went on here in Beata's lifetime—and may still be going on. I know that your marriage was a most unhappy one; and I suppose that must be taken as some sort of excuse——

Rosmer. Oh, how little you really know me——!

Kroll. Don't interrupt me. What I mean is this: if your present mode of life with Miss West is to continue, it is absolutely necessary that the change of views—the unhappy backsliding—brought about by her evil influence, should be hushed up. Let me speak! Let me speak! I say, if the worst comes to the worst, in Heaven's name think and believe whatever you like about everything under the sun. But you must keep your views to yourself. These things are purely personal matters, after all. There is no need to proclaim them from the housetops.

Rosmer. I feel it an absolute necessity to get out of a false and equivocal position.

Kroll. But you have a duty towards the traditions of your race, Rosmer! Remember that! Rosmersholm has, so to speak, radiated morality and order from time immemorial—yes, and respectful conformity to all that is accepted and sanctioned by the best people. The whole district has taken its stamp from Rosmersholm. It would lead to deplorable, irremediable confusion if it were known that you had broken with what I may call the hereditary idea of the house of Rosmer.

Rosmer. My dear Kroll, I cannot see the matter in that light. I look upon it as my imperative duty to spread a little light and gladness here, where the Rosmer family has from generation to generation been a centre of darkness and oppression.

Kroll (looks at him severely). Yes, that would be a worthy life-work for the last of your race! No, Rosmer; let such things alone; you are the last man for such a task. You were born to be a quiet student.

Rosmer. Perhaps so. But for once in a way I mean to bear my part in the battle of life.

Kroll. And do you know what that battle of life will mean for you? It will mean a life-and-death struggle with all your friends.

Rosmer (quietly). They cannot all be such fanatics as you.

Kroll. You are a credulous creature, Rosmer. An inexperienced creature, too. You have no conception of the overwhelming storm that will burst upon you.

MADAM HELSETH *looks in at the door on the left.*

Madam Helseth. Miss West wants to know——
Rosmer. What is it?

Madam Helseth. There's a man downstairs wanting to have a word with the Pastor.

Rosmer. Is it the man who was here yesterday evening?

Madam Helseth. No, it's that Mortensgård.

Rosmer. Mortensgård?

Kroll. Aha! So it has come to this, has it?—Already!

Rosmer. What does he want with me?/ Why didn't you send him away?

Madam Helseth. Miss West said I was to ask if he might come upstairs.

Rosmer. Tell him I'm engaged——

Kroll (to MADAM HELSETH*).* Let him come up, Madam Helseth. [MADAM HELSETH *goes.*

Kroll (takes up his hat). I retire from the field—for the moment. But the main battle has yet to be fought.

Rosmer. On my honour, Kroll—I have nothing whatever to do with Mortensgård.

Kroll. I do not believe you. On no subject and in no relation whatever will I henceforth believe you. It is war to the knife now. We will try whether we cannot disarm you.

Rosmer. Oh,, Kroll—how low—how very low you have sunk!

Kroll. I? And you think you have the right to say that to me! Remember Beata!

Rosmer. Still harping upon that?

Kroll. No. You must solve the enigma of the mill-race according to your own conscience—if you have anything of the sort left.

PETER MORTENSGARD *enters softly and quietly from the left. He is a small, wiry man with thin reddish hair and beard.*

Kroll (with a look of hatred). Ah, here we have the "Beacon"—burning at Rosmersholm! *(Buttons his coat.)* Well, now I can no longer hesitate what course to steer.

Mortensgård (deferentially). The "Beacon" may always be relied upon to light the Rector home.

Kroll. Yes; you have long shown your goodwill. To be sure there's a commandment about bearing false witness against your neighbour——

Mortensgård. Rector Kroll need not instruct me in the commandments.

Kroll. Not even in the seventh?

Rosmer.—Kroll——!

Mortensgård. If I needed instruction, it would rather be the Pastor's business.

Kroll (with covert sarcasm). The Pastor's? Oh, yes, unquestionably Pastor Rosmer is the man for that.—Good luck to your conference, gentlemen!

[*Goes out and slams the door behind him.*

Rosmer (keeps his eyes fixed on the closed door and says to himself). Well, well—so be it then. *(Turns.)* Will you be good enough to tell me, Mr. Mortensgård, what brings you out here to me?

Mortensgård. It was really Miss West I came to see. I wanted to thank her for the friendly note I received from her yesterday.

Rosmer. I know she wrote to you. Have you seen her then?

Mortensgård. Yes, for a short time. *(Smiles slightly.)* I hear there has been a certain change of views out here at Rosmersholm.

Rosmer. My views are altered in many respects. I might almost say in all.

Mortensgård. So Miss West told me; and that's why she thought I had better come up and talk things over with the Pastor.

Rosmer. What things, Mr. Mortensgård?

Mortensgård. May I announce in the "Beacon" that there has been a change in your views—that you have joined the party of freedom and progress?

Rosmer. Certainly you may. In fact, I beg you to make the announcement.

Mortensgård. Then it shall appear in to-morrow's paper. It will cause a great sensation when it's known that Pastor Rosmer of Rosmersholm is prepared to take up arms for the cause of light, in that sense, too.

Rosmer. I don't quite understand you.

Mortensgård. I mean that the moral position of our party is greatly strengthened whenever we gain an adherent of serious, Christian principles.

Rosmer (with some surprise). Then you do not know——? Did not Miss West tell you that, too?

Mortensgård. What, Pastor Rosmer? Miss West was in a great hurry. She said I was to go upstairs and hear the rest from yourself.

Rosmer. Well, in that case I may tell you that I have emancipated myself entirely, and on every side. I have broken with all the dogmas of the Church. Henceforth they are nothing to me.

Mortensgård (looks at him in amazement). Well—if the skies were to fall I couldn't be more——! Pastor Rosmer himself announces——.

Rosmer. Yes, I now stand where you have stood for many years. That, too, you may announce in the "Beacon" to-morrow.

Mortensgård. That too? No, my dear Pastor—excuse me—— I don't think it would be wise to touch on that side of the matter.

Rosmer. Not touch on it?

Mortensgård. Not at present, I mean.

Rosmer. I don't understand——

Mortensgård. Well, you see, Pastor Rosmer—you probably don't know the ins and outs of things so well as I do. But, since you have come over to the party of freedom—and, as I hear from Miss West, you intend to take an active share in the movement—I presume you would like to be of as

much service as possible, both to the cause in general and
to this particular agitation.

Rosmer. Yes, that is my earnest wish.

Mortensgård. Good. But now I must tell you, Pastor
Rosmer, that if you openly declare your defection from the
Church, you tie your own hands at the very outset.

Rosmer. Do you think so?

Mortensgård. Yes; believe me, you won't be able to do
much for the cause, in this part of the country at any rate.
And besides—we have plenty of free-thinkers already, Pastor Rosmer—I might almost say too many. What the party
requires, is a Christian element—something that every one
must respect. That is what we are sadly in need of. And,
therefore, I advise you to keep your own counsel about what
doesn't concern the public. That's my view of the matter,
at least.

Rosmer. I understand. Then if I openly confess my
apostasy, you dare not have anything to do with me?

Mortensgård (shaking his head). I scarcely like to risk it,
Pastor Rosmer. I have made it a rule for some time past not
to support any one or anything that is actively opposed to
the Church.

Rosmer. Then you have yourself returned to the Church?

Mortensgård. That concerns no one but myself.

Rosmer. Ah, so that is it. Now I understand you.

Mortensgård. Pastor Rosmer—you ought to remember
that I—I in particular—have not full liberty of action.

Rosmer. What hampers you?

Mortensgård. The fact that I am a marked man.

Rosmer. Ah—indeed.

Mortensgård. A marked man, Pastor Rosmer. You,
above all men, should remember that; for I have chiefly you
to thank for the scandal that branded me.

Rosmer. If I had then stood where I stand now, I should
have dealt more gently with your offence.

Mortensgård. That I don't doubt. But it is too late now.

You have branded me once for all—branded me for life.
I suppose you can scarcely understand what that means.
But now you may perhaps come to feel the smart of it your-
self, Pastor Rosmer.

Rosmer. I?

Mortensgård. Yes. You surely don't suppose that Rector Kroll and his set will ever forgive a desertion like yours?
I hear the "County News" is going to be very savage in future. You, too, may find yourself a marked man before long.

Rosmer. In personal matters, Mr. Mortensgård, I feel
myself secure from attack. My life is beyond reproach.

Mortensgård (*with a sly smile*). That's a large word,
Mr. Rosmer.

Rosmer. Perhaps; but I have a right to use it.

Mortensgård. Even if you were to scrutinise your conduct
as closely as you once scrutinised mine?

Rosmer. Your tone is very curious. What are you hinting at? Anything definite?

Mortensgård. Yes, something definite. Only one thing.
But that might be bad enough, if malicious opponents got
wind of it.

Rosmer. Will you have the kindness to let me hear what
it is?

Mortensgård. Cannot you guess for yourself, Pastor?

Rosmer. No, certainly not. I have not the slightest idea.

Mortensgård. Well, well, I suppose I must come out with
it then.—I have in my possession a strange letter, dated
from Rosmersholm.

Rosmer. Miss West's letter, do you mean? Is it so
strange?

Mortensgård. No, there's nothing strange about that.
But I once received another letter from this house.

Rosmer. Also from Miss West?

Mortensgård. No, Mr. Rosmer.

Rosmer. Well then, from whom? From whom?

Mortensgård. From the late Mrs. Rosmer.

Rosmer. From my wife! You received a letter from my wife!

Mortensgård. I did.

Rosmer. When?

Mortensgård. Towards the close of Mrs. Rosmer's life. Perhaps about a year and a half ago. That is the letter I call strange.

Rosmer. I suppose you know that my wife's mind was affected at that time.

Mortensgård. Yes; I know many people thought so. But I don't think there was anything in the letter to show it. When I call it strange, I mean in another sense.

Rosmer. And what in the world did my poor wife take it into her head to write to you about?

Mortensgård. I have the letter at home. She begins to the effect that she is living in great anxiety and fear; there are so many malicious people about here, she says; and they think of nothing but causing you trouble and injury.

Rosmer. Me?

Mortensgård. Yes, so she says. And then comes the strangest part of all. Shall I go on, Pastor Rosmer?

Rosmer. Assuredly! Tell me everything, without reserve.

Mortensgård. The deceased lady begs and implores me to be magnanimous. She knows, she says, that it was her husband that had me dismissed from my post as teacher; and she conjured me by all that's sacred not to avenge myself.

Rosmer. How did she suppose you could avenge yourself?

Mortensgård. The letter says that if I should hear rumours of sinful doings at Rosmersholm, I am not to believe them; they are only spread abroad by wicked people who wish to make you unhappy.

Rosmer. Is all that in the letter?

Mortensgård. You may read it for yourself, sir, when you please.

Rosmer. But I don't understand——! What did she imagine the rumours to be about?

Mortensgård. Firstly, that the Pastor had deserted the faith of his fathers. Your wife denied that absolutely— then. And next—h'm——

Rosmer. Next?

Mortensgård. Well, next she writes—rather confusedly —that she knows nothing of any sinful intrigue at Rosmersholm; that she has never been wronged in any way. And if any such rumours should get about, she implores me to say nothing of the matter in the "Beacon."

Rosmer. Is no name mentioned?

Mortensgård. None.

Rosmer. Who brought you the letter?

Mortensgård. I have promised not to say. It was handed to me one evening, at dusk.

Rosmer. If you had made inquiries at the time, you would have learnt that my poor, unhappy wife was not fully accountable for her actions.

Mortensgård. I did make inquiries, Pastor Rosmer. But I must say that was not the impression I received.

Rosmer. Was it not?—But what is your precise reason for telling me now about this incomprehensible old letter?

Mortensgård. To impress on you the necessity for extreme prudence, Pastor Rosmer.

Rosmer. In my life, do you mean?

Mortensgård. Yes. You must remember that from to-day you have ceased to be a neutral.

Rosmer. Then you have quite made up your mind that I must have something to conceal?

Mortensgård. I don't know why an emancipated man should refrain from living his life out as fully as possible. But, as I said before, be exceedingly cautious in future. If anything should get abroad that conflicts with current prejudices, you may be sure the whole liberal movement will have to suffer for it.—Good-bye, Pastor Rosmer.

Rosmer. Good-bye.

Mortensgård. I shall go straight to the office and have the great news put into the "Beacon."

Rosmer. Yes; omit nothing.

Mortensgård. I shall omit nothing that the public need know.

> [*He bows and goes out.* ROSMER *remains stand-*
> *ing in the doorway while he goes down the stairs.*
> *The outer door is heard to close.*

Rosmer (in the doorway, calls softly). Rebecca! Re——
H'm. *(Aloud.)* Madam Helseth,—is Miss West not there?

Madam Helseth (from the hall). No, Pastor Rosmer, she's not here.

> [*The curtain at the back is drawn aside.* REBECCA
> *appears in the doorway.*

Rebecca. Rosmer!

Rosmer (turns). What! Were you in my room? My dear, what were you doing there?

Rebecca (goes up to him). I was listening.

Rosmer. Oh, Rebecca, how could you?

Rebecca. I could not help it. He said it so hatefully— that about my morning gown——

Rosmer. Then you were there when Kroll——?

Rebecca. Yes. I wanted to know what was lurking in his mind.

Rosmer. I would have told you.

Rebecca. You would scarcely have told me all. And certainly not in his own words.

Rosmer. Did you hear everything, then?

Rebecca. Nearly everything, I think. I had to go down-stairs for a moment when Mortensgård came.

Rosmer. And then you came back again——?

Rebecca. Don't be vexed with me, dear friend!

Rosmer. Do whatever you think right. You are mis-tress of your own actions.—But what do you say to all this,

Rebecca——? Oh, I seem never to have needed you so much before!

Rebecca. Both you and I have been prepared for what must happen some time.

Rosmer. No, no—not for this.

Rebecca. Not for this?

Rosmer. I knew well enough that sooner or later our beautiful, pure friendship might be misinterpreted and soiled. Not by Kroll—I could never have believed such a thing of him—but by all those other people with the coarse souls and the ignoble eyes. Oh yes—I had reason enough for keeping our alliance so jealously concealed. It was a dangerous secret.

Rebecca. Oh, why should we care what all those people think! We know in our own hearts that we are blameless.

Rosmer. Blameless? I? Yes. I thought so—till to-day. But now—now, Rebecca——?

Rebecca. Well, what now?

Rosmer. How am I to explain Beata's terrible accusation?

Rebecca (vehemently). Oh, don't speak of Beata! Don't think of Beata any more! You were just beginning to shake off the hold she has upon you, even in the grave.

Rosmer. Since I have heard all this, she seems, in a ghastly sort of way, to be alive again.

Rebecca. Oh no—not that, Rosmer! Not that!

Rosmer. Yes, I tell you. We must try to get to the bottom of this. What can possibly have led her to misinterpret things so fatally?

Rebecca. You are surely not beginning to doubt that she was on the very verge of insanity?

Rosmer. Oh yes—that is just what I can't feel quite certain of any longer. And besides—even if she was——

Rebecca. If she was? Well, what then?

Rosmer. I mean—where are we to look for the determining cause that drove her morbid spirit over the border-line of madness?

Rebecca. Oh, why brood over problems no one can solve?

Rosmer. I cannot help it, Rebecca. I cannot shake off these gnawing doubts, however much I may wish to.

Rebecca. But it may become dangerous—this eternal dwelling upon one miserable subject.

Rosmer (walks about restlessly, in thought). I must have betrayed myself in one way or another. She must have noticed how happy I began to feel from the time you came to us.

Rebecca. Yes but, dear, even if she did——?

Rosmer. Be sure it didn't escape her that we read the same books—that the interest of discussing all the new ideas drew us together. Yet I cannot understand it! I was so careful to spare her. As I look back, it seems to me I made it the business of my life to keep her in ignorance of all our interests. Did I not, Rebecca?

Rebecca. Yes, yes; certainly you did.

Rosmer. And you too. And yet——! Oh, it's terrible to think of! She must have gone about here—full of her morbid passion—saying never a word—watching us—noting everything—and misinterpreting everything.

Rebecca (pressing her hands together). Oh, I should never have come to Rosmersholm!

Rosmer. To think of all she must have suffered in silence! All the foulness her sick brain must have conjured up around us! Did she never say anything to you to put you at all on the alert?

Rebecca (as if startled). To me! Do you think I should have stayed a day longer if she had?

Rosmer. No, no, of course not.—Oh, what a battle she must have fought! And alone too, Rebecca; desperate and quite alone!—and then, at last, that heart-breaking, accusing victory—in the mill-race.

[*Throws himself into the chair by the writing-table, with his elbows on the table and his face in his hands.*

Rebecca (approaches him cautiously from behind). Listen, Rosmer. If it were in your power to call Beata back —to you—to Rosmersholm—would you do it?

Rosmer. Oh, how do I know what I would or would not do? I can think of nothing but this one thing—that cannot be recalled.

Rebecca. You were just beginning to live, Rosmer. You had begun. You had freed yourself—on every side. You felt so buoyant and happy——

Rosmer. Oh yes—I did indeed.—And now this crushing blow falls on me.

Rebecca (behind him, rests her arms on the chair-back). How beautiful it was when we sat in the twilight, in the room downstairs, helping each other to lay out our new life-plans! You were to set resolutely to work in the world —the living world of to-day, as you said. You were to go as a messenger of emancipation from home to home; to win over minds and wills; to create noble-men around you in wider and wider circles. Noble-men.

Rosmer. Happy noble-men.

Rebecca. Yes—happy.

Rosmer. For it is happiness that ennobles, Rebecca.

Rebecca. Should you not say—sorrow as well? A great sorrow?

Rosmer. Yes—if one can get through it—over it—away from it.

Rebecca. That is what you must do.

Rosmer (shakes his head gloomily). I shall never get over this—wholly. There will always be a doubt—a question left. I can never again know that luxury of the soul which makes life so marvellously sweet to live!

Rebecca (bends over his chair-back, and says more softly). What is it you mean, Rosmer?

Rosmer (looking up at her). Peaceful, happy innocence.

Rebecca (recoils a step). Yes. Innocence.

[*A short pause.*

Rosmer (with his elbow on the table, leaning his head on his hand, and looking straight before him). And what extraordinary penetration she showed! How systematically she put all this together! First she begins to doubt my orthodoxy—— How could that occur to her? But it did occur to her; and then it grew to be a certainty. And then—yes, then of course it was easy for her to think all the rest possible. *(Sits up in his chair and runs his hands through his hair.)* Oh, all these horrible imaginings! I shall never get rid of them. I feel it. I know it. At any moment they will come rushing in upon me, and bring back the thought of the dead!

Rebecca. Like the White Horse of Rosmersholm.

Rosmer. Yes, like that. Rushing forth in the darkness —in the silence.

Rebecca. And because of this miserable figment of the brain, you will let slip the hold you were beginning to take upon the living world?

Rosmer. You may well think it hard. Yes, hard, Rebecca. But I have no choice. How could I ever leave this behind me?

Rebecca (behind his chair). By entering into new relations.

Rosmer (surprised, looks up). New relations?

Rebecca. Yes, new relations to the outside world. Live, work, act. Don't sit here brooding and groping among insoluble enigmas.

Rosmer (rises). New relations? *(Walks across the floor, stops at the door and then comes back.)* One question occurs to me. Has it not occurred to you too, Rebecca?

Rebecca (drawing breath with difficulty). Let me—hear —what it is.

Rosmer. What form do you think our relations will take after to-day?

Rebecca. I believe our friendship will endure—come what may.

Rosmer. That is not exactly what I meant. The thing that first brought us together, and that unites us so closely —our common faith in a pure comradeship between man and woman——

Rebecca. Yes, yes—what of that?

Rosmer. I mean, that such a relation—as this of ours— does it not presuppose a quiet, happy, peaceful life——?

Rebecca. What then?

Rosmer. But the life I must now look forward to is one of struggle and unrest and strong agitations. For I will live my life, Rebecca! I will not be crushed to earth by horrible possibilities. I will not have my course of life forced upon me, either by the living or by—any one else.

Rebecca. No, no—do not! Be an absolutely free man, Rosmer!

Rosmer. But can you not guess what is in my mind? Do you not know? Don't you see how I can best shake off all gnawing memories—all the unhappy past?

Rebecca. How?

Rosmer. By opposing to it a new, a living reality.

Rebecca (feeling for the chair-back). A living—— What do you mean?

Rosmer (comes nearer). Rebecca—if I were to ask you —will you be my second wife?

Rebecca (for a moment speechless, then cries out with joy). Your wife! Your——! I!

Rosmer. Come; let us try it. We two will be one. The place of the dead must stand empty no longer.

Rebecca. I—in Beata's place——!

Rosmer. Then she will be out of the saga—completely— for ever and ever.

Rebecca (softly, trembling). Do you believe that, Rosmer?

Rosmer. It must be so! It must! I cannot—I will not go through life with a dead body on my back. Help me to cast it off, Rebecca. And let us stifle all memories in freedom, in joy, in passion. You shall be to me the only wife I have ever had.

Rebecca (with self-command). Never speak of this again. I will never be your wife.

Rosmer. What! Never! Do you not think you could come to love me? Is there not already a strain of love in our friendship?

Rebecca (puts her hands over her ears as if in terror). Don't speak so, Rosmer! Don't say such things!

Rosmer (seizes her arm). Yes, yes—there is a growing promise in our relation. Oh, I can see that you feel it too. Do you not, Rebecca?

Rebecca (once more firm and calm). Listen to me. I tell you—if you persist in this, I will go away from Rosmersholm.

Rosmer. Go away! You! You cannot. It is impossible.

Rebecca. It is still more impossible that I should be your wife. Never in this world can I marry you.

Rosmer (looks at her in surprise). You say "can"; and you say it so strangely. Why can you not?

Rebecca (seizes both his hands). Dear friend—both for your own sake and for mine—do not ask why. *(Lets go his hands.)* Do not, Rosmer.

[*Goes towards the door on the left.*

Rosmer. Henceforth I can think of nothing but that one question—why?

Rebecca (turns and looks at him). Then it is all over.

Rosmer. Between you and me?

Rebecca. Yes.

Rosmer. It will never be all over between us two. You will never leave Rosmersholm.

Rebecca (with her hand on the door-handle). No, perhaps I shall not. But if you ask me again—it is all over.

Rosmer. All over? How——?

Rebecca. For then I will go the way that Beata went. Now you know it, Rosmer.

Rosmer. Rebecca——?

Rebecca (in the doorway, nods slowly). Now you know it.   [*She goes out.*

Rosmer (stares, thunderstruck, at the door, and says to himself). What—is—this?

ACT THIRD

*The sitting-room at Rosmersholm. The window and the
entrance door are open. The sun is shining outside.
Forenoon.*

REBECCA WEST, *dressed as in the first Act, stands at the
window, watering and arranging the flowers. Her
crochet-work lies in the arm-chair.* MADAM HELSETH
*is moving about, dusting the furniture with a feather-
brush.*

Rebecca (after a short silence). I can't understand the
Pastor remaining so long upstairs to-day.

Madam Helseth. Oh, he often does that. But he'll soon
be down now, I should think.

Rebecca. Have you seen anything of him?

Madam Helseth. I caught a glimpse of him when I went
upstairs with his coffee. He was in his bedroom, dressing.

Rebecca. I asked because he was a little out of sorts
yesterday.

Madam Helseth. He didn't look well. I wonder if there
isn't something amiss between him and his brother-in-law.

Rebecca. What do you think it can be?

Madam Helseth. I couldn't say. Perhaps it's that Mortensgård that has been setting them against each other.

Rebecca. Likely enough.—Do you know anything of this
Peter Mortensgård?

Madam Helseth. No indeed. How could you think so,
Miss? A fellow like him?

Rebecca. Do you mean because he edits such a low paper?

Madam Helseth. Oh, it's not only that.—You must have heard, Miss, that he had a child by a married woman that had been deserted by her husband?

Rebecca. Yes, I have heard of it. But it must have been long before I came here.

Madam Helseth. It's true he was very young at the time; and she should have known better. He wanted to marry her too; but of course he couldn't do that. And I don't say he hasn't paid dear for it.—But, good Lord, Mortensgård has got on in the world since those days. There's a many people run after him now.

Rebecca. Yes, most of the poor people bring their affairs to him when they're in any trouble.

Madam Helseth. Ah, and others too, perhaps, besides the poor folk——

Rebecca (looks at her furtively). Indeed.

Madam Helseth (by the sofa, dusting away vigorously). Perhaps the last people you would think likely to, Miss.

Rebecca (busy with the flowers). Come, now, that's only an idea of yours, Madam Helseth. You can't be sure of what you're saying.

Madam Helseth. You think I can't, Miss? But I can tell you I am. Why—if you must know it—I once took a letter in to Mortensgård myself.

Rebecca (turning). No—did you?

Madam Helseth. Yes, indeed I did. And a letter that was written here at Rosmersholm too.

Rebecca. Really, Madam Helseth?

Madam Helseth. Yes, that it was. And it was on fine paper, and there was a fine red seal on it too.

Rebecca. And it was given to you to deliver? Then, my dear Madam Helseth, it's not difficult to guess who wrote it.

Madam Helseth. Well?

Rebecca. It must have been something that poor Mrs. Rosmer, in her morbid state——

Madam Helseth. It's you that say that, Miss, not me.

Rebecca. But what was in the letter? Oh, I forgot—— you can't know that.

Madam Helseth. H'm; what if I did know it, all the same?

Rebecca. Did she tell you what she was writing about?

Madam Helseth. No, she didn't exactly do that. But Mortensgård, when he'd read it, he began questioning me backwards and forwards and up and down, so that I soon guessed what was in it.

Rebecca. Then what do you think it was? Oh my dear good Madam Helseth, do tell me.

Madam Helseth. Oh no, Miss. Not for the whole world.

Rebecca. Oh you can surely tell me. We two are such good friends.

Madam Helseth. Lord preserve me from telling you anything about that, Miss. I can only tell you that it was something horrible that they'd got the poor sick lady to believe.

Rebecca. Who had got her to believe it?

Madam Helseth. Wicked people, Miss West. Wicked people.

Rebecca. Wicked——?

Madam Helseth. Yes, I say it again. They must have been real wicked people.

Rebecca. And who do you think it could have been?

Madam Helseth. Oh, I know well enough what to think. But Lord forbid *I* should say anything. To be sure there's a certain lady in the town—h'm!

Rebecca. I can see that you mean Mrs. Kroll.

Madam Helseth. Ah, she's a fine one, she is. She has always been the great lady with me. And she's never had any too much love for you neither.

Rebecca. Do you think Mrs. Rosmer was in her right mind when she wrote that letter to Mortensgård?

Madam Helseth. It's a queer thing a person's mind, Miss. Clean out of her mind I don't think she was.

Rebecca. But she seemed to go distracted when she learned that she must always be childless. It was that that unsettled her reason.

Madam Helseth. Yes, poor lady, that was a dreadful blow to her.

Rebecca (takes up her crochet and sits in a chair by the window). But after all—don't you think it was a good thing for the Pastor, Madam Helseth?

Madam Helseth. What, Miss?

Rebecca. That there were no children. Don't you think so?

Madam Helseth. H'm, I'm sure I don't know what to say about that.

Rebecca. Oh yes, believe me, it was fortunate for him. Pastor Rosmer is not the man to have crying children about his house.

Madam Helseth. Ah, Miss, little children don't cry at Rosmersholm.

Rebecca (looks at her). Don't cry?

Madam Helseth. No. As long as people can remember, children have never been known to cry in this house.

Rebecca. That's very strange.

Madam Helseth. Yes; isn't it? But it runs in the family. And then there's another strange thing. When they grow up, they never laugh. Never, as long as they live.

Rebecca. Why, how extraordinary——

Madam Helseth. Have you ever once heard or seen the Pastor laugh, Miss?

Rebecca. No—now that I think of it, I almost believe you are right. But I don't think any one laughs much in this part of the country.

Madam Helseth. No, they don't. They say it began at Rosmersholm. And then I suppose it spread round about, as if it was catching-like.

Rebecca. You are a very wise woman, Madam Helseth.

Madam Helseth. Oh, Miss, you mustn't sit there and make fun of me. *(Listens.)* Hush, hush—here's the Pastor coming down. He doesn't like to see dusting going on.   [*She goes out to the right.*

JOHANNES ROSMER, *with his hat and stick in his hand, enters from the hall.*

Rosmer. Good morning, Rebecca.

Rebecca. Good morning, dear. *(A moment after—crocheting.)* Are you going out?

Rosmer. Yes.

Rebecca. It's a beautiful day.

Rosmer. You didn't look in on me this morning.

Rebecca. No, I didn't. Not to-day.

Rosmer. Do you not intend to in future?

Rebecca. Oh, I don't know yet, dear.

Rosmer. Has anything come for me?

Rebecca. The "County News" has come.

Rosmer. The "County News"?

Rebecca. There it is on the table.

Rosmer (puts down his hat and stick). Is there any-thing——?

Rebecca. Yes.

Rosmer. And you didn't send it up?

Rebecca. You will read it soon enough.

Rosmer. Oh, indeed? *(Takes the paper and reads, standing by the table.)*—What!—"We cannot warn our readers too earnestly against unprincipled renegades." *(Looks at her.)* They call me a renegade, Rebecca.

Rebecca. They mention no names.

Rosmer. That makes no difference. *(Reads on.)* "Secret traitors to the good cause."—"Judas-natures, who make brazen confession of their apostasy as soon as they

think the most convenient and—profitable moment has arrived." "Ruthless befouling of a name honoured through
generations"—"in the confident hope of a suitable reward
from the party in momentary power." *(Lays down the
paper on the table.)* And they can say such things of me!—
Men who have known me so long and so well! Things
they themselves don't believe. Things they know there is
not a word of truth in—they print them all the same.

Rebecca. That is not all.

Rosmer (takes up the paper again). "Inexperience and
lack of judgment the only excuse"—"pernicious influence—
possibly extending to matters which, for the present, we
do not wish to make subjects of public discussion or accusation." *(Looks at her.)* What is this?

Rebecca. It is aimed at me, plainly enough.

Rosmer (lays down the paper). Rebecca,—this is the
conduct of dishonourable men.

Rebecca. Yes, they need scarcely be so contemptuous of
Mortensgård.

Rosmer (walks about the room). Something must be
done. All that is good in human nature will go to ruin, if
this is allowed to go on. But it shall not go on! Oh,
what a joy—what a joy it would be to me to let a little
light into all this gloom and ugliness!

Rebecca (rises). Ah yes, Rosmer. In that you have a
great and glorious object to live for.

Rosmer. Only think, if I could rouse them to see themselves as they are; teach them to repent and blush before
their better natures; bring them together in mutual forbearance—in love, Rebecca!

Rebecca. Yes, put your whole strength into that, and
you must succeed.

Rosmer. I think success must be possible. Oh, what a
delight it would be then to live one's life! No more malig-
nant wrangling; only emulation. All eyes fixed on the same
goal. Every mind, every will pressing forward—upward—

each by the path its nature prescribes for it. Happiness for all—through all. *(Happens to look out of the window, starts, and says sadly.)* Ah! Not through me.

Rebecca. Not——? Not through you?

Rosmer. Nor for me.

Rebecca. Oh Rosmer, do not let such doubts take hold of you.

Rosmer. Happiness—dear Rebecca—happiness is above all·things the calm, glad certainty of innocence.

Rebecca (looks straight before her). Yes, innocence——

Rosmer. Oh, you cannot know what guilt means. But I——

Rebecca. You least of all!

Rosmer (points out of the window). The mill-race.

Rebecca. Oh Rosmer——!

MADAM HELSETH *looks in at the door.*

Madam Helseth. Miss West!

Rebecca. Presently, presently. Not now.

Madam Helseth. Only a word, Miss.

[REBECCA *goes to the door.* MADAM HELSETH
*tells her something. They whisper together for
a few moments.* MADAM HELSETH *nods and
goes out.*

Rosmer (uneasily). Was it anything for me?

Rebecca. No, only something about the house-work.— You ought to go out into the fresh air, dear Rosmer. You should take a good long walk.

Rosmer (takes up his hat). Yes, come. Let us go together.

Rebecca. No, dear, I can't just now. You must go alone. But shake off all these gloomy thoughts. Promise me.

Rosmer. I am afraid I shall never shake them off.

Rebecca. Oh, that such baseless fancies should take so strong a hold of you——!

Rosmer. Not so baseless I am afraid, Rebecca. I lay

awake all night thinking it over and over. Perhaps Beata
saw clearly after all.

Rebecca. In what?

Rosmer. In her belief that I loved you, Rebecca.

Rebecca. Right in that!

Rosmer (lays his hat down on the table). The question
that haunts me is this: were we two not deceiving ourselves
all the time—when we called our relation friendship?

Rebecca. You mean that it might as well have been
called——?

Rosmer. ——love. Yes, Rebecca, that is what I mean.
Even while Beata was alive, all my thoughts were for you.
It was you alone I longed for. It was when you were by
my side that I felt the calm gladness of utter content. If
you think it over, Rebecca—did we not feel for each other
from the first a sort of sweet, secret child-love—desireless,
dreamless? Was it not so with you? Tell me.

Rebecca (struggling with herself). Oh—I don't know
what to answer.

Rosmer. And it was this close-linked life in and for each
other that we took for friendship. No, Rebecca—our bond
has been a spiritual marriage—perhaps from the very first.
That is why there is guilt on my soul. I had no right to such
happiness—it was a sin against Beata.

Rebecca. No right to live happily? Do you believe that,
Rosmer?

Rosmer. She looked at our relation with the eyes of her
love—judged it after the fashion of her love. Inevitably.
Beata could not have judged otherwise than she did.

Rebecca. But how can you accuse yourself because of
Beata's delusion?

Rosmer. It was love for me—her kind of love—that
drove her into the mill-race. That is an immovable fact,
Rebecca. And that is what I can never get over.

Rebecca. Oh, think of nothing but the great, beautiful
task you have devoted your life to.

Rosmer (shakes his head). It can never be accomplished, dear. Not by me. Not after what I have come to know.

Rebecca. Why not by you?

Rosmer. Because no cause ever triumphs that has its origin in sin.

Rebecca (vehemently). Oh, these are only ancestral doubts—ancestral fears—ancestral scruples. They say the dead come back to Rosmersholm in the shape of rushing white horses. I think this shows that it is true.

Rosmer. Be that as it may; what does it matter, so long as I cannot rid myself of the feeling? And believe me, Rebecca, it is as I tell you. The cause that is to win a lasting victory must have for its champion a happy, an innocent man.

Rebecca. Is happiness so indispensable to you, Rosmer?

Rosmer. Happiness? Yes, dear,—it is.

Rebecca. To you, who can never laugh?

Rosmer. Yes, in spite of that. Believe me, I have a great capacity for happiness.

Rebecca. Now go for your walk, dear. A good long walk. Do you hear?—See, here is your hat. And your stick too.

Rosmer (takes both). Thanks. And you won't come with me?

Rebecca. No, no; I can't just now.

Rosmer. Very well, then. You are with me none the less.

> [*He goes out by the entrance door.* REBECCA
> *waits a moment, cautiously watching his de-*
> *parture from behind the open door; then she goes*
> *to the door on the right.*

Rebecca (opens the door, and says in a low tone). Now, Madam Helseth. You can show him in now.

> [*Goes towards the window.*

A moment after RECTOR KROLL *enters from the right. He bows silently and formally, and keeps his hat in his hand.*

Kroll. He has gone out?

Rebecca. Yes.

Kroll. Does he usually stay out long?

Rebecca. Yes, he does. But one cannot count on him to-day. So if you don't care to meet him——

Kroll. No, no. It is you I want to speak to,—quite alone.

Rebecca. Then we had better not lose time. Sit down, Rector.

[*She sits in the easy-chair by the window.* RECTOR KROLL *sits on a chair beside her.*

Kroll. Miss West—you can scarcely imagine how deeply and painfully I have taken this to heart—this change in Johannes Rosmer.

Rebecca. We expected it would be so—at first.

Kroll. Only at first?

Rebecca. Rosmer was confident that sooner or later you would join him.

Kroll. I?

Rebecca. You and all his other friends.

Kroll. Ah, there you see! That shows the infirmity of his judgment in all that concerns men and practical life.

Rebecca. But after all—since he feels it a necessity to emancipate himself on all sides——

Kroll. Yes, but wait—that is just what I do not believe.

Rebecca. What do you believe then?

Kroll. I believe that you are at the bottom of it all.

Rebecca. It is your wife who has put that in your head, Rector Kroll.

Kroll. No matter who has put it in my head. What is certain is that I feel a strong suspicion—an exceedingly strong suspicion—when I think things over, and piece together all I know of your behaviour ever since you came here.

Rebecca (looks at him). I seem to recollect a time when you felt an exceedingly strong faith in me, dear Rector. I might almost call it a warm faith.

Kroll (in a subdued voice). Whom could you not bewitch—if you tried?

Rebecca. Did I try——?

Kroll. Yes, you did. I am no longer such a fool as to believe that there was any feeling in the matter. You simply wanted to get a footing at Rosmersholm—to strike root here—and in that I was to serve you. Now I see it.

Rebecca. You seem utterly to have forgotten that it was Beata who begged and implored me to come out here?

Kroll. Yes, when you had bewitched her to. Can the feeling she came to entertain for you be called friendship? It was adoration—almost idolatry. It developed into—what shall I call it?—a sort of desperate passion.—Yes, that is the right word for it.

Rebecca. Be so good as to recollect the state your sister was in. So far as I am concerned, I don't think any one can accuse me of being hysterical.

Kroll. No; that you certainly are not. But that makes you all the more dangerous to the people you want to get into your power. It is easy for you to weigh your acts and calculate consequences—just because your heart is cold.

Rebecca. Cold? Are you so sure of that?

Kroll. I am quite certain of it now. Otherwise you could never have lived here year after year ́without faltering in the pursuit of your object. Well, well—you have gained your end. You have got him and everything into your power. But in order to do so, you have not scrupled to make him unhappy.

Rebecca. That is not true. It is not I—it is you yourself that have made him unhappy.

Kroll. I?

Rebecca. Yes, when you led him to imagine that he was responsible for Beata's terrible end.

Kroll. Does he feel that so deeply, then?

Rebecca. How can you doubt it? A mind so sensitive as his——

Kroll. I thought that an emancipated man, so-called, was above all such scruples.—But there we have it! Oh yes—I admit I knew how it would be. The descendant of the men that look down on us from these walls—how could he hope to cut himself adrift from all that has been handed down without a break from generation to generation?

Rebecca (looks down thoughtfully). Johannes Rosmer's spirit is deeply rooted in his ancestry. That is very certain.

Kroll. Yes, and you should have taken that fact into consideration, if you had felt any affection for him. But that sort of consideration was no doubt beyond you. There is such an immeasurable difference between your antecedents and his.

Rebecca. What antecedents do you mean?

Kroll. I am speaking of your origin—your family antecedents, Miss West.

Rebecca. Oh, indeed! Yes, it is quite true that I come of very humble folk. Nevertheless——

Kroll. I am not thinking of rank and position. I allude to your moral antecedents.

Rebecca. Moral——? In what sense?

Kroll. The circumstances of your birth.

Rebecca. What do you mean?

Kroll. I only mention the matter because it accounts for your whole conduct.

Rebecca. I do not understand this. You must explain.

Kroll. I really did not suppose you could require an explanation. Otherwise it would have been very odd that you should have let Dr. West adopt you——

Rebecca (rises). Ah! Now I understand.

Kroll. ——and that you should have taken his name. Your mother's name was Gamvik.

Rebecca (walks across the room). My father's name was Gamvik, Rector Kroll.

Kroll. Your mother's business must have brought her very frequently into contact with the parish doctor.

Rebecca. Yes, it did.

Kroll. And then he takes you into his house—as soon as your mother dies. He treats you harshly; and yet you stay with him. You know that he won't leave you a half-penny—as a matter of fact, you only got a case full of books—and yet you stay on; you bear with him; you nurse him to the last.

Rebecca (stands by the table, looking scornfully at him). And you account for all this by assuming that there was something immoral—something criminal about my birth?

Kroll. I attribute your care for him to involuntary filial instinct. Indeed I believe your whole conduct is determined by your origin.

Rebecca (vehemently). But there is not a single word of truth in what you say! And I can prove it! Dr. West did not come to Finmark till after I was born.

Kroll. Excuse me, Miss West. He settled there the year before. I have assured myself of that.

Rebecca. You are mistaken, I say! You are utterly mistaken.

Kroll. You told me the day before yesterday that you were nine-and-twenty—in your thirtieth year.

Rebecca. Indeed! Did I say so?

Kroll. Yes, you did. And I can calculate from that——

Rebecca. Stop! You needn't calculate. I may as well tell you at once: I am a year older than I give myself out to be.

Kroll (smiles incredulously). Really! I am surprised! What can be the reason of that?

Rebecca. When I had passed twenty-five, it seemed to me I was getting altogether too old for an unmarried woman. And so I began to lie about my age.

Kroll. You? An emancipated woman! Have you prejudices about the age for marriage?

Rebecca. Yes, it was idiotic of me—idiotic and absurd. But some folly or other will always cling to us, not to be shaken off. We are made so.

Kroll. Well, so be it; but my calculation may be right, none the less. For Dr. West was up there on a short visit the year before he got the appointment.

Rebecca (with a vehement outburst). It is not true!

Kroll. Is it not true?

Rebecca. No. My mother never spoke of any such visit.

Kroll. Did she not?

Rebecca. No, never. Nor Dr. West either; not a word about it.

Kroll. Might not that be because they both had reasons for suppressing a year? Just as you have done, Miss West. Perhaps it is a family foible.

Rebecca (walks about clenching and wringing her hands). It is impossible. You want to cheat me into believing it. This can never, never be true. It cannot! Never in this world——

Kroll (rises). My dear Miss West—why in heaven's name are you so terribly excited? You quite frighten me! What am I to think—to believe——?

Rebecca. Nothing! You are to think and believe nothing.

Kroll. Then you must really tell me how you can take this affair—this possibility—so terribly to heart.

Rebecca (controlling herself). It is perfectly simple, Rector Kroll. I have no wish to be taken for an illegitimate child.

Kroll. Indeed! Well well, let us be satisfied with that explanation—in the meantime. But in that case you must still have a certain—prejudice on that point too?

Rebecca. Yes, I suppose I have.

Kroll. Ah, I fancy it is much the same with most of what you call your "emancipation." You have read yourself into a number of new ideas and opinions. You have got a sort of smattering of recent discoveries in various fields—discoveries that seem to overthrow certain principles which have hitherto been held impregnable and unassailable. But all this has only been a matter of the intellect, Miss West—a superficial acquisition. It has not passed into your blood.

Rebecca (thoughtfully). Perhaps you are right.

Kroll. Yes, look into your own mind, and you will see! And if this is the case with you, one may easily guess how it must be with Johannes Rosmer. It is sheer, unmitigated madness—it is running blindfold to destruction—for him to think of coming openly forward and confessing himself an apostate! Only think—a man of 'his sensitive nature! Imagine him disowned and persecuted by the circle of which he has always formed a part—exposed to ruthless attacks from all the best people in the community! He is not—he never can be the man to endure all that.

Rebecca. He must endure it! It is too late now for him to retreat.

Kroll. Not at all too late. By no means. What has happened can be hushed up—or at least explained away as a mere temporary aberration, however deplorable. But— one measure is certainly indispensable.

Rebecca. And what is that?

Kroll. You must get him to legalise the position, Miss West.

Rebecca. His position towards me?

Kroll. Yes. You must make him do that.

Rebecca. Then you absolutely cannot clear your mind

of the idea that our position requires to be—legalised, as you call it?

Kroll. I would rather not go into the matter too closely. But I believe I have noticed that it is nowhere easier to break through all so-called prejudices than in—h'm——

Rebecca. In the relation between man and woman, you mean?

Kroll. Yes,—to speak plainly—I think so.

Rebecca (wanders across the room and looks out at the window). I could almost say—I wish you were right, Rector Kroll.

Kroll. What do you mean by that? You say it so strangely.

Rebecca. Oh well—please let us drop the subject. Ah, —there he comes.

Kroll. Already! Then I will go.

Rebecca (goes towards him). No—please stay. There is something I want you to hear.

Kroll. Not now. I don't feel as if I could bear to see him.

Rebecca. I beg you to stay. Do! If not, you will regret it by-and-by. It is the last time I shall ask you for anything.

Kroll (looks at her in surprise and puts down his hat). Very well, Miss West—so be it, then.

A short silence. Then JOHANNES ROSMER *enters from the hall.*

Rosmer (sees the RECTOR, *and stops in the doorway).* What!—Are you here?

Rebecca. He did not wish to meet you, dear.*

Kroll (involuntarily). "Dear!"

Rebecca. Yes, Rector Kroll, Rosmer and I say "dear" to each other. That is one result of our "position."

---

* In the original, Rebecca here addresses Rosmer as *"du"* for the first time in Kroll's presence.

Kroll. Was that what you wanted me to hear?

Rebecca. That—and a little more.

Rosmer (comes forward). What is the object of this visit?

Kroll. I wanted to try once more to stop you and win you back to us.

Rosmer (points to the newspaper). After what appears in that paper?

Kroll. I did not write it.

Rosmer. Did you make the slightest effort to prevent its appearance?

Kroll. That would have been to betray the cause I serve. And, besides, it was not in my power.

Rebecca (tears the paper into shreds, crushes up the pieces and throws them behind the stove). There! Now it is out of sight. And let it be out of mind too. For there will be nothing more of that sort, Rosmer.

Kroll. Ah, if you could only make sure of that!

Rebecca. Come, let us sit down, dear. All three of us. And then I will tell you everything.

Rosmer (seats himself mechanically). What has come over you, Rebecca? This unnatural calmness—what is it?

Rebecca. The calmness of resolution. *(Seats herself.)* Pray sit down too, Rector.

[RECTOR KROLL *seats himself on the sofa.*

Rosmer. Resolution, you say? What resolution?

Rebecca. I am going to give you back what you require in order to live your life. Dear friend, you shall have your happy innocence back again!

Rosmer. What can you mean?

Rebecca. I have only to tell you something. That will be enough.

Rosmer. Well!

Rebecca. When I came down here from Finmark—along with Dr. West—it seemed to me that a great, wide new world was opening up before me. The Doctor had taught

me all sorts of things—all the fragmentary knowledge of
life that I possessed in those days. (*With a struggle and in
a scarcely audible voice.*) And then——

Kroll. And then?

Rosmer. But Rebecca—I know all this.

Rebecca (mastering herself). Yes, yes—you are right.
You know enough about this.

Kroll (looks hard at her). Perhaps I had better go.

Rebecca. No, please stay where you are, my dear
Rector. (*To* ROSMER.) Well, you see, this was how it was
—I wanted to take my share in the life of the new era
that was dawning, with all its new ideas.—Rector Kroll told
me one day that Ulric Brendel had had great influence over
you while you were still a boy. I thought it must surely be
possible for me to carry on his work.

Rosmer. You came here with a secret design——?

Rebecca. We two, I thought, should march onward in
freedom, side by side. Ever onward. Ever farther and
farther to the front. But between you and perfect emancipation there rose that dismal, insurmountable barrier.

Rosmer. What barrier do you mean?

Rebecca. I mean this, Rosmer: You could grow into
freedom only in the clear, fresh sunshine—and here you were
pining, sickening in the gloom of such a marriage.

Rosmer. You have never before spoken to me of my
marriage in that tone.

Rebecca. No, I did not dare to, for I should have frightened you.

Kroll (nods to ROSMER*).* Do you hear that?

Rebecca (goes on). But I saw quite well where your
deliverance lay—your only deliverance. And then I went
to work.

Rosmer. Went to work? In what way?

Kroll. Do you mean that——?

Rebecca. Yes, Rosmer—— (*Rises.*) Sit still. You
too, Rector Kroll. But now it must out. It was not you,

Rosmer. You are innocent. It was I that lured—that ended in luring Beata out into the paths of delusion——

Rosmer (springs up). Rebecca!

Kroll (rises from the sofa). The paths of delusion!

Rebecca. The paths—that led to the mill-race. Now you know it both of you.

Rosmer (as if stunned). But I don't understand—— What is it she is saying? I don't understand a word——!

Kroll. Oh yes, Rosmer, I am beginning to understand.

Rosmer. But what did you do? What can you possibly have told her? There was nothing—absolutely nothing to tell!

Rebecca. She came to know that you were working yourself free from all the old prejudices.

Rosmer. Yes, but that was not the case at that time.

Rebecca. I knew that it soon would be.

Kroll (nods to ROSMER). Aha!

Rosmer. And then? What more? I must know all now.

Rebecca. Some time after—I begged and implored her to let me go away from Rosmersholm.

Rosmer. Why did you want to go—then?

Rebecca. I did not want to go; I wanted to stay here, where I was. But I told her that it would be best for us all—that I should go away in time. I gave her to understand that if I stayed here any longer, I could not—I could not tell—what might happen.

Rosmer. Then this is what you said and did!

Rebecca. Yes, Rosmer.

Rosmer. This is what you call "going to work."

Rebecca (in a broken voice). I called it so, yes.

Rosmer (after a pause). Have you confessed all now, Rebecca?

Rebecca. Yes.

Kroll. Not all.

Rebecca (looks at him in fear). What more should there be?

Kroll. Did you not at last give Beata to understand that it was necessary—not only that it would be wisest, but that it was necessary—both for your own sake and Rosmer's, that you should go away somewhere—as soon as possible? Well?

Rebecca (low and indistinctly). Perhaps I did say something of the sort.

Rosmer (sinks into the arm-chair by the window). And this tissue of lies and deceit she—my unhappy, sick wife believed in! Believed in it so firmly! So immovably! *(Looks up at* REBECCA.*)* And she never turned to me. Never said one word to me! Oh, Rebecca,—I can see it in your face—you dissuaded her from it!

Rebecca. She had conceived a fixed idea that she, as a childless wife, had no right to be here. And then she imagined that it was her duty to you to efface herself.

Rosmer. And you—you did nothing to disabuse her of the idea?

Rebecca. No.

Kroll. Perhaps you confirmed her in it? Answer me! Did you not?

Rebecca. I believe she may have understood me so.

Rosmer. Yes, yes—and in everything she bowed before your will. And she did efface herself! *(Springs up.)* How could you—how could you play this ghastly game!

Rebecca. It seemed to me I had to choose between your life and hers, Rosmer.

Kroll (severely and impressively). That choice was not for you to make.

Rebecca (vehemently). You think then that I was cool and calculating and self-possessed all the time! I was not the same woman then that I am now, as I stand here telling it all. Besides, there are two sorts of will in us I believe! I wanted Beata away, by one means or another; but I never really believed that it would come to pass. As I felt my way forward, at each step I ventured, I seemed to hear something within me cry out: No farther! Not a step farther! And yet I could not stop. I had to venture the least little bit farther. Only one hair's-breadth more. And then one more—and always one more.—And then it happened.—That is the way such things come about.

[*A short silence.*

Rosmer (to REBECCA). What do you think lies before you now? After this?

Rebecca. Things must go with me as they will. It doesn't greatly matter.

Kroll. Not a word of remorse! Is it possible you feel none?

Rebecca (coldly putting aside his question). Excuse me, Rector Kroll—that is a matter which concerns no one but me. I must settle it with myself.

Kroll (to ROSMER). And this is the woman you are living under the same roof with—in the closest intimacy! *(Looks round at the pictures.)* Oh if those that are gone could see us now!

Rosmer. Are you going back to town?

Kroll (takes up his hat). Yes. The sooner the better.

Rosmer (does the same). Then I will go with you.

Kroll. Will you? Ah yes, I was sure we had not lost you for good.

Rosmer. Come then, Kroll! Come!

[*Both go out through the hall without looking at* REBECCA.

[*After a moment,* REBECCA *goes cautiously to the window and looks out through the flowers.*

Rebecca (speaks to herself under her breath). Not over the foot-bridge to-day either. He goes round. Never across the mill-race. Never. *(Leaves window.)* Well, well, well!

[*Goes and pulls the bell-rope; a moment after,* MADAM HELSETH *enters from the right.*

Madam Helseth. What is it, Miss?

Rebecca. Madam Helseth, would you be so good as to have my trunk brought down from the garret?

Madam Helseth. Your trunk?

Rebecca. Yes—the brown sealskin trunk, you know.

Madam Helseth. Yes, yes. But, Lord preserve us—are you going on a journey, Miss?

Rebecca. Yes—now I am going on a journey, Madam Helseth.

Madam Helseth. And immediately!

Rebecca. As soon as I have packed up.

Madam Helseth. Well, I've never heard the like of that! But you'll come back again soon, Miss, of course?

Rebecca. I shall never come back again.

Madam Helseth. Never! Dear Lord, what will things be like at Rosmersholm when you're gone, Miss? And the poor Pastor was just beginning to be so happy and comfortable.

Rebecca. Yes, but I have taken fright to-day, Madam Helseth.

Madam Helseth. Taken fright! Dear, dear! how was that?

Rebecca. I thought I saw something like a glimpse of white horses.

Madam Helseth. White horses! In broad daylight!

Rebecca. Oh, they are abroad early and late—the white horses of Rosmersholm. *(With a change of tone.)* Well,— about the trunk, Madam Helseth.

Madam Helseth. Yes, yes. The trunk.

[*Both go out to the right.*

ACT FOURTH

*The sitting-room at Rosmersholm. Late evening. A lighted
lamp, with a shade over it, on the table.*

REBECCA WEST *stands by the table, packing some small
articles in a hand-bag. Her cloak, hat, and the white
crocheted shawl are hanging over the back of the sofa.*

MADAM HELSETH *enters from the right.*

*Madam Helseth (speaks in a low voice and appears ill at
ease).* All your things have been taken down, Miss. They
are in the kitchen passage.

Rebecca. Very well. You have ordered the carriage?

Madam Helseth. Yes. The coachman wants to know
what time he ought to be here.

Rebecca. About eleven o'clock, I think. The steamer
starts at midnight.

Madam Helseth (hesitates a little). But the Pastor? If
he shouldn't be home by that time?

Rebecca. I shall go all the same. If I don't see him,
you can tell him that I will write to him—a long letter.
Tell him that.

Madam Helseth. Yes, writing—that may be all very well.
But, poor Miss West—I do think you should try to speak
to him once more.

Rebecca. Perhaps so. And yet—perhaps not.

Madam Helseth. Well—that I should live to see this! I
never thought of such a thing.

Rebecca. What did you think then. Madam Helseth?

326

Madam Helseth. Well, I certainly thought Pastor Rosmer was a more dependable man than this.

Rebecca. Dependable?

Madam Helseth. Yes, that's what *I* say.

Rebecca. Why, my dear Madam Helseth, what do you mean?

Madam Helseth. I mean what's right and true, Miss. He shouldn't get out of it in this way, that he shouldn't.

Rebecca (looks at her). Come now, Madam Helseth, tell me plainly: what do you think is the reason I am going away?

Madam Helseth. Well, Heaven forgive us, I suppose it can't be helped, Miss. Ah, well, well, well! But I certainly don't think the Pastor's behaving handsome-like. Mortensgård had some excuse; for her husband was alive, so that they two couldn't marry, however much they wanted to. But as for the Pastor—h'm!

Rebecca (with a faint smile). Could you have believed such a thing of Pastor Rosmer and me?

Madam Helseth. No, never in this world. At least, I mean—not until to-day.

Rebecca. But to-day, then——?

Madam Helseth. Well,—after all the horrible things that they tell me the papers are saying about the Pastor——

Rebecca. Aha!

Madam Helseth. For the man that can go over to Mortensgård's religion—good Lord, I can believe anything of him.

Rebecca. Oh yes, I suppose so. But what about me? What have you to say about me?

Madam Helseth. Lord preserve us, Miss—I don't see that there's much to be said against you. It's not so easy for a lone woman to be always on her guard, that's certain. —We're all of us human, Miss West.

Rebecca. That's very true, Madam Helseth. We are all of us human.—What are you listening to?

Madam Helseth (in a low voice). Oh Lord,—if I don't believe that's him coming.

Rebecca (starts). After all then——? *(Resolutely.)* Well well; so be it.

JOHANNES ROSMER *enters from the hall.*

Rosmer (sees the hand-bag, etc., turns to REBECCA, *and asks).* What does this mean?

Rebecca. I am going.

Rosmer. At once?

Rebecca. Yes. *(To* MADAM HELSETH.*)* Eleven o'clock then.

Madam Helseth. Very well, Miss.

                                [*Goes out to the right.*

Rosmer (after a short pause). Where are you going to, Rebecca?

Rebecca. North, by the steamer.

Rosmer. North? What takes you to the North?

Rebecca. It was there I came from.

Rosmer. But you have no ties there now.

Rebecca. I have none here either.

Rosmer. What do you think of doing?

Rebecca. I don't know. I only want to have done with it all.

Rosmer. To have done with it?

Rebecca. Rosmersholm has broken me.

Rosmer (his attention aroused). Do you say that?

Rebecca. Broken me utterly and hopelessly.—I had a free and fearless will when I came here. Now I have bent my neck under a strange law.—From this day forth, I feel as if I had no courage for anything in the world.

Rosmer. Why not? What is the law that you say you have——?

Rebecca. Dear, don't let us talk of that just now.—What happened between you and the Rector?

Rosmer. We have made peace.

Rebecca. Ah yes; so that was the end.

Rosmer. He gathered all our old friends together at his house. They have made it clear to me that the work of ennobling the minds of men—is not for me.—And besides, it is hopeless in itself, Rebecca.—I shall let it alone.

Rebecca. Yes, yes—perhaps it is best so.

Rosmer. Is that what you say now? Do you think so now?

Rebecca. I have come to think so—in the last few days.

Rosmer. You are lying, Rebecca.

Rebecca. Lying——!

Rosmer. Yes, you are lying. You have never believed in me. You have never believed that I was man enough to carry the cause through to victory.

Rebecca. I believed that we two together could do it.

Rosmer. That is not true. You thought that you yourself could do something great in life; and that you could use me to further your ends. I was to be a serviceable instrument to you—that is what you thought.

Rebecca. Listen to me, Rosmer——

Rosmer (seats himself listlessly on the sofa). Oh, what is the use? I see through it all now—I have been like a glove in your hands.

Rebecca. Listen, Rosmer. Hear what I have to say. It will be for the last time. *(Sits in a chair close to the sofa.)* I intended to write you all about it—when I was back in the North. But I daresay it is best that you should hear it at once.

Rosmer. Have you more confessions to make?

Rebecca. The greatest of all is to come.

Rosmer. The greatest?

Rebecca. What you have never suspected. . What gives light and shade to all the rest.

Rosmer (shakes his head). I don't understand you at all.

Rebecca. It is perfectly true that I once schemed to gain a footing at Rosmersholm. I thought I could not fail to

turn thing. to good account here. In one way or the other
—you understand.

Rosmer. Well, you accomplished your ends.

Rebecca. I believe I could have accomplished anything,
anything in the world—at that time. For I had still my
fearless, free-born will. I knew no scruples—I stood in awe
of no human tie.—But then began what has broken my will
—and cowed me so pitiably for all my days.

Rosmer. What began? Do not speak in riddles.

Rebecca. It came over me,—this wild, uncontrollable
passion——. Oh, Rosmer——!

Rosmer. Passion? You——! For what?

Rebecca. For you.

Rosmer (tries to spring up). What is this?

Rebecca (stops him). Sit still, dear; there is more to
tell.

Rosmer. And you mean to say—that you have loved me
—in that way!

Rebecca. I thought that it should be called love—then.
Yes, I thought it was love. But it was not. It was what
I said. It was a wild, uncontrollable passion.

Rosmer (with difficulty). Rebecca, is it really you—you
yourself—that you are speaking of?

Rebecca. Yes, would you believe it, Rosmer?

Rosmer. Then it was because of this—under the influence of this—that you—that you "went to work," as you
call it?

Rebecca. It came upon me like a storm on the sea. It
was like one of the storms we sometimes have in the North
in the winter time. It seizes you—and whirls you along
with it—wherever it will. There is no resisting it.

Rosmer. And so it swept the unhappy Beata into the
mill-race.

Rebecca. Yes; for it was a life-and-death struggle between Beata and me at that time.

Rosmer. Assuredly you were the strongest at Rosmersholm. Stronger than Beata and I together.

Rebecca. I judged you rightly in so far that I was sure I could never reach you until you were a free man, both in circumstances—and in spirit.

Rosmer. But I don't understand you, Rebecca. You—yourself—your whole conduct is an insoluble riddle to me. I am free now—both in spirit and in circumstances. You have reached the very goal you aimed at from the first. And yet——

Rebecca. I have never stood farther from my goal than now.

Rosmer. And yet I say—when I asked you yesterday—begged you to be my wife—you cried out, as if in fear, that it could never be.

Rebecca. I cried out in despair, Rosmer.

Rosmer. Why?

Rebecca. Because Rosmersholm has sapped my strength. My old fearless will has had its wings clipped here. It is crippled! The time is past when I had courage for anything in the world. I have lost the power of action, Rosmer.

Rosmer. Tell me how this has come about.

Rebecca. It has come about through my life with you.

Rosmer. But how? How?

Rebecca. When I was left alone with you here,—and when you had become yourself again——

Rosmer. Yes, yes?

Rebecca. ——for you were never quite yourself so long as Beata lived——

Rosmer. I am afraid you are right there.

Rebecca. But when I found myself sharing your life here,—in quiet—in solitude,—when you showed me all your thoughts without reserve—every tender and delicate feeling, just as it came to you—then the great change came over me. Little by little, you understand. Almost imperceptibly—

but at last with such overwhelming force that it reached to the depths of my soul.

Rosmer. Oh, is this true, Rebecca?

Rebecca. All the rest—the horrible sense-intoxicated desire—passed far, far away from me. All the whirling passions settled down into quiet and silence. Rest descended on my soul—a stillness as on one of our northern bird-cliffs under the midnight sun.

Rosmer. Tell me more of this. Tell me all you can.

Rebecca. There is not much more, dear. Only this—it was love that was born in me. The great self-denying love, that is content with life, as we two have lived it together.

Rosmer. Oh, if I had only had the faintest suspicion of all this!

Rebecca. It is best as it is. Yesterday—when you asked me if I would be your wife—I cried out with joy——

Rosmer. Yes, did you not, Rebecca! I thought that was the meaning of your cry.

Rebecca. For a moment, yes. I had forgotten myself. It was my old buoyant will that was struggling to be free. But it has no energy left now—no power of endurance.

Rosmer. How do you account for what has happened to you?

Rebecca. It is the Rosmer view of life—or your view of life, at any rate—that has infected my will.

Rosmer. Infected?

Rebecca. And made it sick. Enslaved it to laws that had no power over me before. You—life with you—has ennobled my mind——

Rosmer. Oh that I could believe it!

Rebecca. You may safely believe it! The Rosmer view of life ennobles. But—— [*Shaking her head.*] But—but——

Rosmer. But——? Well?

Rebecca. ——but it kills happiness.

Rosmer. Do you think so, Rebecca?

Rebecca. My happiness, at any rate.

Rosmer. Yes, but are you so certain of that? If I were to ask you again now——? If I were to beg and entreat you——?

Rebecca. Dear,—never speak of this again! It is impossible——! For you must know, Rosmer, I have a—a past behind me.

Rosmer. More than what you have told me?

Rebecca. Yes. Something different and something more.

Rosmer (with a faint smile). Is it not strange, Rebecca? Some such idea has crossed my mind now and then.

Rebecca. It has? And yet——? Even so——?

Rosmer. I never believed it. I only played with it—in my thoughts, you understand.

Rebecca. If you wish it, I will tell you all, at once.

Rosmer (turning it off). No, no! I will not hear a word. Whatever it may be—I can forget it.

Rebecca. But I cannot.

Rosmer. Oh Rebecca——!

Rebecca. Yes, Rosmer—this is the terrible part of it: that now, when all life's happiness is within my grasp—my heart is changed, and my own past cuts me off from it.

Rosmer. Your past is dead, Rebecca. It has no hold on you any more—it is no part of you—as you are now.

Rebecca. Oh, you know that these are only phrases, dear. And innocence? Where am I to get that from?

Rosmer (sadly). Ah,—innocence.

Rebecca. Yes, innocence. That is the source of peace and happiness. That was the vital truth you were to implant in the coming generation of happy noble-men——

Rosmer. Oh, don't remind me of that. It was only an abortive dream, Rebecca—an immature idea, that I myself no longer believe in.—Ah no, we cannot be ennobled from without, Rebecca.

Rebecca (softly). Not even by tranquil love, Rosmer?

Rosmer (thoughtfully). Yes—that would be the great thing—the most glorious in life, almost—if it were so. *(Moves uneasily.)* But how can I be certain of that? How convince myself?

Rebecca. Do you not believe me, Rosmer?

Rosmer. Oh Rebecca—how can I believe in you, fully? You who have all this while been cloaking, concealing such a multitude of things!—Now you come forward with something new. If you have a secret purpose in all this, tell me plainly what it is. Is there anything you want to gain by it? You know that I will gladly do everything I can for you.

Rebecca (wringing her hands). Oh this killing doubt——! Rosmer—Rosmer——!

Rosmer. Yes, is it not terrible, Rebecca? But I cannot help it. I shall never be able to shake off the doubt. I can never be absolutely sure that you are mine in pure and perfect love.

Rebecca. Is there nothing in the depths of your own heart that bears witness to the transformation in me? And tells you that it is due to you—and you alone?

Rosmer. Oh Rebecca—I no longer believe in my power of transforming any one. My faith in myself is utterly dead. I believe neither in myself nor in you.

Rebecca (looks darkly at him). Then how will you be able to live your life?

Rosmer. That I don't know. I cannot imagine how. I don't think I can live it.—And I know of nothing in the world that is worth living for.

Rebecca. Oh, life—life will renew itself. Let us hold fast to it, Rosmer.—We shall leave it soon enough.

Rosmer (springs up restlessly). Then give me my faith again! My faith in you, Rebecca! My faith in your love! Proof! I must have proof!

Rebecca. Proof? How can I give you proof——?

Rosmer. You must! *(Walks across the room.)* I cannot bear this desolation—this horrible emptiness—this—this—— [*A loud knock at the hall door.*

Rebecca (starts up from her chair). Ah—did you hear that?

The door opens. ULRIC BRENDEL *enters. He has a white shirt on, a black coat and a good pair of boots, with his trousers tucked into them. Otherwise he is dressed as in the first Act. He looks excited.*

Rosmer. Ah, is it you, Mr. Brendel?

Brendel. Johannes, my boy—hail—and farewell!

Rosmer. Where are you going so late?

Brendel. Downhill.

Rosmer. How——?

Brendei. I am going homewards, my beloved pupil. I am home-sick for the mighty Nothingness.

Rosmer. Something has happened to you, Mr. Brendel! What is it?

Brendel. So you observe the transformation? Yes—well you may. When I last set foot in these halls—I stood before you as a man of substance, and slapped my breast-pocket.

Rosmer. Indeed! I don't quite understand——

Brendel. But as you see me this night, I am a deposed monarch on the ash-heap that was my palace.

Rosmer. If there is anything *I* can do for you——

Brendel. You have preserved your child-like heart, Johannes. Can you grant me a loan?

Rosmer. Yes, yes, most willingly!

Brendel. Can you spare me an ideal or two?

Rosmer. What do you say?

Brendel. One or two cast-off ideals. It would be an act of charity. For I'm cleaned out, my boy. Ruined, beggared.

Rebecca. Have you not delivered your lecture?

Brendel. No, seductive lady. What do you think? Just as I am standing ready to pour forth the horn of plenty, I make the painful discovery that I am bankrupt.

Rebecca. But all your unwritten works——?

Brendel. For five-and-twenty years I have sat like a miser on his double-locked treasure-chest. And then yesterday—when I open it and want to display the treasure—there's none there! The teeth of time had ground it into dust. There was nix and nothing in the whole concern.

Rosmer. But are you so sure of that?

Brendel. There's no room for doubt, my dear fellow. The President has convinced me of it.

Rosmer. The President?

Brendel. Well well—His Excellency then. *Ganz nach Belieben.*

Rosmer. What do you mean?

Brendel. Peter Mortensgård, of course.

Rosmer. What?

Brendel (mysteriously). Hush, hush, hush! Peter Mortensgård is the lord and leader of the future. Never have I stood in a more august presence. Peter Mortensgård has the secret of omnipotence. He can do whatever he will.

Rosmer. Oh, don't believe that.

Brendel. Yes, my boy! For Peter Mortensgård never wills more than he can do. Peter Mortensgård is capable of living his life without ideals. And that, do you see— that is just the mighty secret of action and of victory. It is the sum of the whole world's wisdom. *Basta!*

Rosmer (in a low voice). Now I understand—why you leave here poorer than you came.

Brendel. *Bien!* Then take a *Beispiel* by your ancient teacher. Rub out all that he once imprinted on your mind. Build not thy house on shifting sand. And look ahead—and feel your way—before you build on this exquisite creature, who here lends sweetness to your life.

Rebecca. Is it me you mean?

Brendel. Yes, my fascinating mermaid.

Rebecca. Why am I not to be built on?

Brendel (comes a step nearer). I gather that my former pupil has a great cause to carry forward to victory.

Rebecca. What then——?

Brendel. Victory is assured. But—mark me well—on one indispensable condition.

Rebecca. Which is——?

Brendel (taking her gently by the wrist). That the woman who loves him shall gladly go out into the kitchen and hack off her tender, rosy-white little finger—here—just here at the middle joint. Item, that the aforesaid loving woman— again gladly—shall slice off her incomparably-moulded left ear. *(Lets her go, and turns to* ROSMER.*)* Farewell, my conquering Johannes.

Rosmer. Are you going now? In the dark night?

Brendel. The dark night is best. Peace be with you.

[*He goes. There is a short silence in the room.*

Rebecca (breathes heavily). Oh, how close and sultry it is here!

[*Goes to the window, opens it, and remains standing by it.*

Rosmer (sits down in the arm-chair by the stove). There is nothing else for it after all, Rebecca. I see it. You must go away.

Rebecca. Yes, I see no choice.

Rosmer. Let us make the most of our last hour. Come here and sit by me.

Rebecca (goes and sits on the sofa). What do you want to say to me, Rosmer?

Rosmer. First, I want to tell you that you need not feel any anxiety about your future.

Rebecca (smiles). H'm, my future.

Rosmer. I have long ago arranged for everything. Whatever may happen, you are provided for.

Rebecca. That too, my dear one?

Rosmer. You might surely have known that.

Rebecca. It is many a long day since I have given a thought to such things.

Rosmer. Yes, yes—you thought things would always remain as they were between us.

Rebecca. Yes, I thought so.

Rosmer. So did I. But if I were to go——

Rebecca. Oh, Rosmer—you will live longer than I.

Rosmer. Surely my worthless life lies in my own hands.

Rebecca. What is this? You are never thinking of——!

Rosmer. Do you think it would be so strange? After this pitiful, lamentable defeat! I, who was to have borne a great cause on to victory—have I not fled from the battle before it was well begun?

Rebecca. Take up the fight again, Rosmer! Only try—and you shall see, you will conquer. You will ennoble hundreds—thousands of minds. Only try!

Rosmer. Oh Rebecca—I, who no longer believe in my own mission!

Rebecca. But your mission has stood the test already. You have ennobled one human being at least—me you have ennobled for the rest of my days.

Rosmer. Oh—if I dared believe you.

Rebecca (pressing her hands together). Oh Rosmer,—do you know of nothing—nothing that could make you believe it?

Rosmer (starts as if in fear). Don't speak of that! Keep away from that, Rebecca! Not a word more.

Rebecca. Yes, this is precisely what we must speak about. Do you know of anything that would kill the doubt? For *I* know of nothing in the world.

Rosmer. It is well for you that you do not know.—It is well for both of us.

Rebecca. No, no, no.—I will not be put off in this way! If you know of anything that would absolve me in your eyes, I claim as my right to be told of it.

Rosmer (as if impelled against his will to speak). Then
let us see. You say that a great love is in you; that through
me your mind has been ennobled. Is it so? Is your reckoning just, Rebecca? Shall we try to prove the sum?
Say?

Rebecca. I am ready.

Rosmer. At any time?

Rebecca. Whenever you please. The sooner the better.

Rosmer. Then let me see, Rebecca,—if you for my sake
—this very evening—— *(Breaks off.)* Oh, no, no, no!

Rebecca. Yes, Rosmer! Yes! Tell me, and you shall
see.

Rosmer. Have you the courage—have you the will—
gladly, as Ulric Brendel said—for my sake, to-night—gladly
—to go the same way that Beata went?

Rebecca (rises slowly from the sofa; almost voiceless).
Rosmer——!

Rosmer. Yes, Rebecca—that is the question that will for
ever haunt me—when you are gone. Every hour in the day
it will return upon me. Oh, I seem to see you before my
very eyes. You are standing out on the foot-bridge—right
in the middle. Now you are bending forward over the railing—drawn dizzily downwards, downwards towards the
rushing water! No—you recoil. You have not the heart
to do what she dared.

Rebecca. But if I had the heart to do it? And the will
to do it gladly? What then?

Rosmer. I should have to believe you then. I should
recover my faith in my mission. Faith in my power to
ennoble human souls. Faith in the human soul's power to
attain nobility.

*Rebecca (takes up her shawl slowly, and puts it over her
head; says with composure).* You shall have your faith
again.

Rosmer. Have you the will and the courage—for this,
Rebecca?

Rebecca. That you shall see to-morrow—or afterwards—when they find my body.

Rosmer (puts his hand to his forehead). There is a horrible fascination in this——!

Rebecca. For I don't want to remain down there. Not longer than necessary. You must see that they find me.

Rosmer (springs up). But all this—is nothing but madness. Go—or stay! I will take your bare word this time too.

Rebecca. Phrases, Rosmer! Let us have no more cowardly subterfuges, dear! How can you believe me on my bare word after this day?

Rosmer. I shrink from seeing your defeat, Rebecca!

Rebecca. It will be no defeat.

Rosmer. Yes, it will. You will never bring yourself to go Beata's way.

Rebecca. Do you think not?

Rosmer. Never. You are not like Beata. You are not under the dominion of a distorted view of life.

Rebecca. But I am under the dominion of the Rosmersholm view of life—now. What I have sinned—it is fit that I should expiate.

Rosmer (looks at her fixedly). Is that your point of view?

Rebecca. Yes.

Rosmer (with resolution). Well then, *I* stand firm in our emancipated view of life, Rebecca. There is no judge over us; and therefore we must do justice upon ourselves.

Rebecca (misunderstanding him). Yes, that is true—that too. My going away will save what is best in you.

Rosmer. Oh, there is nothing left to save in me.

Rebecca. Yes, there is. But I—after to-day, I should only be a sea-troll dragging down the ship that is to carry you forward. I must go overboard. Why should I remain here in the world, trailing after me my own crippled life? Why brood and brood over the happiness that my past has forfeited for ever? I must give up the game, Rosmer.

Rosmer. If you go—I go with you.

Rebecca (smiles almost imperceptibly, looks at him, and says more softly). Yes, come with me—and see——

Rosmer. I go with you, I say.

Rebecca. To the foot-bridge, yes. You know you never dare go out upon it.

Rosmer. Have you noticed that?

Rebecca (sadly and brokenly). Yes.—It was that that made my love hopeless.

Rosmer. Rebecca,—now I lay my hand on your head— *(Does so)*—and I wed you as my true wife.

Rebecca (takes both his hands, and bows her head towards his breast). Thanks, Rosmer. *(Lets him go.)* And now I will go—gladly.

Rosmer. Man and wife should go together.

Rebecca. Only to the bridge, Rosmer.

Rosmer. Out on to it, too. As far as you go—so far shall I go with you. For now I dare.

Rebecca. Are you absolutely certain—that this way is the best for you?

Rosmer. I am certain that it is the only way.

Rebecca. If you were deceiving yourself? If it were only a delusion? One of those white horses of Rosmersholm.

Rosmer. It may be so. For we can never escape from them—we of this house.

Rebecca. Then stay, Rosmer!

Rosmer. The husband shall go with his wife, as the wife with her husband.

Rebecca. Yes, but first tell me this: Is it you who follow me? Or is it I who follow you?

Rosmer. We shall never think that question out.

Rebecca. But I should like to know.

Rosmer. We go with each other, Rebecca—I with you, and you with me.

Rebecca. I almost think that is the truth.

Rosmer. For now we two are one.

Rebecca. Yes. We are one. Come! We go gladly.

> [*They go out hand in hand through the hall, and are seen to turn to the left. The door remains open. The room stands empty for a little while. Then the door to the right is opened by* MADAM HELSETH.

Madam Helseth. Miss West—the carriage is—— (*Looks round.*) Not here? Out together at this time of night? Well—I must say——! H'm! (*Goes out into the hall, looks round, and comes in again.*) Not on the garden seat. Ah, well well. (*Goes to the window, and looks out.*) Oh, good God! that white thing there——! My soul! They're both of them out on the bridge! God forgive the sinful creatures—if they're not in each other's arms! (*Shrieks aloud.*) Oh—down—both of them! Out into the mill-race! Help! Help! (*Her knees tremble; she holds on to the chairback, shaking all over; she can scarcely get the words out.*) No. No help here.—The dead wife has taken them.

PEER GYNT

(1867)

A Play in Five Acts

DRAMATIS PERSONÆ

AASE, widow of John Gynt, a peasant.

PEER GYNT, her son.

Two Old Women with corn-sacks.

ASLAK, a blacksmith.

Wedding Guests, a Steward at the Wedding, a Fiddler, etc.

A Stranger and his Wife.

SOLVEIG and little HELGA, their daughters.

The Owner of Hægstad Farm.

INGRID, his daughter.

The Bridegroom and his Parents.

Three Cowherd Girls. A Woman in Green.

The TROLL KING. Several Trolls of his Court.

Troll Boys and Girls. Two Witches. Hobgoblins, **Brownies,** Elves, etc.

An Ugly Urchin. A Voice in the Gloom. Birds' Cries.

KARI, a cotter's wife.

MR. COTTON
MONSIEUR BALLON
HERR VON EBERKOPF } tourists.
HERR TRUMPETERSTRAALE

A Thief and a Receiver of Stolen Goods.

ANITRA, daughter of a Bedouin Chief.

Arabs, Female Slaves, Dancing Girls, etc.

The Statue of Memnon (with song). The Sphinx at Gizeh (dumb).

PROFESSOR BEGRIFFENFELDT, Ph.D., in charge of the Lunatic Asylum at Cairo.

Lunatics with their Keepers.

HUHU, a language-reformer from the Malabar coast.

HUSSEIN, an Eastern Secretary of State.
A Fellah, carrying a royal mummy.
A Norwegian Skipper and his Crew. A Strange Passenger.
A Priest. A Funeral Party. A Button-Moulder. A Thin Man.

(The action, which begins in the early years of the century and ends somewhere about our own day [1867], takes place partly in the Gudbrandsdal and on the surrounding mountain-tops, partly on the coast of Morocco, in the Sahara Desert, in the Cairo Lunatic Asylum, at Sea, etc.)

ACT I

SCENE I

(SCENE.—The wooded mountain-side near *Aase's* farm, with a stream rushing past. On the farther bank stands an old mill. It is a hot summer's day. *Peer Gynt,* a sturdy youth of twenty, comes down the path, followed by his mother *Aase,* who is short and slight. She is scolding him angrily.)

Aase. Peer, you're lying!
Peer Gynt (without stopping). No, I'm not!
Aase. Well then, will you swear it's true?
Peer Gynt. Swear? Why should I?
Aase. Ah, you daren't! Your whole tale's a pack of lies!
Peer Gynt. Every blessed word is true!
Aase (facing him). I wonder you can face your mother! First of all, just when the work is at busiest, off you go to prowl about the hills for weeks after reindeer in the snow; come back with your clothes in rags, game-bag empty—and no gun! Then you have the cheek to think you can make your mother swallow such a pack of lies as this about your hunting!—Tell me, then, where you found this precious buck?
Peer Gynt. West of Gendin.
Aase (with a scornful laugh). I dare say!
Peer Gynt. I was leeward of the blast, and behind a clump of trees he was scraping in the snow for some moss——
Aase (as before). Oh, yes, no doubt!
Peer Gynt. I stood and listened, held my breath, heard the scraping of his hoof, saw the antlers of his horns; then upon my belly crawled carefully between the rocks; peeped from cover of the stones— Such a buck, so sleek and fat, I suppose was never seen!

347

Aase. I expect not!

Peer Gynt. Then I fired! Down the buck came on the ground! But the moment he had fallen I was up astride his back, on his left ear got my grip, and was just in act of thrusting with my knife into his gullet just behind his head—when, hi! with a scream the ugly beggar scrambled up upon his feet. From my hand his sudden back-throw jerked my hunting-knife and scabbard, pinned me to his loins and held me by the legs between his antlers like a pair of mighty pincers; then he rushed with bounds gigantic right along the ridge of Gendin!

Aase (involuntarily). Christ in Heaven—!

Peer Gynt. Have you ever been upon the ridge at Gendin? Fully half a mile it stretches, at the top as sheer and narrow as a scythe-blade. Looking downward—past the slopes and past the glaciers, past the grey ravines and gullies—either side you see the water wrapped in dark and gloomy slumber half a mile at least beneath you. Right along it he and I clove our passage through the air. Never rode I such a steed! Far ahead the peaks were sparkling as we rushed along. Beneath us in the void the dusky eagles fell away like motes in sunshine; you could see the ice-floes breaking on the banks, yet hear no murmur. But the sprites that turn us dizzy danced and sang and circled round us—I could hear and seemed to see them!

Aase (swaying as if giddy). Heaven help us!

Peer Gynt. On a sudden, on the precipice's edge, from the hole where it lay hidden almost at the reindeer's feet, up a ptarmigan rose, cackling, flapping with its wings in terror. Then the reindeer, madly swerving, gave a bound sky-high that sent us plunging o'er the edge and downwards. (*Aase* totters and grasps a tree-trunk. *Peer Gynt* continues.) Gloomy precipice behind us!—Fathomless abyss below us! First through clouds of mist we hurtled, then a flock of gulls we scattered wheeling through the air and screaming. Downward still and ever downwards! But beneath us something glis-

tened whitish, like a reindeer's belly. Mother, 'twas our own
reflection mirrored in the lake beneath us, rushing up, it
seemed, to meet us just as swiftly and as madly as we downwards rushed towards it.

Aase (gasping for breath). Peer! God help me—! Tell me
quickly!

Peer Gynt. Buck from air and buck from water met with
mighty splash together, scattering the foam around us. Then
at last we somehow managed to the northern shore to struggle;
Buck, he swam and dragged me after—so I got home——

Aase. But where's the reindeer?

Peer Gynt. I expect he's where I left him— (Snaps his fingers, turns on his heel and adds): If you find him, you may
keep him!

Aase. And your neck you haven't broken? Nor your legs?
Nor smashed your backbone? Praise and thanks to God be
given for His goodness that has saved you! There's a rent
across your breeches, it is true; but that is scarcely worth a
mention when one thinks what the harm might well have been
from a leap like that of yours— (She suddenly pauses, stares
at him with open mouth, seems to struggle for speech and at
last breaks out.) Oh, you lying little devil!—Christ above
us, what a liar! All that rigmarole you told me is the tale
of Gudbrand Glesnë that I heard when I was twenty. 'Twas ·
to him that all this happened, not to you, you——

Peer Gynt. Yes, it did; history repeats itself.

Aase. Lies, I know, can be so furbished and disguised in
gorgeous wrappings that their skinny carcasses not a soul
would recognize. That's what you've been doing now, with
your wonderful adventures—eagles' wings, and all that nonsense—making up a pack of lies, tales of breathless risk and
danger, till one can no longer tell what one knows and what
one doesn't.

Peer Gynt. If a man said that to me, I would beat him
to a jelly.

Aase (in tears). Would to God that I were dead and buried

in the cold black earth! Prayers and tears have no effect.
You're a hopeless ne'er-do-well!

Peer Gynt (in tears). Dearest pretty little mother, every
word you say is true; so be gay and happy——

Aase. Pshaw! Don't talk nonsense. How could I be happy,
if I wanted to, with such a pig as you for son? Don't you
think it's pretty hard for a poor weak widow never to feel
anything but shame? (Weeps again.) How much is there
left of all that your grandfather enjoyed in his days of
comfort? Where are the well-filled money-bags left by good
old Rasmus Gynt? 'Twas your father emptied them, pouring
money out like sand—buying land in all directions—gilded
coach to ride about in. Where's the stuff so freely wasted at
the famous winter banquet, when each guest sent glass and
bottle crash against the wall behind him?

Peer Gynt. Where are the snows of yester year?

Aase. Hold your tongue when I am speaking! See the farm-
house—scarce a window but is smashed and stuffed with dish-
clout; scarce a hedge or fence is standing; no protection for
the cattle from the wind and wet; the meadows and the fields
all lying fallow; every month distraint on something——

Peer Gynt. That's enough of dismal wailing! Often when
our luck's been drooping it has grown as strong as ever.

Aase. Where it grew, the soil is poisoned. Peer, you certainly don't lack good opinion of yourself. You are just as
brisk and bumptious, just as pert, as when the Parson who had
come from Copenhagen asked you what your Christian name
was, telling you that where he came from lots of men of
highest station would be glad to be as clever; and your father
was so grateful for his amiable praises that a horse and sledge
he gave him. Ah me! All went well in those days. Parsons,
Captains and such people, dropping in to see us daily—filling
up with drink and victuals until they were nearly bursting.
But it's when your fortunes alter that you get to know your
neighbours. Since the day when "rich John Gynt" took the
road with pedlar's pack, not a soul has e'er been near us.

(Wipes her eyes with her apron.) You're a stout and strapping fellow—you should be a staff supporting your old mother in her troubles. You should work the farm for profit, and look after all the little that your father left behind him. (Weeps again.) Heaven knows, it's precious little use you've been to me, you rascal. When you are at home, you're loafing by the fire, or grubbing idly in the ashes and the embers; when you're in the town you frighten all the girls you meet at dances, so that I'm ashamed to own you—fighting with the lowest tramps——

Peer Gynt (moving away from her). Let me be!

Aase (following him). Can you deny you were foremost in the brawling in that dog-fight of a scrimmage down at Lundë? Who but you cracked the blacksmith Aslak's-arm? Or at any rate disjointed one of his ten fingers for him?

Peer Gynt. Who has stuffed you up with that?

Aase (hotly). Why, the cotters heard his howls!

Peer Gynt (rubbing his elbow). Yes—but it was I that howled.

Aase. What!

Peer Gynt. Yes, mother, *I* got thrashed.

Aase. What?

Peer Gynt. Well, he's a lusty chap.

Aase. Who is?

Peer Gynt. Aslak—as I felt!

Aase. Shame! I'd like to spit upon you! To let such a scurvy swiller, such a worthless drunken rascal, beat you! (Weeps again.) Often I've endured shame and scorn on your account, but that this disgrace should happen is the very worst of all. If he *is* a lusty fellow, need that mean that you're a weakling?

Peer Gynt (with a laugh). Well, it doesn't seem to matter if I beat, or if I'm beaten—either way you start your wailing. You may cheer up——

Aase. Are you lying now again?

Peer Gynt. Yes, just this once; so you may as well stop

crying. (Clenches his left hand.) See, 'twas with this pair of pincers that I bent the blacksmith double, while my right hand was my hammer——

Aase. Oh, you brawler! You will bring me to my grave by your behaviour!

Peer Gynt. Nonsense! You're worth something better— better twenty thousand times! Little, homely, dainty mother, just believe what I am saying. All the town shall do you honour; only wait till I have done something—something really great!

Aase (contemptuously). You!

Peer Gynt. Who knows what lies before him!

Aase. If you ever know enough to mend your breeches when they're torn, 'tis the most that I could hope for!

Peer Gynt (hotly). I'll be a King, an Emperor!

Aase. Oh, God help me! Now he's losing what was left him of his wits!

Peer Gynt. Yes, I shall! Just give me time!

Aase. Of course! As the old proverb runs, "Everything comes to him that waits."

Peer Gynt. Mother, you shall see.

Aase. Be quiet! You are as mad as mad can be. After all, it's true enough something might have come of you if you'd thought of something else but your stupid lies and nonsense. Hægstad's daughter fancied you, and you might have won the game if you'd rightly gone to work——

Peer Gynt. Do you think so?

Aase. The old man is too weak to stand against her. He is obstinate enough in a way; but in the end it is Ingrid takes the lead, and where *she* goes, step by step the old hunks comes stumbling after. (Begins to cry again.) Ah, Peer—a richly dowered girl, heir to his lands, just think of it. You might, if only you had liked, in bridegroom's finery be dressed instead of in these dirty rags!

Peer Gynt (quickly). Come on, I'll be a suitor now.

Aase. Where?

Peer Gynt. Why, at Hægstad!

Aase. Ah, poor boy, the right of way is barred to you.

Peer Gynt. What do you mean?

Aase. Alas, alas! You've lost the moment—lost your chance——

Peer Gynt. How's that?

Aase (sobbing). While you were on the hills, riding your reindeer through the air, Mads Moen went and won the girl.

Peer Gynt. What? He? That guy the girls all laugh at?

Aase. Yes. Now she's betrothed to him.

Peer Gynt. Just wait till I have harnessed up the cart—— (Turns to go.)

Aase. You needn't take the trouble. The wedding is to-morrow.

Peer Gynt. Pooh! I'll get there by this evening.

Aase. Fie! Do you want to make things worse? Just think how everyone will mock us!

Peer Gynt. Cheer up! All will turn out right. (Shouting and laughing at the same time.) No, mother! We won't take the cart; we haven't time to put the mare in. (Lifts her off her feet.)

Aase. Let me alone!

Peer Gynt. No, in my arms you shall be carried to the wedding! (Wades out into the water.)

Aase. Help! Help! Oh, Heaven protect me!—Peer, we'll drown——

Peer Gynt. Oh, no, we shan't—I'm born to meet a better death.

Aase. That's true; you'll probably be hanged. (Pulls his hair.) You beast!

Peer Gynt. You'd best keep quiet, for just here the bottom's smooth and slippery.

Aase. Ass!

Peer Gynt. Yes, abuse me if you like, words don't do any harm. Aha! The bottom's sloping upwards now——

Aase. Don't lose your hold of me!

Peer Gynt. Gee up! We'll play at Peer and Reindeer now! (*Prances.*) I am the reindeer, you are Peer!

Aase. I'm sure I don't know what I am!

Peer Gynt. See here, now—here's an even bottom. (*Wades to the bank.*) Now give your steed a pretty kiss to thank him for the ride you've had.

Aase (*boxing his ears*). That's the thanks I'll give him!

Peer Gynt. Wow! That's a scurvy sort of tip.

Aase. Put me down!

Peer Gynt. Not till we get to where the wedding is afoot. You are so clever, you must be my spokesman—talk to the old fool—tell him Mads Moen is a sot——

Aase. Put me down!

Peer Gynt. And tell him, too, the sort of lad that Peer Gynt is.

Aase. Yes, you may take your oath I will! A pretty character I'll give you! I'll draw a faithful portrait, too,—and all your devil's pranks and antics I'll tell them of—in every detail——

Peer Gynt. Oh, will you!

Aase (*kicking him in her temper*). I won't hold my tongue till the old man sets his dog upon you, as upon a tramp!

Peer Gynt. Ah, then I think I'll go alone.

Aase. All right, but I shall follow you!

Peer Gynt. Dear mother, you're not strong enough.

Aase. Not strong enough? I'm so worked up that I could smash a heap of stones! Oh, I could make a meal of flints! So put me down!

Peer Gynt. Yes, if you promise——

Aase. Nothing! I'm going there with you, and they shall know the sort you are!

Peer Gynt. Oh, no, you won't; you'll stay behind.

Aase. Never! I'm going there with you.

Peer Gynt. Oh, no, you aren't.

Aase. What will you do?

Peer Gynt. I'll put you on the mill-house roof! (Puts her up there. She screams.)

Aase. Lift me down!

Peer Gynt. If you will listen——

Aase. Bah!

Peer Gynt. Now, little mother, listen——

Aase (throwing a bit of turf thatch at him). Lift me down this moment, Peer!

Peer Gynt. If I dared I would, indeed. (Goes nearer to her.) Remember to sit still and quiet—not to kick your legs about, nor the tiles to break or loosen—or an accident may happen, and you might fall off.

Aase. You beast!

Peer Gynt. Don't shift!

Aase. I wish you'd been shifted up the chimney, like a changeling!

Peer Gynt. Mother! Shame!

Aase. Pooh!

Peer Gynt. You should rather give your blessing on my journey. Will you?

Aase. I'll give you a thrashing, big as you are!

Peer Gynt. Oh well, good-bye! Only have patience, mother dear; I shan't be long (Is going; but turns, lifts a warning finger, and says): But don't forget you mustn't try to move from there! (Goes.)

Aase. Peer!—Heaven help me, he is gone! Reindeer-rider! Liar! Hi! Will you listen?—No, he's off over the meadows. (Screams.) Help! I'm giddy! (Two *Old Women*, with sacks on their backs, come down the path towards the mill.)

First Old Woman. Who's that screaming?

Aase. Me!

Second Old Woman. Why, Aase, you have had a lift in life!

Aase. One that won't do me much good—I'll be booked for heaven directly!

First Old Woman. Pleasant journey!

Aase. Fetch a ladder! Get me down! That devil Peer——

Second Old Woman. What, your son?

Aase. Now you can say you have seen how he behaves.

First Old Woman. We'll bear witness.

Aase. Only help me—help me to get straight to Hæg-stad——

Second Old Woman. Is he there?

First Old Woman. You'll be revenged; the blacksmith's going to the party.

Aase (wringing her hands). Oh, God help me! My poor boy! They will murder him between them!

First Old Woman. Ah, we know that lot quite well; you may bet that's what will happen!

Second Old Woman. You can see she's lost her senses. (Calls up the hill.) Eivind! Anders! Hi! come here!

A Man's Voice. What?

Second Old Woman. Peer Gynt has put his mother up upon the mill-house roof!

SCENE II

(SCENE.—A little hill covered with bushes and heather. The high-road, shut off by a fence, runs at the back. *Peer Gynt* comes down a foot-path, goes quickly up to the fence, and stands looking out over the landscape beyond.)

Peer Gynt. Yonder lies Hægstad. I shall soon be at it. (Climbs half over the fence, then stops and considers.) I wonder if Ingrid's sitting all alone there? (Shades his eyes and looks along the road.) No, folk with gifts are swarming up like midges. Perhaps I had better turn and go no farther. (Draws his leg back over the fence.) There'll be their grins behind my back for certain—whispers that seem to burn their way right through you. (Moves a few steps away from the fence, and begins absently plucking leaves.) If only I'd a good strong drink inside me—or could just slip into the house unnoticed— Or if no one knew me—. No, some good strong liquor would be best; their laughter wouldn't hurt then.

(Looks round suddenly as if startled, then hides among the bushes. Some *Country Folk*, carrying presents, pass along the road on their way to the wedding.)

A Man (in conversation). With a drunkard for father, and a poor thing of a mother——

A Woman. Yes, it's no wonder the boy is such a wastrel. (They pass on. After a little, *Peer Gynt* comes forward, blushing with shame, and peeps after them.)

Peer Gynt (softly). Was it of me they gossiped? (With a forced shrug.) Oh well, let them! Anyway they can't kill me with their gossip. (Throws himself down on the heather slope, and for some time lies on his back with his hands under his head, staring up into the sky.) What a curious cloud! That bit's like a horse, and there is its rider and saddle and bridle, and behind them an old crone is riding a broomstick. (Laughs quietly to himself.) That's mother! She's scolding and screaming "You beast! Hi! Peer, come back!" (Gradually closes his eyes.) Yes, now she is frightened.—There rides Peer Gynt at the head of his henchmen, his charger gold-shod, silver-crested his harness. Peer carries gauntlets and sabre and scabbard, wears a long coat with a fine silky lining. Splendid the men in his retinue following; but there's not one sits his charger as proudly, not one that glitters like him in the sunshine. The people in groups by the wayside are gathered, lifting their hats as they stare up in wonder; the women are curtseying, everyone knows it is Kaiser Peer Gynt and his thousand retainers. Half-guinea pieces and glittering shillings are strewn on the roadway as if they were pebbles; rich as a lord is each man in the parish. Peer Gynt rides over the seas in his glory; Engelland's Prince on the shore is awaiting, and Engelland's maidens all ready to welcome him. Engelland's nobles and Engelland's Kaiser rise from their seats as he deigns to approach them. Lifting his crown, speaks the Kaiser in welcome——

Aslak the Smith (to some others, as they pass by on the

other side of the fence). Hullo! Look here! Why, it's Peer
Gynt the drunkard!

Peer Gynt (half rising). What, Kaiser—!

Aslak (leaning on the fence and grinning). Get up on your
feet, my young fellow!

Peer Gynt. What the devil—? The blacksmith! Well, pray,
what do *you* want?

Aslak (to the others). He hasn't got over our spree down
at Lundë.

Peer Gynt (springing up). Just let me alone!

Aslak. That I will. But, young fellow, what have you done
with yourself since we parted? It's six weeks ago. Have the
troll-folk been at you?

Peer Gynt. I can tell you I've done something wonderful,
Aslak.

Aslak (winking to the others). Let's hear it then, Peer!

Peer Gynt. No, it won't interest you.

Aslak. Shall we see you at Hægstad?

Peer Gynt. You won't.

Aslak. Why, the gossip says there was a time you were
fancied by Ingrid.

Peer Gynt. You dirty-faced crow!

Aslak. Now don't get in a temper! If the girl *has* refused
you, there surely are others. Remember the goodly John Gynt
was your father! Come along to the farm! There'll be girls
at the wedding as tender as lambkins, and widows well seasoned——

Peer Gynt. Go to hell!

Aslak. You'll be sure to find someone who'll have you.
Good evening. I'll give the bride all your good wishes! (They
go off, laughing and whispering. *Peer* stands for a moment
looking after them, then tosses his head and turns half round.)

Peer Gynt. Well, Ingrid at Hægstad may wed whom she
pleases, for all that I care! I shall be just as happy! (Looks
down at his clothes.) Breeches all torn—all dirty and tattered. If only I had something new to put on me—— (Stamps

his foot on the slope.) If I only could carve at their breasts like a butcher, and tear out the scorn and contempt that they show me! (Looks round suddenly.) What was that? Who is it that's laughing behind there? I certainly thought that I heard—. No, there's no one. I'll go home to mother. (Moves off, but stops again and listens in the direction of Hægstad.) The dance is beginning! (Stares and listens; moves step by step towards the fence; his eyes glisten; he rubs his hands down his legs.) How the girls swarm! Seven or eight of them there for each man! Oh, death and damnation, I must go to the party!—But what about mother, sitting up there on the roof of the mill-house—? (His eyes wander towards the fence again; he skips and laughs.) Haha! I can hear them out dancing a Halling! Guttorm's the boy—how he handles his fiddle! Hear it sparkle and flash like a stream at a waterfall! And think of the girls—all the pick of the neighbourhood—Yes, death and damnation, I'm off to the party! (Vaults over the fence and goes off down the road.)

SCENE III

(SCENE.—The courtyard of the farm at Hægstad. The farm buildings are at the back. A number of guests are assembled, and a lively dance is in progress on the grass. The *Fiddler* is seated on a table. The *Steward* stands in the doorway. Cookmaids pass to and fro between the buildings. The older folk are sitting about, gossiping.)

A Woman (joining a group of guests who are sitting on some logs). The bride? To be sure she is crying a little, but that's not a thing that is out of the usual.

The Steward (to another group). Now then, my friends, you must empty your noggins!

A Man. Ah, thank you kindly—you fill up too quickly!

A Youth (as he flies past the *Fiddler*, holding a girl by the hand). That's the way, Guttorm! Don't spare your fiddle-strings!

The Girl. Scrape till it echoes out over the meadows!

Other Girls (standing in a ring round a youth who is dancing). That's a good step!

A Girl. He's lusty and nimble!

The Youth (dancing). The roof here is high and the walls far apart, you know! (The *Bridegroom* comes up whimpering to his *Father,* who is standing talking to some others, and pulls at this jacket.)

The Bridegroom. Father, she won't! She is not being nice to me!

His Father. What won't she do?

The Bridegroom. She has locked herself in.

His Father. Well, you must see if you can't find the key.

The Bridegroom. But I don't know how.

His Father. Oh, you are a nuisance! (Turns to the others again. The *Bridegroom* drifts across the courtyard.)

A Boy (coming from behind the house). I say, you girls! Now things will be livelier! Peer Gynt's arrived!

Aslak (who has just come on the scene). Who invited him?

The Steward. No one did. (Goes into the house.)

Aslak (to the girls). If he should speak to you, don't seem to hear him.

A Girl (to the others). No, we'll pretend that we don't even see him. (*Peer Gynt* comes in, hot and eager, stops in front of the group and rubs his hands.)

Peer Gynt. Who is the nimblest girl of the lot of you?

A Girl (whom he has approached). Not I.

Another. Nor I.

A Third. No, nor I either.

Peer Gynt (to a fourth). Then *you* dance with me, for want of a better.

The Girl (turning away). I haven't time.

Peer Gynt (to a fifth). You, then.

The Girl (moving away). I'm off homeward.

Peer Gynt. Homeward to-night? Are you out of your senses?

Aslak (after a little in a low voice). Peer, she has taken an old man to dance with.

Peer Gynt (turning quickly to another man). Where are the disengaged girls?

The Man. Go and look for them. (He moves away from *Peer Gynt,* who has suddenly become subdued. He glances furtively and shyly at the group. They all look at him, but no one speaks. He approaches other groups. Wherever he goes there is a sudden silence; when he moves away, they smile and look after him.)

Peer Gynt (in a low voice). Glances—and thoughts and smiles that are cutting—jarring on one like a file on a saw-blade! (He sidles along by the palings. *Solveig,* holding little *Helga* by the hand, comes into the courtyard with her *Parents.*)

A Man (to another, close to *Peer Gynt*). These are the newcomers.

The Other. Living out westward?

First Man. Yes, out at Hedal.

The Other. Ah, yes—of course they are. (*Peer Gynt* advances to meet the newcomers, points to *Solveig* and addresses her *Father.*)

Peer Gynt. May I dance with your daughter?

The Father. You may; but before that we must go indoors and give our hosts greetings. (They go in.)

The Steward (to *Peer Gynt,* offering him a drink). As you're here, I suppose you must wet your whistle.

Peer Gynt (looking fixedly after the newcomers). Thanks, I'm for dancing. I don't feel thirsty. (The *Steward* leaves him. *Peer Gynt* looks towards the house and laughs.) How fair she is! Was there ever a fairer? Eyes glancing down at her shoes and white apron—and the way she held on to her mother's skirt, too—and carried her prayer-book wrapped in a kerchief—! I must have a look at her! (Is going into the house, but is met by several *Youths* coming out.)

A Youth. What, off already? Away from the dance?

Peer Gynt. No.

The Youth. You're on the wrong road, then! (Takes him by the shoulders to turn him round.)

Peer Gynt. Let me get past!

The Youth. Are you frightened of Aslak?

Peer Gynt. I, frightened?

The Youth. Remember what happened at Lundë! (The group laugh and move off to where the dancing is going on. *Solveig* comes to the door.)

Solveig. Are you the boy who wanted to dance with me?

Peer Gynt. Of course I am. Can't you tell by the look of me? Come on!

Solveig. But I mustn't go far—mother said so.

Peer Gynt. Mother said? mother said? Were you only born yesterday?

Solveig. Don't laugh——

Peer Gynt. It is true you are almost a kiddie still. Are you grown up?

Solveig. I shall soon be confirmed, you knôw.

Peer Gynt. Tell me your name—then we can talk easier.

Solveig. My name is Solveig. Tell me what yours is.

Peer Gynt. Peer Gynt.

Solveig (drawing back her hand from his). Oh, heavens!

Peer Gynt. Why, what is the matter?

Solveig. My garter's come loose; I must tie it more carefully. (Leaves him.)

The Bridegroom (pulling at his *Mother's* sleeve). Mother, she won't——

His Mother. She won't? What won't she do?

The Bridegroom. Mother, she won't——

His Mother. What?

The Bridegroom. Unbar the door to me!

His Father (in a low and angry voice). You're only fit to be tied in a stable, sir!

His Mother. Poor boy, don't scold him—he'll be all right

presently. (A *Youth* comes in, with a crowd of others who have been dancing.)

The Youth. Brandy, Peer?

Peer Gynt. No.

Youth. Just a drop!

Peer Gynt. Have you got any?

Youth. Maybe I have. (Pulls out a flask and drinks.) Ah, that's got a bite to it! Well?

Peer Gynt. Let me try it. (Drinks.)

Second Youth. And now have a pull at mine!

Peer Gynt. No.

Youth. Oh, what rubbish! Don't be a simpleton! Have a drink, Peer!

Peer Gynt. Well, give me a drop of it. (Drinks again.)

A Girl (in an undertone). Come, let's be off.

Peer Gynt. Why, are you afraid of me?

Youth. Do you think there is any that isn't afraid of you? You showed us what you could do, down at Lundë.

Peer Gynt. I can do better than that if I'm roused, you know!

Youth (whispering). Now he is getting on!

Others (making a ring round *Peer*) Come on, now—tell us, Peer, what you can do?

Peer Gynt. Oh, I'll tell you to-morrow——

Others. No! Tell us to-night!

A Girl. Can you show us some witchcraft, Peer?

Peer Gynt. Ah, I can conjure the Devil!

A Man. My grandmother, she could do that long before I was born, they say.

Peer Gynt. Liar! What *I* can do, no one alive can do. Why, once I conjured him into a nutshell, right through a wormhole!

Others (laughing). Of course—we can guess that!

Peer Gynt. He swore and he wept and promised to give me all sorts of things——

One of the Group. But had to go into it?

Peer Gynt. Yes; and then, when I'd stopped up the worm-hole, Lord! if you'd heard him buzzing and rumbling!

A Girl. Fancy!

Peer Gynt. 'Twas like a great bumble-bee buzzing.

The Girl. And pray have you got him still in the nutshell?

Peer Gynt. No, the old Devil got right clean away again. It is his fault the blacksmith dislikes me.

A Boy. How's that?

Peer Gynt. Because I took him to the smithy and asked the smith to crack the nutshell for me. He said he would. I laid it on the anvil; but you know Aslak's very heavy-handed, and with a will he laid on with his hammer——

A Voice from the Group. Did he kill the Devil?

Peer Gynt. No; he laid on stoutly, but the Devil looked after himself and just vanished through ceiling and walls in a flame of fire.

Several Voices. And Aslak——?

Peer Gynt. Stood there with his hands well roasted. And since that day we have never been friendly. (General laughter.)

Voices. That's a fine rigmarole!

Others. Easily his best one!

Peer Gynt. Do you suggest that I made it up?

A Man. Oh, no, I know you didn't; for I've heard the story told by my grandfather——

Peer Gynt. Liar! It happened to me, I tell you!

The Man. Oh, well—that's all right.

Peer Gynt (tossing his head). Pooh! I can ride through the clouds on horseback! There are lots of fine things I can do, I tell you! (Roars of laughter again.)

One of the Group. Peer, let us see you ride clouds!

Others. Yes, dear Peer—!

Peer Gynt. Oh, you won't need to beg me so humbly—one day I'll ride like a storm o'er the lot of you! The whole countryside shall fall at my feet!

An Older Man. Why, now he's raving!

Another. Yes, the great booby!

A Third. The braggart!

A Fourth. The liar!

Peer Gynt (threatening them). Just wait and you'll see, then!

A Man (half drunk). Yes, wait and you'll get your jacket well dusted!

Others. A good sound drubbing! A nice black eye, too! (The crowd disperses, the older ones angry and the younger ones laughing and mocking him.)

The Bridegroom (edging up to *Peer*). Peer, is it true you can ride through the clouds, then?

Peer Gynt (shortly). Anything, Mads! I'm the boy, I can tell you!

The Bridegroom. I suppose you've a coat that will make you invisible?

Peer Gynt. An invisible hat, do you mean? Yes, I have one. (Turns away from him. *Solveig* comes across the courtyard leading *Helga* by the hand. *Peer Gynt* goes to meet them, looking happier). Solveig! Ah, I am glad you have come to me! (Grasps her wrists.) Now I shall swing you round most nimbly!

Solveig. Oh, let me go!

Peer Gynt. Why?

Solveig. You look so wildly.

Peer Gynt. The reindeer grows wild when summer's approaching. Come along, girl! Come, don't be sullen!

Solveig (drawing back her arm). No—no, I daren't.

Peer Gynt. Why?

Solveig. No, you've been drinking. (Moves away a little, with *Helga*.)

Peer Gynt. I wish I had stuck my knife in the lot of them!

The Bridegroom (nudging *Peer's* elbow). Can't you help me to get in there where the bride is?

Peer Gynt (absently). The bride? Where is she?

The Bridegroom. In the loft.

Peer Gynt. Oh, is she?

The Bridegroom. Oh, come, Peer—dear Peer—you might try to!

Peer Gynt. No, you must manage to do without me. (A thought strikes him. He says, softly and meaningly): Ingrid! The loft! (Goes up to *Solveig.*) Have you made up your mind, then? (*Solveig* turns to get away, but he bars her path.) I look like a tramp, and so you're ashamed of me.

Solveig (hastily). Oh, no, you don't; that isn't the truth.

Peer Gynt. It is. And it's because you think I am fuddled; but that was for spite, because you had hurt me. Come along, then!

Solveig. I daren't, if I wanted to.

Peer Gynt. Who are you frightened of?

Solveig. Mostly of father.

Peer Gynt. Your father? Oh, yes—he's one of the solemn ones! Sanctimonious, isn't he? Answer me!

Solveig. What shall I say?

Peer Gynt. Perhaps he's a preacher? And you and your mother the same, I dare say? Are you going to answer me?

Solveig. Let me alone.

Peer Gynt. I won't! (In a low but hard and threatening voice.) I can turn myself into a troll! I shall come and stand by your bed at midnight; and if you hear something that's hissing and spitting, don't you suppose it's your cat you are hearing. It is I! And I'll drain your life-blood out of you; and your little sister—I'll eat her up, for I turn to a werewolf whenever the night falls, your loins and your back I'll bite all over—(Changes his tone suddenly and entreats her anxiously.) Dance with me, Solveig!

Solveig (looking darkly at him). Ah—now you are horrid. (Goes into the house.)

The Bridegroom (drifting up to *Peer* again). I'll give you an ox, if you'll help me!

Peer Gynt. Come! (They go behind the house. At the same moment a crowd comes back from dancing, most of them drunk. Noise and confusion. *Solveig, Helga* and their *Parents* come out to the door.)

The Steward (to *Aslak,* who is in the front of the crowd). Be quiet!

Aslak (pulling off his coat). No, here we'll settle the matter. Peer Gynt or I shall get a thrashing.

Some of the Crowd. Yes, let them fight!

Others. No, no, let them argue!

Aslak. No, we must fight; we want no arguing.

Solveig's Father. Be quiet, man!

Helga. Will he hit him, mother?

A Boy. It's better fun with his lies to tease him!

Another. Kick him out, I say!

A Third. No, spit in his face!

A Fourth (to *Aslak*). Are you backing out?

Aslak (throwing away his coat). I'll murder the beggar!

Solveig's Mother (to *Solveig*). You see now what they think of the booby. (*Aase* comes in, with a cudgel in her hand.)

Aase. Is my son here? He shall have such a drubbing! Just wait and you'll see what a thrashing I'll give him!

Aslak (turning up his shirt-sleeves). No, *your* little body's too weak for that.

Voices. Aslak will thrash him!

Others. Slash him!

Aslak (spitting on his hands and nodding to *Aase*). Hang him!

Aase. What? Hang my Peer? Just try, if you dare! This old Aase's got teeth and claws!—Where is he? (Calls across the courtyard.) Peer!

The Bridegroom (running in). Oh, God in Heaven! Come, father! Mother!

His Father. Why, what's the matter?

The Bridegroom. Oh, Peer Gynt! I—!

Aase (with a scream). What? What? Have you killed him?

The Bridegroom. No, Peer Gynt—! Look, up there on the hillside!

Voices. With the bride!

Aase (letting her cudgel fall). The beast!

Aslak (in amazement). Where the hill is steepest he's climbing, by God—like a mountain goat!

The Bridegroom (in tears). And carrying her under his arm like a pig!

Aase (shaking her fist at Peer). I wish he would fall and—! (Screams anxiously.) Take care of your footing!

Ingrid's Father (coming out bareheaded and white with rage). I'll have his life for his rape of the bride!

Aase. No, may God punish me if I let you!

ACT II

SCENE I

(SCENE.—A narrow track high up on the mountain-side. It is early morning. *Peer Gynt* comes hurriedly and sulkily along the path. *Ingrid*, wearing some of her bridal ornaments, is trying to hold him back.)

Peer Gynt. Get away!

Ingrid (in tears). What, after this? Where to?

Peer Gynt. Anywhere you like.

Ingrid (wringing her hands). What deceit!

Peer Gynt. It's no use railing. We must go our own ways —both.

Ingrid. Think what binds us two together!

Peer Gynt. Oh, the devil take all thinking! And the devil take all women—except one—!

Ingrid. And who is she?

Peer Gynt. She's not you.

Ingrid. Who is it, then?

Peer Gynt. Get you back to where you came from! Go back to your father!

Ingrid. Dearest——

Peer Gynt. Pshaw!

Ingrid. You surely can't be meaning what you say.

Peer Gynt. I can and do.

Ingrid. To ruin me, and then forsake me?

Peer Gynt. Well, what have you got to offer?

Ingrid. Hægstad farm, and something more.

Peer Gynt. Is your prayer-book in your kerchief? Where's your mane of hair all golden? Do you glance down at your apron? Do you hold on to your mother by her skirt? Come, answer!

369

Ingrid. No; but——

Peer Gynt. Shall you go to Confirmation very shortly?

Ingrid. No, but, dearest——

Peer Gynt. Are your glances always bashful? If I beg, can you deny me?

Ingrid. Christ! I think he's lost his senses——!

Peer Gynt. Does one feel a holy feeling when one sees you? Answer!

Ingrid. No, but——

Peer Gynt. Then what matter what you offer? (Turns to go.)

Ingrid (confronting him). Remember it's a hanging matter to forsake me now.

Peer Gynt. So be it.

Ingrid. Rich you may be, and respected, if you take me——

Peer Gynt. I can't do it.

Ingrid (bursting into tears). Oh, you tempted——

Peer Gynt. You were willing.

Ingrid. I was wretched.

Peer Gynt. I was mad.

Ingrid (threateningly). You'll pay a heavy price for this!

Peer Gynt. I should call the heaviest cheap.

Ingrid. Is your mind made up?

Peer Gynt. Like stone.

Ingrid. Very well. You'll see who'll win. (Goes down the hill.)

Peer Gynt (is silent for a little; then suddenly calls out). Oh, the devil take all thinking! And the devil take all women!

Ingrid (turns head and calls up mockingly). All but one!

Peer Gynt. Yes, all but one! (They each go their way.)

SCENE II

(SCENE.—By a mountain lake, on boggy moorland. A storm is blowing up. *Aase,* in despair, is calling and searching in every direction. *Solveig* can scarcely keep pace with her.

Her *Parents* and *Helga* are a little way behind. *Aase* beats the
air with her arms and tears her hair.)

Aase. Everything's against me with the might of anger!
The skies and the water and the hateful mountains! Fogs
from the skies are rolling to mislead him—treacherous waters
will delude and drown him—mountains will crush or slip
away beneath him—! And all these people! They are out to
kill him! By God, they shall not! I can't do without him!
The oaf! To think the devil thus should tempt him! (Turns
to *Solveig*.) Ah, my girl, one simply can't believe it. He, who
was always full of lies and nonsense—he, who was only
clever with his talking—he, who had never done a thing worth
telling—he—! Oh, I want to laugh and cry together! We
were such friends in our needs and troubles. For, you must
know, my husband was a drunkard, made us a byword in the
neighbours' gossip, brought all our good estate to rack and
ruin, while I and Peerkin sat at home together—tried to forget—we knew no better counsel; I was too weak to stand up
stoutly to it. It is so hard to face the fate that's coming; and
so one tries to shake one's sorrows off one, or do one's best
to rid one's mind of thinking. Some fly to brandy, others try
romancing; so we found comfort in the fairy stories all about
trolls and princes and such cattle—tales, too, of stolen
brides—but who would ever think that such stories in his
mind would linger? (Becomes terrified again.) Ah, what a
screech! A nixie or a kelpie! Peer! Oh, my Peer!—Up there
upon the hillock—! (Runs up on to a little hillock and
looks over the lake. *Solveig's Parents* come up to her.) Not
a thing to be seen!
    The Husband (quietly). It is worst for him.
    Aase (in tears). Oh, Peer! my Peer! My own lost lamb!
    The Husband (nodding his head gently). Aye, lost indeed.
    Aase. Say no such thing! He is so clever; there's no one
like him.
    The Husband. You foolish woman!

Aase. Oh yes, oh yes, I may be foolish, but he is fine!

The Husband (always quietly and with a gentle expression). His heart is stubborn; his soul is lost.

Aase (anxiously). No, no! God's not so hard as that!

The Husband. Do you think he feels the weight of his sinning?

Aase (hastily). No—he can ride through the air on a reindeer!

The Wife. Christ! Are you mad?

The Husband. What are you saying?

Aase. There's nothing that is too great for him. You'll see, if only he live to do it——

The Husband. 'Twould be best to see him hang on the gallows.

Aase (with a scream). Good God!

The Husband. When he's in the hangman's clutches perhaps his heart may turn to repentance.

Aase (confusedly). Your talk will make me dazed and giddy! We must find him!

The Husband. Save his soul.

Aase. And body! We must drag him out if he's in the marshes, and ring church bells if the trolls have got him.

The Husband. Ah! Here's a track——

Aase. May God repay you if you help me aright!

The Husband. 'Tis our Christian duty.

Aase. All the others are naught but heathens! There was only one that would come and wander——

The Husband. They knew him too well.

Aase. He was much too good for them. (Wrings her hands.) And to think—to think his life is in danger!

The Husband. Here's a footprint.

Aase. That's the way we must go, then!

The Husband. We'll scatter and search below the pastures. (He and his wife go on.)

Solveig (to *Aase*). Tell me some more.

Aase (wiping her eyes). About my son?

Solveig. Yes. Tell me everything!

Aase (smiling and holding her head up). Everything? 'Twould weary you!

Solveig. You'd be sooner wearied with telling me, than I with hearing.

SCENE III

(SCENE.—Low treeless hills below the higher mountains, whose peaks show in the distance. It is late in the day, and long shadows are falling. *Peer* comes running in at full speed, and stops on a slope.)

Peer Gynt. They're after me now—the whole of the parish! And everyone's taken his stick or his rifle. The old man from Hægstad is leading them, howling. It has soon got abroad that Peer Gynt is the quarry! A different thing from a fight with the blacksmith! This is life! All my muscles are strong as a bear's. (Swings his arms about and leaps into the air.) To overthrow everything! Breast a waterfall! Strike! Pull a fir-tree up by the roots! This is life! It can harden and it can exalt! To hell with all my trumpery lying! (Three *Cowherd Girls* run across the hill, shouting and singing.)

The Girls. Trond of Valfjeld! Baard and Kaare! Listen, trolls! Would you sleep in our arms?

Peer Gynt. Who are you shouting for?

The Girls. Trolls! Trolls! Trolls!

First Girl. Trond, come lovingly!

Second Girl. Come, lusty Baard!

Third Girl. All the beds in our hut are empty!

First Girl. Love is lusty!

Second Girl. And lustiness love!

Third Girl. When boys are lacking, one plays with trolls!

Peer Gynt. Where are your boys, then?

The Girls (with a burst of laughter). They can't come!

First Girl. Mine called me dearest and sweetheart too, now he is wed to an elderly widow.

Second Girl. Mine met a gipsy wench up at Lien, now they are both on the road together.

Third Girl. Mine made an end of our bastard brat, now on a stake his head is grinning.

All Three. Trond of Valfjeld! Baard and Kaare! Listen, trolls! Would you sleep in our arms?

Peer Gynt (leaping suddenly among them). I'm a three-headed troll, and the boy for three girls!

The Girls. Can you tackle the job?

Peer Gynt. You shall see if I can!

First Girl. To the hut! To the hut!

Second Girl. We have mead!

Peer Gynt. Let it flow!

Third Girl. This Saturday night not a bed shall be empty!

Second Girl (kissing *Peer*). He gleams and glitters like glowing iron!

Third Girl (kissing *Peer*). Like a baby's eyes from the blackest tarn!

Peer Gynt (dancing with them). Dismal bodings and wanton thoughts, laughter in eyes and tears in throat!

The Girls (making long noses at the mountain-tops, and shouting and singing). Trond of Valfjeld! Baard and Kaare! Listen, trolls! Did you sleep in our arms? (They dance away over the hills with *Peer Gynt* between them.)

SCENE IV

(SCENE.—Among the mountains. The snowy peaks are gleaming in the sunset. *Peer Gynt* comes in, looking wild and distraught.)

Peer Gynt. Palace o'er palace is rising! See, what a glittering gate! Stop! Will you stop!—It is moving farther and farther away! The cock on the weather-vane's lifting its wings as if for a flight—into rifts of rock it has vanished, and the mountain's barred and locked. What are these roots and tree-

trunks that grow from the clefts of the ridge? They are heroes
with feet of herons—and now they are vanished away. A
shimmer like strips of rainbow my sight and mind assails.
Are they bells that I hear in the distance? What's weighing
my eyebrows down? Oh, how my forehead's aching—as if
I'd a red-hot band pressing—! But who the devil put it there
I don't know! (Sinks down.) A flight o'er the ridge at Gendin
—romancing and damned lies! Over the steepest walls with
the bride—and drunk for a day—hawks and kites to fight
with—threatened by trolls and the like—sporting with crazy
lasses—damned romancing and lies! (Gazes upwards for a
long time.) There hover two brown eagles; the wild geese
fly to the south; and I have to trudge and stumble knee-
deep in mud and mire. (Springs up.) I'll go with them!
Cleanse my foulness in a bath of the keenest wind! Up aloft
I'll lave my stains in that glittering christening-font! I'll
away out over the pastures; I'll fly till I'm pure and clean—
fly o'er the ocean waters, o'er the Prince of Engelland's head!
Ah, you may stare, you maidens; I'm flying, but not to you.
It's of no use your waiting—! Yet I might swoop below—
Why, where are the two brown eagles? They've gone to the
devil, I think! See, there's the end of a gable, it's rising bit
by bit; it's growing out of the rubbish—see, now the door
stands wide! Aha! I recognize it, grandfather's farm new
built! Gone are the clouts from the casements and the fence
that was tumbling down; lights gleam from every window;
they are feasting there within. Listen! The Parson's tapping
his knife upon his glass; the Captain's hurled his bottle and
broken the mirror to smash. Let them waste and let them
squander! Hush, mother—there's plenty more! It's rich John
Gynt that is feasting; hurrah for the race of Gynt! What's
all the bustle and rumpus? What are the cries and shouts?
"Where's Peer?" the Captain is calling—the Parson would
drink my health—go in, then, Peer, for the verdict; you
shall have it in songs of praise: Great, Peer, were thy begin-
nings, and in great things thou shalt end. (He leaps forward,

but runs his nose against a rock, falls and remains lying on the ground.)

SCENE V

(SCENE.—A mountain-side, with trees in full leaf through which the wind is whispering. Stars are twinkling through the branches. Birds are singing in the tree-tops. *A Woman in Green* crosses the slope. After her follows *Peer Gynt,* performing all sorts of amorous antics.)

The Woman in Green (stopping and turning round). Is it true?

Peer Gynt (drawing his finger across his throat). As true as my name is Peer; as true as that you are a lovely woman! Will you have me? You'll see how nice I can be; you shall never have to weave or to spin; you shall be fed till you're ready to burst; I promise I never will pull your hair——

The Woman in Green. Nor strike me, either?

Peer Gynt. No; is it likely? We sons of kings don't strike our women.

The Woman in Green. A king's son?

Peer Gynt. Yes.

The Woman in Green. I'm the Dovrë-King's daughter.

Peer Gynt. Are you really? Well, well! How suitable!

The Woman in Green. In the mountains my father has his castle.

Peer Gynt. And my mother a larger one, let me tell you.

The Woman in Green. Do you know my father? His name's King Brosë.

Peer Gynt. Do you know my mother? Her name's Queen Aase.

The Woman in Green. The mountains reel when my father's angry.

Peer Gynt. If my mother begins to scold, they totter.

The Woman in Green. My father can kick to the highest rafters.

Peer Gynt. My mother can ride through the fiercest river.

The Woman in Green. Besides those rags have you other clothing?

Peer Gynt. Ah, you should see my Sunday garments!

The Woman in Green. My week-day garments are gold and silver.

Peer Gynt. It looks to me more like tow and grasses.

The Woman in Green. Yes. There's just one thing to remember: we mountain folk have an ancient custom; all that we have has a double shape. So when you come to my father's palace it would not be in the least surprising if you were inclined to think it merely a heap of ugly stones and rubbish.

Peer Gynt. That's just the same as it is with us! You may think our gold all rust and mildew, and mistake each glittering window-pane for a bundle of worn-out clouts and stockings.

The Woman in Green. Black looks like white, and ugly like fair.

Peer Gynt. Big looks like little, and filthy like clean.

The Woman in Green (falling on his neck). Oh, Peer, I see we are splendidly suited!

Peer Gynt. Like the hair to the comb—or the leg to the breeches.

The Woman in Green (calling over the hillside). My steed! My steed! My wedding steed! (A gigantic pig comes running in, with a rope's end for a halter and an old sack for a saddle. *Peer Gynt* swings himself on to its back and seats the *Woman in Green* in front of him.)

Peer Gynt. Houp-là! We'll gallop right into the palace! Come up! Come up, my noble charger!

The Woman in Green (caressingly). And to think I was feeling so sad and lonely—one never can tell what is going to happen!

Peer Gynt (whipping up the pig, which trots off). Great folk are known by the steeds they ride!

SCENE VI

(Scene.—The Royal Hall of the King of the Trolls. A great assembly of *Troll Courtiers*, *Brownies* and *Gnomes*. The *Troll King* is seated on his throne, with crown and sceptre. His children and nearest relations sit on either side of him. *Peer Gynt* is standing before him. There is a great uproar in the hall.)

Troll Courtiers. Slay him! The Christian's son has tempted the fairest daughter of our King!

A Young Troll. Let me slash him on the fingers!

Another. May I tear his hair out for him?

A Troll Maiden. Let me bite him on the buttocks!

Troll Witch (with a ladle). Let me boil him down for broth!

Another (holding a chopper). Shall he toast on a spit or be browned in a kettle?

The Troll King. Quiet! Keep calm! (Beckons to his counsellors to approach him.) We must not be too boastful. Things have been going badly with us lately; we don't feel sure if we shall last or perish, and can't afford to throw away assistance. Besides, the lad is almost without blemish, and well-built too, as far as I can gather. It's true enough that he has only *one* head; but then my daughter hasn't more than one. Three-headed Trolls are going out of fashion; two-headed, even, nowadays aren't common, and *their* heads usually are not up to much. (To *Peer Gynt*.) And so, my lad, it's my daughter you're after?

Peer Gynt. Yes, if she comes with a kingdom for dowry.

The Troll King. You shall have half while I am living and the other half when I am done for.

Peer Gynt. I'm content with that.

The Troll King. But stop, young fellow, *you've* got to give some pledges also. Break one of them, and our bargain's off and you don't get out of here alive. First, you must promise never to give thought to aught except what within these hills is bounded; shun the day, its deeds, and all the sunlit places.

Peer Gynt. If I'm called King, 'twill not be hard to do it.

The Troll King. Secondly—now I'll see how far you're clever—— (Rises from his seat.)

The Oldest Troll Courtier (to *Peer Gynt*). Let's see if you've got a wisdom tooth that can crack the nut of our monarch's riddle!

The Troll King. What is the difference between Trolls and Men?

Peer Gynt. There isn't any, as far as I can gather; big trolls would roast and little ones would claw you—just as with us if only we dared do it.

The Troll King. True; we're alike in that and other things too. Still, just as morning's different from evening, so there's a real difference between us, and I will tell you what it is. Out yonder under the skies, men have a common saying: "Man, to thyself be true!" But here, 'mongst Trolls, "Troll, to thyself be—enough!" it runs.

Troll Courtier (to *Peer Gynt*). Well, do you fathom it?

Peer Gynt. It seems rather hazy.

The Troll King. "Enough," my son—that word so fraught with meaning—must be the motto written on your buckler.

Peer Gynt (scratching his head). Well, but——

The Troll King. It *must*, if you're to be a king here!

Peer Gynt. All right; so be it. It is not much worse than——

The Troll King. Next you must learn to value rightly our simple, homely way of living. (He beckons two *Trolls* with pigs' heads, wearing white nightcaps, bring food and drink.) Our cows give cakes and our oxen mead; no matter whether their taste is sour or sweet; the great thing to remember is that they're home-made and home-brewed.

Peer Gynt (pushing the things away from him). The devil take your home-brewed drink! I'll never get used to your country's habits.

The Troll King. The bowl goes with it, and it is golden. Who takes the bowl gets my daughter too.

Peer Gynt (thoughtfully). Of course we're told that a man should master his disposition, and in the long run perhaps the drink will taste less sour. So, here goes! (Drinks.)

The Troll King. Now that was sensibly said. But you spit?

Peer Gynt. I must trust to the force of habit.

The Troll King. Next, you must take off all your Christian clothing; for you must know we boast that in the Dovrë all's mountain-made; we've nothing from the valleys except the bows of silk that deck our tail-tips.

Peer Gynt (angrily). I haven't got a tail!

The Troll King. Then you shall have one. (To one of the courtiers.) See that my Sunday tail is fastened on him.

Peer Gynt. No, that he shan't! Do you want to make a fool of me?

The Troll King. Don't try with tail-less rump to court my daughter.

Peer Gynt. Making a beast of a man!

The Troll King. My son, you're wrong there; I'd only make a courtly wooer of you. And, as a mark of very highest honour, the bow you wear shall be of bright flame-colour.

Peer Gynt (reflectively). We're taught, of course, that man is but a shadow; and one must pay some heed to use and wont, too. So, tie away!

The Troll King. You're coming to your senses.

Troll Courtier. Just see how nicely you can wag and wave it!

Peer Gynt (angrily). Now, do you mean to ask anything more of me? Do you want me to give up my Christian faith?

The Troll King. No, to keep that you are perfectly welcome. Faith is quite free, and pays no duty; it's his dress and its cut that a Troll should be known by. If we're of one mind as to manners and costume you're free to believe what would give us the horrors.

Peer Gynt. You are really, in spite of your many conditions, more reasonable than one might have expected.

The Troll King. We Trolls are better than our reputation,

my son; and that is another difference between you and us. But now we have finished the serious part of the present assembly. Our ears and our eyes shall now be delighted. Let the harp-maid waken the Dovrë-harp's strings, let the dance-maiden tread the Dovrë-hall's floor. (Music and a dance.) What do you think of it?

Peer Gynt. Think of it? H'm——

The Troll King. Tell me quite openly. What did you see?

Peer Gynt. See? What I saw was impossibly ugly. A bell-cow thrumming her hoof on a gut-string, a sow in short stockings pretending to dance to it.

The Troll Courtiers. Eat him!

The Troll King. Remember his understanding is only human.

Troll Maidens. Oh, tear his eyes out and cut off his ears!

The Woman in Green (weeping). Are we to endure it, my sister and I, when we've played and danced?

Peer Gynt. Oho, was it you? Well, you know, at a banquet a joke is a joke—no offence was intended.

The Woman in Green. Will you swear to me you were only joking?

Peer Gynt. The dance and the music were both delightful.

The Troll King. It's a funny thing, this human nature; it clings to a man with such persistence. Suppose we fight it and it is wounded, there may be a scar, but it heals up quickly. My son-in-law's now most accommodating; he has willingly cast off his Christian breeches, willingly drunk of the mead-filled goblet, willingly tied on a tail behind him—is so willing, in fact, to do all we ask him that I certainly thought the old Adam banished for good and all; then, all of a sudden, we find him uppermost. Yes, my son, you certainly must undergo some treatment to cure this troublesome human nature.

Peer Gynt. What will you do?

The Troll King. I'll scratch you slightly in the left eye, and then your vision will be oblique, and all you look on will seem to you to be perfection. Then I'll cut out your right-hand window——

Peer Gynt. You're drunk!

The Troll King (laying some sharp instruments on the table). See, here are the glazier's tools. You must be tamed like a raging bullock; then you'll perceive that your bride is lovely, and never again will your sight deceive you with dancing sows or bell-cows thrumming——

Peer Gynt. That's fool's talk.

The Oldest Courtier. It's the Troll King's word; he is the wise man and you the fool.

The Troll King. Just think what a lot of trouble and worry you will be rid of for good and all. Remember, too, that the eye is the source of the bitter, searing flood of tears.

Peer Gynt. That's true; and it says in the family Bible: "If thine eye offend thee, pluck it out." But, tell me, when will my sight recover and be as it is now?

The Troll King. Never, my friend.

Peer Gynt. Oh, really! Then I must decline with thanks.

The Troll King. But what do you mean to do?

Peer Gynt. To leave you.

The Troll King. Softly! It's easy to get within here; but the Troll King's gate doesn't open outwards.

Peer Gynt. You surely don't mean to detain me by force?

The Troll King. Now listen, Prince Peer, and give way to reason. You're cut out for a Troll. Why, look, already you bear yourself quite in a Troll-like fashion! And you want to become one, don't you?

Peer Gynt. Of course. In return for a bride and a well-found kingdom I'm not unwilling to sacrifice something; but all things have their natural limit. I have taken a tail, it is true; but then I can undo the knots that our friend has tied, and take the thing off. I have shed my breeches; they were old and patched; but that won't prevent me from putting them on if I have a mind to. I shall probably find it just as easy to deal with your Trollish way of living. I can easily

swear that a cow's a maiden; an oath's not a difficult thing
to swallow. But to know that one never can get one's freedom—not even to die as a human being—to end one's days
as a Troll of the mountains—never go back, as you tell me
plainly—that is a thing that I'll not submit to.

The Troll King. Now, on my sins, I'm getting angry; I'm
not in the mood to be made a fool of. You scurvy lout! Do
you know who I am? To begin with, you make too free with
my daughter——

Peer Gynt. That's a lie in your throat!

The Troll King. And you have to marry her.

Peer Gynt. Do you dare accuse me of—?

The Troll King. Can you deny that she was the object of
all your desire?

Peer Gynt (whistles). But no more than that. What the
deuce does that matter?

The Troll King. You human beings are always the same.
You are always ready to talk of your souls, but heed nothing
really save what is tangible. You think desires are things that
don't matter? Wait; your own eyes will prove to you
shortly——

Peer Gynt. It's no use baiting your hook with lies!

The Troll King. My Peer, ere the year's out you'll be a
father.

Peer Gynt. Unlock the doors. I'm going.

The Troll King. We'll send you the brat in a goat-skin.

Peer Gynt (wiping the sweat from his brow). I wish I
could wake up!

The Troll King. Shall we send to your Palace?

Peer Gynt. Oh, send to the Parish!

The Troll King. As you like, Prince Peer; it's your affair
solely. But one thing is certain—what's done can't be undone, and you will see how your offspring will grow up! Mon-
grels like that grow remarkably quickly——

Peer Gynt. Oh, come, old chap, don't go at me like a bullock! Fair maiden, be reasonable! Let's come to terms. I have

to confess that I'm neither a prince nor rich; and, however you take my measure, I'm sure you won't find you've made much of a bargain. (The *Woman in Green* faints and is carried out by the *Troll Maidens*.)

The Troll King (looks at him for a while with a contemptuous expression, then says) Dash him to bits on the rocks, my good children!

Young Trolls. Dad, mayn't we first play at Owls and Eagles? Or the Wolf-Game? Or Grey Mouse and Red-Eyed Pussy?

The Troll King. Yes, but be quick. I'm angry and sleepy. Good night! (Goes.)

Peer Gynt (hunted by the *Young Trolls*). Let me go, you young devils! (Tries to climb up the chimney.)

Young Trolls. Hobgoblins! Brownies! Come, bite him!

Peer Gynt. Ow! (Tries to get away through the cellar-flap.)

Young Trolls. Stop all the holes up!

Troll Courtier. How the youngsters enjoy it!

Peer Gynt (fighting with a little *Troll* who has bitten deep into his ear). You filth, let go!

Troll Courtier (rapping *Peer Gynt* over the knuckles). A little respect for a king's son, you scoundrel!

Peer Gynt. Ah! A rat hole! (Runs towards it.)

Young Trolls. Stop up the holes, Brownie brothers!

Peer Gynt. The old man was foul, but the young ones are worse!

Young Trolls. Flay him!

Peer Gynt. I wish I were small as a mouse!

Young Trolls (swarming about him). Don't let him escape!

Peer Gynt. I wish I were a louse!

Young Trolls. Now jump on his face!

Peer Gynt (smothered in *Trolls*). Help, mother, I'm dying! (Church bells are heard afar off.)

Young Trolls. Bells in the Valley! The Blackfrock's Cows! (The *Trolls* disperse in a turmoil and wild shrieks. The Hall falls to pieces. Everything disappears.)

SCENE VII

(Pitch darkness, *Peer Gynt* is heard slashing and hitting about him with a branch of a tree.)

Peer Gynt. Answer! Who are you?

A Voice in the Darkness. Myself!

Peer Gynt. Let me pass, then!

Voice. Go round about, Peer! Room enough on the mountain. (*Peer Gynt* tries to pass another way, but runs up against something.)

Peer Gynt. Who are you?

Voice. Myself. Can you say as much?

Peer Gynt. I can say what I like, and my sword can strike! Look out for yourself! I'm going to smash you! King Saul slew hundreds; Peer Gynt slays thousands! (Hits about him wildly.) Who are you?

Voice. Myself.

Peer Gynt. That's a silly answer, and you can keep it. It tells me nothing. What are you?

Voice. The great Boyg.

Peer Gynt. No, are you really? Things were black before! now some grey is showing. Out of my way, Boyg!

Voice. Go round about, Peer!

Peer Gynt. No, through you! (Hits out wildly.) He's down! (Tries to get on, but always runs up against something.) Ha, ha! Are there more of you?

Voice. The Boyg, Peer Gynt! The one and only. The Boyg that's unwounded, the Boyg that was hurt. The Boyg that was dead and the Boyg that's alive.

Peer Gynt (throwing away his branch). My weapon's bewitched; but I have my fists! (Strikes out in front of him.)

Voice. Yes, put your trust in your fists and strength! Ho, ho! Peer Gynt, they'll bring you out top!

Peer Gynt. Backward or forward, it's just as far— Out or in, the way's as narrow. It's there!—and there!—and all about me! I think I've got out, and I'm back in the midst of it. What's your name! Let me see you! Say what you are!

Voice. The Boyg.

Peer Gynt (feeling round him). Neither dead, nor alive; slime and mistiness; no shape or form! It's as if one were smothered amidst any number of bears that are growling at being waked up! (Shrieks.) Why don't you hit out at me!

Voice. The Boyg's not so foolish as that.

Peer Gynt. Oh, strike at me!

Voice. The Boyg doesn't strike.

Peer Gynt. Come, fight! You *shall* fight with me!

Voice. The great Boyg can triumph without any fighting.

Peer Gynt. I'd far rather it were the Brownies tormenting me! Or even as much as a one-year-old Troll! Just something to fight with—and not this blank nothingness! It's snoring now! Boyg!

Voice. What is it?

Peer Gynt. Show fight, will you!

Voice. The great Boyg can get all he wishes by gentleness.

Peer Gynt (biting his own hands and arms). Oh, for claws and teeth that would tear my flesh! I must see a drop of my own blood flow! (A sound is heard like the beating of wings of great birds.)

Birds' Cries. Is he coming, Boyg?

Voice. Yes, foot by foot.

Birds' Cries. Sisters afar off, fly to meet us!

Peer Gynt. If you mean to save me, girl, be quick! Don't hang your head and look down blushing. Your prayer-book! Hit him straight in the eye with it!

Birds' Cries. He's failing!

Voice. He's ours.

Birds' Cries. Come, sisters, quickly!

Peer Gynt. An hour of torture such as this is too dear a price to pay for life. (Sinks down.)

Birds' Cries. Boyg, he is down! Boyg, seize him! Seize him!

(Church bells and the singing of psalms are heard in the distance.)

Voice (with a gasp, as the *Boyg* gradually dwindles away to nothing). He was too strong. There were women behind him.

SCENE VIII

(SCENE.—On the hillside outside a hut on *Aase's* mountain pasture. It is sunrise. The door of the hut is barred. Everything is empty and still. *Peer Gynt* lies asleep by the hut. Presently he wakes and looks around him with listless and heavy eyes.)

Peer Gynt (spitting). I'd give the world for a pickled herring! (He spits again; then he sees *Helga* approaching, carrying a basket of food.) You here, youngster? What do you want?

Helga. It was Solveig——

Peer Gynt (springing up). Where is she?

Helga. Behind the hut.

Solveig (from behind the hut). If you come any nearer, I'll run away!

Peer Gynt (standing still). Perhaps you're afraid I shall carry you off?

Solveig. For shame!

Peer Gynt. Do you know where I was last night? The Troll King's daughter is hunting me down.

Solveig. 'Twas well done, then, that we rang the bells.

Peer Gynt. Oh, Peer Gynt's not quite the lad to get caught— What's that you say?

Helga (crying). She's running away. (Runs after *Solveig.*) Wait for me!

Peer Gynt (gripping her by the arm). See what I've got in my pocket! A fine silver button! And you shall have it if you speak up for me!

Helga. Oh, let me go!

Peer Gynt. Take it, then.

Helga. Oh, let me go!—and my basket!

Peer Gynt. You had better look out if you don't—!

Helga. Oh, you frighten me!

Peer Gynt (quietly, as he lets her go). No; all I meant was: don't let her forget me! (*Helga* runs off.)

ACT III

SCENE I

(SCENE.—The depths of a pine-wood. It is a grey autumn day, and snow is falling. *Peer Gynt* is in his shirt-sleeves, felling timber. He has just tackled a tall tree with crooked branches.)

Peer Gynt. Oh, yes, you're tough, my ancient friend, but that won't help you; you're coming down! (Sets to work again.) I know you're wearing a coat of mail; but I'll slash through, were it never so strong. Yes, you may shake your crooked arms; I daresay you're both fierce and angry, but all the same you shall bow to me—! (Suddenly breaks off sullenly.) What lies! It's only an ancient tree. What lies! I'm fighting no mail-clad foe; it's only a fir with its bark all cracked. It's toilsome work, this felling timber; but the devil's own job when all the time one's dreams get mixed up with one's working. All that must stop—this daytime dreaming and always being in the clouds. My lad, remember that you're an outlaw! Your only shelter's in this forest. (Works again hurriedly for a while.) An outlaw, yes. You have no mother to bring you food and spread your table. If you want to eat, you must help yourself; get what you can from the woods and the stream, forage for sticks if you want a fire, look to yourself for everything. If you need clothes, you must skin a deer; if you want a wall to put round your house, you must break the stones; if you want to build, you must fell the timber and shoulder it and carry it to the spot you've chosen. (He lets his axe fall and stares in front of him.) I'll build a beauty! Up on the roof I'll have a tower and weather-vane, and on the gable-end I'll carve a lovely mermaid. Vane and locks

shall be of brass, and window-panes shall shine so bright that
from afar people shall wonder what it is that they see gleaming
in the sun. (Laughs bitterly.) Damned lies! Why, there I go
again! Remember that you're an outlaw, boy! (Sets to work
feverishly.) A well-thatched hut is quite enough to keep out
both the frost and rain. (Looks up at the tree.) It's giving
way. One more stroke! There! He's down and fallen all his
length, and all the undergrowth is quivering. (Sets to work to
lop off the branches, all at once he stops and listens, with
uplifted axe.) There's someone coming! Ingrid's father—
Trying to catch me treacherously! (Hides behind a tree and
peeps out.) A boy! Just one. And he looks frightened. He's
glancing round him. What is that he's hiding underneath his
jacket? A sickle. Now he stands and looks— He lays his hand
upon a log— What now? Why does he brace himself—? Ugh!
He has chopped a finger off! And now he's bleeding like a
pig— And now he runs off with his hand wrapped in a clout.
(Comes forward.) He must be mad! Chopped it right off!—
a precious finger! And did it, too, as if he meant it. Oho, I see!
If one's not anxious to serve His Gracious Majesty that is
the only way. So that's it! They would have called him for
the army, but he, I see, would be exempted. Still, to cut off—?
To lose for ever—? The thought, perhaps—the wish—the
will— Those I could understand; but really to *do* the deed!
Ah, no—that beats me! (Shakes his head a little; then resumes
his work.)

SCENE II

(SCENE.—A room in *Aase's* house. Everything is in dis-
order. The clothes-chest is standing open; clothes lie scattered about; a cat is lying on the bed. *Aase* and *Kari* are trying
to put things in order.)

Aase (running to one side of the room). Kari, tell me——
Kari. What is it?
Aase. Tell me— Where is—? Where shall I find—? Oh,

tell me, where is—? What am I looking for? I'm going crazy! Where's the chest key?

Kari. It's in the keyhole.

Aase. What's that rumbling?

Kari. The last load going off to Hægstad.

Aase (weeping). I wish they were taking me in my coffin! What we poor creatures have to suffer! God pity me! The whole house emptied! What Hægstad left, the Judge has taken. They've scarcely left me with a rag to put upon my back. It's shameful to have pronounced so hard a sentence! (Sits down on the edge of the bed.) The farm's gone now, and all our land. He's a hard man, but the Law was harder; no one to help me—none showed mercy— Peer gone, and no one to advise me.

Kari. You've got this house until you die.

Aase. Oh, yes—the bread of charity, for me and for my cat!

Kari. Old mother, God help you! Peer has cost you dear.

Aase. My Peer? I think you've lost your senses! They got their Ingrid, safe and sound. They should have rightly blamed the Devil; he is the culprit, and no other; 'twas he, the ugly beast, that tempted my poor dear boy!

Kari. Had you not better send for the priest? For all you know, things may be worse than you believe.

Aase. Send for the priest? Perhaps I'd better. (Gets up.) No, no—I cannot! I'm his mother; I must help the boy—it's only my duty; I must do my best, when everyone fails me. They've left him that coat. I must get it patched. I wish I had dared to keep the bed-cover! Where are the stockings?

Kari. There, with that rubbish.

Aase (fumbling among the things). What's this? Look here! An old casting-ladle! He used to pretend to mould buttons with this, melt them and shape them and stamp them too. Once, when we'd company, in came the boy and begged of his father a bit of tin. "Not tin," said John, "King Christian's coin! A silver coin to melt, and show that you're the son of rich John Gynt." May God forgive him, for he was drunk; and when he was drunk it was all the same, tin or gold. Ah, here are the stockings! They are all in holes; I must darn them, Kari.

Kari. They certainly need it.

Aase. When that is done, I must go to bed. I feel so bad, so wretchedly ill. (*Joyfully.*) Oh, look here, Kari! Two flannel shirts that they have forgotten!

Kari. Aye, so they have.

Aase. That's a lucky find. You might put one of them aside. Or—no, I think we'll take them both; the one he has on is so thin and worn.

Kari. But, Aase, you know that it's a sin!

Aase. Oh, yes; but you know the parson tells us that all our sins may be forgiven.

SCENE III

(SCENE.—Outside a newly built hut in the forest. Reindeer horns over the door. Deep snow everywhere. It is nightfall. *Peer Gynt* is standing fixing a heavy wooden bolt to the door.)

Peer Gynt (laughing now and then). There must be a bolt, to fasten my door against the Troll-folk and men and women. There must be a bolt, to keep me safe from all the plaguy crowd of goblins. They'll come when it's dark, and I'll hear them knocking: "Open, Peer, we are quick as thoughts! Under the bed, on the hearth in the ashes, you'll hear us creeping and crawling about; we'll fly down the chimney like fiery dragons. Hee-hee! Do you think your nails and planks can save you from plaguy goblin-thoughts?" (*Solveig* comes over the snow on ski; she has a shawl over her head and a bundle in her hand.)

Solveig. God bless your work. You must not reject me. I had your message, and you must take me.

Peer Gynt. Solveig! It can't be—! Yes, it is! And not afraid to come so near me!

Solveig. I had your message from little Helga, and others I had from the winds and the silence. There was one in all that your mother told me, and others that came to me in my dreams. The dreary nights and the empty days brought me the message that I must come. All light had gone from my life down yonder; I had neither the heart to laugh nor to weep. I could not tell what was in your mind; I could only tell what I needs must do.

Peer Gynt. But your father?

Solveig. I've no one on God's wide earth that I can call father or mother now; I've left them for ever.

Peer Gynt. Solveig, my dear— To come to me?

Solveig. Yes, to you alone; you must be all to me—friend and comfort. (In tears.) The worst was leaving my little sister; and worse than that, to leave my father; and worst of all to leave her who carried me at her breast; no, God forgive me, the worst indeed was the bitter sorrow that I must part from all my dear ones!

Peer Gynt. And do you know the heavy sentence the law pronounced? They've taken from me everything that I had or might have.

Solveig. 'Twas not for what you had or might have I give up what was dearest to me.

Peer Gynt. And do you know that if I venture beyond this forest I am forfeit if any man can lay hand on me?

Solveig. When I asked my way as I came hither, they questioned me—where was I going? "I'm going home": that was my answer.

Peer Gynt. Ah, then I need no bolts to guard me, no locks against the powers of evil! My hunter's hut is consecrated if you deign enter it and live there. Dear, let me look at you! Not too near you— I'd only look at you! How lovely, how pure you are! Let my arms lift you! How slim and light you are, my Solveig! I'd carry you for ever, dearest, and never weary! I'll not soil you; I'll hold your warm and lovely body at arms' length from me! Ah, my Solveig, can I believe I've made you love me? Both night and day 'tis what I've longed for. See, I have built this little dwelling— It shall come down; it's cramped and ugly——

Solveig. Little or big, I'm happy here. Here one can breathe, in the buffeting wind. Down yonder 'twas sultry; I felt hemmed in; it was partly that, that drove me away. But here, where one hears the fir-trees soughing— Such song and silence!—I feel at home.

Peer Gynt. But, dear, are you sure? It means for ever!

Solveig. There's no way back on the road I have trodden.

Peer Gynt. You're mine, then! Go in! I would see you within! Go in! I will fetch some wood for a fire, to warm you snugly and flicker brightly; you shall sit soft and never shiver. (He unbars the door, and *Solveig* goes in. He stands silent for a moment, then laughs aloud for joy and leaps into the air.) My princess! Now she is found and won! Now my palace shall spring into being! (Seizes his axe and crosses over towards the trees. At the same moment an elderly woman in a tattered green gown advances out of the wood; an ugly child with a flagon in his hand limps after her, holding on to her skirt.)

The Woman. Good evening, Peer Light-Foot!

Peer Gynt. What is it? Who are you?

The Woman. Old friends, Peer Gynt! My hut is quite near here. We're neighbours.

Peer Gynt. Indeed? I was not aware of it.

The Woman. As your hut grew up, so mine grew beside it.

Peer Gynt (trying to get away). I'm in a great hurry.

The Woman. You always were that; but, trudging along, in the end I come up with you.

Peer Gynt. Old dame, you're mistaken!

The Woman. I know I was once; that day when you made me such wonderful promises.

Peer Gynt. I made you promises? Why, what the devil—?

The Woman. Do you mean you've forgotten the night when you drank at my father's? Do you mean you've forgotten——

Peer Gynt. I mean I've forgotten what never took place to remember! What nonsense is this? And when last did we meet?

The Woman. The last time we met was the first time we met. (To the child.) Give your father a drink; I think he is thirsty.

Peer Gynt. His father? You're drunk! Do you mean that this urchin—?

The Woman. You're not going to say that you can't recognize him? Have you eyes? Can't you see that he's lame in the shanks as you're lame in your mind?

Peer Gynt. Do you mean to pretend—?

The Woman. You can't wriggle out of it!

Peer Gynt. That long-legged brat—?

The Woman. He has grown very fast.

Peer Gynt. Why, you ugly old hag, do you dare to assert that this—?

The Woman. Listen, Peer Gynt; you're as coarse as a bullock. (Weeps.) Oh, how can I help it if I'm not as fair as I was when you tempted me out on the hill-side up there in the mountains? And when in the autumn my travail came on me, I'd only the Devil to act as a midwife; so it isn't surprising I lost all my beauty. But if you would see me as fair as before, you've only to turn out that girl that's in there, out of your house and your mind and your sight; do that, dearest lad, and my ill-looks will vanish!

Peer Gynt. Get away, you old witch!

The Woman. You shall see if I will!

Peer Gynt. I'll break your head for you!

The Woman. Try, if you dare! You'll find me, Peer, a hard nut to crack! Every day I shall be back again, peeping at doors and spying on both of you. When you and your girl are sitting together, and you are inclined for cuddling and fondling, you'll find me beside you, claiming my share of it. She and I will share you—turn about. Good-bye, dear boy. If you like the prospect, then wed her to-morrow!

Peer Gynt. You devil's nightmare!

The Woman. But I had forgotten! You've got to look after your little son—this graceful urchin! Come on, little imp, will you go to your father?

The Boy (spitting at *Peer*). If I had an axe, I'd split you in two with it! Just wait!

The Woman (kissing the *Boy*). What a head he's got on his shoulders! When you've grown up you'll be just like your father!

Peer Gynt (stamping his foot). I wish you——

The Woman. As far off as now we are near you?

Peer Gynt (clenching his fists). And all this comes——

The Woman. Just of thoughts and desires! Hard luck for you, Peer!

Peer Gynt. It's hardest for her—for Solveig—my loveliest, purest treasure!

The Woman. Oh, yes; the innocent always suffer—as the Devil said when his mother thrashed him because his father had come home drunk! (She moves off into the wood with the *Boy*, who throws the flagon behind him.)

Peer Gynt (after a long silence). "Round about," said the Boyg; that's how I must go.—My palace has tumbled about my ears! She was so near me; and now there has risen a wall between us, and all in a moment my joy is gone and everything's ugly. "Round about"—ah, yes; there's no straight road that leads through this from me to her. No straight road? All the same, there might be. If I remember aright, the Bible says something somewhere about repentance—but I've no Bible, and I've forgotten the most of it, and in this forest there's not a thing that will give me guidance. Repent? It might take years to do it before I found the way. And, meanwhile, a life that's empty, ugly, dreary; and in the end from shreds and fragments to try and patch the thing together? One can patch up a broken fiddle, but not a watch-spring. If one tramples on growing things they're spoiled for ever.— But, surely, the old witch was lying! I can put all those ugly

doings out of my sight! But—can I put them out of my mind?
I shall be haunted by lurking memories—of Ingrid—of those
three girls upon the hillside. Will they come too, and jeer and
threaten, and beg of me to hold them closely or lift them
tenderly at arms' length? It's no use! Were my arms as long
as fir-trees' stems or pine-trees' branches, I should be holding
her too near to set her down again unsullied. I must find some
way round about, without a thought of gain or loss; some way
to free me from such thoughts and shut them from my mind
for ever. (Takes a few steps towards the hut, then stops.)
But—go in now? Disgraced and soiled? With all these Troll-
folk at my heels? Speak, and yet not tell all? Confess, and still
be hiding something from her? (Throws away his axe.) No,
no—to go and meet her now, such as I am, were sacrilege.
(*Solveig* appears at the door of the hut.)

    Solveig. Are you coming, dear?

    Peer Gynt (below his breath). "Go round about"!

    Solveig. What do you say?

    Peer Gynt. Dear, you must wait. It's dark, and I've a heavy
load.

    Solveig. I'll come and help you bear the load.

    Peer Gynt. No, do not come! Stay where you are! I'll bear
the whole of it.

    Solveig. But, dear, don't be too long.

    Peer Gynt. Be patient, child; whether the time is long or
short, you must just wait.

    Solveig (nodding to him). Yes, I will wait. (*Peer Gynt*
goes off along the forest path. *Solveig* remains standing at the
half-open door.)

SCENE IV

(SCENE.—*Aase's* house. It is evening. A log fire is burning
on the hearth and lights up the room. A cat is lying on a chair
at the foot of a bed on which *Aase* is lying, fumbling restlessly
with the sheets.)

Aase. Ah me, is my son never coming? The nights are so weary and long. I've no one to take him a message, and so much to say to him now, my time's running short—oh, how quickly! To think that the end should be this! If only I'd known, I would never have said a hard word to the boy! (*Peer Gynt* comes in.)

Peer Gynt. Good evening!

Aase. My boy! Oh, God bless you! My dearest, at last you have come! But how have you dared to come hither? Your life is in danger, you know.

Peer Gynt. My life?—oh, my life doesn't matter. I had to come down to you now.

Aase. And Kari!—she said that you wouldn't! Ah, now I can leave you in peace.

Peer Gynt. Leave me? Why, what are you saying? And where do you think you can go?

Aase. Ah, Peer, it's the end that's approaching; I haven't much longer to live.

Peer Gynt (turning away abruptly and walking across the room). I was running away from my sorrows, and thought at least here I'd be free—! Are you cold? Are your hands and your feet cold?

Aase. Yes, Peer; you'll be done with me soon. When my eyes lose their light you must close them—but tenderly, carefully, Peer. And then you must get me a coffin, and see that it's handsome and fine. Ah, no, I forgot——

Peer Gynt. Do be quiet! Time enough for all that by-and-by.

Aase. Yes, yes. (Looks uneasily round the room.) Do you see what a little they've left me? It's all one to them.

Peer Gynt (with a grimace). There you go! (Harshly.) Yes, I know I am guilty. But what do you think is the good of raking it up to remind me?

Aase. No! It was the drink was to blame. That damnable drink that destroyed you, my boy; for you know you were drunk, and didn't know what you were doing. Besides—that

wild ride on the buck!—I'm sure it was not to be wondered
if you were not right in your head.

Peer Gynt. Never mind all that nonsense and rubbish;
never mind about anything now. Let's put off serious thinking
till later—another day. (Sits down on the edge of the bed.)
Now, mother, let's have a gossip, and talk of all sorts of
things, except what's ugly and horrid and hurts—let's forget
all that. Bless me! Why, there's old pussy! To think that he's
still alive!

Aase. At night he seems so uneasy; and we all know what
that means!

Peer Gynt (turning away). What is the news in the district?

Aase (smiling). They do say that hereabouts there's a
girl that longs for the mountains——

Peer Gynt (hastily). Mads Moen—is he content?

Aase. They say that she will not listen to the old folks'
prayers and tears. You ought to go and see her; maybe you
could find a way——

Peer Gynt. And what's become of the blacksmith?

Aase. Oh, bother the dirty smith! I'd so much rather tell
you her name—that girl's, you know——

Peer Gynt. No, we're going to have a gossip, and talk of
all sorts of things, except what's ugly and horrid and hurts
—let's forget all that. Shall I fetch you a drink? Are you
thirsty? Can you stretch in that little bed? Let me look—
why, this is surely the bed I had as a boy! Do you remember
your sitting beside my bed at night smoothing the bed-spread
over and singing me rhymes and songs?

Aase. Yes, and we played at sleighing, when your father
had gone away—the bed-spread was our apron, and the
floor an ice-bound fjord.

Peer Gynt. Yes, but do you remember the finest bit of it
all—our pair of prancing horses?

Aase. Why, yes—of course I do. 'Twas Kari's cat we bor-
rowed, and put up on a stool.

Peer Gynt. To Soria-Moria Castle, that's westward of the moon and eastward of the sunrise, o'er hill and dale we flew. A stick that we found in the cupboard made you a splendid whip.

Aase. I sat up like the driver——

Peer Gynt. Yes, and you shook the reins; and turned round as we galloped, to ask if I were cold. God bless you, you old scolder! You were a dear to me— Why do you groan?

Aase. It's my back, Peer; it's sore from lying here.

Peer Gynt. Stretch up and I'll support you. There—now you're lying snug.

Aase (uneasily). I want to get away, Peer.

Peer Gynt. To get away?

Aase. Ah, yes—it's what I'm always longing.

Peer Gynt. What senseless talk is that? See, let me smooth the bed-clothes and then sit on the bed,—now, we will make the time fly with singing rhymes and songs.

Aase. No, let me have my prayer-book; my mind is ill at ease.

Peer Gynt. In Soria-Moria Castle they're having a splendid feast. Rest back upon the cushions; I'll drive you quickly there——

Aase. But, dear, am I invited?

Peer Gynt. Of course—and I am, too. (He throws a cord round the back of the chair on which the cat is lying, takes a stick in his hand and sits down on the foot of the bed.) Gee up! Get on with you, Blackie! Mother, you're sure you're not cold? Aha! Now we shall be moving, when Granë kicks up his heels!

Aase. But, Peer—I hear something ringing——

Peer Gynt. It's the glittering sleigh-bells, dear.

Aase. They sound so strange and hollow!

Peer Gynt. We're driving over a fjord.

Aase. I'm frightened! What is it, that sighing and moaning so wild and drear?

Peer Gynt. It's only the firs on the hillside whispering. Just sit still.

Aase. I seem to see lights in the distance. What is it that's glistening there?

Peer Gynt. It's the windows and gates of the Castle. Can you hear the dancers?

Aase. Yes.

Peer Gynt. And outside stands Saint Peter asking you to come in.

Aase. Does he greet me?

Peer Gynt. Yes, with honour, and offers you sweetest wine.

Aase. Wine! Does he offer cakes, too?

Peer Gynt. A plateful of them, yes! And our parson's wife preparing your coffee and your dessert.

Aase. What! Shall I really meet her?

Peer Gynt. As soon and as oft as you please.

Aase. You're driving your poor old mother to a splendid party, Peer!

Peer Gynt (smacking his whip). Gee up! Get on with you, Blackie!

Aase. Are you sure that you know the way?

Peer Gynt (smacking his whip again). I can see the road.

Aase. But the journey makes me feel ill and tired.

Peer Gynt. I can see the Castle before me; the drive will soon be done.

Aase. I'll lie back with my eyes shut, and trust to you, my boy!

Peer Gynt. Now show your paces, Granë! The Castle is all agog; the folk all swarm to the gateway; Peer Gynt and his mother arrive! Why, what's that, Mister Saint Peter? You won't let my mother in? You must look far, I can tell you, to find a worthier soul. Of myself I will say nothing; I can turn back to the gate. I'll take pot-luck, if you'll have me; if not, it's all one to me. Like the Devil in the pulpit, I've told a heap of lies, and have called my dear old mother a silly old hen, I know, because she cackled and scolded; but

things must be different here. You must respect and revere
her, sincerely and honestly; you'll not get anyone better from
our parts nowadays.—Oho! Here's God the Father! Saint
Peter, you'll catch it now! (Speaks in a deep voice.) "Just
stop that bullying, will you! Mother Aase is welcome here!"
(Laughs aloud and turns to his mother.) I knew how 'twould
be! Saint Peter is singing small enough now! (His voice takes
on an anxious tone.) Why do you stare so, mother? Have you
lost your senses, dear? (Goes to the head of the bed.) You
mustn't lie and stare so—! Speak, mother; it's I, your boy!
(Feels her forehead and hands cautiously; then throws the
cord away on to the chair and says in a low voice): So it's
that!—You may rest now, Granë; our journey's over and
done. (Shuts her eyes and bends over her.) Thanks, dear,
for all you gave me, thrashings and kisses alike! And now
it's for you to thank me—(Presses his cheek against her lips.)
There—that was the driver's fee. (Kari comes in.)

    Kari. What? Peer! Then her deepest sorrow and grieving
will be forgot! Good Lord, how sound she is sleeping! Or
is she—?

    Peer Gynt. Hush, she is dead. (*Kari* weeps by *Aase's* body.
Peer Gynt walks to and fro in the room; at last he stops by
the bedside.)

    Peer Gynt. See that she's decently buried. I must try to
escape from here.

    Kari. Where shall you go?

    Peer Gynt. To the sea-coast.

    Kari. So far! Aye, and farther still. (Goes out.)

ACT IV

SCENE I

(SCENE.—A grove of palm-trees, on the south-west coast of Morocco. A dining-table is spread under an awning; rush matting underfoot. Farther back in the grove hammocks are hanging. A steam yacht, flying the Norwegian and American flags, is lying off the shore. A jolly-boat is drawn up on the beach. It is nearly sundown. *Peer Gynt,* now a good-looking middle-aged man, dressed in a neat travelling-suit; with a pair of gold-mounted eyeglasses dangling on his breast, is presiding at table as host to *Mr. Cotton, Monsieur Ballon, Herr von Eberkopf,* and *Herr Trumpeterstraale.* The party have just finished a meal. *Peer Gynt* is passing the wine.)

Peer Gynt. Drink, gentlemen! If man is meant for pleasure, let him take his pleasure. The past's the past—what's done is done—so we are taught. What may I give you?

Herr Trumpeterstraale. As host, dear brother Gynt, you're splendid!

Peer Gynt. The credit's just as much my purse's, my cook's and steward's——

Mr. Cotton. Very well, then here's a health to all the four!

Monsieur Ballon. Monsieur, your taste—your *ton*—is such as nowadays one seldom meets with amongst men living *en garçon*—a certain *je ne sais quoi*——

Herr von Eberkopf. Quite so; a breath, a gleam, of introspection—world-citizenship's inspiration; a glance that pierces clouds, that's free from any narrow prejudices; a glimpse of higher criticism; a simple nature coupled with a life's experience and thereby uplifted to the highest power. I think that's what you meant—eh, Monsieur?

403

Monsieur Ballon. Yes, very possibly. In French it doesn't sound quite so impressive.

Herr von Eberkopf. Of course not. French is somewhat cramped. But if we want to trace the source of this phenomenon——

Peer Gynt. That's easy; it's just because I've never married. Why, gentlemen, the thing's as clear as daylight. What's a man's first duty? The answer's brief: To be himself—to take good care of all that touches himself and what is his. But how can he do this if his existence is that of a pack-camel laden with someone else's weal and woe?

Herr von Eberkopf. But I dare say you've had to fight for this self-centred concentration?

Peer Gynt. Oh, yes, I've had to fight for it, but I have always won the honours; though once I very nearly fell into a trap, for all my cunning. I was a wild, good-looking spark, and let my roving fancy capture a girl who was of royal blood——

Monsieur Ballon. Of royal blood?

Peer Gynt (carelessly). Or very nearly. You know——

Herr Trumpeterstraale (thumping on the table). These damned aristocrats!

Peer Gynt (shrugging his shoulders). These bogus Highnesses, whose pride is to keep off from their escutcheon the slightest speck of what's plebeian.

Mr. Cotton. And so it came to nothing, then?

Monsieur Ballon. The family opposed the match?

Peer Gynt. Quite the reverse!

Monsieur Ballon. Ah!

Peer Gynt (discreetly). Well, you see, things took a turn which made them think that it was high time we were married. But, to be candid, the affair from first to last was most distasteful. In certain things I'm very dainty, and also like my independence; and when her father came and hinted that he would make it a condition that I should change my name and status and lose my own nobility—with lots of similar conditions I could not stomach or accept—I gracefully retired from it, refused the father's ultimatum, and gave my youthful bride her congé. (Drums on the table with his fingers, and says with a pious air) Ah, yes, there is a Hand that guides us, and we poor men can trust to that. It's very comforting to know it.

Monsieur Ballon. So the affair went by the board?

Peer Gynt. No, it took on another aspect. Outsiders meddled in the game and raised an unexpected pother. The youngsters of the family were much the worst. I had to battle with seven of them all at once. I never shall forget that time, though I emerged from it the victor. Some blood was spilt; but still that blood sealed my certificate of valour, and proved what I remarked just now—that there's a Hand that guides us wisely.

Herr von Eberkopf. You have an outlook upon life that proves you a philosopher. For, while an ordinary thinker sees every detail separately and never grasps the whole completely, your vision covers all together. You have a universal standard to measure life with. Your perceptions, like rays of sunlight, emanating from a great central contemplation, pierce every fallacy.—And yet you say you had no education?

Peer Gynt. I am, as I've already told you, a self-taught man in every way. I've never learnt methodically, but I have thought and speculated and read a bit on every subject. I was not young when I began; and so, of course, it wasn't easy to plough the field of knowledge up and do the thing at all completely. I've learnt my history in scraps; for more than that I've had no leisure. And since, when evil days assail, a man needs certain things to trust in, I fitfully absorbed religion; I found that it assimilated much easier if taken that way. No use to glut one's self with reading, but to select what may be useful——

Mr. Cotton. Ah, now, that's practical!

Peer Gynt. Dear friends, just think what my career has been. What was I when I first went westwards? Quite penniless and empty-handed. I had to work hard for my food—

No easy job, believe me, often; but life, my friends, is always sweet, and death, as we all know, is bitter. Well! Luck, you see, did not desert me, and good old Fate was always kindly. Things moved, and I was always careful, and so things went from good to better; and, ten years after that, they called me the Crœsus of the Charlestown traders; my name was known in every port and luck pursued me with my shipping——

Mr. Cotton. What was your trade?

Peer Gynt. I trafficked most in negro slaves for Carolina and idols that were sent to China.

Monsieur Ballon. Oh, fie, for shame!

Herr Trumpeterstraale. Friend Gynt, how could you?

Peer Gynt. You think my enterprise was passing beyond the bounds of what was lawful? I felt the same thing very keenly; I found it hateful in the end. But, once begun, you may believe me 'twas difficult enough to end it. In any case, so big a business affected others by the thousand; to break it off too suddenly would have, of course, been most disastrous. I never like to break things off; but all the same, I must admit I've always fully been alive to what you'd call the consequences; and, when I've overstepped the bounds, it's always made me feel uneasy. Besides, I wasn't growing younger. By that time I was nearly fifty, and by degrees my hair was greying; and, though my health was always perfect, thoughts such as this cropped up to plague me; "who knows how short the time may be before the Great Assize is summoned and sheep from goats are separated?" What could I do? To cease my trade with China was impossible. I found a way. I opened up a second traffic to those waters; and, though each spring I sent to China shiploads of idols, every autumn I sent out Missionaries furnished with everything that could be needful to work conversion—stockings, rum, Bibles and rice——

Mr. Cotton. All at a profit?

Peer Gynt. Oh, well, of course.—The plan worked well. For every idol sold out yonder there was a duly baptized coolie, so one thing neutralized the other. We kept the Missionaries busy, because they had to counteract the idols that we were exporting.

Mr. Cotton. But what about the negro traffic?

Peer Gynt. Why, there my morals triumphed also. I felt the trade was scarcely suited to one whose years were fast increasing; you never know when death may claim you. And then there were the thousand pitfalls dug by our philanthropic friends, besides the chance of being caught and daily risks from wind and weather. By taking thought I found a way. "You'll have to reef your sails, friend Peter, and see"—so I said to myself—"how you can best retrieve your error!" I bought land in a southern state, and held back my last load of niggers (which was of first-class quality) and settled them on the plantation. They throve apace, grew fat and sleek, and they, as well as I, were happy. Yes, without bragging I may say I treated them like any father— And the result was handsome profit. I built them schools, so as to set a standard of morality to be maintained, and saw to it that it was kept well up to mark. And then, to make the change complete, out of the business I retired, and sold, with livestock, as it stood, the whole plantation. When I left, to all alike, both young and old, a gratis gift of grog was issued, and every nigger got a skinful. The widows, as an extra gift, were given snuff. And so I hope— unless the Word is merely froth which says one's deeds are surely good if they are not as surely evil—that all my errors are forgot, and that perhaps in greater measure than in most people's case, my deeds will more than balance out my sins.

Herr von Eberkopf (clinking glasses with him). How edifying 'tis to hear a scheme of life worked out so deftly, freed from the fog of theories and undisturbed by outer clamour!

Peer Gynt (who during the foregoing conversation has been applying steadily to the bottle). We northern men are famous hands at planning a campaign! The secret of life's success is very simple—merely to keep one's ears shut tight to the insidious advances of a pernicious reptile.

Mr. Cotton. Aye, but what's the reptile, my dear friend?

Peer Gynt. A small one, always tempting men to take irrevocable steps. (Drinks again.) A man can venture without fear, and keep his courage, if he's careful not to get definitely caught in any of life's cunning pitfalls—if he looks forward, and beyond the present moment and its chances, and always carefully preserves a bridge behind him to retire on. That theory has held me up and always coloured all my conduct— a theory I inherited and learnt at home from early childhood.

Monsieur Ballon. You're a Norwegian, I believe?

Peer Gynt. By birth, yes; but by disposition I am a citizen of the world. For the good fortune I've enjoyed, I have to thank America; my well-stocked library I owe to Germany's advanced young thinkers; from France I get my taste in dress, my manners, and whatever turn I have for subtleness of mind; England has taught me industry and care for my own interests; the Jews have taught me how to wait; from Italy I've caught a dash of taste for *dolce far niente;* and once, when in a sorry fix, I reached the goal of my desire by trusting to good Swedish steel.

Herr Trumpeterstraale (lifting his glass). Ah, Swedish steel—!

Herr von Eberkopf. Yes, first and foremost we offer homage to the man who is a swordsman. (They clink glasses and drink with *Peer Gynt* who is beginning to get heated with wine.)

Mr. Cotton. All you've said is excellent; but now, sir, pray tell us what you propose to do with all your wealth.

Peer Gynt (smiling). Do with it, eh?

All (drawing nearer to him). Yes, let us hear!

Peer Gynt. Well, first of all, to travel; and that's why, you see, I took you all on board my yacht as company. I had a mind to have a choir to worship at my Altar of the Golden Calf——

Herr von Eberkopf. How witty!

Mr. Cotton. Yes, but no one sails for the mere pleasure of a journey. You have an object, without doubt; what is it?

Peer Gynt. To be Emperor.

All. What!

Peer Gynt (nodding his head). To be Emperor.

All. But where?

Peer Gynt. Of the whole world.

Monsieur Ballon. But how, my friend—?

Peer Gynt. Just simply by the power of gold! It's not a new idea at all; it has inspired my every effort. In boyish dreams I used to travel over the sea upon a cloud; I tried to soar to fancied grandeurs, and then dropped down on to all-fours; but to its goal my mind was constant. Somewhere— I can't remember where—it says that if a man shall win the whole wide world, but lose *himself*, all that he gains is only like a wreath upon an empty skull. That's what it says—or something like it—and, trust me, it is pretty true.

Herr von Eberkopf. But what, then, is the Gyntian Self?

Peer Gynt. The world which lies within my brain; which makes me *me*, and no one else—no more than God can be the Devil.

Herr Trumpeterstraale. Now I can see at what you're driving!

Monsieur Ballon. Sublime philosopher!

Herr von Eberkopf. Great poet!

Peer Gynt (with growing exaltation). The Gyntian Self! —An army, that, of wishes, appetites, desires! The Gyntian Self! It is a sea of fancies, claims and aspirations; in fact, it's all that swells within my breast, and makes it come about that I am I and live as such. But, just as our Good Lord has need of earthly mould to be earth's God, so I have need of lots of gold if I'm to be an Emperor.

Monsieur Ballon. But you are rich!

Peer Gynt. Not rich enough. Enough, perhaps, for me to pose for two or three days as a princeling in some such place as Lippe-Detmold; but I must be *myself*—complete—a Gynt fit for the universe—Sir Peter Gynt from head to heels!

Monsieur Ballon (in transports). To purchase all the loveliest things the world can offer!

Herr von Eberkopf. All the bins of century-old Johannisberger!

Herr Trumpeterstraale. The armoury of Charles the Twelfth!

Mr. Cotton. But, before all, to seize the chance of profitable business.

Peer Gynt. Well, I've found a way to get them all, and that is why we're anchored here! to-night our course will be to northward. The newspapers I've just received have brought me some important news. (*Rises and lifts his glass.*) It shows that fortune always favours those who have confidence to grasp it——

All. Well? Tell us—!

Peer Gynt. Greece is in an uproar.

All (springing to their feet). What, have the Greeks—?

Peer Gynt. They have revolted.

All. Hurrah!

Peer Gynt. And Turkey's in a hole.

Monsieur Ballon. To Greece! The way to glory's open! I'll help them with my sword of France!

Herr von Eberkopf. I with my voice—but at a distance!

Mr. Cotton. I'll get a contract to supply them!

Herr Trumpeterstraale. Let us away! I'll find at Bender Charles the Twelfth's famous spur-buckles!

Monsieur Ballon (falling on *Peer Gynt's* neck). Forgive me, friend, if for a moment I had misjudged you!

Herr von Eberkopf (grasping *Peer Gynt* by the hand). I'm a fool! I almost took you for a scoundrel!

Mr. Cotton. That's much too strong—say, rather, for a simpleton——

Herr Trumpeterstraale (embracing *Peer Gynt*). And I, dear friend, had put you down as an example of the worst type of Yankee rascal! Forgive me!

Herr von Eberkopf. We were all mistaken——

Peer Gynt. What do you mean?

Herr von Eberkopf. We now can glimpse the banners of the Gyntian army of wishes, appetites, desires—!

Monsieur Ballon (admiringly). That's what you meant by "being a Gynt"!

Herr von Eberkopf (in the same tone). A Gynt that's worthy of all honour!

Peer Gynt. But tell me—?

Monsieur Ballon. Don't you understand?

Peer Gynt. I'm hanged if I can take your meaning.

Monsieur Ballon. Why, aren't you going to help the Greeks with money and with ships?

Peer Gynt (whistling). No, thank you! I'm going to help the stronger side, and lend my money to the Turks.

Monsieur Ballon. Impossible!

Herr von Eberkopf. That's very funny!—But you, of course, must have your joke! (*Peer Gynt* is silent for a moment, then leans on a chair and assumes an air of importance.)

Peer Gynt. Gentlemen, we had better part before the last remains of friendship dissolve like wreaths of smoke. The man who hasn't anything may lightly take any chances; those whose all is no more than the scrap of earth they stand on, are the fittest far for sacrifice and cannon-fodder. But when a man's well off, as I am, he risks a greater stake than they. Pray go to Greece. I'll land you there, and furnish you with weapons gratis; the more you fan the flame of strife, the better it will be for me. Strike hard for Freedom and the Right! Attack the Turks and give them hell; and meet a glorious end upon a janissary's spear-point.—But, excuse me if I don't come with you. (Slaps his pockets.) I've money in my pockets, and I am Myself—Sir Peter Gynt. (Puts up his umbrella and goes into the grove where the hammocks are hanging.)

Herr Trumpeterstraale. The swine!

Monsieur Ballon. He has no sense of honour!

Mr. Cotton. Oh, honour—let that pass. But think what

splendid profits we could make if only Greece could free
herself——

Monsieur Ballon. I saw myself acclaimed a victor by crowds
of lovely Grecian women!

Herr Trumpeterstraale. I felt those famous buckles safe
within my Swedish grasp!

Herr von Eberkopf. I saw my glorious fatherland's *Kultur*
spread widely over land and sea——

Mr. Cotton. The actual loss is worst of all. Goddam!—I
feel inclined to cry! I saw myself proprietor of Mount Olym-
pus, which contains (unless what men have said is false) rich
veins of copper to be worked; and the renowned Castalian
stream—its many waterfalls would yield a thousand horse-
power, easily!

Herr Trumpeterstraale. I shall go, all the same! My sword
is worth more, still, than Yankee gold.

Mr. Cotton. Perhaps; but, fighting in the ranks, we should
be merely swamped by numbers. What profit should we get
from that?

Monsieur Ballon. Curse it! So near the heights of fortune—and then to be dashed down again.

Mr. Cotton (shaking his fist at the yacht). To think that
all this nabob's gold, that he has sweated from his niggers,
is in that ship!

Herr von Eberkopf. An inspiration! Come on, and let us
act! His empire shall come to nothing now! Hurrah!

Monsieur Ballon. What will you do?

Herr von Ekerkopf. I'll seize his power! The crew will
easily be bought. On board! I'll commandeer his yacht!

Mr. Cotton. You'll—what?

Herr von Eberkopf. I mean to bag the lot. (Goes towards
the jolly-boat.)

Mr. Cotton. It's clearly to my interest to share with you.
(Follows him.)

Herr Trumpeterstraale. There goes a scamp!

Monsieur Ballon. A proper scoundrel! But—*enfin!* (Follows the others.)

Herr Trumpeterstraale. Well, I suppose I may as well go with them—under protest, though! (Follows.)

SCENE II

(SCENE.—Another part of the coast. Moonlight and passing clouds. Out at sea the yacht is seen steaming at full speed. *Peer Gynt* is running along the shore, now pinching himself in the arm, now staring out to sea.)

Peer Gynt. It's nightmare!—Illusion!—I soon shall wake up! It's heading to sea! And at top of its speed! It's a dream, and I'm sleeping! I'm drunk or I'm mad! (Wrings his hands.) It's impossible that I should perish like this! (Tears his hair.) It's a dream! It *must* be—it *shall* be—a dream! It's terrible! Ah, but alas it is true! My scoundrelly friends—! Oh, hear me, Good Lord! You are Wisdom and Justice—oh, punish them, Lord! (Stretches up his arms.) It is I—Peer Gynt! Do look after me, Lord! Take care of me, Father, or else I shall die! Make them slacken the engines—or cast off the gig! Stop the robbers! Make something go wrong with the works! Do listen! Leave other folk's matters alone! The world will look after itself while You do.—He's not listening. He is as deaf as a post! It's too much! A God that can't think what to do! (Beckons up to the sky.) I say! I've disposed of my negro plantation, and sent heaps of Missionaries out to Asia. Don't You think that one good turn's deserving another? Oh, help me to get on the ship—! (A sudden glare rises into the sky from the yacht, followed by a thick cloud of smoke. A dull explosion is heard. *Peer Gynt* utters a shriek and sinks down on the sand. The smoke gradually disperses and the yacht is seen to have disappeared. *Peer Gynt* looks up, with a pale face, and says in a low voice) 'Twas a judgment! Sunk with all hanks in a moment of time! All thanks to the chances of fortune. (Emo-

tionally.) No, no! There was more than the chance of fortune
in this, that I should be saved while the rest of them perish.
Thanks be to Thee who hast been my protector and kept an
eye on me in spite of my failings! (Takes a deep breath.)
What a wonderful feeling of safety and comfort it gives you
to know that you're specially guarded! But where shall I find
meat and drink in the desert? I don't know, I'm sure. But He
will understand. It *can't* be so dangerous.— (In a loud and in-
sinuating voice.) He will not suffer such a poor little sparrow
as I am to perish! I must humble myself—and allow Him
some time. The Lord will provide; I must not be downhearted.— (Springs to his feet with a cry of terror.) Did I
hear a lion? That growl in the rushes—? (His teeth chatter.)
No, it was no lion. (Pulls himself together.) I'm certain it
was! Those creatures, of course, know to keep at a distance;
they dare not take bites at a lord of creation. They have instinct, of course; it's by instinct they feel that an elephant's
not a safe thing to attack.—All the same, I will see if I can't
find a tree. Ah, there I see palms and acacias waving; if I climb
one of them, I'll get safety and shelter—especially if I can
only remember some psalms to repeat.— (Climbs up a tree.)
"Lo, morning and evening are different things"—that's a
verse that is often discussed and examined. (Settles himself in
the tree.) How pleasant it is to feel that one's soul is so nobly
uplifted! Thoughts that ennoble are worth more than riches.
I'll trust myself to Him. He knows just how far I am able
to drink of the cup of affliction. He takes a most fatherly interest in me— (Looks out over the sea, and whispers with a
sigh): but He's not what you'd call economical over it!

SCENE III

(SCENE.—A Moroccan camp on the edge of the desert, at
night. *Warriors* are resting by a watch-fire.)

A Slave (running in and tearing his hair). Gone is the Emperor's white charger!

Another Slave. The Emperor's sacred garb is stolen!

A Chief of the Warriors (coming in). A hundred strokes of the bastinado to all of you, if the thieves escape! (The *Warriors* spring on to their steeds and gallop off in all directions.)

SCENE IV

(SCENE.—A clump of palm-trees and acacias. It is dawn. *Peer Gynt,* in a tree, is trying to defend himself with a broken-off branch against a swarm of Apes.)

I've spent an extremely uncomfortable night. (Hits about him.) Is that them again? The infernal creatures! They're throwing down fruit. No, it's something else. Apes are the most disgusting beasts! It is written that one must watch and fight; but I can't do it—I'm wearied out. (Is disturbed again. Speaks impatiently.) I must make an end of all this discomfort—try and get hold of one of these creatures, hang him and flay him and dress myself up from head to foot in his shaggy hide; then the others will think I am one of them.— We men are but nothing, after all, and must bow to the force of circumstances.—Another lot! Why, they swarm like flies! Away with you! Shoo! They act like madmen. If only I could get a false tail—or something to make me look like a beast— what's that up there above my head? (Looks up.) An old one —his paws chock-full of filth! (Crouches down nervously and keeps still for a little. The *Ape* makes a movement; *Peer Gynt* tries to coax him, as one would a dog.) Hullo, old man! Is that you up there? He's a good chap, if you speak to him kindly. *He* won't throw things down—will he? No! It's I! Good dog! We're the best of friends. Wuff, wuff! Do you hear, I can speak your language: old man and I are as good as cousins! Would he like a nice bit of sugar—? The dirty beast! He's thrown the lot all over me! Disgusting brute!—Or was

it food, perhaps? Its taste was unfamiliar, certainly. But
taste is mostly a thing of habit. What is it that some philosopher has said: You must just spit, and trust to force of
habit.—Here's the crowd of youngsters now! (Hits about
him.) This is too much! That man, who's his Creator's image,
should have to suffer.—Murder! Help! The old one's foul, but
the youngsters fouler!

SCENE V

(SCENE.—A rocky spot overlooking the desert. It is early
morning. On one side, a ravine with the entrance to a cave. A
Thief and a *Receiver of Stolen Goods* are standing in the
ravine, with the Emperor's charger and robe. The charger,
richly caparisoned, is tied to a rock. *Horsemen* are seen in the
distance.)

Thief. Spear-points, gleaming in the sunshine! See! see!

Receiver. I hear them galloping over the sand! Woe! Woe!

Thief (folding his arms on his breast). My father thieved;
his son must steal.

Receiver. My father received; and so must I.

Thief. We must bear our lot, and be ourselves.

Receiver (listening). Footsteps in the thicket! Away! But
where?

Thief. The cave is deep and the Prophet great! (They fly,
leaving the stolen goods behind them. The *Horsemen* disappear in the distance. *Peer Gynt* comes in, whittling a reed.)

Peer Gynt. Really a most enchanting morning! The beetles
are busy at work in the sand; out of their shells the snails are
peeping. Morning! Ah, morning's worth more than gold! It's
strange what a very remarkable power there is in daylight. In
its beams you feel so safe—your courage waxes—you're ready
to fight wild bulls, if need be. What silence around me! These
rural joys—it's strange that I never appreciated these things
so much till now. To think that men live cooped up in great
cities, just to be pestered and plagued by people. Look at

those lizards, bustling about enjoying the air and thinking of nothing. What innocence in the life of beasts! They perform the behest of their great Creator, their character stamped indelibly on them; they are *themselves,* whether playing or fighting—themselves, as they were when He first said "Be." (Puts on his eye-glasses.) A toad—looking out of a piece of sandstone, only his head peeping out of his chamber. He sits, as if looking out of a window at the world; to himself he is— enough. (Thoughtfully.) Enough? Where have I read that before? Most probably in the Great Book I read as a boy. Or perhaps it was in the Prayer-book? Or else set down in Solomon's Proverbs? Dear me—I notice, as years go on, I cannot remember times and places as once I used. (Sits down in the shade.) Here's a spot that's cool; I'll sit and rest my bones awhile. Ah, here are ferns—one can eat the roots. (Tastes one.) It's really food for beasts; but then the Book says we must subdue our nature, and, further, that pride must be abased. "Who humbleth himself, shall be exalted." (Uneasily.) Exalted? Of course that will happen to me—the contrary's quite unthinkable. Fate surely will help me away from here and set my feet on the road to fortune. This is but a test; if the Lord will grant me strength to endure, I'll be rescued later. (Shakes off such thoughts, lights a cigar, stretches himself out and gazes over the desert.) What an enormous, boundless waste!—Far off, there, I can see an ostrich.—It is hard to perceive the Almighty's purpose in all this dead and empty desert, where there is nothing that is life-giving; a burnt-up waste that profits no one, this bit of the world that's for ever sterile; a corpse that never, since it was shaped, has brought its Creator anything—not even thanks. Why was it made? Nature is ever extravagant.—Is that the sea that glitters yonder, away in the east? No—only mirage. The sea's to the west, where, like a dam, sandhills protect the desert from it. (An idea strikes him.) A dam! Then I might—! The hills are low. A dam! Then a cutting—a canal—and through the gap the rushing waters would fill the desert with a life-flood, and all this empty burnt-up grave become a fresh and rippling ocean! Islands would show in it where now there are oases; to the north, Atlas would fringe the shore with verdure; and to the south, like heedless birds, white sails would skim along, where now the caravans plod painfully; a lively breeze would dissipate this stuffy air, and from the clouds a gentle dew would fall. In time town after town would be established, and grass grow round the swaying palm-trees. The country beyond the Sahara's edge, away in the south, would become a land of busy trade and seamen's ventures. Steam should drive works in Tombuktu, new colonies arise in Bornu, and the explorer should be carried safe in his waggon through the land of Habes to the Upper Nile. Then in the middle of my sea, on the most fertile, rich oasis, I'll settle Norsemen—for the blood of dalesmen is the nearest thing to that of royalty; a cross with Arab blood will do the rest. And on a cape with sloping shore I'll build Peeropolis, the capital! The old world's out of date; and now it is the turn of Gyntiana, my new-born land! (Springs up.) I only need some capital, and the thing is done—a golden key, and the ocean's gate is open! A crusade 'gainst death! That grisly miser shall disgorge the hidden treasure that he's hoarding. There is a world-wide wish for freedom. Like Noah's donkey in the Ark, I'll bray my message to the world; Liberty's baptism I will pour over these prisoned shores, till they grow lovely in their freedom!—Forward! In east or west I'll have to seek the money for the work! My kingdom—or half my kingdom—for a horse! (The horse in the ravine neighs.) A horse! And robes! And ornaments! And weapons! (Goes nearer.) It's impossible—and yet it's true!—I know I've read somewhere that faith can move a mountain, but never thought that it could bring a horse! I must be dreaming— No, it is a fact—there stands the horse! *Ab esse ad posse,* etcetera.— (Puts on the robe and looks himself over.) Sir Peter—and Turk from head to foot! Well, truly one can never tell what's going to happen to one! Come

up, Granë, my steed! (Climbs into the saddle.) Gold stirrups,
too! Great folk are known by the steeds they ride! (Gallops
away across the desert.)

SCENE VI

(SCENE.—The tent of an Arab Chieftain, on an oasis. *Peer
Gynt,* in his oriental robes, is taking his ease on a divan,
drinking coffee and smoking a long pipe. *Anitra* and a troupe of
Girls are dancing and singing to him.)

Chorus of Girls. The Prophet is come! The Prophet, the
Lord, the All-Wise One, to us, to us he has come, riding over
the sea of sand! The Prophet, the Lord, the Infallible, to us,
to us he has come, sailing over the sea of sand! Blow flute!
Sound drum! The Prophet, the Prophet is come!

Anitra. His charger is white as milk in the streams of Paradise! Bend the knee! Bow low! His eyes are stars that flash
and yet are full of love. No earth-born eyes can meet the
flashing of those stars! Across the desert he came, decked with
gold and pearls. Where he rode it was light; behind him all
was dark, drought and the dread simoom. The Mighty One
has come! Over the desert he came, clothed in mortal shape.
Kaaba is empty now! Himself has told us so.

Chorus of Girls. Blow flute! Sound drum! The Prophet, the
Prophet is come! (The girls dance to soft music.)

Peer Gynt. I have read in a book, and the saying's true,
that no man's a prophet in his own country.—This life's a
deal more to my liking than that which I led as a Charlestown
trader. There was something false about it all, something
foreign to me, and shady; I never could feel myself at home,
or feel I had chosen the right profession, *Qu'allais-je faire
dans cette galère,* grubbing about with business matters? I
can't understand it, the more I try—it simply happened, and
that is all. To climb up the world on money-bags is just like
building a house on sand. If you wear rings and a watch and
so forth, people will curtsey and bow to you, take off their

hats if you wear a breast-pin; but the rings and the pin are
not yourself. Now a Prophet—he has a definite status; you
know exactly where you're standing, if a man salutes you, it's
for *yourself*, and not because of your pounds and shillings.
You are what you are without pretence. Owing nothing to
chance or accident, independent of patents or concessions.
A Prophet—yes, that's the life for me. And it happened so
unexpectedly—simply from riding across the desert and
coming upon these children of nature. The Prophet had come;
it was clear to them. But indeed it was not my design to deceive them—an official reply from a Prophet is one thing,
and a lie quite another; in any case, too, I can always retire
from my present position. I'm in no way bound; so it's not
so bad. It's all, so to speak, like a private arrangement. I can
go as I came; my steed's standing ready; in short, I am
master of the situation.

Anitra (at the door of the tent). Prophet and Master!

Peer Gynt. What is it, my slave?

Anitra. At the door of the tent stand sons of the desert,
craving to look on the face of the Prophet——

Peer Gynt. Stop! You can tell them they must keep their
distance; I will receive their petitions at a distance. Tell them
no man may set his foot within here! Menfolk, my child, are
but a set of scoundrels—they are, in fact, a filthy lot of rascals.
You, my Anitra, cannot well imagine with what barefaced
impertinence they cheat one—h'm!—I should say, how griev-
ously they sin. Now, no more of that! Come, dance for me, my
children! I would forget these thoughts that make me angry.

The Girls (as they dance). The Prophet is good! His heart
is distressed for the sins that the sons of earth have committed.
The Prophet is kind! All praise to his kindness which leads
such poor sinners to Paradise!

Peer Gynt (whose eyes have followed *Anitra* through the
dance). Her legs flit about like nimble drumsticks! She's
really a tasty morsel, the baggage! It's true her figure's pronounced in some ways—not quite in accord with the stand-

ards of beauty; but what is beauty? A mere convention, a
currency coined for a special purpose. And it's just these
extravagances that tickle a palate that's sated with what is
normal. In marriage there's always something wanting; she's
either too fat or else too scraggy, annoyingly young or alarm-
ingly ancient; and if she's between the two, she's insipid.—
Her feet, it is true, might well be cleaner, also her arms
—especially that one. But, after all, that's nothing to matter;
one might rather call it a qualification.—Anitra, come here!

Anitra. Thy slave, my Master!

Peer Gynt. You attract me, child! The Prophet is moved.
If you don't believe me, I'll prove it to you—I'll make you
a Houri in Paradise!

Anitra. Impossible, Master!

Peer Gynt. You don't believe me? As I am alive, I'm in real
earnest!

Anitra. But I've no soul!

Peer Gynt. Then you shall have one!

Anitra. How shall I, Master?

Peer Gynt. That's my affair. I shall look after your education. No soul? It's true you are pretty stupid; I've noticed
that fact with some regret; but there's room enough in you
for a soul. Come here! Let me measure your head. Oh, yes,
there's plenty of room, as I knew there was. True enough,
you'll never be anything much; a great soul will be quite
beyond you. But, pshaw! it really doesn't matter; you'll have
enough to prevent your feeling ashamed of it——

Anitra. My Lord is kind——

Peer Gynt. You're hesitating? What is the matter?

Anitra. I'd rather have——

Peer Gynt. Speak out, at once!

Anitra. I don't care so much about having a soul; I'd rather
have——

Peer Gynt. What?

Anitra (pointing to his turban). That lovely opal!

Peer Gynt (in raptures, as he hands her the jewel). Anitra,

you're one of Eve's true daughters! Your charm attracts me—
for I am a man; and, as a noted writer puts it: *"Das ewig
weibliche ziehet uns an."*

SCENE VII

(SCENE.—A grove of palm-trees outside *Anitra's* tent. The
moon is shining. *Peer Gynt,* with an Arabian lute in his hands,
is sitting under a tree. His beard and hair have been trimmed,
which makes him look considerably younger.)

Peer Gynt (plays and sings)

> I locked the gate of Paradise
> And took away the key.
> > My bark afar the north wind bore,
> > While lovely women on the shore
> Were weeping there for me.
>
> Southward I sailed the salty depths
> Before the die was cast;
> > Where palms were waving proud
> > > and free
> > Around an inlet of the sea,
> I burned my ship at last.
>
> A desert-ship I mounted then—
> A four-legged ship, I trow—
> > To bear me o'er the desert dark.
> > I am a bird of passage! Hark!
> I'm twittering on a bough!
>
> Anitra, thou art like the wine
> Of palm-trees, sparkling clear!
> > Angora-goats'-milk cheese is good,
> > But it's not half so sweet a food
> As thou, Anitra dear!

(Slings the lute over his shoulder and approaches the tent.) All is silent! Now I wonder if she heard my little song? Is she there behind the curtain, peeping out with nothing on? What's that sound? It's like a bottle someone is uncorking!— There! There again I heard it—Is it sighs of love?—a lover's song?—No, it's clearly someone snoring. Lovely sound! Anitra sleeps! Nightingales, desist from singing! You shall suffer if you dare with your silly cluck and gurgle.—Oh, well, after all—sing on! Every nightingale's a songster, just as I am one myself; with their notes, like me, they capture tender, delicate young hearts. Night's cool hours are meant for singing; singing is our common sphere; singing is the art of being *us*—Peer Gynt and nightingale. And to hear Anitra sleeping is the topmost bliss of love; it's like lifting up a goblet to the lips, but drinking naught.—Oh, but here she comes! Well, really, after all that is the best.

Anitra (at her tent door). Did I hear my Master calling?

Peer Gynt. Yes, my dear, the Prophet called. I was wakened by a hubbub; cats were fighting all around——

Anitra. Ah, they were not fighting, Master. It was something worse than that.

Peer Gynt. What was it?

Anitra. Oh, spare me!

Peer Gynt. Tell me!

Anitra. I am blushing!

Peer Gynt (going close to her). Do you mean the emotion I was feeling when you had my opal, dear?

Anitra (horrified). Don't compare yourself, great Master, to an old disgusting cat!

Peer Gynt. Child—considered just as lovers, there's perhaps not much to choose 'twixt a tom-cat and a Prophet.

Anitra. Honeyed jests, great Master, fall from your lips.

Peer Gynt. My little friend, you, like other girls, pass judgment solely by a great man's looks, I am really very playful—especially when *tête-à-tête*. My position makes it needful for me to put on a mask of most serious behaviour; I'm

constrained by daily duties, and the nature of the business
relative to my great office, to assume a weighty manner, and
at times may seem to others too prophetically abrupt; but
'tis all upon the surface.—Away with all that bosh! In private
I am Peer—that's who I am. Come, now, I will drop the
Prophet; you shall know my very self! (Sits down under a
tree and draws *Anitra* closer to him.) Come, Anitra, let us
dally underneath this waving palm! You shall smile and I
shall whisper nothings in your ear; and then we'll reverse the
parts we're playing, your sweet lips shall whisper love in my
ear while I sit smiling!

Anitra (lying at his feet). All you say is sweet as music,
though I don't quite understand. Tell me, Master, can your
daughter get a soul by listening?

Peer Gynt. Presently you shall be dowered with the light
of life—a soul; when upon the rosy portals of the dawn we
see in gold "I am daybreak" clearly written,—then it will be
time enough to begin your education. But for me to play
schoolmaster, and to waste this lovely night trying to collect
together weatherbeaten bits of lore, would be stupid altogether, even if I wanted to. And, besides, considered rightly,
souls are not the chiefest things in our lives; it's hearts that
matter.

Anitra. Speak on, Master! When you speak, it's like opals
flashing fire.

Peer Gynt. Too much cleverness is folly; and the fruit of
cowardice pushed too far, is cruelty. Truth, if it's exaggerated,
is no more than wisdom's self turned hind-foremost.—Yes, my
child, you may take my word for it, there are people in the
world gorged with soul but dull of vision. I once knew a chap
like that; he seemed brighter than his fellows; yet he let
resounding phrases which he did not understand quite mislead him from his business.—Look around this fair oasis, at
the desert; if my turban I took off and fluttered gently once
or twice, the mighty ocean at my bidding would invade it,
filling up its every corner. But I'd be a silly cuckoo if I set

about creating seas and continents. Do you know, my child, what life is?

Anitra. No, instruct me.

Peer Gynt. Life means passing safe and dry-shod down the rushing stream of time. Manly strength is what is needed to be what I am, my dear. Age makes eagles lose their feathers, makes old fogies' footsteps fail, sets an old crone's teeth decaying, gives an old man withered hands,—and they all get withered souls. Give me youth! I mean as Sultan, ardent and vigorous, to rule—not the realms of Gyntiana with their palm-trees and their vines—but the realm of fresh young beauty that lies in a maiden's thoughts. So you see, my child, the reason why I graciously was pleased to bestow my love upon you; why I chose your little heart, so to speak, to be the empire that shall be my caliphate. None but I shall know your longings; in the empire of my love I must reign supreme, unquestioned! For you must be mine alone. I shall be your gentle gaoler, binding you with gold and gems. If we part, life will be empty—or, at any rate, for you! Not a fibre of your being, not an instinct of your will, but shall know me as their master—you shall be so filled with me. And your raven locks—your beauty—all in you that can allure—these shall be a pleasant garden for your Sultan's foot to tread. And that's why it's really lucky you've an empty little head. Souls are apt to make their owners too absorbed about themselves. And—while we're upon the topic—if you like, I'll seal the pact by bestowing on your ankle this fine bangle. That, I think, fairly meets the situation. Me—instead of soul—you'll have; otherwise, the *status quo.* (*Anitra* snores.) What? Is she sleeping? Have my words fallen on unheeding ears? No; it shows the power lying in my words—that, like a stream, they transport her gently with them to the land of dreams. (Gets up and puts some jewels in her lap.) Anitra! Here are jewels! Here are more! Sleep, Anitra! Dream of Peer! Sleep, for in your sleep you've set a crown upon your Emperor's head! Peer Gynt has won a victory of personality to-night.

SCENE VIII

(SCENE.—A caravan route. The oasis is visible in the remote background. *Peer Gynt,* on his white horse, is galloping over the desert, holding *Anitra* before him on the pommel of his saddle.)

Anitra. Let go! I'll bite you!

Peer Gynt. You little rogue!

Anitra. What do you want to do?

Peer Gynt. To play at dove and falcon! To carry you off, and do all sorts of reckless things!

Anitra. For shame! An old Prophet, too!

Peer Gynt. Oh, bosh! The Prophet is not old, you goose! Do you think this looks as if he were old?

Anitra. Let me go! I want to go home!

Peer Gynt. You flirt! Home! To father-in-law! That's good! We birds that have flown out of our cage dare not be seen by him again. Besides, my child, no one should stay too long in the same place; he's apt to lose as much in estimation as he can gain by making friends; and this is especially the case when he's a Prophet, or the like. His should be flying visits—seen as snatches of a song are heard. It was time that my visit should come to an end; these sons of the desert are shifty creatures,—incense and gifts have both been lacking for some days.

Anitra. Yes, but *are* you a Prophet?

Peer Gynt. I am your Emperor! (Tries to kiss her, but she draws back. (Oh, come! Don't be a proud little birdie, now!

Anitra. Give me the ring that's on your finger.

Peer Gynt. Take the lot if you wish, dear!

Anitra. Your words are like life-giving music!

Peer Gynt. What happiness 'tis to be loved like this! Let me dismount! I will lead the horse and be your slave! (Hands her the whip and dismounts.) See now, my pretty, my beautiful rose—here am I now, and here I'll tread the sands until

I get a sunstroke and have to stop. I am young, Anitra! Remember that! You mustn't look at my deeds too closely; jokes and fun are what youth is known by! And, if you were not quite so stupid, my graceful flower, you'd understand that, since your lover is full of fun, *ergo* he's young!

Anitra. Yes, you are young. Have you any more rings?

Peer Gynt. Of course I'm young! Look, I am bounding like a deer! If there was any green-stuff handy, I'd make myself a wreath! Aha! Of course I'm young! Just see me dance! (Dances and sings.)

> I am a happy little cock!
> Peck me, my little pullet!
> Houp-là! Just see me foot it!
> I am a happy little cock!

Anitra. You're sweating, my Prophet; I'm afraid you will melt. Let me carry that bag that weighs down on your belt.

Peer Gynt. What tender concern! You shall carry the purse; hearts that are loving have no need of gold! (Dances and sings again.)

> He is a madcap, your little Peer!
> He doesn't know what he is doing!
> And doesn't care—if he keeps going!
> He is a madcap, your little Peer!

Anitra. How joyful 'tis to see the Prophet dancing!

Peer Gynt. Oh, drop that "Prophet" nonsense! Let's put on each other's clothes! Come on! You take yours off!

Anitra. Your caftan is too long, your belt too roomy, your stockings much too small.

Peer Gynt. Eh bien! Instead, inflict some pain upon me; for 'tis sweet for loving hearts to suffer for their love! And, when we come to where my castle stands——

Anitra. Your Paradise? Have we got far to ride?

Peer Gynt. A thousand miles or so!

Anitra. Oh, what a way!

Peer Gynt. Then you shall have the soul I promised you——

Anitra. No, thanks; I think I'll do without the soul. But you were asking for some pain——

Peer Gynt. Ah, yes! Something severe but brief—a passing pang—!

Anitra. Anitra must obey the Prophet! So—farewell! (Hits him smartly over the fingers with the whip, and gallops back over the desert at full speed.)

Peer Gynt (after standing for a long time as if thunder-struck). Well, I am—!

SCENE IX

(SCENE.—The same as the preceding, an hour later. *Peer Gynt* is taking off his Turkish dress bit by bit, deliberately and thoughtfully. When he has finished, he takes a travelling-cap out of his coat pocket, puts it on, and stands once more in European dress. He flings the turban far away from him.)

Peer Gynt. There lies the Turk, and here stand I! A pagan existence is no good at all. It's lucky that I can throw it away with the clothes, and that it's not bred in the bone. *Qu'allais-je faire dans cette galère?* It's certainly best to live as a Christian, avoid the temptation of sumptuous garments, fashion your life by what's lawful and moral; in fact, be yourself—and deserve at the last a funeral oration and wreaths on your coffin. (Takes a few steps.) The baggage!—Only a little more, and I believe she'd have turned my head. But I'll be hanged if I understand what it was in her that so upset me. I am well out of it! If the joke had been pursued a little farther, it would have made me ridiculous.—I have erred, no doubt; but it's comforting to feel that my erring was the result of the position I had assumed; it was not I, myself, that erred. It was, as a fact, the prophetic life—devoid of any

savouring salt of active work—that caused in me these lapses
into want of taste. It's a sorry business being a Prophet! In
the course of your duties you're apt to get heedless. You're
sober and dignified; all of a sudden you find you're nothing
of the sort. I certainly gave proof of it by paying homage to
that goose, still, all the same— (Bursts out laughing.) Just
think of it! Spending the time in wanton dancing! Trying
to stem the stream of life by fooling like that!—sweet music,
caresses, sighs—and in the end be plucked like any silly hen!
Prophetically wild behaviour!—Plucked!—To my shame,
I've been plucked badly! Still, I've a little left in hand,—
some in America, and some safe in my pocket; so I'm not
quite on the rocks. And, after all, a moderate amount of
wealth is best. I am no longer tied by horses, coachmen and
the like; I've neither carriages nor luggage to give me trouble.
In a word, I'm master of the situation.—Which way shall I
choose? Many are open. It's in such choice that wisdom
counts. My business life is a finished chapter; my love affairs,
discarded garments; and I have no mind to retrace my steps.
"Forward or back it's just as far; out or in, it's just as narrow"
—as I think it says in some clever book. I must find some
new, some ennobling task; an object that's worth my pains
and money. Suppose I wrote, without concealment, the story
of my life—a book to serve as a guide and an example to
others after me? Or, wait—! I've lots of time at my com-
mand—suppose I become a travelling scholar, making a study
of bygone ages? That, I believe, is the thing for me! I'd
always a fancy for history, and lately I've improved my
knowledge. I'll trace the story of mankind! Float like a
feather upon the stream of history; and live again, as in a
dream, the days of old; see the fierce fights the heroes waged
—but from a vantage-point that's safe, that of an onlooker;
see how thinkers were slaughtered, martyrs bled; how kingdoms rose and kingdoms fell; watch epochs of world-history
grow from their birth; and, in a word, skim all the cream of
history.—I must try and get hold of a book of Becker's, and

go chronologically about it. It's true that my previous knowledge is sketchy, and history's rather an intricate matter,— but what is the odds! It frequently happens that very unusual methods of starting lead to the most original outcome.—To see one's goal and drive towards it, steeling one's heart, is most uplifting! (With restrained emotion.) Breaking through every bond that hinders, sundering ties of home and friendship, bidding adieu to love's soft promptings, to solve the mystery of truth! (Wipes a tear from his eye.) *That* is the test of a real enquirer! It makes me happy beyond measure to feel I have solved the great enigma of my destiny. I've only, now, to hold my course through thick and thin! I think I may be well forgiven if I feel proud, and call Peer Gynt a Man, and Manhood's Emperor! The Past shall be a lock to which I have the key; I will desert the sordid paths of modern life. The Present is not worth a shoe-lace. The ways of men are empty, faithless; their minds are dull, their deeds are futile—(Shrugs his shoulders.) And women—well their name is frailty! (Moves on.)

SCENE X

(SCENE.—Outside a hut in a forest in the far north of Norway. It is a summer's day. The door, which stands open, is furnished with a massive wooden bolt; above the door a pair of reindeer horns is fixed. A herd of goats are feeding by the wall. *Solveig,* now a fair and handsome middle-aged woman, is sitting spinning in the sunshine.)

Solveig (looks down the path and sings).
      It may not be till winter's past,
      And spring and summer—the whole long year;
      But I know that you will come at last,
      And I shall wait, for I promised you, dear.
(Calls to her goats, then resumes her spinning and singing.)

God guard you, dear, where'er you be!
If in Heaven, God have you in His care!
I shall wait till you come back to me;
If you're waiting above, I shall meet you there!

SCENE XI

(SCENE.—In Egypt, at the foot of the statue of Memnon, at dawn. *Peer Gynt* comes walking along, stops, and looks around him.)

Peer Gynt. I think that this place will do for a start.— Now, for a change, I'm an Egyptian; but Egyptian always upon the basis of the Gyntian Self. I'll wander later into Assyria. I'll stop short of going back to the Creation, for that would only lead to danger. I'll skirt the edges of Bible history. No doubt I'll discover certain traces that will confirm it; but to go minutely into it is not according to my plan of action. (Sits down on a stone.) I'll rest awhile and wait with patience until I've heard the Statue singing its customary morning song; and, after I have had my breakfast, I'll climb the Pyramid, and then, if I have time I'll look inside it. Then to the Red Sea, where perhaps I shall discover King Potiphar's grave. Then I will be an Asiatic; in Babylon I'll seek the famous Hanging Gardens and Concubines—the fairest products, that's to say, of civilization. Then a leap, and I'll be at the walls of Troy; and then the sea-route is direct to beautiful old Athens. There, I shall examine, stone by stone, the pass Leonidas defended; I'll make myself familiar with all the best philosophies; find out the gaol where Socrates laid down his life as sacrifice—but, stop a minute, I forgot—! Greece is at war, so for the present I must put Hellenism aside. (Looks at his watch.) What a ridiculous time the sun takes in rising! My time's precious. Well, then,—from Troy—that's where I'd got to—(Gets up and listens.) I wonder what that curious murmur—? (The sun rises.)

The Memnon Statue (singing).

From the demi-god's ashes arise new-born
Singing birds.
Zeus, the all-knowing,
Shaped them for conflict.
Owl of Wisdom,
Where sleep my birds?
You must die if you read not
The Riddle of the Song!

Peer Gynt. I really do believe I heard sounds from the Statue! That would be the music of the past. I heard the rise and fall of the Statue's voice. I'll note that down for consideration at experts' hands. (Makes a note in his pocket-book.) "The Statue sang. I heard the sounds quite plainly, but could not completely understand the words. I have, of course, no doubt the whole thing was hallucination. Otherwise, I have not observed anything of importance so far." (He moves on.)

SCENE XII

(Scene.—Near the village of Gizeh, by the great Sphinx carved out of the rocks. In the distance are seen the spires and minarets of Cairo. *Peer Gynt* arrives; he examines the Sphinx carefully, sometimes through his eye-glass, sometimes through the hollow of his hand.)

Peer Gynt. Now where in the world have I met before something I only half remember that this ugly thing reminds me of? For met it I have—either north or south. Was it a man? And, in that case, who? The Memnon Statue reminded me of the Troll King of our fairy tales, sitting like that, all stiff and rigid, resting his rump on a piece of rock; but this remarkable mongrel here, this monster, half lion and half woman—have I known it, too, in a fairy tale? Or have I some real recollection of it? A fairy tale?—No, I know the chap! It's the Boyg, if you please, whose skull I cracked—I meant to say that I dreamt I did, for I was lying ill of a fever. (Goes nearer to the Sphinx.) The selfsame eyes, the selfsame lips! Not quite so sluggish—a bit more cunning—but in the main points just the same. Well, Boyg, old fellow, you're like a lion, seen from behind and in the daylight! Are you still full of riddles? We'll try, and see; we'll see if you answer as you did before. (Calls to the Sphinx.) Hi, Boyg! Who are you?

Voice (from behind the Sphinx). *Ach, Sfinx, wer bist du?*

Peer Gynt. What's that? An echo in German? Astounding!

Voice. Wer bist du?

Peer Gynt. It's got a perfect accent! The observation's new, and my own. (Makes a note in his book.) "Echo in German—with Berlin accent." (*Begriffenfeldt* comes from behind the Sphinx.)

Begriffenfeldt. A man!

Peer Gynt. Oh—it was *he* that was talking. (Makes a further note.) "Came later to another conclusion."

Begriffenfeldt (with signs of great excitement). Excuse me, sir—! A vital question—! What was it brought you here to-day?

Peer Gynt. A visit. I'm greeting a friend of my youth.

Begriffenfeldt. The Sphinx?

Peer Gynt. Yes, I knew him in days gone by.

Begriffenfeldt. Splendid!—And after the night I've spent! My forehead is throbbing as if it would burst!—You know him, sir? Then speak! What is he? Can you tell me that?

Peer Gynt. What is he? Yes, I can tell you that. He is *himself*.

Begriffenfeldt (with a start). Ha! Like a flash I see the answer to life's enigma!—Is it certain that he's himself?

Peer Gynt. Yes; at least, he said so.

Begriffenfeldt. Himself! The great awakening's come! (Takes off his hat.) Your name, sir?

Peer Gynt. I am called Peer Gynt.

Begriffenfeldt (with an air of quiet amazement). Peer Gynt! Allegorical! What one expected. Peer Gynt? That means: the Great Unknown—the Messiah that was announced to me——

Peer Gynt. No—really? And you came here to find him—?

Begriffenfeldt. Peer Gynt! Profound! Enigmatic! Incisive! Each word is full of deepest teaching! What are you?

Peer Gynt (modestly). I have always tried to be myself. And, for the rest, my passport——

Begriffenfeldt. Enigmatic too! All an enigma! (Grasps him by the hand.) Come to Cairo! Come! I have found the Emperor of Exegesis!

Peer Gynt. Emperor?

Begriffenfeldt. Come!

Peer Gynt. Am I really known—?

Begriffenfeldt (dragging him away with him). The Emperor of Exegesis—based on Self!

SCENE XIII

(SCENE.—In a lunatic asylum at Cairo. A big courtyard surrounded by high walls and buildings with barred windows. Iron cages on the ground level. Three of the *Keepers* are in the courtyard. A fourth comes in.)

Fourth Keeper. I say, Schafmann—where's the Director?

Another Keeper. He went out this morning, long before dawn.

Fourth Keeper. I'm afraid something's happened that has upset him, because in the night——

Another. Hush! Here he comes! (*Begriffenfeldt* shows *Peer Gynt* in, locks the gate and puts the key in his pocket.)

Peer Gynt (aside). He is a remarkably learned man; almost all that he says is beyond understanding. (Looks round him.) So this, then, is your Savants' Club?

Begriffenfeldt. Yes, here you'll find them, bag and baggage —the coterie of seventy professors of Exegesis. Lately a hundred and three new ones joined them.—(Calls to the *Keepers.*) Mikkel, Schlingelberg, Schafmann, Fuchs—into the cages with you! Quick!

The Keepers. We!

Begriffenfeldt. Yes—who else? Get on! get on! As the world's topsy-turvy, we must follow suit! (Shuts them up in the cage.) The mighty Peer has come to us to-day; so you can join the others.—I will say no more. (Locks the cage and throws the key into a well.)

Peer Gynt. But why—my dear Director—?

Begriffenfeldt. Don't call me that! I *was* Director until— Sir, can you keep a secret? I must unburden myself——

Peer Gynt. What is it?

Begriffenfeldt. Promise me that you will not tremble.

Peer Gynt. I will try not to.

Begriffenfeldt (takes him into a corner and whispers). Absolute Reason expired at eleven o'clock last night!

Peer Gynt. God help us—!

Begriffenfeldt. Yes, it's a great disaster. In *my* position, too, you see, it's doubly disagreeable; because this place, until it happened, was known as a lunatic asylum.

Peer Gynt. A lunatic asylum!

Begriffenfeldt. Ah, not *now*, you understand!

Peer Gynt (aside, growing pale). I see exactly how it is; this fellow is mad—and not a soul suspects it. (Moves away.)

Begriffenfeldt (following him). I hope you have really understood me? To say it's dead is not accurate. It has left itself—got out of its skin like my friend Baron Munchausen's fox.

Peer Gynt (trying to get away). Excuse me——

Begriffenfeldt (holding on to him). No, it was like an eel, not a fox. A nail right through its eye—and there it was, squirming on the wall——

Peer Gynt. How on earth am I to save myself?

Begriffenfeldt. Just one slit round the neck—and pop! Out of its pelt it came!

Peer Gynt. Quite mad!

Begriffenfeldt. And now the fact is evident that this same exit-from-itself entails a revolution in all the world. All persons who up to that time were known as mad at eleven o'clock last night became normal; this, in conformity with Reason in its newest phase. And, if you consider the matter farther, it's clear that from the selfsame hour our so-called wise men all went mad.

Peer Gynt. Speaking of time, my time is precious——

Begriffenfeldt. Your time? You've jogged my memory! (Opens a door and calls out.) Come out! The appointed time has come! Reason is dead. Long live Peer Gynt!

Peer Gynt. No, my dear friend—! (The mad folk come one after another into the courtyard.)

Begriffenfeldt. Good morning to you! Come out and greet the dawn of freedom! Your Emperor's here!

Peer Gynt. Their Emperor?

Begriffenfeldt. Certainly!

Peer Gynt. It's too great an honour—far more than——

Begriffenfeldt. No false modesty at such a time as this!

Peer Gynt. At least give me some respite!—I'm not fit for such a task; I'm quite dumbfounded!

Begriffenfeldt. The man who guessed the Sphinx's riddle! Who is himself!

Peer Gynt. That's just my trouble. I am myself in every way; but here, so far as I can see, everyone gets outside themselves.

Begriffenfeldt. Outside themselves? Oh, no, you're wrong. It's here that men are most themselves—themselves and nothing but themselves—sailing with outspread sails of self. Each shuts himself in a cask of self, the cask stopped with a bung of self and seasoned in a well of self. None has a tear for others' woes or cares what any other thinks. We are ourselves in thought and voice—ourselves up to the very limit; and, consequently, if we want an Emperor, it's very clear that you're the man.

Peer Gynt. I wish to goodness—!

Begriffenfeldt. Don't be downhearted; everything that's new, at first seems strange to one. "One's self"—well, as a specimen, I'll choose the first that comes to hand. (To a gloomy figure that is passing.) Good morning, Huhu! Still, my lad, looking the picture of misery?

Huhu (a Language-Reformer from Malabar). What can I do, when generation after generation dies lacking an interpreter? (To *Peer Gynt.*) You're a stranger; will you listen?

Peer Gynt (bowing). By all means.

Huhu. Then pay attention.—Away in the East, like a bridal crown, lie the shores of Malabar. Portuguese and Hollanders try to civilize the place, where there still survive a lot of original Malabari. These good folk have muddled up their language, and now rule supreme in that land. But, long ago, that same countryside was ruled by Orang-outangs. The woods were all theirs; and they could fight, growl and snarl to hearts' content—live, in fact, as Nature made them; they could screech without permission, and were lords of all the country. Then there came this horde of strangers and disturbed the primal language that was spoken in the forests. Now four hundred years have passed—that means many generations—and so long a time as that, as one knows, can easily stamp out aborigines. The forest cries have long been dumb, not a growl is ever heard; if we want to speak our minds, we must have recourse to words. It applies to all alike —Portuguese and Hollanders, Hybrid races, Malabari—all are equally affected. I have tried my best to fight for our real forest-tongue; tried to bring its corpse to life; upheld people's right to screech, screeched myself, and pointed out the necessity of screeching in our folk-songs. But my efforts met with no result whatever.—Now I think you understand what my grievance is. I thank you for your courtesy in listening. If you think you can advise me what to do, I beg you'll tell me!

Peer Gynt (aside). They say that when you are in Rome you should do as the Romans do. (Aloud.) My friend, if I remember rightly, there are forests in Morocco where there are Orang-outangs that have neither songs nor teacher; and their language much resembles that of Malabar; if you were, like many other statesmen, to expatriate yourself for the good of these same people, it would be a noble action and a fine example also.

Huhu. Let me thank you, sir, for listening; I will follow your advice. (With an impressive gesture.) In the east they flout their singer! The west has its Orang-outangs! (Goes out.)

Begriffenfeldt. Now, surely you'll say that *he's* himself! He's full of himself and nothing else; himself in every word he says—himself when he's beside himself. Come here! I want to show you another, who's been no less conformable to Reason since last night's occurrence. (To a *Fellah* who is carrying about a Mummy on his back.) King Apis, how goes it, my noble sir?

Fellah (fiercely, to *Peer Gynt*). Am I King Apis?

Peer Gynt (getting behind *Begriffenfeldt*). I'm afraid I'm not quite qualified to say; but I should think, if I may judge from what your voice suggests to me——

Fellah. Now you are lying, too!

Begriffenfeldt. Your Highness must kindly deign to let us have an explanation.

Fellah. Well, I will. (Turns to *Peer Gynt.*) You see this man I'm carrying? King Apis was his name. They call him now a Mummy; and, what is more, he's dead. He built up all the Pyramids, and carved the mighty Sphinx, and fought —so the Director says—with Turks on every side. And therefore the Egyptians worshipped him as a God, and set up in their temples his statue as a bull. But *I* am that King Apis —it's just as clear as day; if you don't understand it, I'll make you very soon. King Apis was out a-hunting, and got down from his horse, and stepped aside for a moment in my grandfather's field. The soil King Apis fertilized has nourished *me* with corn; and, if more proof is needed, I have invisible horns. Then don't you think it's damnable that I can't get my due? By my birth I am King Apis, but only a Fellah here. If you think you can advise me, tell me, without delay, what I'm to do to make myself like Apis, the great king.

Peer Gynt. Your Highness must build Pyramids and carve a mighty Sphinx, and fight—as the Director says—with Turks on every side.

Fellah. Yes, that's a likely story! A Fellah! A hungry louse! It's all I can do to keep my hut clear of the rats and mice. Come, think of something better, to make me great and safe, and also make me look like King Apis that's on my back.

Peer Gynt. Suppose your Highness hanged yourself, and then, deep in the ground, within a coffin's sheltering walls, behaved like one that's dead——

Fellah. I'll do it! Let me have a rope! To the gallows with my head! I'll not be quite like him at first, but time will alter that. (Goes away and makes preparations to hang himself.)

Begriffenfeldt. A great personality that, my friend—a man with method——

Peer Gynt. Yes, so I see.—But he really *is* hanging himself! God help us! I feel quite sick—and my brain is turning!

Begriffenfeldt. A transitional stage; it won't last long.

Peer Gynt. Transition? To what? I really must go——

Begriffenfeldt (holding him back). Are you mad?

Peer Gynt. Not yet! Mad? God forbid! (Amidst an uproar, *Hussein*, a Minister of State, pushes his way through the other lunatics.)

Hussein. They tell me an Emperor's come to-day. (To *Peer Gynt.*) Is it you?

Peer Gynt (desperately). They've settled that it is!

Hussein. Good.—Here are papers that need an answer.

Peer Gynt (tearing his hair). Aha! Go on! The more the merrier!

Hussein. Perhaps you will honour me with a dip? (Bows low.) I am a pen.

Peer Gynt (bowing still lower). And I am merely a trumpery imperial parchment.

Hussein. My history, sir, is briefly this: they think me a sand-box, and not a pen.

Peer Gynt. And mine, Sir Pen, succinctly told: I'm a paper that's never been written on.

Hussein. They never will understand what I'm meant for; they all want to use me to sprinkle sand!

Peer Gynt. I was a book with silver clasps, when I belonged to a woman once. Madness or wisdom is merely a misprint.

Hussein. But, think—how wretched to be a pen that never has tasted the edge of a knife!

Peer Gynt (leaping into the air). Think what it is to be a reindeer that's always jumping down from a height and never reaching solid ground!

Hussein. A knife! I am blunt; I need repairing! The world will perish if I'm not mended!

Peer Gynt. That would be sad when, like all that He made, our Heavenly Father admired it so much.

Begriffenfeldt. Here's a knife!

Hussein (grasping it). Ah, how I shall lick up the ink! How lovely to cut one's self! (Cuts his throat.)

Begriffenfeldt (moving to one side). Don't splash me!

Peer Gynt (with growing terror). Hold him!

Hussein. Yes, hold me! That's the word! Hold! Hold the Pen! Is the paper there—? (Falls.) I'm worn out. A postscript—don't forget it: He was a pen in the hands of others.

Peer Gynt. What shall I—? What am I? Oh, Thou—keep hold! I am what Thou wilt—a Turk, a Sinner, a Troll; only help me! Something has burst within me! (Shrieks.) I cannot remember Thy name—help me, Thou—Guardian of all madmen! (Sinks down in a swoon. *Begriffenfeldt,* holding a straw crown in his hand, leaps on to *Peer Gynt* and sits astride of him.)

Begriffenfeldt. See how he sits enthroned in the mud!— He's out of himself! Let us crown him now! (Puts the crown on *Peer Gynt's* head, and shouts) Long live the Emperor of Self!

Schafmann (in the cage). *Es lebe hoch der grosse Peer!*

ACT V

SCENE I

(SCENE.—On board a ship in the North Sea, off the coast
of Norway. Sunset and a threatening sky. *Peer Gynt,* now a
vigorous old man with grey hair and beard, is on the poop.
His clothes, which are somewhat the worse for wear, are half
sailor-like; he wears a pilot-jacket and sea-boots. He looks
weatherbeaten, and his expression has hardened. The *Captain* is at the wheel with the *Helmsman.* The crew is forward.
Peer Gynt is leaning his arms on the gunwale and gazing at
the land.)

Peer Gynt. There's Hallingskarven in winter dress; he
shows up well in the evening light. And there's his brother
Jöklen behind, still wearing his ice-green glacier cap; and,
like a lady dressed in white, lies Folgefond behind them
both.—Don't try any follies, my ancient friends! Stay where
you are—you are made of stone.

Captain (calling forward). Two men to the wheel—and
hoist the light!

Peer Gynt. It's blowing.

Captain. Aye, we'll have a storm.

Peer Gynt. Can one see Rondë from the sea?

Captain. No—it lies hidden behind Faanen.

Peer Gynt. Or Blaahö?

Captain. No; but, from aloft, Galdhöpiggen when the
weather's clear.

Peer Gynt. Which way's Harteigen?

Captain (pointing). Over there.

Peer Gynt. Of course.

Captain. You seem to know the country.

442

Peer Gynt. I passed this way when I sailed from home; and early impressions, as they say, last longest. (Spits over the side, and continues gazing at the coast.) It is over there—where the hillside glens are blue, in the dark and narrow valleys, and along the open fjords—that is where the people live. (Looks at the *Captain.*) Not many houses on this coast.

Captain. No, they are few and far between.

Peer Gynt. Shall we be in by morning?

Captain. Aye, I hope so, if the night is not too bad.

Peer Gynt. It's gathering in the west.

Captain. It is.

Peer Gynt. Oh, by the way, look here—remind me, when we're settling up, that I intend to make a present to the crew——

Captain. You're very good.

Peer Gynt. It will only be a small one. I made money, but I've lost it; Fate and I have fallen out. You know what I have got on board; well, that's the lot. The rest of it has taken wings and flown away.

Captain. Oh, what you've got is quite enough to win respect from folk at home.

Peer Gynt. I have no folk. There's no one waiting for this rich ugly uncle.—Well, I shall be spared some fuss at landing.

Captain. The storm is brewing.

Peer Gynt. Now remember, if any of you need it badly I'm not close-fisted with my money.

Captain. That's kind. They're mostly badly off; they all have wives and families—can scarcely live upon their pay—and, if your kindness sends them home with something extra in their pockets, to-morrow's home-coming will never be forgotten.

Peer Gynt. What's all that? Do you say they've wives and children? Married?

Captain. Yes, married—all the lot. The poorest of them all's the Cook; his house is never free from hunger.

Peer Gynt. Married? And someone waiting there to greet them when they come? Is that it?

Captain. Of course, like all poor folk.

Peer Gynt. Supposing it's evening when they come—what then?

Captain. Then I expect that something tasty will have been got for the occasion——

Peer Gynt. A lamp upon the table?

Captain. Aye, and maybe two; a dram to drink——

Peer Gynt. They'll sit at ease, in warmth and comfort, with children round them? And such hubbub in the room that no one hears half the other says to them, just because they are so happy?

Captain. Very likely; and that's why it's so kind of you to promise they shall have a little present.

Peer Gynt. (banging his fist on the gunwale). No, I'm damned if they shall have it! Do you think me such a fool as to fork out for the pleasure of helping other people's children? I've worked too hard to get my money! No one's waiting for old Peer Gynt.

Captain. Just as you please; it's your own money.

Peer Gynt. Quite so. It's mine and no one else's. Directly you have cast your anchor I'll settle up for what I owe you for my cabin passage hither from Panama; and then I'll give you something for a dram of brandy for the crew; but not a penny more than that. You may have leave to knock me down if I give more!

Captain. You'll get my receipt, and nothing else. Now please excuse me; the storm is rising. (He crosses the deck. It has become dark, and the cabin lamps are being lit. The sea grows rougher. Fog and thick clouds gather.)

Peer Gynt. Provide for a crowd of others' children—? Fill others' hearts with happiness, and so be always in their thoughts—? There's no one wasting thoughts on me. Lamps on their tables? I'll put them out! I'll find some way—! I will make them drunk; not one of these fellows shall go home sober. They shall go drunk to their wives and children; they shall swear—bang loudly on the table—frighten their families out of their wits! Their wives shall scream and run out of the house, and their children too! I'll spoil their pleasure! (The ship rolls heavily; he stumbles, and has difficulty in holding on.) That was a bad one! The sea's as busy as if it were paid for what it's doing. It's the same always, up here in the north; the sea to fight with, fierce and angry— (Listens.) What was that cry?

The Watch (forward). A wreck to leeward!

Captain (amidships). Starboard the helm! Keep her close to the wind!

Helmsman. Are there men on the wreck?

The Watch. I can make out three.

Peer Gynt. Lower a boat—!

Captain. It would only capsize. (Goes forward.)

Peer Gynt. Who thinks of that? (To the crew.) If you're men, you'll save them! You're surely not afraid of a wetting?

Boatswain. It's impossible in such a sea as this.

Peer Gynt. They're calling again! The wind is raging.— Cook, won't you try? Come on! I'll pay you——

Cook. Not if you gave me twenty guineas.

Peer Gynt. You dogs! You cowards! Don't you know that these are men that have wives and children who are waiting—?

Boatswain. Patience will do them good.

Captain. Keep her stern to the breakers!

Helmsman. The wreck's gone under.

Peer Gynt. Was that sudden silence—?

Boatswain. If they are married, as you suggest, then the world's the richer by three newly-created widows. (The storm increases in violence. *Peer Gynt* goes aft.)

Peer Gynt. There's no more Faith among men any longer —no more Christianity worth the name; there's little that's good in their words or their deeds, and they pay no heed to the Powers Above. In a storm like to-night's, one may very well be afraid of God; these brutes should cower and remember that, as the saying goes, it's risky to play with elephants, —and then they defy Him openly! *I'm* guiltless enough; if it comes to judgment, I can prove that I made an offer to pay them. But what do I get in return for that? I know they say that your head lies easy if your conscience is clear. That may be true on *terra firma;* but on the sea, where an honest man's quite the exception, I don't consider it worth a rush. At sea you never can be yourself; you simply sink or swim with the others; should the hour of vengeance chance to strike for the Cook and the Boatswain, I most likely should be swept along to perdition with them: there's no respect for individuals,—you're nothing more than one of the crowd. My mistake has been that I've been too meek, and get the blame for all that has happened. If I were younger, I do believe I'd change my tune and play the boss. There's time for it yet! It shall get abroad that Peer has come overseas a winner! By hook or crook I'll get back the farm; I'll build on it— it shall look like a castle. But not a soul shall come into my house! They shall stand at the door and twiddle their caps, they shall beg—I'll let them do *that* with pleasure—but I'll not give them a single farthing. If I've had to smart from the lash of fortune, they'll find out that I can hit back again— (A *Stranger* is seen standing beside *Peer Gynt* in the gloom, bowing politely to him.)

Stranger. Good evening!

Peer Gynt. Good evening! What—? Who are you?

Stranger. Your fellow-passenger, at your service.

Peer Gynt. Indeed? I thought I was the only one.

Stranger. A wrong impression, corrected now.

Peer Gynt. But it's very strange I have never seen you until this evening——

Stranger. I don't go out in daytime.

Peer Gynt. Perhaps you are not well? You're as white as a sheet——

Stranger. I'm quite well, thank you.

Peer Gynt. What a storm!

Stranger. Yes, what a blessing, man!

Peer Gynt. A blessing?

Stranger. The waves are mountains high. It makes one's mouth water to think of the wrecks that there will be to-night!—of the corpses that will be washed ashore.

Peer Gynt. God forbid!

Stranger. Have you ever seen a man that has been strangled —or hanged—or drowned?

Peer Gynt. What on earth do you mean?

Stranger. There's a grin on their faces; but the grin is ghastly, and for the most part they've bitten their tongues.

Peer Gynt. Do go away!

Stranger. Only one question! Suppose, for instance, that the ship should run aground to-night and sink——

Peer Gynt. Then do you think there's danger?

Stranger. I really don't know what to answer. Suppose I'm saved and you get drowned——

Peer Gynt. Oh, bosh—!

Stranger. Well, it's just possible. With one foot in the grave, a man inclines to charitable thoughts——

Peer Gynt (putting his hand in his pocket). I see, it's money that you want!

Stranger. No; but if you would be so kind as to present me with your corpse—?

Peer Gynt. This is too much!

Stranger. Merely your corpse! It's for a scientific pur-pose——

Peer Gynt. Get out!

Stranger. But, my dear friend, consider—the thing would be to your advantage! I'd have you opened and laid bare. It really is the seat of dreaming that I am seeking; but, be-sides, I'd have you thoroughly examined——

Peer Gynt. Get out!

Stranger. But, sir—a mere drowned corpse!

Peer Gynt. Blasphemous man! You encourage the storm!

What folly! In all this wind and rain and heavy seas and every sign that some fatality may happen—here are you asking for something worse!

Stranger. I see that you're not disposed, for the moment, to carry the matter farther. But time so very often will alter things. (Bows politely.) We shall meet when you're sinking, if not before; then, perhaps, you'll be in a better humour. (Goes into the cabin.)

Peer Gynt. Unpleasant fellows, these men of science! Freethinkers, too— (To the *Boatswain* who is passing.) A word, my friend! Who is that lunatic passenger?

Boatswain. I did not know we had any but you.

Peer Gynt. No other? Why, this gets worse and worse. (To a *Sailor* who comes out of the cabin.) Who went into the cabin just now?

Sailor. The ship's dog, sir! (Passes on.)

The Watch (calling out). Land close ahead!

Peer Gynt. My trunk! My box! Bring them up on deck!

Boatswain. We have something else to think about now.

Peer Gynt. Captain, I wasn't serious in what I said! I was only joking! Of course I'm going to help the Cook—!

Captain. The jib has gone!

Mate. There went the foresail!

Boatswain (calling from forward). Breakers ahead!

Captain. She'll go to pieces! (The ship strikes. Noise and confusion.)

SCENE II

(SCENE.—Off the coast, amongst rocks and breakers. The ship is sinking. Through the mist, glimpses are caught of a boat with two men in it. A breaking wave fills it; it capsizes; a scream is heard, then all is still for a while. Soon afterwards the boat comes into sight, floating keel uppermost. *Peer Gynt* comes to the surface near the boat.)

Peer Gynt. Help! Help! A boat!—Help! I shall sink! God save me—as the Bible says! (Clings tight to the keel of the boat. The *Cook* comes to the surface on the other side of the boat.)

Cook. Oh, God—for my dear children's sake be pitiful! Let me be saved! (Holds on to the keel.)

Peer Gynt. Let go!

Cook. Let go!

Peer Gynt. I'll push you off!

Cook. I'll push *you* off!

Peer Gynt. I'll kick you off! Let go your hold! It won't bear two!

Cook. I know. Get off!

Peer Gynt. Get off yourself!

Cook. Not likely! (They fight. The *Cook* gets one hand hurt, but clings fast to the boat with the other hand.)

Peer Gynt. Take your hand away!

Cook. Be kind! Be merciful!—Just think of my young children there at home!

Peer Gynt. I have more need to live than you, for I have got no children yet.

Cook. Let go! You've had your life; I'm young!

Peer Gynt. Be quick and sink; you're much too heavy.

Cook. Have mercy! For God's sake let go! There's no one that will mourn for you—(Shrieks and slips down.) I'm drowning!

Peer Gynt (catching hold of the *Cook's* hair). No, I've got you tight by your back hair; repeat "Our Father"!

Cook. I can't remember—all seems dark——

Peer Gynt. Say what is most essential! Quick!

Cook. "Give us this day"——

Peer Gynt. Oh, skip all that; you have got all that you will need.

Cook. "Give us this day"——

Peer Gynt. The same old song! It's easy seen you were a cook— (His grip gives way.)

Cook (sinking). "Give us this day our"— (Goes under.)

Peer Gynt. Amen, lad! You were yourself up to the end. (Swings himself up on to the keel of the boat.) Where there is life there's always hope— (The *Stranger* is seen in the water, catching hold of the boat.)

Stranger. Good morning!

Peer Gynt. Eh!

Stranger. I heard a cry; it's funny I should find you here. Well? Do you see I spoke the truth?

Peer Gynt. Let go! There's barely room for one!

Stranger. I'll swim quite well with my left leg. I'll float if only I insert my finger-tip into this crack. But what about your corpse?

Peer Gynt. Be quiet!

Stranger. The rest is absolutely done for——

Peer Gynt. Do hold your tongue!

Stranger. Just as you wish. (Silence.)

Peer Gynt. Well?

Stranger. I am silent.

Peer Gynt. Devil's tricks!—What are you doing?

Stranger. I am waiting.

Peer Gynt (tearing his hair). I shall go mad! What are you?

Stranger (nodding to him). Friendly!

Peer Gynt. Go on! What more?

Stranger. What do you think? Don't you know anyone that's like me?

Peer Gynt. I know the Devil——

Stranger (lowering his voice). Is he wont to light us on the darkest paths of life when we're beset by fear?

Peer Gynt. Oh! So it seems, on explanation, that you're a messenger of the light?

Stranger. Friend, have you known—say, twice a year— what terror really means?

Peer Gynt. Of course. One is afraid when danger threatens; but your words are ambiguous——

Stranger. Well, have you ever, even once, triumphed as the result of terror?

Peer Gynt (looking at him). If you have come to guide my steps, 'twas stupid not to come before. It's not much good to choose the time when I'm most likely to be drowned.

Stranger. And would your triumph be more likely if you sat snugly by your fire?

Peer Gynt. Perhaps not; but your talk was foolish. How could you think it would affect me?

Stranger. Where I come from, they think a smile worth quite as much as any pathos.

Peer Gynt. There is a time for everything. Things which a publican may do are most disgraceful in a bishop.

Stranger. The souls of those bygone days whose ashes rest in funeral urns aren't always in a solemn humour.

Peer Gynt. Leave me, you bugbear! Get away! I won't die! I must get to land!

Stranger. As far as that goes, make your mind quite easy; no one ever dies until he's seen the fifth act through. (Disappears.)

Peer Gynt. Ah, it slipped out of him at last;—he was a wretched Moralist.

SCENE III

(Scene.—A churchyard high up in the mountains. A funeral is going on. The *Priest* and the *Mourners* are just finishing the last verse of a hymn. *Peer Gynt* is passing on the road, and stops at the churchyard gate.)

Peer Gynt. Here's another man going the way of all flesh. Well, God be praised that it isn't me! (Goes into the churchyard.)

Priest. Now that his soul has gone to meet its God, and this poor dust waits like an empty husk,—let us, dear friends, in a few words recall the dead man's journey on this earth of

ours. He wasn't rich, nor was he very clever; his voice was
weak, his bearings scarcely manly; he had no strength of
mind, nor much decision; nor in his own home did he seem
the master. His manner when he came to church was such
as if he felt he must request permission to take his seat among
the congregation. Of Gudbrandsdal he was, you know, a native, and he was scarce a boy when he came hither; and, to
the last, as you no doubt have noticed, he always kept his
right hand in his pocket. That same peculiarity I mention was
probably the only thing that stamped his picture on our
minds; that, and the shyness—the almost shamefaced diffi-
dence—with which he bore himself when he came in amongst
us. But, though he was so diffident and quiet, and to the last
was almost like a stranger, you know quite well, in spite of
his concealment, the hand he hid had no more than four
fingers.—I well remember, many years ago, during the war,
one morning a Conscription was held at Lundë. Everyone
was full of Norway's troubles and her doubtful future. Behind a table, I remember, sat a Captain and the Mayor, and
several Sergeants; and one by one our lads came in, were
measured, enrolled, and duly sworn in to the army. The room
was full; and outside in the courtyard was heard the noise
of the young people's laughter. A man was called out, and
a lad came in with face as white as snow upon the hilltops.
They told him to come forward to the table. His right hand
was all swathed up in a napkin; he gasped and swallowed—
tried to find his voice—but seemed as if he had no words to
answer the Captain's questions. Still, at last, he did; and
then, with crimson face and faltering tongue that sometimes
let the words out with a rush, he mumbled some tale of an
accident—a reaping-hook that slipped and cut his finger
clean off his hand. There was a sudden silence. Men exchanged glances; lips were curled in scorn; looks of disdain
were flashed upon the lad, who stood there staring with un-
seeing eyes; he felt their scorn although he did not see it.
And then the Captain, an old grey-haired man, stood up, and

spat, and pointed to the door and said: "Begone!"—and so
the lad went out. Those in the room divided to make way,
so that he ran the gauntlet of them all. He reached the door,
and then took to his heels; ran up the hillside—through the
woods and pastures, up over rocks and stones, stumbling and
slipping—to where his home was, far up in the mountains.
'Twas six months after that when he came hither, bringing
his mother, children and betrothed. He leased some land upon
the mountain-side near to where Lomb is bounded by the
moor. As soon as it was possible, he married the mother of
his children; built a house; broke up the stony ground with
such success that yellow grain in patches soon appeared
amidst the rocks. It's true that when he went to church he
kept his right hand in his pocket; but on his farm I know he
worked as well with nine fingers as others with their ten.—
Then, one wet spring, a flood swept all away. They saved
their lives, but nothing else; and, poor and naked as he was,
he set to work to clear the soil afresh; and by the autumn
he'd built himself a house on safer ground. Safer? Yes, from
the flood but not the mountains. For, two years later, in an
avalanche all that he had was overwhelmed again. But even
avalanches had no power to daunt his soul. He set to work to
dig and clear the snow and save what might be left; and,
ere the winter's snow had come again, he'd built his little
house a third time up. Three sons he had—three fine young
lads—and they must go to school, and school was far away;
and so, from where the public roadway ended, he had to cut
a steep and narrow path through the hard snow. And then—
what did he do? The eldest boy had to climb up and scramble as best he could; and where it was too steep his father
roped him to him for support. The other two he carried in his
arms and on his back. And thus, year after year, he drudged;
and his three sons grew to be men. Then came a time when he
might surely ask for something in return from them; but
they, three prosperous men in far America, had quite forgotten their Norwegian father and how he used to help them to

the school. He was a man whose vision never saw farther than what lay nearest to his hand. Words which resound in other people's hearts were meaningless to him as tinkling bells; Family, Country—all that's best and brightest—was blurred and hidden by a veil of tears. But never did I know a man so humble. From that Conscription Day he carried with him the sense of guilt, which showed as plainly on him as did the blush of shame upon his cheek and his four fingers hidden in his pocket. A breaker of his country's laws? Perhaps! But there is something that outshines the law as certainly as Glittertinde's peaks stand gleaming in the sun above the clouds. He was a bad citizen, no doubt; for Church and State alike, a sterile tree; but up there on the rocky mountainside, in the small circle of his hearth and home, where his work lay, *there* I say he was great, because he was himself. 'Twas only there the metal he was made of could ring true. His life was like a melody that's played on muted strings.— And therefore, peace be with you, poor silent warrior, who fought and fell waging the little war of peasant's life! We will not seek to search the heart and reins; that's not a task for us, but for his Maker. Still, this I hope—and hope with confidence: that this man, as he stands before the Throne, is not a cripple in the eyes of God! (The congregation disperses. *Peer Gynt* remains alone.)

Peer Gynt. Well, *that's* what I call Christianity! Nothing in it to make one feel uneasy. Indeed the theme of the Priest's address—that we should all strive to be ourselves—is really extremely edifying. (Looks into the grave.) Was it he, I wonder, who slashed his knuckles when I was felling trees in the forest? Who knows? If I were not standing here by the grave of this congenial spirit, I might believe that it was myself that was sleeping there and was listening in dreams to praises that I deserved. It's really a beautiful Christian practice to take a kindly retrospect of the whole life of the departed. I'd readily accept a verdict from this most worthy priest.—However, I've still some time left, I expect, before the sexton comes and claims me; and, as the Scripture says: "The best is still the best"; and, in like manner: "Sufficient for the day is the evil thereof"; and, further: "Do not borrow trouble."—The Church is the only comforter. Up till now I have never given the credit to it that is its due; but now I know what good it does you to hear authority proclaim: "As you have sowed, so must you reap." We must be ourselves; in everything, both great and small, we must look after ourselves and what concerns ourselves. Though Fortune fail us we shall win respect, if our careers have been shaped in accordance with this doctrine.—And now for home! What though the way be steep and narrow—what though Fortune be still malicious—old Peer Gynt will go his own way, and remain, as always: poor but virtuous. (Goes.)

SCENE IV

(SCENE.—A hillside showing the dried-up bed of a stream, by which stands a ruined mill. The ground is torn up, and everything is in a ruinous state. Outside the mill an auction is taking place; there is a large and noisy gathering of people, and drinking is going on. *Peer Gynt* is sitting on a heap of rubbish near the mill.)

Peer Gynt. Backward or forward, it's just as far; out or in, the way's as narrow. Time destroys and the stream cuts through. "Round about," said the Boyg; and we needs must, here.

A Man in Mourning. Now there's nothing left but the rubbish. (Looks at *Peer Gynt.*) Strangers, too? God save you, sir!

Peer Gynt. Well met! This is a merry scene; is it a christening, or a wedding?

Man in Mourning. I should rather say a house-warming; the bride, poor thing, is food for worms.

Peer Gynt. And worms are fighting for rags and scraps.

Man in Mourning It's a finished story, and this is the end.

Peer Gynt. Every story ends the same; I've known them all since I was a boy.

A Young Boy (holding a casting-ladle). Look what a fine thing I have bought! Peer Gynt used to mould buttons with this.

Another. I got a fine purse for a farthing!

A Third. A pedlar's pack for twopence halfpenny!

Peer Gynt. Peer Gynt? Who was he?

Man in Mourning. I only know he was brother-in-law to the bridegroom, Death, and also to the blacksmith Aslak.

A Man in Grey. You're forgetting me; you must be drunk!

Man in Mourning. You're forgetting the loft-door at Hægstad.

Man in Grey. So I was; but you were never dainty.

Man in Mourning. If only she doesn't play Death a trick——

Man in Grey. Come on! Have a drink with your relation!

Man in Mourning. Relation be damned! Your drunken fancies——

Man in Grey. Oh, nonsense! Blood is thicker than that; at least we're both Peer Gynt's relations. (They go off together.)

Peer Gynt (aside). I'm meeting old friends.

A Boy (calling after the *Man in Mourning*). My poor dead mother will come after you, Aslak, if you get drinking.

Peer Gynt (getting up). The Agriculturalists are wrong; it doesn't smell better the deeper you dig.

A Boy (with a bearskin). Here's the Dovrë-Cat!—or at least his skin! It was he chased the Troll on Christmas Eve.

Another (with a pair of reindeer-horns). Here's the fine buck on which Peer Gynt rode right along the ridge of Gendin.

A Third (with a hammer, calls to the *Man in Mourning*). Hi! Aslak! Do you know this hammer? Was it this you used when the Devil escaped?

A Fourth (showing his empty hands). Mads Moen, here's the invisible cloak in which Peer Gynt and Ingrid vanished.

Peer Gynt. Some brandy, boys! I'm feeling old; I'll hold an auction of all my rubbish.

A Boy. What have you got to sell?

Peer Gynt. A castle; it's up at Rondë, and solidly built.

Boy. I bid one button!

Peer Gynt. A drink with it, then; it's a sin and a shame to offer less.

Another Boy. He's a merry old chap! (The crowd gathers round *Peer Gynt*.)

Peer Gynt. Granë, my horse!—Who bids?

One of the Crowd. Where is he?

Peer Gynt. Away in the West! Near the sunset, boys! He can trot as fast as Peer Gynt could make up his lies.

Voices. What more have you?

Peer Gynt. Both gold and rubbish! I bought them at a loss, and now I'll sell them at a sacrifice.

A Boy. Put them up!

Peer Gynt. A vision of a prayer-book! You may have it for a hook and eye.

Boy. Deuce take your visions!

Peer Gynt. Then—my Empire! I throw it to you; you may scramble for it!

Boy. Does a crown go with it?

Peer Gynt. A lovely crown of straw, and it will fit the first that puts it on.—Here's something more! An empty egg! Grey hair of a madman! The Prophet's beard!—You may have them all, if you'll only show me on the hillside a sign-post marked: "This is the way"!

The Mayor (who has come up). The way you're going on, my man, I think will lead you to the lock-up.

Peer Gynt (with his hat in his hand). Very likely. But, tell me, who was Peer Gynt?

The Mayor. Oh, bother—!

Peer Gynt. Excuse me—I want to know—!

The Mayor. Well,—they say, an incurable romancer.

Peer Gynt. Romancer?

The Mayor. Yes; romanced about all sorts of glorious deeds as if he had done all of them himself. Excuse me now, my friend, I'm busy— (Goes away.)

Peer Gynt. And where's this wonderful fellow now?

An Elderly Man. He went oversea to a foreign land, and came to grief as one might have expected. It's many years now since he was hanged.

Peer Gynt. Hanged? Dear me! I was sure of it; the late Peer Gynt was himself to the last. (Bows.) Good-bye. I'm much obliged to you all! (Takes a few steps, then stops.) You merry boys and lovely women, may I tell you a story in return?

Voices. Yes, if you know one!

Peer Gynt. Certainly. (Comes back to them. His face takes on an altered expression.) I was in San Francisco, gold-digging, and the whole town was full of freaks; one played the fiddle with his toes, one danced fandangoes on his knees, a third, I heard, kept making verses while holes were bored right through his skull. To this freak-show the Devil came, to try his luck like so many others. His line was this: he could imitate the grunting of a pig exactly. His personality attracted although he was not recognized. The house was full, and on tenterhooks of expectation. In he strode, dressed in a cape with flowing wings; *Man muss sich drappieren,* as the Germans say. But no one knew that in his cape he had a little pig concealed. And now he started his performance. The Devil pinched; the pig gave tongue. The whole was a fantasia on a pig's life, from birth to slaughter, ending up with a shriek like that which follows on the slaughterer's stroke; with which, the artist bowed and went.—Then there arose a keen discussion among the experts in the audience. The noises were both praised and censured; some found the

tone of them too thin. Others declared the dying shriek was
far too studied; but they all were of the same mind on one
point: That the performance was, *qua* grunt, exceedingly exaggerated. You see, that's what the Devil got, because he'd
made the sad mistake of reckoning without his public. (Bows
and goes away. An uneasy silence falls on the crowd.)

SCENE V

(SCENE.—A clearing in a great forest, on the Eve of Pentecost. In the background is seen a hut, with a pair of reindeer-
horns over the door. *Peer Gynt* is on all-fours on the ground,
grubbing up wild onions.)

Peer Gynt. This is one standpoint. Where is the next? One
should try all things and choose the best. I have done that;
I've been a Cæsar, and now I'm behaving like Nebuchad-
nezzar. So I might go through Bible history. This old boy's
back to mother earth. I remember the Book says: "Dust
thou art." The great thing in life is to fill your belly. Fill it
with onions? It matters little; I'll fit some cunning traps
and snares. There is a brook; I'll not go thirsty; and all wild
things shall do my bidding. And, suppose I die—which perhaps may happen—I'll creep beneath a fallen tree; like the
bear, I'll cover myself with leaves, and scratch in the bark,
in great big letters: "Here lies Peer Gynt, a decent chap,
who was Emperor of all the Beasts."—Emperor? (Laughs
to himself.) You absurd old humbug! You're not an emperor, you're an onion! Now, my dear Peer, I'm going to peel
you, however little you may enjoy it. (Takes an onion and
peels it, layer by layer.) There's the untidy outer husk;
that's the shipwrecked man on the wreck of the boat; next
layer's the Passenger, thin and skinny—still smacking of
Peer Gynt a little. Next we come to the gold-digger self;
the pith of it's gone—someone's seen to that. This layer with

a hardened edge is the fur-hunter of Hudson's Bay. The next one's like a crown. No, thank you! We'll throw it away without further question. Here's the Antiquarian, short and sturdy; and here is the Prophet, fresh and juicy; he stinks, as the saying goes, of lies enough to bring water to your eyes. This layer, effeminately curled, is the man who lived a life of pleasure. The next looks sickly. It's streaked with black. Black may mean missionaries or negroes. (Pulls off several layers together.) There's a most surprising lot of layers! Are we never coming to the kernel? (Pulls all that is left to pieces.) There isn't one! To the innermost bit it's nothing but layers, smaller and smaller. Nature's a joker! (Throws the bits away from him.) Deuce take all thinking! If you begin that, you may miss your footing. Well, anyway, *I* don't run that risk as long as I'm down on all-fours here. (Scratches the back of his head.) Life's an uncommonly odd contraption; it plays an underhand game with us; if you try to catch hold of it, it eludes you, and you get what you didn't expect—or nothing. (Goes closer to the hut, looks at it, and starts.) That hut? In the forest—! Eh? (Rubs his eyes.) I'm certain I must have seen that hut before. The reindeer-horns there, over the door—! A mermaid carved on the end of the gable—! That's a lie! No mermaid—just logs and nails—and the bolt that should keep out plaguy thoughts—! (*Solveig's* voice is heard from the hut.)

    Solveig (singing).

> Now all is ready for Pentecost.
> Dear lad far away, are you coming near?
> If your burden's heavy, then rest awhile;
> I shall wait, because I promised you, dear.

    (*Peer Gynt* rises to his feet, deathly pale and quiet.)

    Peer Gynt. One who remembered—and one who forgot; one who has kept what the other has lost. Life's serious, not a foolish jest! Ah, misery! *Here* my Empire lay! (Runs into the wood.)

SCENE VI

(SCENE.—A moor with firs, at night. A forest fire has laid it waste. Charred tree-trunks for miles around. Patches of white mist are lying here and there over the ground. *Peer Gynt* comes running over the moor.)

Peer Gynt. Ashes, mists and dust-clouds flying—fine material to build with! Stench and rottenness within them; all a whited sepulchre. Fancies, dreams and still-born wisdom for a base, while lies shall serve for a staircase for the building of a lofty pyramid. Flight from everything that's worthy; no repentance—only terror; these shall cap a building labelled: "Petrus Gyntus Cæsar fecit"! (Listens.) What is that sound like children's weeping?—Weeping that is half a song? What are these that I see rolling at my feet, like balls of thread? (Kicks his feet about.) Get away! You block the path up!

The Threadballs (on the ground).

We are thoughts;
You should have thought us;
Little feet, to life
You should have brought us!

Peer Gynt (going round them.) I've only brought *one* thought to life,—and it was wry and bandy-legged!

The Threadballs.

We should have risen
With glorious sound;
But here like threadballs
We are earth-bound.

Peer Gynt (stumbling). Threadballs! You infernal rascals! Are you tripping up your father? (Runs away.)

Withered Leaves (flying before the wind).

We are a watchword;
You should have used us!
Life, by your sloth,

Has been refused us.
By worms we're eaten
All up and down;
No fruit will have us
For spreading crown.

Peer Gynt. Still, you have not been born for nothing; lie still, and you will serve for manure.

A Sighing in the Air.

We are songs;
You should have sung us!
In the depths of your heart
Despair has wrung us!
We lay and waited;
You called us not.
May your throat and voice
With poison rot!

Peer Gynt. Poison yourselves, you silly doggerel! Had I any time for verse and twaddle? (Goes to one side.)

Dewdrops (dropping from the branches).

We are tears
Which were never shed.
The cutting ice
Which all hearts dread
We could have melted;
But now its dart
Is frozen into
A stubborn heart.
The wound is closed;
Our power is lost.

Peer Gynt. Thanks!—I wept at Rondesvalen, and got a thrashing on the backside!

Broken Straws.

We are deeds
You have left undone;
Strangled by doubt,
Spoiled ere begun.

At the Judgment Day
We shall be there
To tell our tale;
How will you fare?

Peer Gynt. Rubbish! You can't condemn a man for actions
that he *hasn't* done!

Aase's Voice (from afar off).

Fi, what a driver!
Ugh! You've upset me
Into a snowdrift,
Muddied and wet me.
Peer, where's the Castle?
You've driven madly;
The whip in your hand
The Devil's used badly!

Peer Gynt. I'd best be off while I am able. If I have to
bear the burden of the Devil's sins, I'll sink into the ground.
I find my own quite a heavy enough load. (Runs off.)

SCENE VII

(SCENE.—Another part of the moor.)

Peer Gynt (singing).

A sexton! a sexton! Where are you all?
Open your bleating mouths and sing!
We've bands of crape tied round our hats,
And plenty of corpses for burying!

(The *Button Moulder,* carrying his box of tools and a big
casting-ladle, comes in by a side path.)

Button Moulder. Well met, gaffer!

Peer Gynt. Good evening, my friend!

Button Moulder. You seem in a hurry. Where are you
going?

Peer Gynt. To a funeral.

Button Moulder. Really? My sight's not good—excuse me—is your name by any chance Peer?

Peer Gynt. Peer Gynt's my name.

Button Moulder. What a piece of luck! It was just Peer Gynt I was looking for.

Peer Gynt. Were you? What for?

Button Moulder. Well, as you see, I am a button moulder; and you must be popped into my Castle-ladle.

Peer Gynt. What for?

Button Moulder. So as to be melted down.

Peer Gynt. Melted?

Button Moulder. Yes; it's clean and it's empty. Your grave is dug and your coffin ordered; your body will make fine food for worms; but the Master's orders bid me fetch your soul at once.

Peer Gynt. Impossible! Like this?—without the slightest warning?

Button Moulder. Alike for funerals and confinements the custom is to choose the day without giving the slightest warning to the chief guest of the occasion.

Peer Gynt. Quite so. My head is going round! You are—?

Button Moulder. You heard; a button moulder.

Peer Gynt. I understand! A favourite child is called by lots of names.—Well, Peer, so *that's* to be the end of your journey!—Still, it's a scurvy trick to play me. I deserved something a little kinder. I'm not so bad as perhaps you think; I've done some little good in the world. At worst I might be called a bungler, but certainly not an out-and-out sinner.

Button Moulder. But that is just the point, my man. In the highest sense you're not a sinner; so you escape the pangs of torment and come into the Casting-ladle.

Peer Gynt. Oh, call it what you like—a ladle or the bottomless pit—it's just the same! Ginger is always hot in the mouth, whatever you may be pleased to call it. Satan, away!

Button Moulder. You are not so rude as to think that I've a cloven hoof?

Peer Gynt. Cloven hoof or fox's claws—whichever you like. So now pack off! Mind your own business, and be off!

Button Moulder. My friend, you're under a great delusion. We're both in a hurry; so, to save time, I'll try to explain the matter to you. You are, as you yourself have said, nothing great in the way of a sinner—scarcely a middling one, perhaps——

Peer Gynt. Now you are talking reasonably.

Button Moulder. Wait a bit!—I think it would be going too far to call you virtuous——

Peer Gynt. I certainly don't lay claim to that.

Button Moulder. Well, then, say, something betwixt and between. Sinners in the true grand style are seldom met with nowadays; that style of sin needs power of mind—it's something more than dabbling in mud.

Peer Gynt. That's perfectly true; one should go at it with something of a Berserk's fury.

Button Moulder. You, on the contrary, my friend, took sinning lightly.

Peer Gynt. Just, my friend, a little mud-splashed, so to speak.

Button Moulder. Now we're agreed. The bottomless pit is not for you who played with mud.

Peer Gynt. Consequently, my friend, I take it that I may have your leave to go just as I came?

Button Moulder. Oh, no, my friend—consequently you'll be melted down.

Peer Gynt. What's this new game that you've invented while I have been abroad?

Button Moulder. The practice is just as old as the Creation, and was invented for the purpose of keeping things up to the standard. You know in metal work, for instance, it sometimes happens that a casting turns out a failure, absolutely—buttons are turned out without loops. What would you do in such a case?

Peer Gynt. I'd throw the trash away.

Button Moulder. Exactly. Your father had the reputation of reckless wastefulness as long as he had anything to waste. The Master, on the other hand, is economical, you see, and therefore is a man of substance. He never throws away as useless a single thing that may be dealt with as raw material. —Now, *you* were meant to be a gleaming button on the world's waistcoat, but your loop was missing; so you've got to go into the scrap-heap, to be merged into the mass.

Peer Gynt. But do you mean that I've got to be melted down with any Tom and Dick and Harry and moulded fresh?

Button Moulder. That's what I mean. That's what we've done to not a few, it's what they do at the mint with the money when the coin is too much worn with use.

Peer Gynt. But it's simply disgusting niggardliness! My dear friend, won't you let me go? A loopless button—a smooth-worn coin—what are they to a man of your master's substance?

Button Moulder. The fact of your having a soul's enough to give you a certain intrinsic value.

Peer Gynt. No, I say! No! With tooth and nail I'll fight against it! I'd rather, far, put up with anything than that!

Button Moulder. But what do you mean by "anything"? You must be reasonable, you know; you're not the sort that goes to heaven——

Peer Gynt. I'm humble; I don't aim so high as that; but I'm not going to lose a single jot of what's myself. Let me be sentenced in ancient fashion; Send me to Him with the Cloven Hoof for a certain time—say, a hundred years, if the sentence must be a very severe one. That's a thing I dare say one might put up with; the torture would then be only moral, and perhaps, after all, not so very tremendous. It would be a transition, so to speak, as the fox said. If you wait, there comes deliverance and you may get back; meanwhile you

hope for better days. But the other idea—to be swallowed
up like a speck in a mass of strange material—this ladle business—losing all the attributes that make a Gynt—*that* fills
my inmost soul with horror!

Button Moulder. But, my dear Peer, there is no need for
you to make so great a fuss about so small a thing; because
you never yet have been yourself. What difference can it
make to you if, when you die, you disappear?

Peer Gynt. *I've* never been myself! Haha! You almost
make me laugh. Peer Gynt anything but himself!—No, no,
friend Button Moulder, you are wrong; you're judging
blindly. If you searched my inmost being, you would find
I'm Peer right through, and nothing else.

Button Moulder. Impossible. Here are my orders. See,
they say: "You will fetch Peer Gynt. He has defied his destiny. He is a failure, and must go straight into the Casting-
ladle."

Peer Gynt. What nonsense! It must surely mean some
other Gynt. Are you quite sure that it says Peer?—not John,
or Rasmus?

Button Moulder. I melted them down long ago. Now, come
along and don't waste time.

Peer Gynt. No, that I won't! Suppose to-morrow you found
that it meant someone else? That would be pleasant! My
good man, you must be careful, and remember what a responsibility——

Button Moulder. I've got my orders to protect me.

Peer Gynt. Give me a little respite, then!

Button Moulder. What for?

Peer Gynt. I will find means to prove that, all my life,
I've been myself; that is, of course, the point at issue.

Button Moulder. Prove it? But how?

Peer Gynt. With witnesses and testimonials.

Button Moulder. I fear that you won't satisfy the Master.

Peer Gynt. I'm quite sure that I shall! Besides, we'll talk
about that when the time comes. Dear man, just let me have

myself on loan for quite a little while. I will come back to
you. We men are not born more than once, you know, and
naturally we make a fight to keep the self with which we
came into the world.—Are we agreed?

Button Moulder. So be it. But, remember this: At the next
crossroads we shall meet. (*Peer Gynt* runs off.)

SCENE VIII

(SCENE.—Another part of the moor.)

Peer Gynt (running in). Time is money, as people say.
If I only knew where the crossroads are—it may be near, or
it may be far. The ground seems to burn my feet like fire.
A witness! A witness! Where shall I find one? It's next to
impossible, here in the forest. The world's a bungle! It's
managed wrong, if it's necessary for a man to prove his rights
that are clear as the noonday sun! (A bent *Old Man,* with a
staff in his hand and a bag on his back, hobbles up to *Peer
Gynt.*)

Old Man. Kind sir, give a homeless old man a penny!

Peer Gynt. I'm sorry—I have no change about me——

Old Man. Prince Peer! Can it be that we meet at last?

Peer Gynt. Why, who—?

Old Man. He's forgotten the old man at Rondë!

Peer Gynt. You surely are never—?

Old Man. The King of the Dovrë.

Peer Gynt. The Troll King? Really? The Troll King?—
Answer!

Old Man. I'm he, but in different circumstances.

Peer Gynt. Ruined?

Old Man. Aye, robbed of everything; a tramp, and as
hungry as a wolf.

Peer Gynt. Hurrah! Such witnesses as this don't grow on
every tree!

Old Man. Your Highness has grown grey too since last we met.

Peer Gynt. Worry and age, dear father-in-law. Well, let's forget our private affairs; and, above all, our family squabbles. I was a foolish youth——

Old Man. Yes, yes; you were young, and youth must have its fling. And it's lucky for you that you jilted your bride; you've escaped a lot of shame and bother, for afterwards she went clean to the bad——

Peer Gynt. Dear me!

Old Man. Now she may look after herself. Just think—she and Trond have gone off together.

Peer Gynt. What Trond?

Old Man. Of the Valfjeld.

Peer Gynt. He? Aha, I robbed him of the cowherd girls.

Old Man. But my grandson's grown a fine big fellow and has bouncing babies all over the country.

Peer Gynt. Now, my dear man, I must cut you short; I am full of quite a different matter.—I'm in rather a difficult position, and have to get a certificate or a testimonial from someone; and I think you'll be the very person. I can always raise the wind enough to stand you a drink——

Old Man. Oh! Can I really be of assistance to Your Highness? Perhaps, if that is so, you'll give me a character in return?

Peer Gynt. With pleasure. I'm a little short of ready money and have to be careful in every way.—Now, listen to me. Of course you remember how I came that night to woo your daughter——

Old Man. Of course, Your Highness!

Peer Gynt. Oh, drop the title! Well, you wanted to do me violence—to spoil my sight by cutting my eyeball, and turn Peer Gynt into a Troll. What did I do? I strongly objected; swore I would stand on my own feet; gave up my love, and power and honours, simply and solely to be myself. I want you to swear to that in court——

Old Man. I can't do that!

Peer Gynt. What's that you're saying?

Old Man. You'll surely not force me to swear a lie? Remember that you put on Troll breeches, and tasted our mead——

Peer Gynt. Yes, you tempted me. But I resolutely made up my mind that I would not give in. And *that's* the way a man shows what he's worth. A song depends on its concluding verse.

Old Man. But the conclusion, Peer, was just the opposite of what you think.

Peer Gynt. What do you mean?

Old Man. You took away my motto graven on your heart.

Peer Gynt. What motto?

Old Man. That compelling word——

Peer Gynt. Word—?

Old Man. —that distinguishes a Troll from Mankind: "Troll, to thyself be— *Enough*"!

Peer Gynt (with a shriek). *Enough!*

Old Man. And, ever since, with all the energy you have, you've lived according to that motto.

Peer Gynt. I? I? Peer Gynt?

Old Man (weeping). You're most ungrateful. You've lived like a Troll, but have kept it secret. The word I taught has enabled you to move in the world like a well-to-do man; and now you begin abusing me and the word to which you owe gratitude.

Peer Gynt. Enough!—A mere Troll! An egoist! It must be nonsense—it can't be true!

Old Man (producing a bundle of newspapers). Don't you suppose that we have our papers? Wait; I will show you in black and white how the *Bloksberg Post* has sung your praises; the *Heklefjeld News* has done the same ever since the winter you went abroad. Will you read them, Peer? I'll be pleased to let you. Here's an article signed: "Stallion's Hoof." Here's one: "On the National Spirit of Trolldom"; the writer shows how true it is that it doesn't depend upon horns or tails, but on having the spirit of Trollhood in one. "Our 'Enough,' " he concludes, "is what gives the stamp of Troll to Man"; and he mentions you as a striking instance.

Peer Gynt. I—a Troll?

Old Man. It seems quite clear.

Peer Gynt. Then I might have stayed where I was, and lived in peace and comfort at Rondë! I might have saved shoe leather, and spared myself much toil and trouble! Peer Gynt —a Troll! It's a pack of lies! Good-bye! Here's a penny to buy tobacco.

Old Man. But, dear Prince Peer—!

Peer Gynt. Oh, drop this nonsense! You're mad, or else you're in your dotage. Go to a hospital.

Old Man. Aye, it's that I'm looking for. But, as I told you, my grandson's very influential in all this part, and tells the people I don't exist except in legends. The saying goes that one's relations are always the worst; and now, alas, I feel the truth of it. It's sad to be looked on as being merely a legendary personage——

Peer Gynt. Dear man, you're not the only one to suffer that mishap.

Old Man. And then, we Trolls have nothing in the way of Charities or Savings Banks or Alms-boxes; such institutions would never be acceptable at Rondë.

Peer Gynt. No; and there you see the work of your confounded motto—your fine "To thyself be *enough*"!

Old Man. Your Highness has no need to grumble. And if, in some way or another—?

Peer Gynt. You're on the wrong scent altogether; I'm at the end of my resources.

Old Man. Impossible! Your Highness ruined?

Peer Gynt. Cleared out. Even my princely self is now in pawn. And that's your fault, you cursed Trolls! It only shows what comes of evil company.

Old Man. So there's another of my hopes destroyed!—

Good-bye! I'd better try and beg my way down to the town——

Peer Gynt. And when you're there, what will you do?

Old Man. I'll try and go upon the stage. They're advertising for National Types in the papers.

Peer Gynt. Well, good luck to you!— And give my kind regards to them! If I can only free myself, I'll go the same way too. I'll write a farce that shall be both profound and entertaining, and its title shall be: "Sic Transit Gloria Mundi." (Runs off along the path, leaving the *Old Man* calling after him.)

SCENE IX

(Scene.—At crossroads.)

Peer Gynt. This is the tightest corner, Peer, you've ever been in. The Trolls' "Enough" has done for you. Your ship's a wreck; you must cling to the wreckage—anything—to avoid the general rubbish heap.

Button Moulder (at the parting of the ways). Well, Peer Gynt? And your witnesses?

Peer Gynt. What, crossroads here? This is quick work.

Button Moulder. I can read your face as easily as I can a book, and know your thoughts.

Peer Gynt. I'm tired from running—one goes astray——

Button Moulder. Yes; and, besides, what does it lead to?

Peer Gynt. True enough; in the woods, in this failing light——

Button Moulder. There's an old man trudging alone; shall we call him?

Peer Gynt. No, let him alone; he's a drunken scamp.

Button Moulder. But perhaps he could——

Peer Gynt. Hush! No—don't call him!

Button Moulder. Is that the way of it?

Peer Gynt. Just one question: What is it really to "be one's self"?

Button Moulder. That's a strange question for a man who just now——

Peer Gynt. Tell me what I ask you.

Button Moulder. To be one's self is to slay one's self. But as perhaps that explanation is thrown away on you, let's say: to follow out, in everything, what the Master's intention was.

Peer Gynt. But suppose a man was never told what the Master's intention was?

Button Moulder. Insight should tell him.

Peer Gynt. But our insight so often is at fault, and then we're thrown out of our stride completely.

Button Moulder. Quite so, Peer Gynt. And lack of insight gives to our friend with the Cloven Hoof his strongest weapon, let me tell you.

Peer Gynt. It's all an extremely subtle problem.—But, listen; I give up my claim to have been myself; it very likely would be too difficult to prove it. I'll not attempt to fight the point. But, as I was wandering all alone over the moor just now, I felt a sudden prick from the spur of conscience. I said to myself: "You are a sinner——"

Button Moulder. Oh, now you're back to where you started——

Peer Gynt. No, not at all; I mean a *great* one,—not only in deed, but in thought and word. I lived a dreadful life abroad——

Button Moulder. May be; but have you anything to show to prove it?

Peer Gynt. Give me time; I'll find a priest, and get it all in writing, properly attested.

Button Moulder. If you can do that, it will clear things up, and you will be spared the Casting-ladle. But my orders, Peer——

Peer Gynt. They're on very old paper; it certainly dates

from a long time back, when the life I lived was loose and foolish. I posed as a Prophet and Fatalist.—Well, may I try?

Button Moulder. But——

Peer Gynt. Be obliging! I'm sure you have no great press
of business. It's excellent air in this part of the country they
say it adds years to the people's lives. The parson at Justedal
used to say: "It is seldom that anyone dies in this valley."

Button Moulder. As far as the next crossroads—no farther.

Peer Gynt. I must find a parson, if I have to go through
fire and water to get him!

SCENE X

(SCENE.—A heathery slope. A winding path leads up to the
hills.)

Peer Gynt. You never can tell what will come in useful as
Esben said of the magpie's wing. Who would have thought
that one's sinfulness would, in the end, prove one's salvation?
The whole affair is a ticklish business, for it's out of the frying-
pan into the fire; but still there's a saying that's very true—
namely, that while there's life there's hope. (A *Thin Person,*
dressed in a priest's cassock which is well tucked up, and
carrying a bird-catcher's net over his shoulder, comes running
down the hill.) Who's that with the bird-net? It's a parson!
Hurrah! I am really in luck to-day!—Good afternoon, sir!
The path is rough——

Thin Person. It is; but what would not one put up with
to win a soul?

Peer Gynt. Oh, then there's someone who's bound for
heaven?

Thin Person. Not at all; I hope he's bound for another
place.

Peer Gynt. May I walk with you a little way?

Thin Person. By all means; I'm glad of company.

Peer Gynt. Something is on my mind——

Thin Person. Speak on!

Peer Gynt. You have the look of an honest man. I have always kept my country's laws and have never been put under lock and key; still, a man misses his footing sometimes and stumbles——

Thin Person. That's so, with the best of us.

Peer Gynt. These trifles, you know——

Thin Person. Only trifles?

Peer Gynt. Yes; I have never gone in for wholesale sinning.

Thin Person. Then, my dear man, don't bother me. I'm not the man you seem to think. I see you're looking at my fingers; what do you think of them?

Peer Gynt. Your nails seem most remarkably developed.

Thin Person. And now you're glancing at my feet?

Peer Gynt (pointing). Is that hoof natural?

Thin Person. Of course.

Peer Gynt (lifting his hat). I would have sworn you were a parson. And so I have the honour to meet—? What luck! If the front door is open, one doesn't use the servants' entrance; if one should meet the King himself, one need not seek approach through lackeys.

Thin Person. Shake hands! You seem unprejudiced. My dear sir, what can I do to serve you? You must not ask me for wealth or power; I haven't such a thing to give you, however willing I might be. You wouldn't believe how bad things are with us just now; nothing goes right; souls are so scarce—just now and then a single one——

Peer Gynt. Have people, then, improved so wonderfully?

Thin Person. No, just the reverse,—deteriorated shamefully; the most of them end in the Casting-ladle.

Peer Gynt. Ah! I've heard a little about that; it really was on that account that I approached you.

Thin Person. Speak quite freely!

Peer Gynt. Well, if it's not too much to ask, I'm very anxious to secure——

Thin Person. A snug retreat, eh?

Peer Gynt. You have guessed what I would say before I said it. You say you're not doing much business, and so perhaps my small suggestion may not be irksome——

Thin Person. But, my friend——

Peer Gynt. I do not ask for much. Of course I shouldn't look for any wages, but only as far as possible to be treated as one of the family.

Thin Person. A nice warm room?

Peer Gynt. But not too warm. And, preferably, I should like an easy access, in and out, so that I could retrace my steps if opportunity should offer for something better.

Thin Person. My dear friend, I really am extremely sorry, but you can't think how very often exactly similar requests are made to me by people leaving the scene of all their earthly labours.

Peer Gynt. But when I call to mind my conduct in days gone by, it seems to me I am just suited for admittance——

Thin Person. But they were trifles——

Peer Gynt. In a sense; still, now that I remember it, I did some trade in negro slaves——

Thin Person. I have had folk who carried on a trade in minds and wills, but still did it half-heartedly,—and they didn't get in.

Peer Gynt. Well—I've exported idols of Buddha out to China.

Thin Person. Rubbish! We only laugh at those. I have known folk disseminating uglier idols, far—in sermons, in art and literature—and yet not getting in.

Peer Gynt. Yes, but—look here! I've passed myself off as a Prophet!

Thin Person. Abroad? That's nothing! Such escapades end mostly in the Casting-ladle. If you've no stronger claim than that, I can't admit you, however much I'd like to do it.

Peer Gynt. Well, but—listen! I had been shipwrecked, and was clinging fast to a boat that had been capsized. "A drowning man clings to a straw," the saying goes; but there's another; "Everyone for himself";—and so the fact that the ship's cook was drowned was certainly half due to me.

Thin Person. It would have been more to the point if you had been responsible for stealing half a cook-maid's virtue. Begging your pardon, what's the good of all this talk of half a sin? Who do you think, in these hard times, is going to waste expensive fuel on worthless rubbish such as that? Now, don't be angry; it's your sins and not yourself I'm sneering at. Excuse my speaking out so plainly. Be wise, my friend, and give it up; resign yourself to the Casting-ladle. Suppose I gave you board and lodging, what would you gain by that? Consider—you are a reasonable man; your memory's good, it's very true; but everything you can recall, whether you judge it with your head or with your heart, is nothing more than what our Swedish friends would call "Very poor sport." There's nothing in it that's worth a tear or worth a smile, worth boasting or despairing of, nothing to make one hot or cold—only, perhaps, to make one angry.

Peer Gynt. You can't tell where the shoe is pinching unless you've got it on, you know.

Thin Person. That's true; and—thanks to so-and-so—I only need one odd one. Still, I'm glad you mentioned shoes, because it has reminded me that I must push along. I've got to fetch a joint I hope will prove a fat one. I haven't any time to spare to stand here gossiping like this——

Peer Gynt. And may I ask what sort of brew of sin this fellow has concocted?

Thin Person. As far as I can gather, he has been persistently himself by day and night; and that is what is at the root of the whole matter.

Peer Gynt. Himself? Does your domain include people like *that?*

Thin Person. Just as it happens; the door is always left ajar. Remember that there are two ways a man can be himself; a cloth has both a right side and a wrong. You know they've lately invented in Paris a method by which they can take a portrait by means of the sun. They can either make a picture like the original, or else what is called a negative, the latter reverses the light and shade; to the casual eye it's far from pretty; but the likeness is in it, all the same, and to bring it out is all that is needed. If in the conduct of its life a soul has photographed itself so as to make a negative, they don't on that account destroy the plate; they send it on to me. I take in hand the rest of the process, and proceed to effect a transformation. I steam it, dip it, burn it, clean it, with sulphur and other ingredients, till I get the likeness the plate should give, —that's to say, what is called a positive. But when, as in your case, it's half rubbed out, no sulphur or lye is of any use.

Peer Gynt. So, then, one may come to you like soot and depart like snow?—May I ask what name is on the particular negative that you're on the point of converting now into a positive?

Thin Person. Yes—Peer Gynt.

Peer Gynt. Peer Gynt? Indeed! Is Peer Gynt himself?

Thin Person. He swears he is.

Peer Gynt. He's a truthful man.

Thin Person. You know him, perhaps?

Peer Gynt. Just as one knows so many people.

Thin Person. I've not much time; where did you see him last?

Peer Gynt. At the Cape.

Thin Person. The Cape of Good Hope?

Peer Gynt. Yes—but I think he's just on the point of leaving there.

Thin Person. Then I must start for there at once. I only hope I'm in time to catch him! I've always had bad luck at the Cape—it's full of Missionaries from Stavanger. (Goes off southwards.)

Peer Gynt. The silly creature! He's off at a run; on a wrong scent, too. He'll be disappointed. It was quite a pleasure to fool

such a donkey. A nice chap, he, to give himself airs and come
the superior over me! He has nothing to give himself airs
about! He won't grow fat on his trade, I'll warrant; he'll lose
his job if he isn't careful. H'm! *I'm* not so very secure in the
saddle; I am out of the "self"-aristocracy for good and all, as
it seems to me. (A shooting-star flashes across the sky. He
nods to it.) Peer Gynt salutes you, Brother Star! To shine,—
to be quenched, and lost in the void—. (Pulls himself together apprehensively and plunges deeper into the mist. After
a short silence he calls out) Is there no one in the universe—
nor in the abyss, nor yet in heaven—? (Retraces his steps,
throws his hat on the ground and tears his hair. By degrees
he grows calmer.) So poor, so miserably poor may a soul
return to the darkling mists and become as nothing. Beautiful
earth, forgive me for having trodden thee all to no purpose.
Beautiful sun, thy glorious rays have shone upon an empty
shell—no one within to receive warmth and comfort from
thee, the owner never in his house. Beautiful sun, beautiful
earth, 'twas but for naught you warmed and nourished my
mother. Nature is a spendthrift, and the Spirit but a greedy
miser. One's life's a heavy price to pay for being born.—I
will go up, up to the highest mountain-tops; I'll see the sun
rise once again, and gaze upon the promised land until my
eyes are weary. Then the snow may fall and cover me, and
on my resting-place be written as epitaph: "The tomb of *No
One*"! And—after that—well, come what may.

    Churchfolk (singing on the road).

        Oh, blessed day when the Gift of Tongues
        Descended on earth in rays of fire!
        O'er all the world creation sings
        The language of the heavenly choir!

    Peer Gynt (crouching down in terror). I will not look!
There's nothing there but desert waste.—I am in terror of
being dead long ere my death. (Tries to steal into the thickets,
but finds himself standing at crossroads.)

SCENE XI

(SCENE.—Crossroads. *Peer Gynt* is confronted by the *Button Moulder*.)

Button Moulder. Good morning, Peer Gynt! Where's your list of sins?

Peer Gynt. I assure you that I have shouted and whistled for all I knew!

Button Moulder. But you found no one?

Peer Gynt. Only a travelling photographer.

Button Moulder. Well, your time is up.

Peer Gynt. Everything's up. The owl smells a rat. Do you hear him hooting?

Button Moulder. That's the matins bell——

Peer Gynt (pointing). What's that, that's shining?

Button Moulder. Only a light in a house.

Peer Gynt. That sound like wailing?

Button Moulder. Only a woman's song.

Peer Gynt. 'Tis there—there I shall find my list of sins!

Button Moulder (grasping him by the arm). Come, set your house in order. (They have come out of the wood, and are standing near *Solveig's* hut. Day is dawning.)

Peer Gynt. Set my house in order? That's it!—Go! Be off! Were your ladle as big as a coffin, I tell you 'twould not hold me and my list!

Button Moulder. To the third crossroads, Peer; but *then*—! (Moves aside and disappears.)

Peer Gynt (approaching the hut). Backward or forward, it's just as far; out or in, the way's as narrow. (Stops.) No! Like a wild unceasing cry I seem to hear a voice that bids me go in— go back—back to my home. (Takes a few steps, then stops again.) "Round about," said the Boyg! (Hears the sound of singing from the hut.) No; this time it's straight ahead in spite of all, however narrow be the way! (Runs towards the hut. At the same time *Solveig* comes to the door, guiding her steps with a stick [for she is nearly blind]. She is dressed for church and carries a prayer-book wrapped up in a handkerchief. She stands still, erect and gentle.)

Peer Gynt (throwing himself down on the threshold.) Pronounce the sentence of a sinner!

Solveig. 'Tis he! 'Tis he! Thanks be to God. (Gropes for him.)

Peer Gynt. Tell me how sinfully I have offended!

Solveig. You have sinned in nothing, my own dear lad! (Gropes for him again, and finds him.)

Button Moulder (from behind the hut). Where is that list of sins, Peer Gynt?

Peer Gynt. Cry out, cry out my sins aloud!

Solveig (sitting down beside him). You have made my life a beautiful song. Bless you for having come back to me! And blest be this morn of Pentecost!

Peer Gynt. Then I am lost!

Solveig. There is One who will help.

Peer Gynt (with a laugh). Lost! Unless you can solve a riddle!

Solveig. What is it?

Peer Gynt. What is it? You shall hear. Can you tell me where Peer Gynt has been since last we met?

Solveig. Where he has been?

Peer Gynt. With the mark of destiny on his brow—the man that he was when a thought of God's created him! Can you tell me that? If not, I must go to my last home in the land of shadows.

Solveig (smiling). That riddle's easy.

Peer Gynt. Tell me, then—where was my real self, complete and true—the Peer who bore the stamp of God upon his brow?

Solveig. In my faith, in my hope and in my love.

Peer Gynt. What are you saying? It is a riddle that you are speaking now. So speaks a mother of her child.

Solveig. Ah, yes; and that is what I am; but He who

grants a pardon for the sake of a mother's prayers, He is his father. (A ray of light seems to flash on *Peer Gynt*. He cries out.)

Peer Gynt. Mother and wife! You stainless woman! Oh, hide me, hide me in your love! (Clings to her and buries his face in her lap. There is a long silence. The sun rises.)

Solveig (singing softly).

> Sleep, my boy, my dearest boy!
> I will rock you to sleep and guard you.
>
> The boy has sat on his mother's lap.
> The two have played the livelong day.
>
> The boy has lain on his mother's breast
> The livelong day. God bless you, my sweet!
>
> The boy has lain so close to my heart
> The livelong day. He is weary now.
>
> Sleep, my boy, my dearest boy!
> I will rock you to sleep and guard you.

(The *Button Moulder's* voice is heard from behind the hut.)

Button Moulder. At the last crossroads I shall meet you, Peer; *then* we'll see—whether—! I say no more.

Solveig (singing louder in the sunshine). I will rock you to sleep and guard you! Sleep and dream, my dearest boy!

THE END